The Alienated Mind
The Sociology of Knowledge in Germany 1918–1933

The Alienated Mind
The Sociology of Knowledge in Germany 1918–33

David Frisby

Heineman Educational Books · London
Humanities Press · New Jersey

Heinemann Educational Books Ltd
22 Bedford Square, London WC1B 3HH

Published in the USA by Humanities Press Inc.,
Atlantic Highlands, New Jersey 07716

© David Frisby 1983
First published 1983

British Library Cataloguing in Publication Data
Frisby, David
  The alienated mind.
  1. Knowledge, Sociology of
  I. Title
  306'.42   BD175
  ISBN 0-435-82321-3

ISBN 0-391-02822-7 (Humanities Press)

Printed in Great Britain.

Contents

Acknowledgements	vi
Preface	vii
1 The Sociology of Knowledge in Weimar Germany: Its Background and Context	1
2 Max Scheler: From the Sociology of Culture to the Sociology of Knowledge	26
3 Georg Lukács: From Reification to the Critique of Ideology	68
4 Karl Mannheim: From the Critique of Ideology to the Sociology of Knowledge	107
5 The Contemporary Controversy Surrounding the Sociology of Knowledge: 1918–33	174
Conclusion	225
References and Notes	230
Bibliography	260
Index of Names	267

Acknowledgements

Since this study embodies the results of library research, my major debt must be to the following libraries and their staffs who made their facilities available to me: University of Glasgow Library, British Library of Political and Economic Science, Stadt und Universitätsbibliothek, Frankfurt am Main, Universitätsbibliothek Konstanz and Universitätsbibliothek Heidelberg. Thanks are due to the Kanzler and the staff of the Universitätsarchiv Heidelberg for access to Karl Mannheim's files. David Kettler (Trent University) kindly made available to me two then unpublished Mannheim manuscripts as well as drafts of his own study of Mannheim. Dr Siebeck (Mohr Verlag, Tübingen) allowed me to consult Mannheim's correspondence in the Mohr archives.

I also wish to thank the Leverhulme Trust for awarding me a European Fellowship, spent at the Universities of Konstanz and Heidelberg during the summers of 1976 and 1977 respectively. In this connection, I am grateful to Horst Baier (Konstanz) and Wolfgang Schluchter (Heidelberg) for their assistance and hospitality. Finally, I wish to acknowledge the encouragement of John Eldridge during the writing of the earlier draft of this study, which was accepted for a Ph.D. at Glasgow University in 1979. Thanks are also due to Tannia McLaren, who typed the original manuscript, and Pru Larsen for the much revised one.

Responsibility for the views contained in this study remain my own.

David Frisby
Glasgow
1982

Preface

The following study does not pretend to be a comprehensive guide to the sociology of knowledge in Weimar Germany; rather, it concentrates upon the works of three writers, two of whom, Max Scheler and Karl Mannheim, are usually associated with its development. The early work of Georg Lukács down to the publication of *History and Class Consciousness* is also presented since it provides the most forceful Marxist presentation of some of the central problems in the sociology of knowledge. This is quite apart from the relationship between Lukács' work and that of Mannheim.

Rather than summarising the many other contributions to the sociology of knowledge in Weimar Germany, attention is focused upon the central debates surrounding this tradition, since they illuminate its basic features. Even if we include Lukács within the discourse concerning the sociology of knowledge, it is apparent that a starting point for all three central figures is a theory of culture and cultural crisis. In each case, the reflections that we associate with the sociology of knowledge emerge out of a theory of culture, usually a critique of contemporary culture that is seen to be in a state of crisis.

However, the diversity of reflections upon the relationship between knowledge and society is mirrored in the plurality of terms used to denote this area: 'Erkenntnissoziologie', 'Soziologie des Erkennens', 'Soziologie des Denkens', 'Soziologie des Wissens', 'Soziologie des Geistes' and 'Wissenssoziologie'. The act of cognition, thought, the mind, and simply knowledge, were all seen to be related to diverse aspects of society: 'group soul', 'social group', 'social strata', 'constellations of experience', and 'social classes'.

Nonetheless, there are some common features of the sociology of knowledge in Weimar Germany aside from its origins in various theories of cultural crisis. As the various debates surrounding its development make clear, deliberations upon the relationship between knowledge and society invoked in the Weimar context — unlike other traditions in say France or the United Sates — a confrontation with Marxism and, specifically, with a theory of ideology. Whether they involved a confrontation with Marx's work and whether they grew out of a critique of ideology remains to be investigated. The sociology of knowledge developed, in part, as a reaction to particular Marxist traditions. This reaction is clearly negative in Scheler's case, whereas

Mannheim's relationship to Lukács' version of Marxism is more ambiguous. Whatever the relationship between Marxism and the sociology of knowledge, it remained at the centre of the debates surrounding the latter, and especially following publication of Mannheim's *Ideologie und Utopie*, in 1929.

From a very different direction, the sociology of knowledge in Weimar Germany often saw itself as contributing towards, if not itself constituting, a foundation for the social sciences as a whole. It sought to raise the issue of the nature of social knowledge and how this might best be grasped. It further raised the question of the role of the social sciences and, especially, of sociology within society. This ambitious project is most apparent in Mannheim's work, but Scheler's account of the role of values and his claims for a study of world views also move in this direction. Indeed, Scheler's account of the three types of knowledge — religious, metaphysical and scientific — seems to raise the question of cognitive interests that has animated much recent work by Habermas and Apel on the foundations of social scientific knowledge.

More specifically, the meta-theoretical concerns of the sociology of knowledge can be viewed as an extension of the earlier debates on the nature of social scientific knowledge that had raged in the decades before the First World War. One of Mannheim's early papers must certainly be understood as a confrontation with the earlier *Methodenstreit*. The aim of the sociology of knowledge, to examine critically evaluative standpoints — a feature of both Scheler's and Mannheim's paradigms — can also be read as an extension of the *Werturteilsstreit*. Finally, the debate surrounding the role of science itself — the so-called *Wissenschaftsstreit* — which was initiated by Max Weber shortly before his death, animated some of Scheler's earlier Weimar writings.

But although these themes are confronted in the following study, its mains focus lies elsewhere. Our title 'The Alienated Mind' refers to the centrality of theories of alienated consciousness that run through the Weimar tradition in the sociology of knowledge. The mind or consciousness as detached from 'real' circumstances, and indeed as determined by them, is an important implication of a base-superstructure model of society having its origins not only in a mechanistic Marxism but in the philosophy of culture prevalent in Germany before the First World War. When contemporaries reacted to what they took to be the Marxist theory of base and superstructure, they were responding to earlier conceptions of cultural alienation prevalent in German sociology and philosophy. In very different ways, Scheler, Lukács and Mannheim all started out from a theory of culture whose origins lay not only in contemporary Marxism but also in the philosophy of culture found in the works of Simmel, Weber, Nietzsche and Dilthey. In turn, all three writers viewed the contemporary period as one of cultural crisis whilst, at the same time, reacting to that crisis largely within the confines set by these earlier traditions.

The sociology of culture and knowledge and the critique of ideology developed by Scheler, Lukács and Mannheim confronted these traditions in different ways. But the concern of each writer was still with the alienation of consciousness. In Scheler's case, and as has been most forcefully argued by Kurt Lenk, this took the form of a commitment to a 'powerlessness of the mind' thesis. For Lukács. the problem of the alienation of modern culture assumed its most radical form in the conception of reified consciousness. This theme forms the central chapter of his *History and Class Consciousness*. Amongst the reviewers of Mannheim's *Ideologie und Utopie*, Hannah Arendt astutely pointed to Mannheim's 'homelessness of the mind' thesis, which made so urgent his search — via the sociology of knowledge — for a 'diagnosis of the times'.

On the other hand, to present these as the only theses of the three major writers under consideration would be an oversimplification. It is for this reason that other themes mentioned earlier have also been covered in this study. Otherwise the many claims made for the sociology of knowledge in this period would be unintelligible. Although the various meta-theoretical intentions of the three writers, and especially their philosophies of history, are important to the sociology of knowledge and the critique of ideology, the intellectual project upon which its central figures were engaged should not be reduced to these intentions. Even if the various claims made for a sociology of knowledge are not subjected here to the kind of epistemological critiques so common for several decades now, in this area of Anglo-American sociology and philosophy, this does not means that many of the criticisms cannot be made. Rather, the main concern here is with a reconstruction of the original texts in order to illuminate both their intellectual and social sources.

1 The Sociology of Knowledge in Weimar Germany: Its Background and Context

I

Any serious attempt to understand the distinctive nature of the German tradition of the sociology of knowledge in the Weimar Republic, must take into account not merely the immediate theoretical and practical context of its emergence but also its antecedents.[1] Our particular concern will be with those philosophical and sociological traditions that inform the sociology of knowledge as it developed in Weimar Germany: the Marxism of the Second International, Dilthey's philosophy of the human sciences, Nietzsche's critique of ideology, Simmel's theory of alienation, Weber's theory of values, and Troeltsch's historicism. Some of these traditions also permeate the theoretical crises in Weimar Germany — such as 'the crisis of historicism' (Troeltsch) or the *Wissenschaftsstreit*.[2] Indeed, the whole atmosphere of crisis informs much of the writing on the sociology of knowledge in Weimar Germany. Mannheim, for instance, saw his *Ideologie und Utopie* as itself 'conscious of an intellectual crisis situation'.

Whereas, Mannheim, however, often viewed this crisis as an intellectual one, there is little doubt that it was itself a part of a wider social and political crisis in Weimar Germany of the kind that surfaces in various forms in the sociology of knowledge. Often, the sociology of knowledge itself can be seen to emanate from these practical crises. For instance, one cannot fully comprehend Mannheim's theory of political ideologies without being aware that *Ideologie und Utopie* was written in the context of a crumbling political structure in the latter stages of the Weimar Republic.

Taking a simplified model of the socio-political and economic constellation in Weimar Germany, we can pick out three basic periods. The first is the aftermath of the First World War 'defeat', the Revolution of 1918/19, and the political and economic upheaval down to 1923, including the uprising of March 1921. This is the period in which the essays that make up Lukács' *History and Class Consciousness* were written. For Lukács, of course, his role in the Hungarian Revolution, participation in Bela Kun's short-lived revolutionary government, and subsequent exile are also of central importance. This was the period of Lukács' adherence to what he later termed messianic Marxism. The second period, characterised as that of 'relative stabilization', extends from 1924 and the Dawes Plan down to the financial collapse of 1929. Lukács, in a later account of German philosophy and social theory, located Scheler's sociology of knowledge within this period.[3] One might add that most of Mannheim's work on the sociology of knowledge also falls within this period. The third period, from 1929 to 1933, is characterised by the collapse of the German economy and the increasing disintegration of the political structure. The fragmentation that characterized the parliamentary political scene gave way to an increasing polarisation and, what was crucial for Mannheim, to the collapse of parties occupying the middle ground of the political spectrum. Though, strictly speaking, this final period cannot be said to inform Mannheim's *Ideologie und Utopie*, which was completed in 1928, Mannheim nonetheless incorporated the fragmentation of the political structure into his sociology of knowledge, both in his paper on competition and in *Ideologie und Utopie*. Furthermore, the publication of the work in 1929 ensured that Mannheim's contemporaries would recognize that the 'intellectual crisis' of which he spoke was itself part of a much deeper crisis permeating the Weimar Republic.

What this suggests is that the sociology of knowledge was not merely viewed as an academic discipline concerned with broad theoretical issues but that it contained practical and sometimes overtly political aims. Scheler and Mannheim both saw a significant pedagogic role either for a *Weltanschauungslehre* or for the sociology of knowledge. Much of Mannheim's later work seeks to relate the insights gained from his sociology of knowledge to the contemporary situation. This is most explicit in *Ideologie und Utopie*, where one of the work's immediate aims — and that of the sociology of knowledge — is 'a diagnosis of the times'. In Lukács' case, the practical, political intentions of the critique of ideology contained in *History and Class Consciousness* are presented openly. But in Mannheim's *Ideologie und Utopie*, too, the problem of ideology is also located within the context of a discussion of theory and practice. Thus, wherever possible, it is important to investigate these contexts initially in the light of the interests of the sociology of knowledge itself. In this way, they are no longer 'external' contexts, but a constituent element of our textual understanding. Conversely, the works themselves must be seen as interventions in the crises — controversies of both the theoretical and practical domains — and not merely writings about these crises.

II

Within the various philosophical and sociological traditions adopted by the sociology of knowledge there can be seen important modes of reflection upon issues that were taken up by the sociology of knowledge at a later date. A sociology of culture, a theory of ideology, hermeneutic and historicist reflection upon the problem of interpretation, a sociological-biological critique of reason, a base-superstructure model of society, a theory of cultural alienation, *Weltanschauungsanalyse*, and the relativist problematic — are some of the central themes in the sociology of knowledge in Weimar Germany. All of them were developed within the various philosophical and sociological traditions that the sociology of knowledge was to take up in Weimar Germany. At the end of one of his essays Mannheim very briefly reviews the development of the sociology of knowledge and highlights the most important of its forerunners: Marx, Nietzsche, Dilthey and, more recently, Lukács and Scheler.[4] Lukács and Scheler, and their association with this tradition, are examined in detail in chapters 2 and 3. It would thus seem reasonable to consider how important were the others listed in the development of the sociology of knowledge in Germany. But this, in itself, would not give us a sufficiently clear focus upon the specific problems raised by the sociology of knowledge and its distinctive mode of dealing with them. Rather, we need to know in advance what the common features of the sociology of knowledge were.

There is little doubt that one of its central features was either a confrontation with the theory of ideology or an attempt to develop it further or, finally, an attempt to transform it into a sociology of knowledge. It might be thought, at first, that the source of this theory of ideology, and its extension in the sociology of knowledge, lay in Marx's critique of ideology. But even in the case of Lukács, whose *History and Class Consciousness* appears to be a Hegelian-Marxist reinterpretation of Marx's critique of ideology, we find that his theory of ideology and reification is deeply embedded in the German sociological tradition, however critical of it he might be. In the case of Mannheim it has often been assumed that the roots of his sociology of knowledge lay in Marx. Grünwald, for instance, suggests that Mannheim's philosophical position '. . . is that of a historicism derived from Marx and Dilthey interspersed with phenomenological elements'.[5] In the course of the discussion surrounding Mannheim's paper on competition, he himself agreed that 'Marx has influenced me but . . . in association with Dilthey's spirit'.[6] In Scheler's case — and he was less obviously concerned with the development of a theory of ideology — one is confronted with a bewildering array of influences. For instance, Coser suggests,

> As one proceeds to read his work, one is struck even more forcibly by the

variety of his intellectual forebearers. Besides Husserl, influences of Dilthey, Bergson, of German neo-vitalism, and *above all of Nietzsche* (italics added: D.F.), are unmistakable. But Scheler's thought is also deeply marked by Saint Augustine and Pascal, by Cardinal Newman and Saint Francis.[7]

Of course, not all of these are responsible for Scheler's quasi-biological base-superstructure theory of knowledge and ideology; it is probably Nietzsche who is central to this aspect of his work.

Thus, whereas at first sight it seems as if the theory of ideology in the sociology of knowledge is derived from Marx's work, the situation is indeed more complex. The specific constellation of intellectual currents is well expressed by Barth with reference to the theory of ideology in Weimar Germany:

> The problems that emerge with the concept of ideology in the present period, their scope and comprehensiveness, become intelligible primarily through the intellectual-historical background which had been formed with the amalgamation of motifs of recent historicism and philosophy of life, together with Nietzsche's socio-biological critique of reason and Marx's base-superstructure doctrine.[8]

Barth highlights four central strands that are important for an understanding of the German tradition in the sociology of knowledge: Marx, Dilthey (*Lebensphilosophie*), historicism and Nietzsche. In order to give some indication of the specific form which the theory of ideology (*Ideologienlehre*) took in Weimar Germany, we may point to Barth's account of its four basic presuppositions. He highlights them as follows:

> 1 In the anthropological conception, the irrational will and drives take over the leading functions. Intellect and reason appear as epiphenomena that owe their emergence to human beings' need for orientation to the world and are created and prove successful as instruments in the service of the life-struggle. Human intellectual capacity is a form of adaptation to the general struggle for the maintenance and development of existence.

> 2 By means of the primacy of the will over reason, the main body of human activity is situated in this practical behaviour that is to be characterised, in the broadest sense of the word, as the economy. The recognition of the predominance of the will over the mind and reason, confirms the view that the will, directed toward life's welfare and the institutional forms in which it operates, relates to human intellectual functions and their creations in the same way as the material base relates to the ideological superstructure. This viewpoint is dangerous in so far as it supports the tendency to believe that cognitive and concrete-practical behaviour can be separated from one another and in so far as it encourages the impression that the economic welfare of life takes place without the co-operation of intellectual functions. Yet, as Marx correctly remarked, the economy is always composed of both intellectual and mental labour . . .

> 3 Since intellectual activity develops originally in the closest contact with the provision of life and orientation to the world, since therefore it is

assumed that it is linked with concrete-practical interests, there emerges the belief that, in its apparently 'pure' development, its primary function — to operate in the service of life — is not sacrificed.

4 There exists a relationship of dependency between the world of objective and subjective mind, on the one hand, and the socio-economic basis, on the other. This dependency is embodied in an insidious and dubious metaphor: it is maintained that the contents and forms of the mind are the 'expression' of these material existential foundations and their organisation.[9]

Even from this brief outline, it is clear that it would be erroneous to assume that the theory of ideology embodied in the sociology of knowledge is simply taken from Marx. Therefore, one of the tasks of illuminating the context within which this theory of ideology is developed in the sociology of knowledge will be to examine this understanding in the light of its mediation through the Marxism of the Second International and through German sociology itself.

In his study of the reception of Marx's work in the sociology of knowledge in Weimar Germany, Lenk demonstrates how far this tradition relied for its understanding of Marx's critique of ideology upon interpretations of Marx that had already gone some way towards 'destroying' Marx's critique of ideology.[10] Lenk argues that the sociology of knowledge in Weimar Germany derived its interpretation of Marx either from the Marxism of the Second International or from German sociology itself through the writings of Simmel, Max Weber and Troeltsch. Despite the fact that Lenk seeks to draw a sharp demarcation line between Marx's and Engels' notions of ideology and those base-superstructure notions that have proved difficult to maintain in the light of recent analyses by Wellmer,[11] Böhler[12] and others, his account of the Marxism of the Second International and of Engels' own later work suggests that the development of vulgar Marxism was already well underway before the substantive development of sociology in Germany. The base-superstructure model of society, Lenk argues, which itself presupposes two realms of existence, was already present in Marxism itself.

> In comparison with Marx, Engels exhibits a preference for concepts that signify a causal or interactional relation between base and ideology, expressions such as 'mirror-image', 'reflection', 'economic reflection', . . . etc, that in part are also already applied by Marx but which do not yet possess this dominating character as in Engels.[13]

The simple reduction of the superstructure to a material base, and the absence of reflection upon the nature of the truth of this 'consciousness' in the superstructure, are thus to be found in Marxism itself. Similarly, the naturalization of society in the scientific and positivistic interpretation of Marxism also reduces any dialectical notion of the subject-object relationship to that of 'interaction'. Socialism as a scientific world view sought to understand Marxism as a world view

> that encompassed nature, history and society. In it, science and politics, theory and practice are identical in the sense that politics is merely the application of scientific knowledge.[14].

A second tendency towards the 'scientisation' of Marxism lay in a contrary orientation towards separating empirical propositions and normative implications within Marxism itself. The implications for the sociology of knowledge of this 'scientific' Marxism, especially in its first variant, are probably already evident. Lenk maintains:

> If law-like regularities are valid for nature and society to the same extent, then the social base must be explained as the authentic reality — in the sense of an ontologised *ens realissimum*; the superstructure however, must be explained as a relatively insignificant epiphenomenon with regard to the real movement of history and the social process.[15]

But it is not merely the reduction of the 'superstructure' to an epiphenomenon that is problematic in the Marxism of the Second International. The original critical intention of Marx's critique of ideology is lost when the material historical 'base' is naturalized. This has recently been argued by Wellmer in relation to Engels' substitution of the naturalisation of history for the historicization of nature.

> The uncritical, ontological conception of dialectics in Engels' theory no longer supports a critical concept of 'ideology'. 'Ideology' is bound to degenerate into a notion designating contents of consciousness in general. As Habermas puts it, 'the dependence of consciousness on social being becomes a special case of a general ontological law according to which the higher is dependent on the lower and ultimately everything is dependent on its material "substratum" '. Consequently the concept of ideology loses the unique strategic significance which it had in Marx's theory, namely, that of a concept signifying a *false* consciousness which *in its falseness adequately expresses* and reflects a 'false' social reality.[16]

The original relationship between theory and practice posited in such a critique of ideology is thus severed. In other words, the naturalisation of society according to this world-view must also lead to the demise of the significance of human practice, an approach that Lukács criticized under the rubric of 'orthodox' Marxism. In the sociology of knowledge, the two-sphere notion of reality is at the centre of Scheler's sociology of knowledge. In its extreme form, this ontological separation of base and superstructure leads to what Scheler himself termed 'the powerlessness of the mind', or, in a different context, to Mannheim's notion of 'the homelessness of the mind'.

Within German sociology, the reception of Marx's work was also problematical. Bosse, in his study of the relationship between the sociology of religion and the treatment of Marx's critique of ideology in the work of Max Weber and Troeltsch, suggested that

> Troeltsch and Weber, with their critique of 'economism' and 'materialism' claim to have refuted the core of the Marxist critique of ideology. They presuppose the unity and continuity of the Marxist critique of ideology from Marx to their Marxist contemporaries.[17]

This is not to suggest that they did not differentiate between their Marxist contemporaries or to deny that Weber, as Löwith argued,[18] was primarily concerned with a critique of orthodox Marxists such as Kautsky. Nonetheless, Marxism as the 'materialist interpretation of history' was criticized for its economic mono-causality whilst, at the same time, it was viewed as a fund of possible working hypotheses. Its approach to the study of society became one of many possible approaches. Specific aspects of Marx's theory, such as the theory of alienation, and commodity fetishism, were — with the exception of Simmel[19] — almost completely ignored in both German sociology and orthodox Marxism. Both were taken up by Lukács as central themes in his *History and Class Consciousness*. But in the sociology of knowledge, insofar as it either remained fixed upon this earlier interpretation of Marxism (Scheler) or failed to take up these aspects of Lukács' work whilst retaining others (Mannheim), a theory of alienation was developed that had its origins not in Marx but in various traditions in German philosophy and sociology.

The reduction of Marx's critique of ideology to a base-superstructure theory of society in which the causal relationships posited between the two result in the superstructure being viewed as an epiphenomenon, could also lead to the substitution of a *theory* of ideology for its critique. The simple positing of connections between base and superstructure as a theory of ideology reduces the truth claims of propositions, theories, etc., in the superstructure to mere assertions that are invalidated just by virtue of their being socially rooted in the base. In other words, their truth claims are ignored. To what extent this was the direction in which the sociology of knowledge moved must be examined later.

Although not systematically developed in his work, a critique of ideology can also be found in the writings of Nietzsche. This critique is perhaps as significant for the German tradition as is the caricature of a Marxist theory of ideology.[20] In our examination of the relevance of Nietzsche's work for the sociology of knowledge, it will not be possible to do more than outline some of the salient features of his critique of ideology and his philosophy of history. Its significance for the sociology of knowledge, however, is particularly evident in Scheler's work. Mannheim too argued that, aside from Marx,

> The other source of the modern theory of ideology and the sociology of

knowledge is to be found in the flashes of insight of Nietzsche, who combined his concrete observations in this area with a theory of drive-structures and a theory of knowledge that is reminiscent of pragmatism. Though he too employed sociological imputation, it is largely the categories 'aristocratic and democratic cultures' to which he imputed specific modes of thought.[21]

Is this, in fact, where the relevance of Nietzsche's work for the sociology of knowledge lies?

In his examination of Nietzsche's theory of ideology, Barth draws attention to the connection between Nietzsche's biological and sociological critique of reason and truth, on the one hand, and his theory of ideology on the other. The latter is a constituent element of the former. Nietzsche's critique of reason is one that reduces the whole cognitive apparatus back to a biological basis, and in particular to 'the will to power'. He engages in a radical destruction of logical forms and laws, which he views as merely manifestations of the will to power. In more general terms, the search for knowledge in all its forms is reduced to a function of the will to power: hence, questions of truth become questions of power.

Though this quest for truth and knowledge is itself an essential social need, the intellect creates a world that is of value to us but is at the same time a world of illusions. As Nietzsche puts it: 'We only live through illusions', or 'The fundamental aspect of all that is great and lively rests upon illusion. The pathos of truth leads to decline.'[22] Hence, the most general consequence of the intellect is delusion about one's self and the world, since its creations ignore the fact that it is itself merely an organ of the will. Human beings are not interested in 'the truth' as such but merely in the use to which it may be put. In their theories and their morality, people seek to establish timeless and reified (the concept of *Verdinglichung* occurs often in Nietzsche's work) notions that ignore 'the eternal flux of all things', 'the eternal transformation'. Hence, 'There are no eternal facts: just as there are no absolute truths'.[23] The 'relative' truths that we produce are the result of our pragmatic interests. In this connection, Habermas has suggested that

> Nietzsche's 'theory of knowledge' . . . consists in the attempt to comprehend the categorial framework of the natural sciences . . . , the operational basis of experience . . . , and the rules of logic and calculation as the relative apriori of a world of objective illusion that has been produced for the purposes of mastering nature and thus of preserving existence.[24]

This 'world of objective illusion' — that also exists in the moral sphere too — is relative because both intellect and drives are, for Nietzsche, 'reducible to the will to power'. It is also 'a perspectivistic illusion', since this world

> . . . can be *interpreted* differently, it does not have a meaning behind it, but innumberable meanings — 'Perspectivism'. It is our needs *that interpret the world*; our instincts and their pro and con.[25]

The theory of knowledge must therefore be replaced by a theory of perspectives — a task not carried out by Nietzsche but by a doctrine of world views (*Weltanschauungslehre*) and the sociology of knowledge.

The key to Nietzsche's critique of ideology lies in his 'universal reduction of psychological, intellectual and social forms and contents of life to the will to power'.[26] We may take morality as an instance of one of the forms that is a central focus of attack in Nietzsche's critique of ideology. Nietzsche posits a diversity of moral systems that both fulfils the needs of various social strata, is related to the diversity of their creators and agents, and takes a hierarchical form:

> Each class and each strata possess the morality that is appropriate to its interests and its will to power. For Nietzsche, the principle of this social order rests in the polarity of domination and subordination, command and commanded, leaders and led . . . The sociological aspect of his critique is thus manifested in the fact that he investigates the notions of moral behaviour as to whether they are the expression of an elite or a mass.[27]

Barth goes on to suggest that the whole of the 'superstructure' in Nietzsche's critique of ideology possess an instrumental character; it is the instrument of vital interests of the organism and especially of the will to power. It thus robs both reason and the mind of any autonomy and removes any questions of truth from this 'superstructure'. The mind is always 'directed' (*dirigiert*) by the will to power even in a period of the devaluation and inversion of values — itself a central theme in Scheler's social philosophy.[28] In such a period there exists a 'war of the mind', a struggle for power but in the form of a struggle between 'value-judgements' and an attempt to devalue those of one's opponent. These value-judgements change with the conditions of life but can, in turn, be reduced to drives and impulses, that is, to a biological basis. Hence, the mind is merely a part of a larger organism and is distinguished from biological processes only by its 'sophistication'. As Nietzsche put it, the mind is 'merely a means or an instrument in the service of higher life'.

Nietzsche's radical critique of ideology, with its socio-biological reductionism, its elite-mass model of society, its destruction of truth claims, and hence its predication of relativism (or 'perspectivism'), is important in understanding Scheler's and, to a lesser extent, Mannheim's sociology of knowledge. But in Mannheim's sociology of knowledge Nietzsche's philosophy of history, as an early instance of historicism, is also relevant.[29] History is significant for Nietzsche only insofar as 'history serves life'. It too is instrumentalized. In his critique of ideology, perspectivism plays a central role. Historical knowledge, too, is possible only through perspectivism. Each approach to history presupposes an interest structure that is dependent upon specific life-situations. But more significant for Mannheim's development is the work of Wilhelm Dilthey, as Mannheim himself acknowledged.[30] Commenting on Dilthey's work, Grünwald argues that in it

> there lie contained *in nuce* all the difficulties with which, subsequently, historicism and the sociology of knowledge that was founded upon it had to grapple.[31]

These difficulties include the delineation of the form of existence to which knowledge is related, the understanding of expressions of that existence, the interpretation of world views, the relativity of world views, and the attempt to synthesize them.[32]

In both his theory of the human sciences and his critique of historical reason, Dilthey takes as his starting point a cognitive subject that is not, as in Kant, a transcendental ego but 'the whole human being' as a historical and psychological reality that exists within a real life-process. The activity of consciousness is related, therefore, to effective life. The human sciences are to be grounded in the context of experience (*Erlebnis*), expression (*Ausdruck*) and understanding (*Verstehen*). Experience is the fundamental 'fact of consciousness'. The contents of this individual experience are contextual in character. They are located within the context of the 'course of life' (*Lebensverlauf*). This flow of life contains 'our notions, evaluations and purposes'. Life is thus more comprehensive than experience, and individual experiences are to be interpreted in the context of life as a totality. Schnädelbach describes their status as follows:

> If, following Dilthey, one interprets experience as the unity of inner and outer, subjectivity and objectivity and as an element in the context of life, then 'life' too must also be understood as such a unity, i.e. *not* as a transcendental metaphysical principle [but] . . . after Hegel, i.e. after the discrediting of absolute idealism, 'life' is the concept of totality that . . . precisely replaces Hegel's 'absolute spirit'.[33]

Hence, the concept of life becomes both the transcendental basis for the critique of knowledge and the constitution of the historical world, and a metaphysical principle (later developed by numerous philosophers as a *Lebensphilosophie*).

However, what is of significance for the sociology of knowledge is not merely this attempt to ground historical knowledge but also the importance of the hermeneutic problem of interpretation and understanding (*Verstehen*). Individual experiences, for Dilthey, are manifestations of life. The relationship between the two is reflexive since the interpretation of experiences and their objectifications in terms of life is itself to return to human beings themselves who constitute this life. Hence, the totality of human studies constitutes the scientific self-understanding of life, that is, the self-knowledge of humanity. The orientation of the knowing subject, therefore, and its attitude with regard to its objects is what constitutes the human sciences. The cognitive subject interprets the objectifications of life in the light of his or her own life-experiences, namely within the context of life itself.

But this interpretation of the objectifications of life is also located historically and temporally. For Dilthey, the model of historical understanding is the autobiography, since

> The autobiography is the highest and most instructive form in which the understanding of life confronts us . . . here we approach . . . the roots of all historical interpretation.[34]

Historical understanding, therefore, must be rooted in individual experience. The instance of the autobiography is also instructive in that it is one in which

> the distance between the subject of understanding and the object of understanding is here demonstrably mediated by the 'living' identity of subject and object, a phenomenon that, according to Dilthey, is constitutive for historical knowledge as such.[35]

In other words, the relationship between subject and object posited here is unproblematic. In order to comprehend the significance of Dilthey's concept of historical knowledge for the sociology of knowledge, we must examine his notion of history and historicity further.

Dilthey's tendency, at least, in his earlier writings, to provide a psychological foundation of history in the individual human subject leads him into considerable difficulties since, as Lieber suggests,

> the attempt to make psychology the foundation of history and to view the origin of all historical-social differentiation in a general psychological structure as a dynamic form of life, in fact leads him back to a strangely unhistorical view of history and society.[36]

In his later writings, Dilthey attempts to deal with the temporality of life. Time, as something concretely experienced, is located in life:

> In life . . . the present encompasses the notion of the past in memory and that of the future in fantasy, which follows its possibilities, and in the activity that, within these possibilities, sets purposes. Thus, the present is filled with the past and carries the future in itself.[37]

Each of these dimensions of time are to be apprehended in different ways since

> When we look back in memory, we comprehend the context of the past element of the flow of life with the category of meaning (*Bedeutung*). When we live in the present that is filled with realities we experience in intuitive understanding their positive or negative value, and as we hold out the future before us there emerge out of this process the categories of purpose.[38]

In short, the past is apprehended through the category of meaning or significance, the present through that of value and the future through purpose. Of these categories, that of meaning is crucial since

Only the category of meaning overcomes the mere juxtaposition, the mere
subordination of aspects of life. And just as history is memory and this
memory belongs to the category of meaning then, so too, is this the genuine
category of historical thought.[39]

Lieber draws the implication from this that 'history must always have already occurred in order for it to be able to be comprehended as a significant context of meaning'.[40] The problems of *ex post* interpretation and the imputation of meaning are central to Mannheim's sociology of knowledge. Similarly, Mannheim's analysis of the past (ideology), the future (Utopia) and the present ('diagnosis of the times') might also be related to Dilthey's distinctions. The past requires interpretation of meaning, the present requires evaluation and the future purposive, transformative action.

However, within the context of Dilthey's philosophy of history, there exists another set of problems that are central to the German tradition in the sociology of knowledge: the analysis of world views.[41] Since a particular philosophy is bound up with the times in which it emerged, different philosophical systems — at this level of analysis, philosophy, too, is reduced to a world view — confront one another in their 'historical anarchy'. Since they strive towards universally valid knowledge, this confrontation and 'anarchy' are inevitable. As we shall see, Mannheim's critique of existing epistemologies is precisely that they claim absolute validity and yet are existentially bounded. But the similarities between Dilthey's *Weltanschauungslehre* and Mannheim's sociology of knowledge of knowledge go much deeper.

Dilthey produces a theory of the development of world views that is not confined merely to philosophy. At the roots of elementary world-views lies the experience that

Every great impression shows man a particular side of life; the world appears
in a new light; our attitudes towards life develop as such experiences are
repeated and combined.[42]

Dilthey distinguishes between these lower forms of world-view (perhaps what Mannheim would also term 'world-view') and a higher form (what Mannheim would term an 'ideology') as follows:

Such attitudes towards life . . . form the lower stratum for the formation of
world-views. These try to solve the enigma of life on the basis of the experiences in which the individual's varied relationships to life are reflected. In
the higher forms of world-views, one procedure is particularly prominent–
understanding something which cannot be grasped as it is given to us by
means of something more distinct.[43]

It is in this second level that philosophy belongs, and it is here that 'the historical anarchy of these systems' of philosophy exists. Dilthey argues that

'In each of the definitions of philosophy, only one aspect of its essence appears. Each of them is merely the expression of a standpoint which philosophy adopted at one stage in its history. Each states what to one or more thinkers in a certain context seemed requisite and possible as its role. Each of them defines a particular group of phenomena as philosophy, excluding from this group the other things often so-called. The great oppositions of standpoints, contending with *equal* [italics added: D.F.] force, gain expression in the definitions. They assert themselves over against one another *with equal justification. And the dispute can be settled only if a standpoint above the factions can be found* [italics added, D.F.].'[44]

Dilthey's solution is to provide a 'philosophy of philosophy' that will examine, and presumably evaluate, existing philosophies. This is possible because, despite the 'historical anarchy' of philosophies, the same types of world-view continually recur in the historical process. They are confined to naturalism, subjective idealism and objective idealism. Since they confront one another 'with equal justification', no rationally groundable decision can be made in favour of any one of them; any decision can only be an existential one. Lieber draws a further implication from Dilthey's analysis of world-views; namely, that within the history of philosophy, 'what has become fact and objectivated in this history becomes the irreducible norm for the historical self-interpretation and self-creation of men.'[45] This constancy in the recurrence of the same types of world-views probably derives from Dilthey's notion of human nature, as when he maintains that

A common human nature and the arrangement by which individuality is produced are vitally related to reality which is always and everywhere the same; life always shows the same sides.[46]

This would appear to conflict with his own view that, once 'voluntary theory' developed we became aware of 'the relativity of every historical form of life'.[47] But perhaps, for Dilthey, 'human nature' is prior to 'life'.

In Mannheim's sociology of knowledge, the situation of conflicting, irreconcilable world-views is one of the starting points for his theory of ideology. The synthesis of world-views to be undertaken by a 'philosophy of philosophy' in Dilthey's work is carried out by the sociology of knowledge in relation to competing ideologies. As Gadamer has argued, many of Dilthey's own problems arise from his 'entanglement in the impasses of historicism'.[48] Dilthey's historicism and that of later writers constitutes a further significant dimension in the sociology of knowledge.

Indeed, Lenk has argued that historicism, along with the reception of Marxism, is one of the essential impulses in the sociology of knowledge. Lenk argues that the whole *Lebensphilosophie* tradition had an important influence upon the concept of historical development. The elements of directedness and progression, are lost in a merely formal dynamism of 'dull will and drive'.[49] History ceases to have a meaning. Its meaning and truth are instead derived from the soul of creative individuals. As we have already seen in Dilthey's work, the search for a synthesis within — or rather from without — this stream of life is a central intention of his *Weltanschauungslehre*. In other writers, this cultural synthesis is to be one not merely of streams of thought but is also to be relevant for practice. It is most fully developed perhaps in Troeltsch's writings on historicism.

In the period around and shortly after the First World War, historicism, as a mode of thought and philosophical position that interpreted the validity of concepts and norms only in terms of the historically given and which accepted a thoroughgoing historical relativism,[50] was seen by many to be in a crisis. This crisis, it was assumed, could be overcome. In his essay on the crisis of historicism, Troeltsch defines historicism as

> the historicisation of our whole knowledge and experience of the intellectual world, as it emerged in the course of the nineteenth century. We see here everything in the flux of becoming, in the endless and ever-new individualism, in the determination by what has passed and in the direction of an unrecognised future. The state, law, morality, religion and art are dissolved in the flux of the historically emergent. . .[51]

Noticeably, it is the 'superstructure' that is historicised here, the whole of the cultural and intellectual apparatus. In the period around the First World War, 'all previously self-evident standards were shaken and thereby all images of development'.[52] It was a period of 'general historical relativism', scepticism towards history and often deep pessimism. More specifically, the crisis of historicism had to deal with the epistemological and logical problems of the study of history, to confront the introduction of sociological elements into historical research and explanation and 'the shaking of ethical systems of value'. This last was seen to result in 'the anarchy of values' and the struggle of value systems one with another. Troeltsch sees the solution to this crisis in 'a new contact between history and philosophy'' 'Historicism longs for ideas, philosophy for life. Both can be helped by such a connection.'[53] Elsewhere, Troeltsch calls more forcefully for a cultural synthesis. But it is clear that such solutions remain firmly anchored within the historicist problematic. This is the starting pointing for one of the key dimensions of the sociology of knowledge. In its final form, in Mannheim's work, we are still confronted with the demand for a cultural synthesis as its solution.

III

Lenk has argued that, from the beginning of the century at least,

German sociology was permeated by a 'tragic consciousness'.[54] He suggests that it may be summarised in the form of three central motifs:

> Firstly, in the first quarter of our century sociology reflects the process of independence of circumstances and institutions created by individuals from human needs. State organisations, bureaucratic apparatuses and political institutions have, . . . to a considerable extent, taken on a self-dynamic that is hardly controllable any more . . . (theory of alienation): secondly, in these sociological outlines, the sphere of economic, political and social relations and decisions of power ('real factors', interests, 'social being') confronts the sphere of values ('ideal factors') that is relatively unbounded by the former (two-realm-theory); thirdly, the intellectual-ideal sphere, measured against the 'massivity' of the social base, takes on a more or less unreal, powerless character (thesis of powerlessness).[55]

Included within this 'tragic consciousness', and as one of its central strands, is the sociology of knowledge itself. Lenk even goes so far as to suggest that this tragic consciousness is also characteristic of the whole of the crisis symptoms of the German cultural and human sciences in the inter-war period, themselves rooted in 'the collapse of German imperialism'. Insofar as this is the case, Lenk's interpretation loses its specific interpretative value for the sociology of knowledge in Germany. On the other hand, these tragic dualisms do recur continually in the sociology of knowledge — especially in the work of Scheler — even though they do not have their origins there. Within the German sociological tradition, the theories of Georg Simmel and Max Weber are significant in this context.

In Simmel's case, we can point to the importance of his theory of cultural alienation not merely for Mannheim's sociology of knowledge but also for Lukács' theory of culture. In *The Philosophy of Money* and elsewhere, Simmel presents us with a theory of cultural alienation and an unbridgeable subject-object duality that is manifested in the gulf between subjective and objective culture.[56] This duality within his theory of cultural crisis gives it its tragic pathos. Though there are many apparent similarities between Simmel's theory of alienation and that of Marx, the central thrust of his argument is against historical materialism. Simmel makes this clear in the preface to his *Philosophy of Money* where he explicitly states his intention

> to construct a new storey beneath historical materialism such that the explanatory value of the incorporation of economic life into the causes of intellectual culture is preserved, whilst these forms themselves are recognised as *the result of more profound valuations and currents of psychological, even metaphysical preconditions* [italics added, D.F.].[57]

Such an intention ensures that the forms of alienation and estrangement that Simmel discusses will constitute merely a part of a wider tragic situation.

Even where Simmel is most explicit in his account of alienation, as when he examines the consequences of the division of labour, the instances that he provides — though reminiscent of Marx's early writings — are located within the context of the development of a theory of subjective and objective culture. This theory is predicted upon an inevitable dualism of subject and object that can no longer be united dialectically. Thus, Simmel is here concerned with the increase in 'material culture' and the lag in 'individual culture', with the

> accentuation of the enigmatic relationship which prevails between social life and its products on the one hand and the *fragmentary* life-contents of individuals on the other.[58]

Hence, when Simmel produces instances of the alienation of the producer from his product and where 'the product is completed at the expense of the development of the producer', they are to be located within this context. One must concur with Lenk that,

> Where Marx speaks of the 'development of forces of production', Simmel moves in the direction of the development of the 'history of culture' that is dependent upon this sphere but has become detached from it. 'Objectified labour' becomes transformed into 'forms of historical expression of life'. 'Living labour', however, is enlarged with 'ever flowing . . . ever extending life'.[59]

Similarly, the development of the money economy and the various instances of alienation, although we can often see them as being located only within capitalism, are given no historical location by Simmel. Instead, as Kracauer suggests, 'he introduces examples from all periods of history or he works with the super-historical significance of intellectual types'.[60]

In his later writings, the location of these fragments and indeed all social phenomena within 'life' becomes more apparent:

> Life becomes to him an absolute principle out of which all phenomena can be explained and to which the many forms of existence, objective structure and norms as well as the subjective interpretations of diverse entities must equally be traced back. . . He was indeed convinced that from a *single* standpoint the world can never be fully comprehended.[61]

For this reason, too, 'a science of the totality of events' is not possible: it would lack 'viewpoint' (*Gesichtspunkt*) from which one could satisfactorily view the totality.[62] The totality is to be found, rather, in 'the absolute flowing movement' of life. The relativist problematic permeates Simmel's work too.

Another theme in his later writings is the crisis of culture, a crisis that is to be located once more in our alienation from culture. As Ludwig Marcuse expressed this alienation: 'Simmel suffered from the powerlessness of thought (*Ohnmacht des Denkens*) before life'.[63] More clearly than in his *Philosophy of Money*, concrete forms of alienation become merely part of a 'very general cultural predicament'. The paradoxical 'fate of the contents of culture' is that

> they were originally created by subjects and for subjects: but in their intermediate form of objectivity, which they take on . . ., they follow an immanent logic of development. In so doing they estrange themselves from their origin as well as from their purpose.[64]

This separation of subjective and objective culture, of 'ideal' and 'real' factors, as well as the explicit relativism of particular perspectives, constitutes a significant strand of the sociology of culture and knowledge in Weimar Germany.

Max Weber's work is certainly significant for the development of a sociology of culture in Germany, and although neither Scheler nor Mannheim ascribe to Max Weber a major role in the development of the sociology of knowledge in Germany, nonetheless, certain aspects of his work are relevant to its emergence. If we include Lukacs within the context of this tradition, then Weber's theory of rationality and the process of rationalisation are much in evidence in Lukacs' delineation of reification in *History and Class Consciousness*. This is quite apart from the use that Lukacs makes of the notion of 'imputation' (*Zurechnung*) and 'objective possibility' both in his earlier works and in his studies on class consciousness.

Lenk points to two aspects of Weber's work that are important for an understanding of the context of the sociology of knowledge — his individualistic methodology and his postulate of value-freedom. Sociology, for Weber, is to commence from individual social action, and not from collective action by, for instance, social classes or parties. If individual social action is the basis for a sociology, then methodologically it must also be individualistic in its orientation. As Weber wrote in 1920:

> If I am now a sociologist . . . I am so essentially in order to put an end to the use of collective concepts, a use which still haunts us. In other words: even sociology can only start from the action of one or a few, or many individuals, i.e. pursue a strictly 'individualistic' method.[65]

On this basis, it is possible to understand part of his critique of historical materialism. Meaningful social behaviour takes place between individuals. Any teleological understanding of history and any notion of developmental tendencies in history are the result of, as Lenk put it, the 'hypostatisation of particular value-judgments into quasi-scientific propositions'.[66]

Within the context of a theory of individual social action, it is not surprising that Weber should have seen as the greatest threat to the individual the progressive rationalisation of all spheres of life — a theme already developed by Simmel. In particular, the inevitable bureaucratisation of the political sphere and, under socialism, the economic sphere left little to choose between the two. On balance, Weber remained committed, as Mommsen has shown, to 'the principle of individual enterprise'.[67] The process of rationalisation, the increasing 'disenchantment of the world', and the all-pervasive bureaucratisation of modern society, together made it increasingly difficult to conceive of individual social action. The individual becomes, as in the Simmel's theory of alienation, increasingly powerless. Scheler, in this context, spoke of Weber's 'exaggerated love of darkness, of tragic insoluble tension in life, a love for the irrational as such'.[68]

However, Lenk sees a further consequence of Weber's methodological individualism and, in particular, his neo-Kantian tendencies, in the strict separation of fact and value. He suggests that

> Insofar as . . . the realm of value, in which particular acting individuals participate, is located in an extra-social sphere, that, for its part, possesses no visible connection with social realities, the possibility of a critical analysis of social relations disappears in favour of an immanent-theoretical critique of knowledge.[69]

This immanent-theoretical critique operates with abstract ideal-types that are elevated to 'objects' of knowledge. The realm of value is excluded from the scientific examination of social phenomena, which is governed by the principle of value-freedom. From a very different starting point, the preservation of an autonomous realm of values is also one of Scheler's central aims.

A prominent theme in Mannheim's sociology of knowledge is the conflict and competition between world views and ideologies. For Weber, at least in 'Wissenschaft als Beruf', the postulate of *Werturteilsfreiheit* was essential 'because the diverse orders of value in the world stand in an insoluble struggle with one another',[70] and it is here that

> the diverse Gods also struggle with one another and indeed for ever more . . . The old plurality of Gods, disenchanted and therefore in the form of impersonal forces, rise from their graves, strive to gain power over our lives and again resume their eternal struggle with one another.'[71]

Science itself can never bridge or overcome this eternal struggle. Hence, the scientist must perform a kind of internal division of labour between his scientific activity and his activity as a concrete individual. Within the scientific realm, the social scientist's task must be 'to render problematic what is given as conventionally self-evident'. For Weber, this could only be achieved by adherence to the postulate of value-freedom. Ironically, it is also a central task of any critique of ideology.

Nonetheless, Mannheim's sociology of knowledge, and in particular his analysis in *Ideologie und Utopie*, attempts to grapple with the value-freedom of the social sciences — and politics in particular — as well as calling for a cultural and political synthesis. His theory of ideology also posits the development of a value-free concept of ideology. But, much more so than Weber, Mannheim is concerned to advance beyond the separation of theory and practice that is evident in Weber's scientific demarcations. This, however, can only highlight the extent to which the sociology of knowledge had not only theoretical but practical intentions.

IV

As indicated earlier, the sociology of knowledge in Germany was conceived of not merely as an academic contribution to another branch of sociology but also as a response to various crises in German intellectual life and society. These crises were not necessarily ones that would spring readily to mind after a detailed analysis of Weimar Germany but they represent those crises in intellectual life and society that were perceived to be urgent and significant by those who developed the sociology of knowledge.

Perhaps nowhere is this crisis situation more acutely stated than in Mannheim's retrospective examination of German sociology which he published in 1934. There he argues that

> '*German sociology is the product of one of the greatest social dissolutions and reorganisations, accompanied by the highest form of self-consciousness and of self-criticism* . . . a process of social dissolution and crisis is not simply a negative process. For the significance of crises lies in the fact that they are not simply disintegrations but are, rather, the attempts which society makes to overhaul the whole of its organisation . . . In this context, then, sociology is seen to be not only the product of this process of dissolution but also a rational attempt to assist in the reorganisation of human society, to help in the reorganisation and readaption of the individual himself . . . If the function of a period of crisis and upheaval is defined in this sense, then the period since 1918 may be truly described as the most dynamic period in the history of German society . . . because these two decades saw a continuous and incessant shifting and displacement of social forces.'[72]

However, when we come to examine writings on the sociology of knowledge for an investigation of these 'social dissolutions', we find that it is hardly in evidence. Indeed, in Mannheim's case, the crises are almost always seen as intellectual. Thus, in *Ideologie und Utopie*, the most overtly political of Mannheim's German writings, the author is concerned with the 'crisis situation of thought'. — this despite the fact that he also argues that the concepts of ideology and utopia reveal 'the possibility of false consciousness'.

In a similar vein, Mannheim's description of the 'three debts to the dynamic forces of the last fourteen years' owed by German sociology comes nowhere near to grasping the significance of the 'dynamic forces' and crises of Weimar Germany. Instead, they too are located within the realm of consciousness. These three forces are:

> 1 The awareness that every social fact is a function of the time and place in which it occurs. . .
> 2 . . . the whole sphere of spiritual life appears in the new light of this constant variability. . .
> 3 Besides this visible interdependence between objective facts and ideas, this social mobility and dissolution reacts upon the human psyche; thus a period of social upheaval has its psychic aspect too. . .[73]

Only the third of these forces comes close to raising at least the possibility of an examination of the recent changes in German society.

Elsewhere, Mannheim can only relate the development of German sociology — and with it the sociology of knowledge — and its distinctive concerns, to the most general of social changes. In his essay on sociology in Germany, for instance, he attributes its emergence to two factors. The first is that

> the new sociology arose at an hour when the economy broadened into a world economy, when nations and countries were brought closer, but also were ranged against one another, when the occident broke into the orient. . .[74]

This led to a radical questioning of our position and situation in the world. The second factor lay within German society itself:

> social strata and classes which in decisive matters were previously present only in a passive capacity and whose will, range of instincts, thoughts, and habits had been passed by, broke into the power structure and into the sphere of consciously attended culture with claims of their own.[75]

This is presumably an oblique reference to the emergence of the working class — ard possibly the middle classes too — into the political and cultural structure of the Weimar Republic after their exclusion in Imperial Germany. But once again, the result of this intervention is merely seen as raising the question, 'Who are we?', both in terms of the present and also historically,[76] and does not differ markedly from Scheler's assumption that the individual had become totally problematical in Weimar Germany. Within Mannheim's writings on the sociology of knowledge, it is difficult to gain a clear conception of his notion of society. This is perhaps all the more surprising in view of his close friendship with the economist Emil Lederer in Heidelberg. Mannheim must have been aware of Lederer's analysis of German society, and especially his work on the role of white collar workers.[77]

The search for such a conception is necessary in terms of Mannheim's own programme for the sociology of knowledge. As a 'diagnosis of the times', it is remarkably reticent about the composition and structure of the society within which that 'diagnosis' is to take place. For instance, in his essay 'Competition as a Cultural Phenomenon' Mannheim adopts a pluralist notion of the composition of German society. Society is composed of competing strata and social classes who objectify their world-view within various institutional arrangements such as political parties. In much of *Ideologie und Utopie*, Mannheim is reluctant to delineate the composition and structure of the society within which these ideologies hold sway. On occasion, they are located within the context of class antagonism, but, in the main, world-views and ideologies are seen to be competing rather than conflicting with one another. This would give support to the view that Mannheim operates with a market model of society, at least with regard to world-views and ideologies, though in his chapter on Utopia he more often applied a model of society based upon domination and subordination even though its features remained unclear.

If we turn to Scheler's sociology of knowledge and his contemporary writings, there can be little doubt about his conception of German society. It, too, is a vision of the crises and dissolution of the social structure, but from a distinctive perspective. It springs from a conviction that society, including its rulers, has become decadent. It is a model of society that is firmly based upon a division between incapable elites and 'unruly' masses. Shortly before the First World War, Scheler argued that the basis and fundamental direction of society is provided by elites. It is

> Not an impersonal 'ideal' (Hegel), not a free-floating 'set of laws of reason' or the rational will (Kant and Fichte), not a law-like . . . ongoing development of reason and science (Comte), not the dark, hardly noticeable fate of blood-mixing (that) determines, in the last instance, what exists and what will be the structure and development of social groups but the existing dominant minority of those who set the pattern and leaders.[78]

This view of the primacy of elites is retained in his post-war writings and within the context of the increasing threat to aristocratic and higher values by the masses. The elite is necessary to overcome the perversion of values that has taken place with industrialization. Scheler's critique of capitalism is that of the neo-romantic anti-capitalist, a critique that is constantly wary of the masses and their susceptibility to ideologies. Marxism, for instance, is 'a *typical ideology of the oppressed and a critical protest ideology*'.[79] Scheler consistently describes the German economy as 'capitalist'. Its problems, however, are most often viewed as religious or psychological in origin. Thus, in a lecture in 1920, Scheler asks

> How can and should new, living *religious* and *moral motors* be developed in the soul of our people that will give back to them once more the will, energy and desire and satisfaction of work.[80]

German society is then, for Scheler, a capitalist society containing social classes, but they are not the most significant social groupings. In an 'age of adjustment' to the increasing proletarianisation and massification of society, it is elites and masses that are Scheler's central categories, just as it is presumably an intellectual elite that, by developing the sociology of knowledge, will seek to preserve 'essential' values. In fact, Scheler saw the sociology of knowledge as itself emerging out of a confrontation with the extreme relativism that has its origins in democratisation and the development of parliamentarianism, since

> The new relativistic study of world-views is the theoretical reflection of this democratic parliamentarianism which extends to world-views.[81]

This process of democratisation threatens the maintenance of absolute values held by a traditional intellectual elite which is faced with 'the increasing unruliness and uncontrollability of the masses and of capitalistic finance grown independent of its creators'.[82] In this age of adjustment or adaptation (*Zeitalter des Ausgleichs*), one is confronted with a bewildering array of adaptations:

> mutual adaptation of *race* tensions; mutual adaptation of the *mentalities* and the ways of regarding oneself, the world and God in all the great cultures, mutual adaptation between the special capacities of the *male* and *female* principles in Man; mutual adaptation between comparatively *primitive* and *hypercivilized* mentality; relatively mutual adaptation between *youth* and *age* in the sense of adequate evaluation of each other's spiritual attitudes; mutual adaptation between *class*-logics, class conditions and the rights of the upper and lower classes. . .[83]

In such an age of adaptation, it becomes all the more important to preserve traditional elites from the threat of extinction.

Such a metaphysical vision of contemporary German society is far removed from Lukács' estimation of the crises facing German society in the period after the First World War. There is no doubt at all that Lukács' analysis of German and other central European societies — such as Hungary — was in terms of the crises of capitalist societies. This is true, at least, for his post-1917 analyses after his 'conversion' to Marxism.[84] What Lukács took to be the crisis of European and, particularly from 1921 onwards, German society was located for him in the 'ideological crisis of the proletariat'. As Grunenberg argues, after the events of March 1921 in Germany and the failure of the workers' uprising,

> Lukács took up the 'ideological crisis of the proletariat' as *the* fundamental problem as such and, in contrast, placed the analysis of the *objective* factors in the background.[85]

The development of a revolutionary consciousness should be a precondition of any revolutionary strategy that deals with naked class conflict. Empirically-existent class consciousness or 'everyday' class consciousness is not Lukács' concern. With the increasing failure of the working class movements in Germany and elsewhere, Lukács could only develop the notion of an 'imputed' class consciousness that was based on a social class's 'objective possibilities'.

Hence, Lukács' analysis of the crisis of capitalism also appears to centre around a crisis of 'consciousness' though, unlike Mannheim's, this crisis is specifically located within a particular class, the proletariat. What this means, however, is that we cannot turn to Lukács for an account of the crisis of German society that Mannheim saw as the source of German sociology and the sociology of knowledge. The 'ideological crisis of the proletariat', however, is the source of a critique of ideology that sought to overcome this crisis through the postulated development of a revolutionary class consciousness.

Yet, when we argue that the sociology of knowledge and the critique of ideology have not merely theoretical but practical aims, then this is nowhere more apparent than in Lukács' *History and Class Consciousness*. Lukács himself saw this work as an attempt 'to clarify the theoretical problems of the revolutionary movement' and to re-examine the methodology of critique. The methodological dispute surrounding Marx's mode of procedure in his critique of political economy, for instance, is not a merely theoretical issue. Rather, Lukacs maintains that

> the logical conclusion for the dialectician to draw . . . is not that he is faced with a conflict between different scientific methods, but that he is in the presence of a *social phenomenon* and that by conceiving it as a socio-historical phenomenon he can, at once refute it and transcend it dialectically.[86]

Lukács' practical intention lies, then, in an examination of the relationship between the process of reification and the generation of a false praxis, the relationship between the 'ideological crisis of the proletariat' and the development of a revolutionary class consciousness, and the relationship between a critique of ideology and the organisation of revolutionary party activity. The critique of ideology, for Lukács, is decidedly concerned with the relation between theory and practice. The question of whether Lukács was successful in his aims must be left to a later chapter.

For Mannheim, too, the sociology of knowledge is not merely a theoretical discipline but has specific practical intentions. When commenting on the contemporary development of sociology in Germany, Mannheim suggests that sociology itself exceeds the narrow confines of an academic discipline, since

> the sociological problem constellation in the narrower sense transcends itself in two directions — in the direction of philosophy and in the direction of a *politically active world orientation* [italics added, D.F.][87]

This is because German sociology possessed a 'metaphilosophical tradition that was alive, as well as Marxism as a perspective that was politically activated in all its elements'.[88]

With regard to the sociology of knowledge itself, Mannheim provides substantial evidence for the view that it has overtly practical aims. The longest chapter of *Ideologie und Utopie* is not merely concerned with the possibility of politics as a science, but is also subtitled 'the problem of theory and praxis'. The sociology of knowledge's aim in overcoming the limitations of ideologies is not merely to provide a 'diagnosis of the times' but to aid our 'adjustment' to the present social situation. Ideologies prevent certain forms of social action and block a 'correct' understanding of the present situation. By 1932, Mannheim was claiming *practical* success for his sociology of knowledge. In the course of his review article on American sociology, he argues that

> a closer contact with central political problems involves the danger that judgments of value creep into science, reducing it to mere political propaganda. In fact, this danger constantly threatens German sociology just because it is closely in touch with political problems. However, if we know about this danger, we can take precautions against it, evolving methods which help to detect and eliminate political bias. . . The desire to treat politically important problems without being a victim to bias was responsible for the development in Germany of a new branch of social science, *Wissenssoziologie*. *This new branch of research, intended to be an organ of critical self-control, has already succeeded in detecting and subjecting to control important groups of sources of error* [italics added, D.F.][89]

What these sources of error were which this new discipline had successfully combated is not made clear. Mannheim saw the sociology of knowledge as extending the critical intention of sociology as a whole, since it too 'has from its beginnings been an organ of self-reflection and self-enlargement'.[90] Whether Mannheim's residual positivist intention of removing political bias by means of the sociology of knowledge was successful remains to be seen.

V

In examining the writings on the sociology of knowledge in Germany, an apparent paradox recurs. On the one hand, there is evidence to suggest that the sociology of knowledge is a response to crises in German society and that the key figures who developed the sociology of knowledge saw its concrete practical aims as being every bit as important as the theoretical aims. On the other hand, there is nowhere a concrete analysis of the crises of German society. This suggests that, in fact, the perception of these crises is largely in theoretical terms. In his introduction to *Ideologie und Utopie*, for example, Mannheim asserts that 'this book is itself conscious of an intellectual crisis situation' to which he can provide no ready solution. The crisis to which he alludes arises out of the conflict and struggle between systems of world-views, ideologies and forms of life. Since, as we shall see, any delineation of these forms of life by Mannheim is largely absent, we are left with the conflict of world-views and ideologies as constituting what Mannheim actually viewed as the crisis. This is not to suggest that he saw the sociology of knowledge as merely an empirical analysis of world-views and ideologies; it was also, for Mannheim, a new form of orientation to life and a possible means of synthesising world-views and ideologies.

The crisis is a crisis for intellectuals. They play a substantial role within the sociology of knowledge, not merely as its creators but also as the source of the resolution of the crisis. This is true not only for Scheler's notion of a cultural elite but also for Mannheim's relatively detached intelligentsia and for Lukács' intellectual vanguard. Within the context of the practical intentions of the sociology of knowledge and the critique of ideology, the intelligentsia play a central role. In Scheler's case, they are concerned with the preservation of the essential order of values, for Mannheim with a cultural synthesis, and in Lukács' case with the revolutionary party's mission. The role of the intelligentsia does not emerge out of a sociological analysis of German society. Its origins lie elsewhere. As Lenk argues,

> Mannheim's theory of the 'free-floating intelligentsia' does not arise out of a sociological context of problems but out of a postulate in the philosophy of culture and history. The structural analogy between the formal-logical narrow strata that is to form the archimedean point from which a transcendence of the relativistic consequences of historicism becomes possible, and the determination of the 'social-intellectual middle' is obvious.[91]

The intelligentsia are thus an essential part of the contemporary diagnosis of society and the attempt to construct a sociology of the modern era. But, in Mannheim's case, this remains merely a programme that is never fulfilled.

2 Max Scheler: From the Sociology of Culture to the Sociology of Knowledge

I

Max Scheler was the principal founder of the sociology of knowledge in Germany. His early articles in this sphere — in which he spoke of an 'Erkenntnissoziologie' and a 'Soziologie des Wissens' — were published in 1921 and 1922.[1] Despite Wilhelm Jerusalem's claim to have been the first to have discussed this area of sociology in an article in 1909,[2] it is clear that he did not develop these ideas in any detail. This Scheler did, in his edited collection *Versuche zu einer Soziologie des Wissens*, published in 1924,[3] as well as in his two-volume collection of essays *Schriften zur Soziologie und Weltanschauungslehre*, published in 1923 and 1924.[4] In 1924, Scheler presented a paper on 'Science and Social Structure's to the Fourth German Sociology Congress, which was published the year after.[5] This was followed, in 1926, by the publication of his major work on the sociology of knowledge, *Die Wissensformen und die Gesellschaft*.[6]

Yet despite the extent of Scheler's output in this area, few sociologists among either his contemporaries or successors have developed his theses on the sociology of knowledge or taken up his orientation in this field of study. Moreover, there are very few published works directly concerned with Scheler's sociology of knowledge — despite the existence of several hundred contributions to other aspects of his work[7] — and the reason for this may well lie in the nature of his conception of this field of study. Many writers have pointed to the difficulty of extracting a specifically *sociological* study of knowledge from his work in this area. Already in 1924, the sociologists who heard Scheler's paper 'Science and Social Structure' complained of the absence of a sociological content. Scheler's referent, Max Adler, asked

> is what has been presented here sociological? Of course, Professor Scheler has at various points in his presentation thrown in sociological observations. But the standpoint from which the speaker has commenced his work, the guiding direction of his thought which is the basis of that work, is itself not a sociological but an intellectual-historical (*geistesgeschichtlicher*) standpoint.[8]

But perhaps this is to overlook the relationship between Scheler's conception of the sociology of knowledge both to his sociology of culture and to his philosophical anthropology. Indeed, it has often been suggested that Scheler's sociology of knowledge cannot be understood except in terms of his philosophical intentions. Grünwald, for instance, comments:

> It is certainly no coincidence that, for Scheler, the sociology of knowledge stands in particularly close contact to the philosophical total system: for it is precisely Scheler's philosophy that contains in substantial measure the presuppositions which alone could meaningfully establish a system of the sociology of knowledge. A complete understanding of the sociology of knowledge developed by Scheler is therefore only possible by recourse to these ultimate meta-empirical premises, to which Scheler — in contrast to any form of positivism — openly and proudly refers.[9]

Such a judgment could certainly be substantiated by reference to the response of other contemporaries.

More recently, some commentators have sought, in contrast, to suggest that Scheler's work is fundamentally sociological in its nature. Bühl, for example, argues that despite the philosophical and theological interest in his writings, 'Scheler's work is . . . quite fundamentally sociology'.[10] More specifically, in his introduction to Scheler's *Problems of a Sociology of Knowledge*, Stikkers claims that 'Scheler can properly be credited with being the father of phenomenological sociology . . . And he offered the first significant alternative approach to sociology since August Comte's conception of that discipline as a positive science.'[11] Such interpretations of Scheler's work, however, totally overlook his own intentions. It might be possible to extract, in an abstract manner, the strictly 'sociological' propositions from Scheler's work but, in so doing, we would necessarily be unable to grasp the precise manner in which the problems of the sociology of knowledge were presented. Therefore our investigation of Scheler's work commences with an outline of his metaphysics and philosophical anthropology, before proceeding to his sociology of culture and knowledge.

However, Scheler's metaphysical standpoint should not be understood as part of our background knowledge that illuminates his sociology of knowledge but, rather, as a constituent element of it. On this point, Scheler himself is quite explicit. In the preface to the first edition of *Die Wissensformen und die Gesellschaft*, he states that 'One can only understand the author's metaphysics when one has read this book', which is itself 'an *introduction* to the metaphysics of the author'.[12] As one recent commentator maintains,

> the results of his philosophy are decisive for Scheler's empirical sociology; for these [metaphysical D.F.] theses are introduced into the sociology without discussion, largely as an axiomatic.[13]

Indeed, Scheler sees the two contributions which form the major part of *Die Wissenformen und die Gesellschaft* as providing the basis 'for strict *methodical metaphysical cognition* and thought'.[14] The reasons for the strong reassertion of the role of metaphysics in Scheler's sociology — ultimately a fusion (*'Verschmelzung'*) of metaphysics and sociology — must itself be sought in the nature of Scheler's aims in developing a sociology of knowledge.

Furthermore, what the major contributions to the German tradition in the sociology of knowledge have in common is their attempt to relate epistemological problems to sociology and to establish the social determination of epistemological problems. This has been one of the decisive areas of dispute in Mannheim's contribution to this area. Scheler too seeks to investigate the relationship between the two spheres and, in the foreword to *Die Wissenformen und die Gesellschaft*, states that

> The simultaneous consideration of a contribution to the *sociology of knowledge* and an extensive *epistemological* and ontological study in one and the same work might, at first glance, evoke surprise. It has its deeper basis in my fundamental guiding conviction that epistemological investigations without the *simultaneous investigation of the social-historical development* of the highest types of human knowledge and cognition are condemned to emptiness and unfruitfulness . . . An absolute historical *constancy* of 'human' forms of reason and principles, which the major part of all previous epistemologies has naively presupposed as the unchangeable object of their research, is, according to the conviction present in this book, an *idol*.[15]

That the results of Scheler's investigation of the relationship between epistemology and sociology is to substantially reduce the importance of epistemological concerns — since they are socially and historically varied — and to assert instead the primacy of ontology, and indeed a static ontological stability, can only be clearly seen once we have examined Scheler's metaphysics.

II

Kurt Lenk argues that the key to Scheler's philosophy is 'the question of the relationship of "Geist" and "Leben". It is the key to his metaphysics and anthropology. The determination of the nature of "Geist" and "Leben" is the central theme of any critical presentation of Scheler's philosophy'.[16] It would be true to say that the whole of Scheler's metaphysics not only rests upon this dualism — and this dualism was, of itself, not peculiar to Scheler — but that it forms the basis for the other dualisms that animate his metaphysics and his sociology. In his metaphysics, the dichotomies of *Sosein* and *Dasein*, essence and existence, absolute and relative, spirit and nature, and spirit and history, play a crucial role. In his sociology, ideal factors and real factors, ideal sociology and real sociology, and *Geistlehre* and

Trieblehre, are crucial to his development of a sociology of culture. In his view of society, a biological base and an idealised superstructure, elites and masses are central dichotomies.

Grünwald, too, has argued that this 'powerlessness of the spirit' (Scheler's own phrase) lies at the centre of Scheler's metaphysics and that this position is to be derived from the ontological dualisms we have just indicated. However, Grünwald suggests that Scheler held this position in common with many of his contemporaries — and he includes Mannheim here — so that

> this conviction of the unreality of the spirit is a characteristic not only of the sociology of knowledge but of the whole intellectual climate of the present period. One can see the contrast most sharply when one contrasts the theses of the sociology of knowledge with, for instance, Hegel's statement of the 'powerlessness of nature' and the omnipotence of the spirit.[17]

Hence, we need to ask, what was distinctive about the way in which these fundamental dualisms basically shaped Scheler's sociology of knowledge. Lieber, for example, argues that at the basis of Scheler's philosophy 'lies the ontologically interpreted separation of existence and essence, nature and spirit as two ultimate ontological givens which, in their development in his sociology of knowledge, are basically directed against the Marxist superstructure-base thesis'.[18] Indeed, any examination of the manner in which this relationship between base and superstructure is treated and the actual content of those two elements will reveal how far away from any kind of Marxist position — even a mechanistic one — Scheler really is.

Scheler's metaphysics seeks to reverse what he takes to be erroneous and decadent tendencies in modern thought and life, that is, it seeks to correct what he saw as the 'subversion of values'.[19] In particular, Scheler attempts to oppose the tendency in *Lebensphilosophie* to reduce consciousness to a stage in the development of life, to reduce consciousness to existence. He seeks to assert the irreducibility of the human mind. Since human beings are the ones who carry out mental acts and realise them in a concrete form, it is the concept of the autonomous person who confronts his environment that is crucial to Scheler's preservation of the autonomy of the mind. Yet the human being as such has become a problematic entity for Scheler. In 1926 he wrote:

> We are the age in roughly ten thousand years of history in which the human being has become completely and absolutely 'problematic'; in which he no longer knows what he is, whilst at the same time he also *knows that* he does not know.[20]

Furthermore, to see the human mind as a timeless essence that is embodied in the concrete form of the person in the temporal life process is to give to the very entity that Scheler seeks to preserve an element of unreality. Hence, 'the denaturalisation of the mind expresses . . . its impotence in relation to historical reality.'[21] The mind seems at times to be reduced to a passive receptacle. This difficulty in preserving the autonomy of the mind is compounded by Scheler's assertion of the identity of physiological and psychic life processes. He speaks of the 'functional identity of psyche and physiology.'[22] In so doing, Lenk argues, 'the psychic self is . . . reduced to a mere "consciousness correlate of the vital impulses and life processes" '.[23] Similarly, a contemporary of Scheler's detected in his work the 'biologization of the self'.[24] Not only does this imply a separation of consciousness and *Geist* but it leads Scheler into establishing what was precisely the opposite of his original intention, namely, that the mind is subordinate to life. With reference to this dualism, Cassirer asks how the quite disparate worlds of life and spirit can accomplish a homogeneous work and how the spirit is able to exert any effect upon a world to which it does not itself belong.[25] The spirit is unable to affect anything beyond itself; it is a testimony to 'the powerlessness of the mind'.

This paradoxical conclusion is also evident in Scheler's relationship to phenomenology. The distinction between essence and existence, between *Sosein* and *Dasein*, is central to Scheler's ontology. Scheler adopts an essentialist notion of truth, that is, he sees a truth as being revealed through a phenomenological reduction, through a bracketing of existential phenomena. He views his phenomenology as one which 'goes behind all causal connections and reveals the absolute facts'. How much Scheler's epistemology rests upon this pervasive dichotomous standpoint may be seen from the schema of propositions which Lenk extracts from Scheler's later writings.

> 1 The distinction between essence [*Wesen*] and existence [*Dasein*] within all that is relatively existent is not only one that is taken from the phenomenological method but is also an ontic one, that is, it exists in the nature of phenomena themselves.
>
> 2 This division is universally valid for all possible forms of being.
>
> 3 The evidence for the duality of essence [*Essenz*] and existence [*Existenz*] can, in principle, be shown for any possible intentional object.
>
> 4 Knowledge of essence and knowledge of existence are qualitatively distinguished both with regard to evidence for them and with regard to their attainability for cognitive consciousness.
>
> 5 Existential knowledge, both in its scope and content, is more limited than essential knowledge.
>
> 6 As well as Kant's formal a priori there exists a material a priori, an a priori of essence that emerges out of the phenomenological standpoint. This material a priori belongs to the phenomenal givens themselves.[26]

This ontological notion of knowledge leads Scheler back into the powerlessness of the mind. In this and other respects, Scheler cannot be described as an orthodox phenomenologist since his philosophy is in many respects antithetical to the phenomenology developed by Husserl.[27] To take but one important difference between Husserl and Scheler,

> Scheler enlarges the division between knowledge of facts and knowledge of essences that Husserl only intended to be a logical-epistemological division in the sense of the phenomenological method into an ontologically conceived dualism of spirit (*Geist*) and drives (*Drang*). To the metaphysics of the spirit there corresponds a doctrine of drives (*Dranglehre*) that provides the foundation for his theory of reality . . . Scheler's dualism allows the sphere of what is real to appear ultimately as the manifestation of impulsive blind drives.[28]

Not only is Scheler's phenomenological standpoint inconsistent with that advanced by Husserl and many of his followers, but he also seeks to ground phenomenology itself in the ontological premises of his metaphysics. The cognitive subject who might engage in phenomenological reductions and apply the phenomenological method to reality is, as it were, imprisoned in that reality through his vital drives and impulses.

Scheler's theory of reality has important implications for the nature of the knowledge that the sociology of knowledge investigates and itself produces. This knowledge cannot be of the same order as that which is produced in other phenomenological accounts that do not share this ontologically-grounded, dualistic metaphysics. The objects which Scheler's phenomenology reveals are not those that would be recognised in an orthodox phenomenological analysis. As Bracht comments,

> Scheler's phenomenology . . . contradicts itself since it does not bring the object to self-givenness but rather *determines* its object as ideal being. The established ideal sphere stands quite unrelated over against the free human being.[29]

But it is not only in relation to the phenomenological method that the nature of the object of Scheler's analyses is questionable. More significantly, perhaps, for his sociology of knowledge are Scheler's notions of history and society.

Scheler's interpretation of history has its basis in the Catholic doctrine of the Fall and in Nietzsche's theory of decadence. For Scheler, the notion of progress is completely rejected. In his sociological writings, this is manifested in his analysis of decadence and in his assertion of the inversion of the hierarchy of human values such that the highest values are now given the lowest estimation. Honigsheim suggests that one of the basic negative impulses in Scheler's work is his 'insight into the pervertedness of the whole modern bourgeois world'.[30] In other words, it is a continuation of that tradition of social theory derived largely from Nietzsche which contains a conception of human alienation that rests upon the inversion of human values. In

Ressentiment, for example, Scheler castigates the domination of a technological ethos in the modern world but within the context of a set of categories that could never be used to grasp the real source of this alienation. Scheler argues that

> With the development of modern civilization, *nature* . . . and objects have become *man's lord and master,* and *the machine* has come to dominate *life.* The 'objects' have progressively grown in vigor and intelligence, in size and beauty — while man, who created them, has more and more become a cog in his own machine . . .
>
> If we consider the transvaluation of the relation between tool and organ in its totality, we must conclude that the spirit of modern civilization does not constitute 'progress' (as Spencer thought) but a *decline* in the evolution of mankind. It represents the rule of the weak over the strong, of the intelligent over the noble, the rule of mere quantity over quality. It is a phenomenon of decadence.[31]

The critique of this alienation remains within the confines of Scheler's valuations. Specifically, it has no historical referent. Where Scheler does examine something approaching historical events, his account of them rapidly becomes biological or psychological. For instance, referring to contemporary mass movements and specifically the youth movement of the post First World War period — which, for Scheler, represent a 'systematic revolt of impulse and instinct' — he sees its origins as follows:

> I hold this movement to be in no way an ephemeral 'after-the-War' apparition — it began, undoubtedly, before the War, as the fact of Nietzsche shows — no, I hold it to be a mass movement, channelled deep in the previous course of Western history, towards *a new distribution of Man's total energy between the cerebral cortex and the rest of the organism.*[32]

The change in Scheler's argument from an actual social movement to an account of this movement in terms of a change in human physiological constitution demonstrates Scheler's desire to explain social change in terms of changes in basic drives.

This theme of the decadence of the modern world both abounds in Scheler's post-First World War writings and coincides with his attempt to develop a sociology of knowledge. In the essay just quoted, Scheler speaks of 'the increasing unruliness and uncontrollability of the masses and of the machinery of capitalistic finance grown independent of its creators'.[33] Scheler's solution is posed not in terms of a change in the nature of social, political and economic institutions but in terms of a balancing of technical intelligence and mechanisation by 'a new art of contemplation and *patientia*'. In other words, there is seldom a sociological explanation of social phenomena. Instead, the social reality Scheler describes continues to dominate, as it were, behind people's backs.

What is absent in Scheler's philosophical anthropology is a notion of society, social system, social structure and other related concepts that might mediate between these notions of spirit and drives and impulses. The individual person, though a central category in Scheler's philosophy, is so robbed of active characteristics — the individual's consciousness is reduced to physiological impulses, the individual's actions are regulated by drives — that it is insufficient to fulfil this mediatory role. Similarly, in *Ressentiment*, Scheler adheres to a residual concept of society that is also incapable of fulfilling this mediatory role. There he states that

> 'society' is not the inclusive concept, designating all the 'communities' which are united by blood, tradition, and history. On the contrary, it is only the *remnant*, the *rubbish* left by the inner *decomposition* of communities. Whenever the unity of communal life can no longer prevail, whenever it becomes unable to assimilate the individuals and develop them into its living organs, we get a 'society' — a unity based on mere contractual agreement. When the 'contract' and its validity ceases to exist, the result is the completely unorganised 'mass', unified by nothing more than momentary sensory stimuli and mutual contagion.[34]

The components of Tönnies' *Gemeinschaft-Gesellschaft* distinction are here emptied of even more content. Elsewhere, society is seen as being composed of helpless elites and unruly masses. The masses threaten the preservation of the aristocratic order of values whilst the elites are unable to regenerate themselves to face the challenge from below. In 1925 Scheler speaks again of 'our age of disunity and of masses who are no longer controllable' and says that 'I know of no time in history when the guiding elites were in greater need of true culture and when it was harder to attain'.[35] This elites-masses dichotomy again expresses Scheler's own 'powerlessness of the mind' thesis and, at a more concrete level, parallels the abstract *Geist-Leben* dichotomy.

The categories of history and society are absent from Scheler's philosophical anthropology except as empty receptacles or vehicles for more basic forces. Where the dualistic view of the world is established as a dichotomy between a base and a superstructure and where the relationship between the two is viewed in a mechanistic manner — either as a mechanistic Marxist base-superstructure model or, here, as a *Geist-Leben* duality — this leads to a notion of the superstructure as unreal. Specifically, what is absent in Scheler's philosophical anthropology is any notion of conscious human activity, of praxis. Instead, Scheler presents us in his writings with a rhetoric of passivity — the individual is no longer an actor but a mere medium for the manifestation of other forces. Human beings are not conceived in terms of their societal relationships and connections but in terms of irrational drives and impulses, against which the ideal sphere, the value hierarchy, is powerless.

As Troeltsch puts it, 'thus, as with Nietzsche, the human being is a dead end of biological evolution, the sick animal that can only develop itself in an intellectual direction and thus absorb its animal drives'.[36] The rhetoric of passivity — 'essential being is revealed' to the individual; free will is a 'negative power to *control and release* the impulses of drives'; '*experiences* of all kinds *happen*' to individuals, etc. — is instructive in that it shows how the individual as creator, as actor, as transformer, is absent from Scheler's anthropology. As Lenk has pointed out, this central feature of Scheler's philosophical anthropology leads him into a conservative position:

> The assertion that the realisation of the highest ranked values can never, in whatever manner, be influenced by what is socially given, that their manipulability extends only to the relatively low values leads, *eo ipso*, to the view that there is no point in striving for an improvement in social circumstances.[37]

Though Scheler most fully advanced the thesis of the powerlessness of the mind (*Ohnmacht des Geistes* and also *Machtlosigkeit des Geistes*)[38] within his sociology of knowledge, the wider issue of the alienation of the mind is already present in his pre-War writings. To give but two instructive examples, we may turn to Scheler's review of Werner Sombart's *Der Bourgeois* (January 1914) and his article, 'The Future of Capitalism' (February 1914).[39] The first of these opens with a dramatic statement on the alienation of the mind, the inversion of fundamental values and the perversion of intellectual energies. Scheler announces that

> Amongst the many signs that demonstrate to us the death of the system of life under whose energy and direction we still live, I can see none more convincing than the deep alienation that today lies in its specific system of life. The history of this alienation is still quite young.[40]

This alienation, Scheler says, is manifested in such writers as Nietzsche and the poet Stefan George and extends today to those in control of economic life such as Walther Rathenau. However, what all of them have experienced in common is that

> the totality of forces that have erected what is typical of the whole of our contemporary system of life could only rest upon a deep perversion of all basic intellectual energies, upon a delusory subversion of all meaningful orders of value.[41]

This alienation is so pervasive that it threatens 'the human type' that was responsible for the existence and maintenance of this system of life.

Although Scheler is extremely vague about the nature of this alienation, it is possible to see some central elements of his thesis of the alienation and powerlessness of the mind. Firstly, it is clear that this alienation is intellectual and spiritual. Secondly, it involves the inversion of intellectual energies and value systems that were previously part of some natural relationship to nature and society. And finally, this alienation does not, for example, threaten an economic order but 'the human type' which gave rise to capitalism. All this is to suggest that the alienation of the mind has become all-pervasive. But elsewhere in his review, and with reference to the 'spirit of capitalism', he argues that the intellectual sphere is the most significant historically since 'the change in dominant *ideals* and images of desires . . . is much more fundamental than that in the historical reality of events'. Thus, on the one hand, the intellectual sphere is the most significant in historical change whilst, on the other, it is threatened by a deep alienation that renders it powerless.

However, Scheler's review already points to a kind of psycho-biological reductionism that is accentuated in Scheler's sociology of knowledge. This is already evident in Scheler's notion of capitalism:

> Capitalism is, in the first place, not an economic system of property distribution but a whole system of life and culture. This system has sprung up out of the goals and value preferences of a specific biopsychic *type of human being*, in fact the bourgois type.[42]

Hence, the decline in capitalism comes about with the decline in the superiority of this type of human being. But even the state socialism and its hoped-for maximization of welfare that Scheler sees Germany moving towards 'with full sails' is itself-one of the 'crudest *consequences of the domination* of the capitalist spirit'. The only hope of overcoming capitalism is through a new human type that Scheler sees emerging in the youth movements. They are 'not limited to specific *social classes* or *parties* but penetrate *all* classes with their new spirit'.[43] Similarly, in his wartime writings, Scheler sees the war as not being the result of rationalisable interests but as having its 'roots in the essence of life itself'. Indeed, Scheler views the war as strengthening the intellectual existence of a nation, no doubt as a way out of this deep alienation and sickness.[44] This vitalism extends into Scheler's sociology of culture and sociology of knowledge. Paradoxically, the alienation of the mind is then explained by a theory that itself has as one of its central presuppositions the alienation of the mind.

This brief account of the metaphysics, philosophical anthropology and earlier social philosophy of Scheler has brought us to the point at which we can commence an examination of his sociology of culture which Scheler sees as being the foundation for his sociology of knowledge.

III

Scheler views the sociology of knowledge as an intrinsic part of a wider study of the sociology of culture. That is, the problems in the sociology of knowledge — such as the social determination of thought — are to be seen within the context of the determination of culture by social, 'real' factors. Scheler seeks to integrate the sociology of knowledge within the broader context of a sociology of culture. In the foreward to *Die Wissensformen und die Gesellschaft*, he states that 'the "sociology of knowledge" is, in its first part, concerned with the "essence and order of historical causal factors", at the same time with the first positive attempt to basically *overcome* the one-sidedness and fundamental errors of both the naturalistic study of history, primarily the economism of Karl Marx, and the ideological and scientistic interpretations of history (Hegel and Comte).'[45]

With this as his central aim, Scheler seeks to develop a '*basic law [Grundgesetz[* of the changing forms — temporally and according to epochs of culture — of the *interplay of the intellectual-ideal* and *impulse driven-real determining and influencing factors* of historical-social life.'[46] It is worth pointing out here that what Scheler takes as his central areas of attack — Comte's law of three stages and his positivism, Marxism, etc. — are also reproduced in a different manner in Scheler's own work. For example, in many places, Scheler adopts a base-superstructure distinction and this becomes more pronounced in his sociology of culture; in countering positivism, Scheler too asserts the possibility of basic laws and provides their axiomatic foundation; in attacking Comte's law of the three stages of knowledge, Scheler adopts his own three types of knowledge, but ranks them differently — almost in reverse order — to Comte. Scheler also suggests that, 'ultimately we fully accept Karl Marx's statement that it is man's *being* (though not only his economic, "material" being as Marx takes it to be) which directs all their possible "consciousness", "knowledge" and the boundaries of their understanding and experience'.[47] However, agreement with Marx on this point is only apparent.

Scheler announces that he will investigate 'the fundamental fact of the *social nature* of all knowledge' and will also take into account the sociology of knowledge's relationship to epistemology and logic, to psychology, to the history of knowledge, to the sociology of culture and to 'real sociology (sociology of race, power, and economic groups and their changing "organisation")'. The sociology by means of which these investigations will be undertaken is one that is concerned 'not with individual facts and events . . . but with *rules*, types (average and logical ideal types) and, where possible, with *laws*'.[48] This sociology is concerned with '*factual*, thus not "normative" . . . determination'. Sociology is to be divided into a sociology of culture (*Kultursoziologie*) and a sociology of what is real (*Realsoziologie*), that is, a 'sociology of the *superstructure* and *base* of the whole of human life's contents'.[49] This duality of the sociological domain presupposes certain kinds of investigations in each of these realms; '*a necessary presupposition for the sociology of culture is a doctrine of the human mind* (*Geistlehre*) *and for the sociology of what is real a doctrine of human drives* (*Trieblehre*)'. Though this distinction might seem an arbitrary one, for Scheler, 'this distinction is . . . an *ontologically* and not merely "methodically" grounded distinction'.[50]

Already, however, Scheler's widening of the base of 'the whole of human life's contents' into a study of drives and impulses removes the independence of the societal dimension from the centre of a theory of society and replaces it with a psycho-biological base. This is exemplified in Scheler's assertions that 'without the drive for subsistence and the objective goal that it biologically serves — nourishment — there would be no economy' or that 'without a drive for power there would be no state'.[51] Yet Scheler argues that sociology will study not merely these two realms of the ideal and the real but also the '*interaction* of the ideal *and* the real, the intellectually and drive-conditioned determining factors'.[52] Hence, in the case of the economy and the state, they are not merely determined by drives and impulses since 'without the mind and its normative rules there would be no economy, no state'. This would already suggest that Scheler's social categories remain uneasily suspended between the ideal and real spheres.

However, the key to an understanding of these two spheres lies in the nature of the interaction between them. Scheler argues that the goal of 'causal sociology' is the search for the factors that determine 'the realization of the ideal and the real' spheres; more specifically, the search for '*a law of ordering the realization of ideal factors and real factors*'.[53] Not only should this law be capable of accounting for historical development in the life process but it should also be 'a law of the *potential* dynamic emergence' of the life-contents of social groups. Such a law deals with '*the basic type of co-operation* between ideal and real factors, objective mind and real-life relationships'.[54]

Scheler argues that the mind can affect what might potentially emerge but not what will emerge. In itself it lacks 'power' or 'effectiveness' in relation to existence. Though it is a 'determining factor', it is not 'a "factor of realization" of possible cultural development. *Negative* realization factors or real *selective* factors . . . are rather the real, drive-determined life circumstances, i.e. the particular combination of real factors.'[55] Scheler freely admits that one consequence of this thesis is that 'the "purer" the intellectual sphere, the more powerless it is in the sense of dynamic effects in society and history', and that, conversely, 'the lowering in the evaluative level of any intellectual entity . . . through increased *dissemination* and gaining of power amongst the masses is thus an inescapable law of all human realization of meanings and values.'[56] In order to become effective, therefore, the intellectual realm must attach itself to real forces and tendencies in society, otherwise it will remain a mere potentiality. Therefore, 'It is only where "ideas" of whatever form *unite* with interests, drives, collective impulses or . . . "tendencies" that they gain *indirect* power and the possibility of being realized . . . The *positive* realization factor of a purely cultural constellation, however, is always the *free act* and the free will of a "small number" of *persons*, primarily the leader, the exemplary figure, the pioneer' who can show a majority how to copy and imitate the new cultural trend. The extent of influence exerted by the intellectual realm is therefore strictly limited; it can aid or modify real factors but cannot realise itself without the aid of these factors:

> Thus, in the intellectual-cultural sphere, there exists 'freedom' and autonomy for what occurs according to its essence, meaning and value — but always in the real expression suspendable by the specific causality of the 'base'; one might term this *liberté modifiable* ('suspensible'). Conversely, in the sphere of real factors there exists only that *'fatalité' modifiable*, of which A. Comte has aptly and correctly spoken.[57]

It is here that Scheler's own thesis of the 'powerlessness of the mind' achieves one of its clearest expressions. The intellectual-cultural sphere may be realized in those directions which the real factors permit; the real factors can only be modified by the intellectual-cultural sphere, they cannot be fundamentally changed or removed. One important vehicle for the realization of ideal factors is the relationship between the elite that creates the intellectual cultural realm and the masses who assimilate it and, by implication, make possible its realization. The elite, too, is powerless without the masses. The human cultural realm is thus anchored in the realm of real factors. There can be no genuine possibility for mutual interaction or for a dialectical relationship.

Scheler amplifies his sociology of culture by delineating the ideal and real spheres and provides a series of axioms with regard to the content and changes that occur within each sphere. This exposition is prefaced by a second conjuncture of causal factors that is located in the relationship between the various conditioning factors, the relationship of the ideal factors to one another (for example, whether they are static or dynamic), the relationship of individual forms of real factors to one another and, finally, the relations between the major groups of real factors to the individual forms of ideal factors.

Hintze, a contemporary commentator, aptly remarks that although 'the objective just as much as the subjective human mind, the individual just as much as the collective mind, is quite incapable of producing anything in the real world through its own free creation' and although 'the real factors certainly form the base of all culture, yet the content and essence of the ideal superstructure is not explicable in terms of these real factors but in terms of its autonomous, independent qualities'.[58] Thus, for Scheler, there exists a set of axioms or laws for the nature and development of the ideal and the real spheres. There also exists a fundamental contradiction here since these independent laws governing the ideal factors cannot themselves be truly independent since, as a form of social knowledge, they are themselves governed by the laws which determine the real factors.

Within the ideal sphere, Scheler distinguishes between an 'objective mind' that is a 'meaning content embodied in some material substance or in reproducible psycho-physical entities such as tools, works of art, language, written works, institutions, morals, customs, rites, ceremonies', and a corresponding subjective mind, '*a changing structure of the "mind" of the group* which, for the individual member, possesses a more or less binding importance or power and is experienced as "obligatory" '.[59] These various forms of objective mind and these ideal factors exist in a definite relationship to one another; there exists between them 'essential and not merely fortuitous empirical dependencies', for example, between 'religion, metaphysics, positive science, between philosophy and positive science', and so on. These relationships and dependencies, however, are a manifestation of their different origins in the directions of human drives and impulses. The mind or spirit thus exists '*only in a concrete plurality* of infinitely varied groups and culture'.

Scheler here explicitly rejects any Enlightenment notion of a unified rationality or earlier notion of a single human nature (a single human nature must come into question since the plurality of ideal factors rests ultimately upon real factors): 'To speak of some kind of factual "unity of human nature" as a presupposition of history and sociology is thus useless, even pernicious.' A common structure only exists within the 'cultural elements of *a* group', with '*a* cultural concretion'. Similarly, the a priori notion of a universal human reason is also to be rejected on the same basis: '. . . rather, the pluralism of groups and forms of culture is the starting point from which all sociology commences.'[60]

At first sight, this assertion of the plurality of groups and forms of cultures may appear to be soundly based and not liable to confront Scheler with fundamental problems. But if we consider, further, that these groups have diverse intellectual apparatuses and these cultural forms developed by diverse groups are ultimately grounded in different human drives, then the problem of relativism seems to arise at least at a factual level. This Scheler recognizes, but goes on to argue that such a view may still be opposed to philosophical relativism, though not by subsuming the plurality of values and cultural forms under the values of one culture — as Scheler argues is the case for Troeltsch — but rather by asserting that, 'similar to Einstein's theory within its realm — the essential idea of man with regard to the *absolute realm of ideas and values* quite firmly stands much higher above all *factually* existent historical value systems'.[61]

It is a feature of all relativist positions, Scheler argues, that they are always solved by the assertion of the existence of something absolute that stands outside, or above, them. This is not the case with Einstein's theory, however, since nothing stands outside the relativities of which he speaks; rather, these relativities are in the world. For Scheler, relativities are in the world but, because of their determination by real factors, they must be seen to be based on something outside both the real and ideal spheres in order to enjoy any independent existence. It is at this point that Scheler asserts the existence of a sphere above that of the ideal and the real — a transcendental sphere that can have no relation to human beings since it would itself be part of one of the two spheres. This sphere is, for Scheler, a 'prepresupposition (*Urvoraussetzung*) of human history, even of human beings themselves'.

Besides the existence of a 'functionalization' of genuine ideas as a result of their being taken up by the masses and therefore becoming capable of being realized, Scheler develops a series of axioms that deal with the cumulative development within a single intellectual structure. The 'differentiation and integration of intellectual spheres' should be the subject of investigation — as was undertaken by Spencer — but the ordering of the levels of this differentiation led to many spurious claims. In particular, Scheler seeks to counter Comte's claim that the different spheres of knowledge can be viewed in a hierarchy of historical progression. At the same time, Scheler argues that only Comte, Spencer and other positivist philosophers have 'brought epistemology into closer connection with sociological statics and dynamics'.[62] Comte's mistake, however, was to take the three forms of knowledge — religious, metaphysical and positive — and to attempt to show that each grew out of the other in a historical sequence commencing with the religious form. Comte treated as 'temporal stages of development what is de facto only a process of *differentiation* in the mind'.[63] According to Scheler, 'religious, metaphysical, and positive thinking and knowing are not historical stages of the development of knowledge but permanent attitudes of mind and forms of knowledge given with the human mind as essential features of it'.[64]

Scheler does accept the importance of the classification of knowledge into these three types, and subsequently attempts to provide an investigation of their features and development that is based, ostensibly, on his sociology of knowledge in *Die Wissensformen und die Gesellschaft*. But he also seeks to separate the three forms of knowledge, which he sees as resting on 'three different motives, on three entirely different groups of acts of the knowing mind, three different aims, three different personality types, and three different social groups. Also, the historical forms of movement of these three mental powers are essentially different.'[65]

A second section of the sociology of the culture therefore has to deal with 'the social forms of intellectual co-operation'. The religious form of knowledge is organised into 'holy knowledge, religious communities, churches, sects'; the metaphysical into *'schools of wisdom'* and *'educational* communities in the ancient sense'; the positive form, based on the division of labour, rests on 'teaching and research organisations'. Each form develops its own linguistic conventions and axioms and Scheler takes each of these forms of knowledge to be genuine, independent forms of knowledge.

He argues that such forms are to be sharply distinguished from the 'common *mixed* forms of collective *interests* and (supposed) contents of *knowledge* derived from people's membership of strata, occupations, classes and parties, strata, occupational, class and party prejudices which we wish to subsume under the general title of *"prejudices"*.'[66] The specific quality of this *'illusory* knowledge' lies in the fact that the roots of the collective interest in this knowledge always remain 'unconscious'.

These prejudices, which do not constitute genuine knowledge, are also to be distinguished from ideologies which have a different origin. He argues that where 'these systems of automatic and unconscious "prejudices" consciously seek to justify themselves behind a particular tendency in religious, metaphysical or positive scientific thought or even by drawing upon dogmas, principles and theories that emerge out of those higher organisations of knowledge, the new mixed form of *"ideologies"* emerges, whose most powerful example in recent history is Marxism as a form of "ideology of the oppressed" '.[67] In this early formulation of the notion of ideology, Scheler views ideology as having its roots in collective prejudices that are formulated within the context of a higher form of knowledge. Ideologies are therefore linked to both base and superstructure.

Hence there are at least three types of potential or apparent knowledge. Firstly, there are the genuine forms of religious, metaphysical and positive knowledge that form the centre of his field of interest in his sociology of culture and knowledge. But there exist two other, subordinate types of pseudo-knowledge. One is the body of supposed knowledge that is, in fact, a bundle of prejudices that are unconsciously absorbed by certain groups in society. The second is, for Scheler, a mixture of these prejudices with genuine forms of knowledge, a mixture that leads to the distorted form of ideologies. These ideologies emerge out of the attempt to legitimate or justify the prejudices of a specific social group and are, in contrast to prejudices, conscious constructs.

Scheler's examination of the axioms necessary for developing an account of the ideal sphere proceeds in a very schematic manner. As well as considering the forms of intellectual co-operation, Scheler argues that we must also examine the basic forms of human grouping as such —

'the fluctuating *horde*', 'the ongoing life community', 'society' and the form of personalistic systems of solidarity amongst individuals. A sociology of culture must investigate how particular phases of knowledge emerge with distinctive categorial structures such as the organic and the mechanical-technical forms of thought. It must examine the forms of movement in cultural spheres such as that of cumulative progress or decline. Scheler hints at a whole series of problems which the sociology of culture must consider, but does so in only the most programmatic manner, in a manner that is somewhat akin to Gurvitch's axiomatic and taxonomical incursions into the sociology of knowledge.[68] Thus far, however, we have only examined the one side of this ideal-real factor dualism. We must now turn to the real factors.

The axioms relating to the ideal sphere are secondary when compared with 'the deepest and most fruitful questions in the sociology of culture', concerned with the nature of the regular order of effects that the structures of drives and real constitutions have upon the development of the 'ideal world of meaning'. This refers to the constant difference between the potentially realizable and the actually realised elements of the ideal sphere, to the 'effectiveness of the real factors in the history of the mind'. But this does not mean that one should subscribe to the fallacy of all naturalistic explanations of history and seek to reduce the ideal to the real sphere or, as Scheler puts it, to assert that 'this ideal world can even be "explained" from the *real* historical world'.[69]

Similarly, one need not subscribe to its idealist converse, that real history constitutes an unfolding of the human mind. Rather, Scheler argues that the mind guides or directs an already ordered phase of the human will but cannot itself overrule the movement of real history. Thus, 'where ideas find no forces, interests, impulses, drives that are objectivated in institutions, then, in terms of real history, they [these ideas] are . . . completely unimportant'.[70] Historical study has to explain the difference between the potentially possible work and the realized work, but real history does not determine 'the positive *meaning content* of the work of the mind'; rather, 'in a definite manner and order it opens and closes the *sluices* to the intellectual stream'. Part of that order in which real factors influence the ideal spheres refers to Scheler's three major phases of a culture — its youthful phase, where guidance is rejected, its collectivistic moment of fatality in which the sense of human determination grows, and its last phase, the massification of life. Implicit in this cycle of development is a theory of decline, and of a decadence that culminates in its mass dissemination.

However, the key question for the sociology of culture is whether there exists in human history a constant or a systematically changing order in the effectiveness of the real factors. The three potential determining factors Scheler sees as being racial, political and economic, each of which has been used to provide naturalistic accounts of the determination of human culture. Scheler argues that at various stages of human history each of these factors has been important, and that in the course of a circumscribed cultural process there exist three phases which correspond to the predominance of racial, political and economic relationships. However, with regard to the general question of the possibility of a single factor always being dominant, Scheler maintains that

> there exists in the course of history *no constant* independent variable amongst the three highest main groups of real factors: race, power, the economy; but, nonetheless, there does exist a *law of ordering of respective primacies* of them for the intellectual historical restriction or encouragement of realisation, that is, there does exist a *diverse* law of ordering for specific *phases* of the course of the history of a culture.[71]

Scheler asserts that not only can he establish this law of ordering of the three factors inductively by an examination of the course of human history but that this law can be established deductively from the study of the origins of human drives: to race relationships there corresponds a sexual and propagatory drive, to political relationships there corresponds a drive for power, and to economic relationships there corresponds a drive for survival. As Scheler makes clear in many passages, a central motive for his construction of a sociology of culture and a sociology of knowledge in this manner is to counter what he takes to be the one-sided economic determination of society and the ideal sphere that is advanced by Marx. He specifically argues that, in contrast to Marx's position,

> *There exists no constancy in the primary effectiveness of real factors; rather, there exists here an ordered variability*. Nonetheless, there does exist a *fundamental relationship of the ideal factors to the real factors as a whole* . . ., that possesses the strictest *constancy* in all human history and in no way permits a reversal or even merely a change.[72]

However, the constancy of this relationship between ideal and real factors testifies once more not only to the powerlessness of the mind but also to the strength of the structure of drives. This material base is not, strictly speaking, social but psycho-biological. At the same time, Scheler assumes that he is preserving some degree of autonomy for the ideal sphere over against social existence, although this is obtained only at the price of a de-historicization of society. Thus, we return to the problem stated earlier, namely, the absence of any mediating concepts between the ideal and the real, the absence of any notion of human praxis and engagement. This deficiency is what makes Scheler's analysis appear so formalistic and static. Potentially mediating categories are, as it were, trapped in the dualistic metaphysics which Scheler has constructed and which lies at the basis of both his sociology of culture and his sociology of knowledge. It is the latter to which we must now turn.

IV

An examination of Scheler's most fully developed position on the sociology of knowledge in *Die Wissensformen und die Gesellschaft* should begin by tracing the outline of the conception of the sociology of knowledge he developed both within that work and in other related writings. By 1926, Scheler has already made a number of contributions to the sociology of knowledge. 'Über die positivistische Geschichtsphilosophie des Wissens' and a reply to Jerusalem's critique of that essay appeared in 1921,[73] and in 1922 an important article entitled 'Weltanschauungslehre, Soziologie und Weltanschauungssetzung',[74] dealing not merely with the study of world views but also relating directly to the debate surrounding Max Weber's 'Wissenschaft als Beruf' essay — the so-called *Wissenschaftsstreit*. These two essays and many others appeared in three small volumes in 1923 and 1924 under the title *Schriften zur Soziologie und Weltanschauungslehre*[75] and, though they are not all equally relevant to an understanding of Scheler's sociology of knowledge, some are worthy of attention.

In 1924 Scheler edited a collection of contributions to the sociology of knowledge by a whole variety of authors under the title *Versuche zu einer Soziologie des Wissens*.[76] At the beginning of the work there appeared Scheler's 141-page introduction entitled 'Probleme einer Soziologie des Wissens'. This long contribution — with important additions — is also the first essay in *Die Wissensformen und die Gesellschaft* (1926). One of the most significant additions to the original is an extension of Scheler's discussion of the sociology of science that arose out of his contribution to the fourth German Sociological Association congress in 1924 entitled 'Wissenschaft und soziale Struktur'.[77] Another addition is Scheler's discussion of ideologies in relation to the class structure. The volume also contains a long examination of the relationship between knowledge and work which Scheler sets within the framework of a critique of pragmatism.

The second section of Scheler's major essay 'Probleme einer Soziologie des Wissens' is concerned with his attempt to develop a sociology of knowledge on the basis of his sociology of culture. This section is itself in two parts: the first concerned with formal problems, the second with material or substantive problems. As instances of substantive problems, Scheler deals with a sociology of the three major forms of knowledge that he has already enumerated — religion, metaphysics and positive science — and with the reassertion of metaphysics in the face of the domination of science and technology. The discussion of the development of knowledge in relation to political development, and specifically what Scheler terms the 'logic of classes' and the 'sociological study of idols', is enlarged in the 1926 version. The section concludes with reflections upon the effects of the World War upon the intellectual structure of European societies.

The sociology of knowledge raises a number of formal problems which both relate directly to the theory of knowledge, logic and developmental psychology, and are formulated in three basic axioms of the sociology of knowledge. The first is that 'the knowledge that each human being has of being a "member" of a society as such is not empirical but a priori knowledge. It genetically *precedes* the stages of his so-called self- and self-evaluative consciousness: No "I" without a "We" and the "We" is always genetically filled with content before the "I".'[78] Commenting on this first axiom, Schilpp suggests that its basis lies in two of Scheler's earlier works, to only one of which Scheler refers.[79]. In *The Nature of Sympathy*, Scheler argued that

> in the case of the development both of the individual and of primitive man there is, to begin with, no differentiation between *ego*-experiences and *alter*-experiences . . . at first both flow on together as an undifferentiated stream of experiences. And if there is a tendency in one direction more than in the other it is rather in the direction of the *alter*.[80]

However, much research in developmental psychology would suggest that the reverse is the case, namely, that whilst there may be little ego-alter differentiation in the early stages of development the child incorporates the alter with its identity, and not conversely. Schilpp also suggests that this axiom has its roots in an even more dubious line of argument found in *Der Formalismus in der Ethik und die materiale Wertethik* where

> Scheler had already shown that an hypothetical Robinson Crusoe, who had never in his life seen or heard any of his own (human) kind, would nevertheless have this (a priori) social consciousness because of certain act-intentions which would be his by virtue of his very nature as man and which are intentions directed toward others of his kind (even though there be no such 'others' actually present or empirically known to him).[81]

It is difficult to see how the knowledge that each person has as a member of a society is not empirical. Scheler can here do no more than assert the a priori nature of this knowledge in order to proceed with a quasi-phenomenonological account of social knowledge.

The second axiom is that 'the empirical relations of a person's participation in the experiences of his fellow human beings are realised *in various ways* according to the basic structure of the group'.[82] These may be represented ideal-typically along a continuum from complete identification — as found amongst 'primitive peoples, the masses, hypnosis, in certain pathological states, in the relationship of mother and child' — to inference by analogy. The implication of Scheler's association of such groups and relationships as instances of complete identification would suggest that, to take but one example, the masses are not capable of reflective thought — which in turn implies that they do not participate in the generation of the world of meaning in the ideal sphere. As well as enumerating other possible modes of apprehension, Scheler goes on to suggest that the basis for the acquisition of knowledge, apart from instances of genius, is hereditary. Scheler is convinced that inherited

> 'talents' for the acquisition of knowledge are *different in origin* not only for individuals but also for genealogical hereditary races — and that the chief basis for the specific composition of fundamental differentiation of castes, estates and occupations lies in these differences in peoples rather than in differences in class situation, social need or any kind of effects on the part of the social milieu.[83]

Once again, Scheler develops an axiom that apparently deals with the 'sociology' of knowledge but whose actual basis lies not in society but in biology or, at least, in some sphere to which sociology cannot contribute.

As part of this second axiom, Scheler puts forward 'two categories without which the sociology of knowledge cannot develop: namely, the *group soul* and the *group mind*'.[84] Scheler insists that these two categories 'are not metaphysical entities that basically precede joint living and experiencing'. The group soul refers solely to 'those mental activities which are not carried out "spontaneously" but "act themselves out", such as expressive reactions or other automatic or semi-automatic psychophysical functions'. In contrast, the group mind refers to 'the subject that constitutes itself in the joint performance of fully conscious *spontaneous acts* with an objective-intentional direction'. As examples of phenomena based on the group soul, Scheler gives myths and fairy tales, customs, folk songs and other similar phenomena; as examples of phenomena based on the group mind, he gives the state, the law, philosophy, science, etc.

Though Scheler has insisted that these two notions are not metaphysical, his account of the differences between the two readily recalls his earlier distinction between ideal and real factors: 'The group soul "lives and grows", as it were, in all human beings even while they sleep; only *its* effects are "organic" in the Romantics' sense. In its origins, the group soul is *impersonal*, anonymous.' It is

> always determined in its content, values, aims, and direction by personal leaders and examples, at any rate by a 'small number' (von Wiese), an 'elite' (Pareto) . . . the group *soul* is effective in the group from 'below' to 'above', the group *mind* from 'above' to 'below'.[85]

Thus, that part of the sociology of knowledge which deals with the dissemination of knowledge from the apex of society down to the masses, and with the distribution of knowledge, is concerned with the group mind. Though Scheler does not make this clear, such an examination must necessarily be restricted by consideration of the real factors that limit the reception of such products of the mind and seem only to emerge out of a societal elite. It is also unclear whether the group soul is to be the concern primarily of a sociology of culture or a substantive (*real*) sociology.

The third axiom in Scheler's sociology of knowledge, 'which is also an axiom in epistemology, states that there exists a fixed law that orders the origin of our knowledge of reality . . . and orders the fulfilment of the individual spheres of knowledge and correlated objects that are constants in human consciousness'.[86] These spheres, which are not reducible to one another, comprise:

(a) the *absolute* sphere, of the real and valuable, of the sacred;
(b) the sphere of a *co-world* [*Mitwelt*], pre-world and after-world in general, i.e. the spheres of society and history or of the 'others';
(c) the spheres of the *outer world and the inner world*, and the sphere of one's own *body and its environment*;
(d) the sphere of what is thought to be 'alive';
(e) the sphere of the corporeal world which is inanimate and appears as 'dead'.[87]

Whereas philosophy has unceasingly attempted to reduce these spheres to one another, Scheler argues that they are '*irreducible*; and, as spheres, all are *equally genuinely* given within every human consciousness'. Nonetheless, there does exist '*a fundamental essential order in the givenness and pregivenness of these spheres* which remains *constant* in all possible human development'.[88]

The most basic of these orders of pregivenness for a sociology of knowledge is that 'the social sphere of the co-world and historical sphere of the ante-world is pregiven to all subsequent spheres with respect to (a) reality, (b) content and concreteness of content'. It is this particular order of pregivenness that is central to the sociology of knowledge, since it already anticipates the conclusions which he derives from these axioms, namely that

> the *sociological character of all knowledge*, of all the forms of thinking, perception, cognition is incontestable: *not*, of course, the content of all knowledge and still less its objective validity, but the *selection* of the objects of knowledge according to the *predominant social perspective of interests*; that, further, the '*forms*' of mental acts within which knowledge is gained are always *necessarily sociologically co*-conditioned, i.e. through the structure of society.[89]

Scheler expresses the second of these conclusions somewhat differently in the unpublished notes for this article: 'There exists a sociological and historical *interest perspective* for the world of meaning. But this world itself does not emerge out of society and history — only its *selection*.'[90] The first of the propositions — 'the sociological character of all knowledge' — would, in its unqualified form, lead Scheler into sociologism, especially as it is not the 'social' character of knowledge that is at issue but the sociological. But the second proposition immediately qualifies the first since it is only the process of selection of objects of knowledge that is at issue and not the content or the validity of that knowledge. Even this highly qualified proposition remains unclear since Scheler does not illuminate at this point his notion of *Interessenperspektive*. Scheler assumes that it is his third proposition — that forms of mental acts are sociologically co-conditioned (*mitbedingt*) — which saves his sociology of knowledge from the charge of sociologism or, as he charges Durkheim, 'positivistic sociologism'. But this escape is only at the price of accepting a timeless and ahistorical essentialism. Sociologism can be avoided

> if one regards all functional *forms* of thought as leading back to the *functionalisation of the interpretation of essences* in the *things themselves*, and views only the particular *selection* which lies beneath this functionalisation as the work of *society* and its *interest perspective* as against the 'pure' realm of meaning.[91]

Aside from pointing to the problems associated with establishing this 'pure' realm of meaning and with the persistence of timeless essences, Scheler is confronted with two other difficulties.

Firstly, he nowhere exhibits much interest in delineating either the nature of society or its structure, nor the nature of these interests. Again, it can only be assumed that such categories are to be filled out by recourse to the real factors. In additional notes Scheler argues that the selection is 'dependent on the construction of the typical drive-structure of society'.[92] Scheler does acknowledge that empirical studies have already demonstrated the co-conditioning of the classification of the world by the divisions and classifications of groups and that 'these structural identities of world-views, images of the soul, of God with social levels of organisation' are 'a particularly fascinating object of the sociology of knowledge', but, in a contradictory manner, he appears not to accept basic categories such as the division of labour, except as being based on biological factors. Thus, in his reply to criticism from Wilhelm Jerusalem, he takes issue with Jerusalem's assertion that all social differentiation derives from the division of labour. Scheler offers his own account of social differentiation and asserts that

> the primary ground for social differentiation is differentiation in the innate endowments and skills of groups (according to race, inheritance, etc.) and it is primarily within the differentiation of racial tendencies and the political power positions of groups co-determined by them that the division of labour brings about differentiation. 'Castes' and 'estates' and their cognitive communities do *not* emerge from the division of labour.[93]

Once more we see that the real factors are to be reduced to the biological level.

Secondly, Scheler fails to confront a more important but related problem. In his sociology of culture, he had already asserted the plurality of cognitive apparatuses in opposition to Kant's standpoint. In the *Zusätze*, Scheler argues that three basic propositions must be rejected:

1. The constancy of a categorial system that is immanent to consciousness,
2. historical relativism and interpretation of all world views as the *fable convenue* of a historical group,
3. the 'ignorant' making of an exception for *our* world view.[94]

Scheler also asserts that the relativist standpoint is itself related to a particular type of society when he states that 'the new relativistic study of world views . . . is the theoretical reflection of this democratic parliamentarianism that extends into the world-view according to which one discusses the meaning of all possible opinions without asserting them, one acts without deciding'.[95] Scheler's solution to the relativist problem is an essentialist conception of truth that lies behind relativist standpoints, and in his lecture 'The Forms of Knowledge and Culture' (1925), he is quite explicit about this:

> *Knowledge is an ontological relationship*, one which assumes that entity and part are forms of being. In this relationship, one being *partakes* in the circumstance of another, without causing this circumstance to change. What is 'known' becomes 'part' of the person who 'knows' but without displacing the other person and without itself changing in any way. This ontological relationship is established without reference to time, space and causality.[96]

In the *Zusätze* Scheler speaks of 'a system of relativity of logic, ethics, aesthetics — *as a consequence of genuine absolutism.* Yet this relativity is transcended through the same history which creates it . . . Every standpoint in the stream of history has its history which is objective — regardless of whether one recognises it.'[97] Thus, behind historical relativities there lies an essential truth which we can grasp. Scheler seeks to clarify this by a graphic analogy to the effect that, 'just as Einstein has to locate the absolute objects of nature, the object of theoretical physics, behind the changing determination of mass and measurement of bodies in terms of their form, scope and time, so we locate the value, order and truth behind the changing *historical* perspectivism'.[98] Scheler's solution to the relativist problem lies in rejecting 'a cheap absolutism' and substituting a 'genuine absolutism'.

Having examined the basic axioms of a sociology of knowledge, Scheler investigates the major types of knowledge under three aspects; their identification, social origin and changing forms. He takes the major types of knowledge to be the '*absolutely constant* natural world-view', 'the *relatively* natural world-view' and the '*relatively artificial*' or "educated" world-view'. In his earlier essay on 'Weltanschauungslehre' (1921), Scheler appeared to take the absolutely natural world-view as being derived from genuine and living traditions. By 'genuine traditional contents of thought' he meant 'only that content of a tradition which obviously survives as contemporary but which to its bearers is completely unconscious and unrecognised as a tradition'.[99]

There, too, he saw such a world-view to be descriptively delineated by philosophy and, from a historical-sociological standpoint, he saw such a world-view as being 'unchangeably "constant" '. In *Die Wissensformen und die Gesellschaft*, however, this concept is taken to be a limited one — limited in its usefulness, not in its actual usage — that is taken by epistemologists to be the basis for all knowledge, 'to be the minimum constant found at any time and any place where "human beings" happen to live'. It possesses, Scheler argues, the same weakness as that philosophical notion of the state of nature that figures so prominently in such 'typical ideologies' as those of Hobbes, Rousseau and Marx. Therefore the 'traditional concept of an *absolutely constant* natural world-view must be completely rejected by the sociology of knowledge'.[100]

Instead, the sociology of knowledge is to commence from the '*relatively* natural world-view' that arises in the following manner:

> To the relatively natural world-view of a group subject (originally to unity of common descent) belongs everything that is accepted as 'given' *without question* in that group, as well as every object and content of meaning in the structural forms of that 'given' without special spontaneous acts, which is generally held and felt to be something that *cannot and need not be justified*. But it is precisely this view which can be *fundamentally different* for different groups, or for one group in different stages of its development.[101]

There exists, therefore, a plurality of relatively natural world-views the diversity of which 'extends into the categorial *structure* of the *given itself*'. Yet this diversity is 'to be explained neither historically, nor psychologically nor sociologically. Only a study of racial inheritance that extends to psychic inheritance' can form the starting point for such an investigation. Similarly, in explaining changes in relatively natural world-views, Scheler argues that they are 'natural growths' which advance only '*in very great* temporal dimensions' and 'can probably only be changed in a more than superficial sense through racial mixing and possibly the mixing of language and culture. At any rate, they belong to the lowest centres of the automatically functioning "group soul" — and not at all to the group "mind".'[102]

Scheler thus makes perfectly clear that it is the real factors which, at every stage, determine the types of knowledge that he subjects to analysis — in this case, the diversity and transformation of the relatively natural world-views are both to be explained largely in terms of biological factors. In a different formulation of the problem of accounting for the changes in the relatively natural world-views, Scheler suggests that such an explanation will only be forthcoming 'if the sociology of knowledge establishes the closest relationship with *developmental psychology* and uses for its own purposes the *parallel co-ordination* of stages of development already discovered in that field.'[103] The examples of 'parallel co-ordination' which Scheler views as already empirically established, illustrate not only his frequent recourse to dubious empirical studies but also the deep-seated nature of his elite-masses dichotomy. We cite three examples of parallel co-ordination for which Scheler provides no evidence, but which were presumably to have been substantiated in his *Philosophical Anthropology*:

8 between the behaviour of masses and that of children; . . .

11 between the psychic life of children and that of women ('constitutional' infantilism of the female psycho-physical organism) . . .

12 between the mentality and educational situation of the lower classes and the educational condition of the elites of two, three or more generations earlier (stratification theory of knowledge and class structure).[104]

From such 'empirical' evidence, we know that masses behave like children, women react like children and the masses are mentally at least two generations behind the elite. All are — apparently — encapsulated within the lowest centre of the group soul. Nonetheless, they are at least worthy of investigation by the sociology of knowledge, which is concerned not merely with 'truth but also the sociology of social delusion, superstition, sociologically conditioned errors and forms of deception'.

It is only the completely abstract extraction of this concept of the relatively natural world-view from its context that enables Schutz or Berger and Luckmann to see the notion as a fundamental one for the establishment of a sociology of knowledge, or for Werner Stark to argue that 'Scheler's whole theory, which seems to us the most satisfactory approach to the basic problem of the sociology of knowledge that has yet been tried, is summed up in one crowning concept — the concept of the "relatively natural" (i.e. normal) world-view'.[105] This is all the more remarkable in view of the fact that, in his discussion of the relatively natural world-view, Scheler seldom expands upon its 'sociological' dimensions but rather concentrates on its deep-seated roots in biological and psychological factors. But then this is precisely what constitutes his 'real' sociology.

The third major type of knowledge, which itself rests upon the 'great solidity' of the relatively natural world-views, is that of the *'relatively artificial* or *"educated" world-views'*.[106] It is some of these that form the major part of Scheler's subsequent examination of concrete material problems in the sociology of knowledge. When Scheler assembles these relatively artificial world-views according to their degree of artificiality, he seems to be doing so on the basis of a hierarchy of proximity to the group soul. That hierarchy is arranged as follows:

1 myth and legend
2 natural folk language
3 religious knowledge
4 mystical knowledge
5 philosophical-metaphysical knowledge
6 positive knowledge (including the *Geisteswissenschaften*)
7 technical knowledge.

Each develops its own special language (except the mystical) and its own distinctive style. But one problem associated with this hierarchy was stated by Schilpp, who asks:

> if Scheler insists on such a sharp distinction between 'group soul' and 'group mind' and also insists that the relatively natural *Weltanschauungen* 'belong to the lowest centres of the automatically working group soul and not at all to the group mind', one cannot help wondering just where in his 'Division of the Higher Forms of Knowledge' the 'group soul' ceases to function and the activity of the 'group mind' belongs.[107]

Schilpp provides here yet another indication of the powerlessness of the mind; on this occasion, the group mind.

The arbitrariness of the hierarchical arrangement of these forms of knowledge, and the problem raised by Schilpp, are by no means resolved by Scheler's discussion of the origin of such types of knowledge, which forms the final aspect of Scheler's treatment of the formal problems in the sociology of knowledge. The 'chief types of knowledge' are the religious, metaphysical and positive scientific knowledge. In all these instances 'the striving for knowledge . . . grows out of an inherent drive-impulse (*Triebimpuls*), which the human being has in common with the higher vertebrates, especially the apes'.[108] Once more, the highest forms of knowledge are in fact rooted — at least as far as our search for that knowledge is concerned — in the real factors, in psychobiological drives.

Scheler argues that there are three basic drives responsible for our striving after the three highest forms of knowledge:

> 1 There is the urge 'primarily of the *whole group* and only secondarily of the individual, to "rescue", to "serve", their existence, fate and welfare and to get in touch with a reality seen as "all-powerful and sacred" '.[109] This is the source of the search of religious knowledge.

> 2 There is also 'the more intentional sense of wonder . . . This act of wonder and the feelings that accompany it are the abiding source of all searching for *metaphysical knowledge*'.

> 3 Finally, there is 'the striving for power and domination over nature, over men and events in society, over psychic and organic processes'. This is the

source of our search for positive knowledge, and the source of 'all forms of technology'.[110]

Scheler is particularly concerned with the third of these drives since it has important implications for philosophy and for positivism. Firstly, Scheler argues that it is neither pure reason nor sense experience that is the source of the positive sciences but rather 'that *completely biological — and in no way rational or "intellectual" — drive for domination and power*'[111] which determines both intellectual and practical behaviour in this sphere. Secondly, it follows from the equivalent status of these three forms of knowledge that 'the positivism of Comte and Spencer — which is not a philosophy but merely a specific West European ideology of late western industrialism — acknowledged only the third of the roots of man's desire for knowledge, without, however, clearly perceiving its biological origin'.[112] One might add that, nonetheless, Scheler still does adhere to three basic types of knowledge even though he does not view their effectiveness in terms of an historical sequence. His intention is to challenge the hegemony of the third form of knowledge and reassert the importance of the metaphysical and religious forms.

Scheler concludes by arguing that an understanding of the roots of these three types of knowledge is essential in order to be able to go on to examine:

1. the different ideal typical forms of leadership in these three areas of knowledge . . .
2. the different *sources* and *method of their acquisition of knowledge* . . .
3. the different *forms of movement* of their development
4. the different *basic social forms* in which the acquisition and conservation of knowledge is presented
5. their different *functions* in human society
6. their different sociological origin in classes, occupations, strata . . .[113]

It is clear from this list of areas of research that the study of the drives responsible for these types of knowledge in fact precedes a 'sociological' examination of their origin. In other words, the biological, psychological and emotional origins should be examined *before* taking up a sociological investigation, and this implies that the sociological dimension by no means plays a primary role.

In the substantive section of his study, Scheler examines the central features of the three major types of knowledge — religion, metaphysics and science — and the social bases for changes in these forms. However, since we shall later be considering his treatment of one of these types of knowledge — positive science — in some detail, we now turn to Scheler's examination of the relationship between social stratification, social classes and group knowledge and, on a more general level, the relationship between the sociology of knowledge and the critique of ideology.

Though one of the central problematics in the German tradition in the sociology of knowledge is precisely its relationship to the critique of ideology, it is remarkable, as Barth suggests, 'that the discussion of ideology and ideological consciousness in Germany was not provoked earlier in connection with Max Scheler's work, *Die Wissensformen und die Gesellschaft*'.[114] One reason may be that the discussion of ideology was introduced into that volume only in 1925 (Scheler's preface is dated November 1925) as an insertion of eight pages into the already existing 1924 manuscript. As such, this discussion of ideology did not assume the central place in his work that it did, for example, in Mannheim's *Ideologie und Utopie*. Nonetheless, Scheler had already alluded to this problem in his 'Weltanschauungslehre' article of 1921 and in his discussion of the sociology of culture which first appeared in 1924.

It is clear from many remarks in *Die Wissensformen und die Gesellschaft* and elsewhere that the emergence of the proletariat as a class with its own political parties and world-view (Scheler views Marxism exclusively in terms of a world-view) is seen by Scheler as a threat to his value-order of the world and to his assertion of the key role of elites. The economic and political emergence of the lower classes and their role in the development of '*political and social "democracies"*' brings about a retreat from 'the aristocratic-metaphysical spirit', an increasing 'dogmatisation' of religion, and accelerated progress in the 'positive scientific and technical spirit'.[115] As we shall see, Scheler links the emergence of science with the emergence of new social groups who generate mere ideologies that legitimate their activities. Thus, for Scheler, 'scientific rationalism and intellectualism (which views all technology merely as the application of pure theory), just as much as the proletarian manual-worker pragmatism, is false . . . both of them represent *ideologies of interests*: the former of the liberal bourgeoisie, the latter of the proletariat'.[116]

Already, Scheler opposes to ideology some non-class-specific set of ideas, perhaps related to the salvation of humanity, or perhaps to some notion of 'genuine' science. It must also be presumed that both religion and metaphysics do not 'represent ideologies of interests'. Scheler adopts a position in which the legitimation and justification of the sciences can be ideological, but not the contents of the sciences themselves. Earlier, in opposing the notion of a 'new proletarian science', Scheler had argued that 'there are bourgeois and proletarian "ideologies" (i.e. constructions of history and programmes of action directed by hidden and preconscious class interests); but there exists only "the sciences", which have nothing in the least to do with such "ideologies" '.[117]

Scheler attempts to show that the class relativism derived from attributing ideological determination to the thought of all classes can be overcome by the argument he has already advanced against philosophical relativism, namely, that it is only the selection and choice of categorial systems that is socially determined. Scheler states the relativist problem in relation to class ideologies as one which leads to its resolution in a form of transcendence:

> If there were really no instance in the human mind that was capable of raising itself *above* all class ideologies, then all possibilities for true knowledge would be an illusion. All knowledge would then be . . . *merely a function of the outcome of class struggles*. The form of logic and the form of cognition would also be merely a function of class situation itself or an option open to such a situation. On the other hand, it is certainly a readily ascertainable fact that class situation *largely determines* both the *ethos* and the *mode of thought* [*Denkart*].[118]

Scheler thus maintains that it is possible to rise above class ideologies and that the forms of logic and cognition are not a function of class situation. Yet he does concede the 'class related determinism of formal modes of thought' and provides a schema of such formal modes as they relate to upper and lower social classes:

Lower Class	*Upper Class*
1. Value prospectivism of consciousness of time	Value retrospectivism
2. Contemplation of becoming	Contemplation of being
3. Mechanical view of world	Teleological view of world
4. Realism (the world predominantly as 'resistance)	Idealism (the world predominantly as the 'realm of ideas')
5. Materialism	Spiritualism
6. Induction, empiricism	A priori knowledge, rationalism
7. Pragmatism	Intellectualism
8. Optimistic view of the future and pessimistic view of the past	Pessimistic view of the future and optimistic view of the past ('the good old days')
9. A mode of thought that looks for contradictions or a 'dialectical' mode of thought	A mode of thought that seeks identity
10. Thought concerned with theories of the milieu	Nativistic thought[119]

As has been argued elsewhere, 'this schema of lower and upper class . . . is much too crude' and displays 'the absence of any historical consciousness' as well as being 'inadequate to the concreteness of social differentiation' and 'to the formation of ideologies'.[120] It might also be said that the reason why Scheler's categories of social class are so crude is that for him social classes are not fundamental groups in society, since he more readily views society as composed of elites and masses.

The schema also reflects the impossibility of the emergence of the problem of false consciousness in Scheler's discussion of ideology and class-determined modes of thought, not merely because the examination of modes of thought is totally without reference to a social class's actual activity in society but because, as the ninth formulation suggests, Scheler believes that, unlike Marx or Lukács, the lower class *already* possess a ' "dialectical" mode of thought', and so are already in a state of true consciousness as far as their own position in society is concerned. Finally, Scheler has already made it clear that such inclinations are unconscious, and so these modes of thought can have no possible relationship to class consciousness of the kind that Marx or Lukács discuss. Moreover, this schema is not concerned with philosophical theories, but rather with

> *living modes of thought* and *forms* of viewing the world *themselves in their functioning* — not with reflexive knowledge of these forms. These are *class determined inclinations of an unconscious type* to conceive the world predominantly in one or the other form. They are not class 'prejudices', but rather they are more than prejudices; they are the *formal laws* of the *formation* of prejudices and specifically formal laws, which, as laws of the predominant inclinations to form certain prejudices, are rooted solely in class situations — quite regardless of individuality, occupation and the mass of knowledge of human beings as well as their race, nationality, etc.[121]

These 'class determined inclinations' are rooted in the classes themselves, not in social class relationships nor in their relationship to a particular form of society. In this sense, they are subjectively determined by the nature of one's class position; they do not relate to activity but to views, conceptions, notions; they are unconscious reactions to the world.

Scheler suggests that if these 'formal laws' of the formation of 'prejudices' were fully comprehended then this would form a constituent part of the sociology of knowledge:

> If they were fully known and their *necessary* deviation from class situation were understood, then they would actually constitute a new doctrine of the sociology of knowledge which, in analogy to Bacon's doctrine of the idols (doctrine of delusions) of external perception and my doctrine of idols of inner perception, I would like to designate as the '*sociological doctrine of the idols*' of thought, contemplation and judgement.[122]

In contrast to Bacon's doctrine, however, 'these sociologically determined idols are *more* than errors . . . These idols are *traditional* to the classes — they are absorbed, as it were, with the mother's milk.' Yet again Scheler argues that such idols are peculiar to a class situation without reference to the relationship which that class has with other classes. The idols are erroneous views into which social classes are automatically socialised.

Despite the traditional and seemingly necessary nature of such idols and class conceptions, Scheler assumes that they can be overcome. He argues that the errors of the 'economistic theory of knowledge' emerge

> when one equates these class conditioned systems of idols with the ontological and emergent forms of things, and, secondly, with the objective forms of thought, interpretation and evaluation and judges them by analogy with these categorial perspectives of class interests; thirdly, when one takes them to be not merely 'necessary' *inclinations* of thought and interpretative *impulses* — which is what they actually are — but also takes them to be causally necessary as well.[123]

However, for Scheler, these systems of idols are not necessarily and causally binding. Rather 'the class prejudices and also the formal laws of the formation of class prejudices are . . . *in principle transcendable* for each individual member of a class. They can — the more they are recognised by the sociological study of idols in their sociological lawfulness — be withdrawn from use by any person, whatever their class position.' It is thus 'a practical-educational central value of a *sociology of knowledge of classes*' to reveal these idols and to make people aware of them. It is legitimate to suggest that what Scheler has in mind here, although he does not use the phrase, is the 'unmasking of ideologies' which plays a central role in some of Mannheim's accounts of ideology. Scheler, like Mannheim, seeks to show that the sociology of knowledge has a practical role to play in this respect but he fails to show how *individuals* can escape from these idols and to take account of any notion of social classes as a whole overcoming their illusions. Scheler had argued earlier, however, in his essay on 'Weltanschauungslehre' that the study of world-views is 'a very important and rich discipline', one which could

> serve to increase the understanding of our people and its strata; it can possess a high value for the contrasting learning to understand and coming to self-understanding of the families, classes and parties of our political fatherland that has largely disintegrated too much into irresponsible parties based on maxims and opinions. For the *Volkshochschule*, for example, the *study* of world views is, moreover, the fundamental discipline [*Grunddiziplin*].[124]

This practical educative role of the study of world-views is certainly a forerunner of Scheler's subsequent claims for the sociology of knowledge, and perhaps also for one of the practical intentions of Mannheim's claims for the sociology of knowledge as a fundamental science (*Grundwissenschaft*).

It is very doubtful, then, if Scheler has any conception at all of a critique of ideology. Rather, he substitutes for that activity a doctrine of ideologies which remains undeveloped. This substitution has its deeper origins in his sociology of culture in that Scheler's sociology of knowledge establishes the essential form of knowledge as an

> element that is undisturbed by the historical-social process; in so doing, both the concept of false consciousness and that of truth lose their meaning. The

bridge to a critique of ideology is broken, and the sociology of knowledge that results from this can only confirm even more the irrationality of the social process it has itself abandoned, especially as it grounds that process — in association with the historical-social explanation of the powerlessness of the mind — in the natural structures of drives.[125]

Indeed, instead of a historical-social analysis of the process by which ideologies develop out of systematic features of the nature of exploitation and domination in society, we are presented with an account of ideologies that is fundamentally subjectivist. We might add here that it is not only the notion of ideology that is subjectivist in origin. It has already been shown that Scheler's concept of society is a merely residual one and therefore plays no central role in his sociology of knowledge. If we were to attempt to integrate Scheler's doctrine of ideologies into a theory of exploitation and domination in society, then we would be confronted with a further difficulty; namely, that the designation of particular societies is itself arbitrary, and ultimately related to a theory of drives. We could not use the concept of a capitalist society, for instance, because Scheler argues that 'the capitalist *economy* is based upon the *will to unlimited acquisition* (as an *actus*), and not upon *acquisition* (as an increasing *ownership* of objects).'[126] So capitalism, too, is rooted in individual or collective drives.

Similarly, ideologies cannot emerge out of such a form of society but must have their origin elsewhere. Ideologies are endemic to social classes and yet have a basis that is hardly social; rather, they originate out of automatically stimulated prejudices, however much they may be formulated in such a way as to hide this origin. Likewise, the process by which we can, as individuals, escape from ideologies is hardly touched upon, except in the form of an assertion that the sociology of knowledge can make people aware of them. Yet this awareness is in no way related to human action but has instead a passive connotation. Scheler's *Idolenlehre* (or *Ideologienlehre*) remains a doctrine which views ideologies as emerging from within social groups in a quasi-automatic manner as drives or as views or inclinations.

It has been suggested by Staude that 'the notion of ideology was crucial to Scheler's sociology of knowledge' and that Scheler's discussion of ideology is, in part, a response to Lukács' *History and Class Consciousness*.[127] Yet the notion of ideology does not appear to play a central role in Scheler's sociology of knowledge. It was only in 1926 that Scheler devoted more than a paragraph to its discussion in his works. Even then, this account of ideology is not only inserted into the wider context of a sociology of knowledge and culture but also can only be understood as a continuation of themes already raised by Scheler in that wider sphere of a sociology of culture and of knowledge. Further, Scheler's discussion of ideology, unlike his central themes in the sociology of culture, did not permeate his other writings.

V

In contrast to his treatment of ideology, Scheler devoted considerable attention to science. His examination of the role of science and its relationship to the social structure — the instance of the application of the sociology of knowledge we will examine — betrays its origins in his attempt to combat positivism as exemplified not only in Comte's, but also in Marx's, presumed, positivist account of the role of science. Scheler's concern with science is a consistent theme in his sociology of knowledge. In his essay on the positivist philosophy of history (1921), Scheler sought to challenge the status that positivists such as Comte, Mill, Spencer, Mach and Avenarius had given to science and to restore the importance of religion and metaphysics as forms of knowledge. These three forms of knowledge, 'rest on three *different* motives, three completely different groups of acts of the knowing mind, three different aims, three different personality types, and three different social groups. The historical forms of movement of these three mental forces are also basically different.'[128] In this early article, Scheler also related science to the emergence of the working class and to work activity.

In *Die Wissensformen und die Gesellschaft*, Scheler provides a detailed account of some social aspects of positive science and, in a long article entitled 'Erkenntnis und Arbeit', takes up the theme of pragmatism as a legitimation of science and work. The discussion of science in this volume relies heavily upon Scheler's paper 'Science and Social Structure' delivered at the fourth meeting of the German Sociological Association in 1924. His paper commences with the by now familiar argument on the three types of knowledge. He states that 'the problem of the origin of types of knowledge is a problem for the sociology of knowledge of the first rank', and asserts that he is seeking 'laws of the development and connection' between the cultural realm and social life.[129]

In contrast to the positivists, Scheler argues that, as a form of knowledge, science stands 'in the innermost and creative connection' to metaphysics, even though science is concerned with 'existential relativity' and metaphysics with the human totality and 'absolute values'. Science and metaphysics also differ in their social origin in that, whereas metaphysics is the work of an educated upper stratum, positive science has its origins in 'two social strata . . . the one a stratum of free contemplative people and the other a stratum of people who have rationally gathered together the experiences of work and craftsmanship'.[130] That is, science and 'the formal-mechanical principle, the explanation of nature' cannot emerge merely from contemplation but from those people 'who must move diverse things from place to place and whose activities of transport and work create increasingly new experiences of the nature of bodies and forces. The economic work and transport communities of patrilineal expansive cultures . . . are universally the *primary* sociological origin of positive science.'[131]

By arguing that positive science has its social origins in two social groups — one philosophical and contemplative, the other concerned with work activity and practical interests — Scheler intends to show the one-sidedness and erroneousness of both the 'Marxist interpretation of the relations between labour and science (Boltzmann, E. Mach, W. James, Schiller, etc.)' — a truly remarkable collection of authors who are said to hold a Marxist interpretation — and the purely intellectualist account that sees science as arising solely out of contemplation. Rather, in his view, science is 'the child of the *marriage of philosophy* and work experience'.[132]

The more fundamental distinction between Scheler's account of the origin of science and that of the Marxists lies not merely in the social groups out of which science is said to emerge but in the nature of the relationship between science and material factors. Scheler argues that

> the forms of production techniques of human labour (in the technical sense) each form a *parallel* to the form of positive-scientific thought, without one being able to say that one of the formal worlds is the cause or independent variable of the other. The independent variable which determines both sequences of forms of knowledge and work techniques is that of the existing *drive structure* of the highest leaders of society . . . in the closest relationship with what I term 'ethos', . . . with the leading values and ideas upon which the leaders of groups and, in and through them, the groups themselves are commonly directed.[133]

The introduction of the will and drive structure is, once more, Scheler's corrective to pragmatism and economism. This is expressed for Scheler in 'one of the most important statements that the sociology of knowledge has to offer', namely, that 'the *will to domination and control* co-determines both the methods of thought and perspective and the goals of scientific thought — and this means co-determination, as it were, behind the backs of individuals' consciousness, whose personal motives for research are thus completely irrelevant'.[134] Perhaps nowhere else in Scheler's sociology of knowledge is the contradictory nature of his intention to create an empirical discipline that searches for the laws governing forms of knowledge so apparent — since he interprets these laws in the very same naive positivist manner as the groups which he opposes. On the one hand, Scheler persistently avoids giving any causal, social explanations and substitutes notions such as 'parallel', 'affinity', 'homology', etc, whose explanatory power is much weaker; on the other, every social form of knowledge is seen to be determined in a rigid manner, not by these parallels, which exist at a social level, but by the structure of drives, the will, the emotions — biological impulses which are so deeply rooted in the ontology of human beings (one cannot even say their 'psyche' since that too is a physiological phenomenon for Scheler) — that this second, deeper level of determination is in no way open to investigation by a *sociology* of knowledge.

Hence, it is not surprising that when Scheler comes to examine the 'sociological-historical connection between technology and science' precisely the same dualism in his account of that relationship appears. He makes his position clear in the following statement when he claims that

> Marx speaks of the direct, or at least determining, causal dependency of not only positive science but also all intellectual products upon the economic relations of production; we only refer to positive science and even here only to a *parallelism* that has a *third common higher cause*, namely the hereditary drive-structure of the leader, ultimately of a racial origin and a corresponding new ethos.[135]

Thus, however interesting and insightful Scheler's parallels may be, and however fruitful in a social-historical context, their real determination lies not at this socio-historical level but at a biological level.

Nevertheless, Scheler attempts to show that the early origins of modern science display close links with technology and that this can, in part, be traced to the connections between, and ultimately the fusion of, the two social groups responsible for the emergence of science. More specifically, he seeks to show that modern science originates in the nascent bourgeoisie's challenge to traditional religion during and after the Reformation, in the emergence of a nominalist form of thought, in the increased concentration upon worldly labour and occupations — documented by Weber — and in the growing separation of church and state as a guarantee for the freedom of science.

Scheler also seeks to account for the emergence of modern science by utilizing a second 'sociological law of knowledge (*Wissensgesetz*)', namely 'the pioneering activity of the "devotion of those who are knowledgeable", dilettantism prior to the establishment of rigorous scientific disciplines, and the "love of knowledge" '.[136] In the early modern period, science is associated with a 'new emotional relationship to animals and plants', with the emergence of new generations — 'according to the law of generations, thus according to a basically biological rhythm'. This dilettantism is 'unmethodical, erratic' and vastly overestimates the value of any newly discovered area. The new theoretical world-view and the practical real world both have their origin in 'the new ethos and structure of drives'. The extent of this new ethos is manifested in the analogies of style when comparing art, philosophy and science. Scheler generalizes such new, culturally emergent phenomena into a quality of human history whereby they awaken and activate the 'sleeping forces of the soul'. But, as well as referring to the importance of such constant phenomena in accounting for the growth of modern science, Scheler points to a second positive factor, namely, the desire of the emergent urban bourgeoisie systematically to dominate nature and capitalise upon the kind of knowledge that would facilitate such domination. A consequence of the successful realisation of this idea is to absolutize this world-view (provided by positive science) into the sole image of the world. Scheler argues that such a tendency is not only prevalent in these sciences but in those interpretations of science, such as positivism, pragmatism and Marxism, which accept the hegemony of the scientific world view. All such accounts are intrinsically deterministic.

It is against such standpoints that Scheler adopts the notion of parallelism and analogy. Besides arguing for the 'parallelism' of forms of knowledge and society, he also asserts that the sociology of knowledge should investigate 'the series of analogies of meaning [*Sinnentsprechungen*] between the structure of modern science, on the one hand, and technology on the other, as well as between technology itself and the economy'.[137] Analogies of this kind are not to be understood as providing from the outset an 'explanation of a causal type', though subsequently 'a causal explanation can and must be sought'. Such analogies may be seen in the transition from feudalism to the modern period, in the transition from a power drive over human beings to a new form of drive over nature. That is, Scheler deliberately argues against concrete historical explanation and passes over to meanings, and ultimately to the structure of drives, as when he clarifies the analogy between science and technology:

> it is not technical needs that determine the new science, nor the new science that determines technical progress but rather both the original transformation of the logical system of categories of the new science and the new simultaneously emerging technical drive towards the domination of nature as grounded in the new *type* of bourgeois man and his *new structure of drives* and his new *ethos*.[138]

Since both science and technology are the result of this '*single* psychoenergetic process'. they must complement one another and interact. Scheler is not only at pains to undermine the pragmatist and Marxist interpretations which, he argues, seek to make science dependent upon technology, but is also insistent that, in the last resort, they are both grounded in the same structure of drives.

It is evident, in Scheler's analysis of the sociology of science, that not only is his 'powerlessness of the mind' thesis further confirmed but also the unreality of the socio-historical structures in his base-superstructure model. The socio-economic and historical structures do not themselves possess a concrete existence, but are instead grounded in drives and impulses. In his discussion of the relationship between the economy and science, Scheler maintains that

> the capitalist economy is based upon the will towards unlimited acquisition (as an *actus*) and not upon acquisition (as an increasing ownership of objects). Modern science, too, administers neither a given stable possession of truth nor does it engage in research in order to find solutions to specific tasks that are determined by needs, but rather it is primarily a striving towards 'methods'.[139]

Modern science is thus 'a type of logical machinery'. Scheler wishes to preserve science as one form of knowledge amongst others, which he sees as being preferable to a positivist interpretation that not only asserts the primacy of scientific knowledge over all other forms but also implies 'the tendency of science to sink into technicism (*Technizismus*)'. Rather, Scheler hopes that the sociology of knowledge will be able to demonstrate the need for a new 'cultural synthesis' of metaphysics and science, of the techniques of the soul and the techniques of domination.

Scheler's treatment of the relationship between science and social structure once more reflects his metaphysical preoccupations just as much as his sociological intentions. Positive sciences as one 'form' of knowledge amongst others rests upon the drive structure of pioneers in science. Scheler's analysis is insensitive to the nature of the object he is investigating. The object becomes subservient to his wider metaphysical intentions, such as the restoration of a primary role for metaphysics. On a social-political level, Scheler is intent on preserving elites at the apex of society, viewing them as the prime creators of cultural innovation. Hence, the socio-political regime most favourable to science would be 'an enlightened aristocracy and monarchy'[140] — the regime which, perhaps, Scheler conceived as being the best in all other respects too. At almost every stage of his analysis, Scheler conceives of his object of investigation within a set of preconceptions which provide little room for the independent development of potentially interesting 'parallels' and 'analogies of meaning'. These preconceptions also rule out the possibility of his examining issues such as science in relation to the production process, or to cognitive interests.

VI

Scheler conceived of his sociology of knowledge as a discipline that could permanently combat what he took to be the erroneous tendencies in social, political and philosophical theory — positivism, Marxism, historicism and relativism. Yet, the very tendencies he opposes shape, to a considerable extent, the nature of his own project. The positivist law of three stages, for instance, as Alfred Weber showed, continues to animate Scheler's sociology of knowledge even though the categories are discussed at a different level.

At the methodological level, Scheler hardly takes seriously his attempt to establish an explanatory model for the sociology of knowledge. His resorting to supposed empirical evidence is erratic and often based on a desire to support his metaphysics. On the other hand, Scheler's rigid adherence to his metaphysical position, with all its contradictions, prevents him from establishing empirically-analysable relationships between knowledge and society. This is not to suggest that a causal-analytical paradigm is the appropriate one for the sociology of knowledge, but since Scheler at times appears to assume that he is establishing such a sociology of knowledge it is legitimate to ask whether he is capable of doing so. Even the sympathetic interpretation of his work by Bühl is forced to conclude that

> Scheler, who . . . still sought to produce a contribution to a 'causal sociology', although his whole work is permeated by process oriented-cybernetic explanations . . ., instead is faced with the danger that his central guiding cognitive principles can be misinterpreted as a metaphysics of history.[141]

Yet the accounts which Scheler provides of the development of forms of knowledge hardly warrant the label 'process oriented-cybernetics'. His metaphysical aims remain central to his sociology of knowledge. The same problem arises with regard to Scheler's presumed phenomenological foundation for the sociology of knowledge. Not only is Scheler a most unorthodox phenomenologist but it is true to say his metaphysical position seriously prevents him from establishing a consistent phenomenological approach. Hence, it is only with the greatest difficulty, and with the most spurious level of abstraction, that one can claim that Scheler did establish a phenomenological basis for the *sociology* of knowledge. Such a positive evaluation is provided by Alfred Schutz, though his arguments are not convincing.[142] Scheler can certainly be counted as a significant phenomenological philosopher, but the insights from his phenomenology of *ressentiment* or sympathy, for instance, do not permeate his much more formalistic sociology of knowledge.

It is, perhaps, the fusion of sociological and metaphysical intentions which led many of his contemporaries to question whether he had provided a sociology of knowledge. Hintze, in the most detailed contemporary review of Scheler's sociology of knowledge, questioned whether he had established in his sociology of culture, the crucial mediating societal categories between the ontologically grounded dualism.[143] Eleutheropulos, reviewing *Die Wissensformen und die Gesellschaft*, suggests that 'in fact, a very large part of this contribution really has nothing to do with the "sociology of knowledge" '.[144] Müller-Freienfels, in a brief but positive review, also states that the work is 'without a doubt not a "sociology" in the specific scientific sense', and suggests that the volume marks Scheler's deep separation from Husserl and phenomenology.[145]

The most thoroughgoing and perceptive examination of Scheler's sociology of knowledge — or at least of a section of it — is provided by Mannheim in his essay 'The Problem of a Sociology of Knowledge', published in 1925 and therefore written with reference to Scheler's introduction to *Versuche zu einer Soziologie des Wissens*.[146] As an indication of Scheler's lack of influence upon the development of the sociology of knowledge in Germany, it is worth noting that Mannheim's critique is the only detailed one to appear from within that tradition if we except Adler's reply to Scheler's paper on science and social structure. Mannheim is the only contemporary critic who points to Scheler's use of a schematic phenomenology to justify Catholicism and 'Catholic concepts of "timelessness", "eternity", with new arguments'. Mannheim's major criticism of Scheler's sociology of knowledge is that it is rooted in a static dualism in which the determining factor, the base, is a 'supra-temporal, unchanging entity'.[147] In Mannheim's terms, Scheler's sociology of knowledge cannot be dynamic since it commences with the absolute as its starting point.

It is not difficult to see why Scheler's sociology of knowledge was not taken up by other sociologists and developed in other directions. Firstly, it is impossible to extract Scheler's sociology of knowledge from his metaphysics, and few sociologists have been at all convinced by Scheler's metaphysical position. Secondly, it is clear that Scheler himself seems only to have taken up the sociology of knowledge for a short time, from 1921 to 1926, and then to have moved on to the development of a philosophical anthropology. His writings after 1926, however brief (Scheler died in 1928), do not betray a continuing interest in the sociology of knowledge.[148] Thirdly, those writers who might have found Scheler's sociology of knowledge appealing — and this is perhaps especially true of phenomenologists — did not adopt aspects of his work until much later. The central notion of 'the relatively natural worldview', taken up by Schutz as the world-taken-for-granted, and widened into the basic for a sociology of knowledge concerned with everyday knowledge by Berger and Luckmann, was only developed much later in the post Second World War period. This is also true of Stark's attempt to construct a sociology of knowledge on the basis, at least in part, of Scheler's work. The positive review of his work in 1942 by Becker and Dahlke concluded that, 'we may regard Max Scheler as among the greatest exponents of that *substantive* sociology of knowledge which is slowly winning its way'.[149] Yet, for the reasons given earlier, it would be inappropriate to ascribe to Scheler's 'sociology' the description 'substantive'.

This is not to suggest that there was no development at all arising out of Scheler's sociology of knowledge. The one positive exception was, in fact, the volume which Scheler himself assembled and published in 1924 as *Versuche zu einer Soziologie des Wissens*. As well as Scheler's long introduction, the volume included articles divided into two areas, in much the same way as Scheler's own introduction though with a different emphasis. The first section included articles by, amongst others, Jerusalem, von Wiese and Honigsheim, dealing with the 'formal sociology of knowledge and epistemology'. The second section comprised articles on material (substantive) sociology of knowledge and 'historical types of scientific co-operation' by Landsberg, Honigsheim, Plessner and others. It consisted largely of an examination of various types of thought, (e.g., Honigsheim on the 'sociology of realistic and nominalistic thought') or on institutions concerned with intellectual activity, such as Plessner's important essay 'Towards a sociology of modern research and its organisation in German universities'. But the volume did not prove to be the start of a cumulative interest in Scheler's version of a sociology of knowledge. More importantly, hardly any of the contributors shared Scheler's perspective on this area of study.

It has already been suggested that one central aspect of Scheler's social theory is an account of the sense of alienation in modern society, as experienced especially by its elite. At the centre of this notion of alienation is the concept of the alienated mind and its powerlessness. For instance, in a discussion largely taken up with Mannheim's sociology of knowledge,[150] Siegfried Marck argued that in Scheler's work

> the whole realm of the substantive study of value and the ontological metaphysics that is built upon it is divorced from any existential relativisation. Material values and their rank order, as well as the ontological reality in which they are grounded, are independent in their pure essence [*Sosein*] from the transformations of existence [*Dasein*]. According to the interpretation of Scheler's later philosophy, the mind is indeed powerless over against real transformations. It requires sublimated power factors in order to have an indirect influence upon real events.[151]

Though Marck here points to the significance of the powerlessness-of-the-mind thesis for the preservation of essential values, he is also aware of its implications for human subjects themselves. As he goes on to suggest, the mind

> is also independent of these real events — as the realm of pure essentiality it is detached from existential determination. What is typical of this sphere of Scheler's 'mind' is his interpretation of it as divorced from the opposition of subject and object. To him, the mind means a purely ontic structure; its a priori nature has nothing to do with the formative human subject but rather rests upon the substance itself . . . the whole world of historically conditioned qualities and purposes are relativised by him in contrast with the world of pure values.[152]

This dualism can only lead to the absence of any notion of interaction, of dialectic between mind and society. As such, it is an instance of one of the many dualisms that permeates Scheler's philosophy: absolute/relative, essential/existential, ideal factors/real factors, superstructure/base, mind/life, elites/masses, etc. It is as if the dynamic of intellectual activity and society are frozen and solidified, in an attempt to preserve what Scheler takes to be the essential human values. But the price paid for this preservation is the absence of human actors, the absence of a dialectic between engagement and reflection, between knowledge and society.

Lenk has argued that Scheler's theory of history is permeated with an uneasy resignation before the permanent fall of higher values. It is a form of capitulation to alienation that is exemplified in the powerlessness-of-the-mind thesis. In this thesis

> thought has already alienated itself to such an extent that it can no longer recognise reification as being produced by human beings, as socially necessary illusion, but has hypostatised it into the essence of things themselves.[153]

The implications for a sociology of knowledge are that, since its categories are derived from an ahistorical anthropology, it cannot itself analyse this alienation, it can only reflect it. For an attempt to analyse the alienation of consciousness in a very different context we must turn to Lukács' writings.

3 Georg Lukács: From Reification to the Critique of Ideology

I

Since Georg Lukács did not explicitly write upon the sociology of knowledge, we need to inquire into the relevance of his early work, down to and including *History and Class Consciousness*, for the sociology of knowledge in Germany. The central task of his major work, 'to understand the essence of Marx's method and to apply it correctly,' seems far removed from the concerns of the sociology of knowledge. In *History and Class Consciousness*,[1] Lukács provides a critique of the orthodox Marxism of the Second International whilst at the same time restoring to Marxism the dialectical dimension which lay in Hegel's philosophy and in Marx's own writings. Lukács aligned himself (however temporarily, in view of his rapid retraction of his views) with attempts at the development of a dialectical and historical theory of society, such as those of Korsch and Gramsci, which ran counter to the increasingly dominant mechanistic materialism. His major work also pointed towards the rejection of a simple base-superstructure theory of ideology with its attendant naive reflection theory of truth. This is important in terms of the development of the sociology of knowledge since it was this caricature of the Marxist position — one also shared by many Marxists — which was the subject of critiques by Scheler, Mannheim and others.

But Lukács' work is significant in other respects. Firstly, many of the roots of his early writings on the sociology of culture and the critique of ideology lie within a tradition of German sociology (Simmel, Weber) and philosophy (Dilthey and neo-Kantians such as Rickert and Lask) that is shared by many of the writers in the sociology of knowledge. Of course, such a statement is more true for Mannheim than it is for Scheler. Nonetheless, when commentators such as Lenk offer an account of the German tradition in the sociology of knowledge in terms of its commitment to a 'tragic consciousness' that derives from, amongst others, Simmel and Weber, it is difficult not to extend this line of argument to Lukács, whose thought certainly exemplifies, at various stages, a 'tragic consciousness'. Lenk also argues, quite correctly, that the sociology of knowledge in Germany must be understood within the context of a wider sociology of culture. This concern, too, applies not only to Scheler and Mannheim but also to Lukács. In some respects, even, it might apply more to Lukács than to either of the other two. Siegfried Marck, one of the reviewers of *History and Class Consciousness*, suggests that Lukács' philosophy of Marxism does not rest upon methodological questions of sociology and economics, as in the case of writers like Max Adler, but rather 'provides a comprehensive philosophy of culture, indeed from Lukács' standpoint, implies the sole possible solution to the fundamental cultural philosophical problems of the present time. This basic problem however is the "crisis" of contemporary culture'.[2]

A theory of bourgeois culture and its critique — especially in the analysis of reification — was certainly a central concern of Lukács' work, at least down to 1923. Indeed, not only does much of Lukács' early work uphold a theory of cultural alienation, but in *History and Class Consciousness* this alienation, in the form of reification, appears to be total. Perhaps it is this all-pervasive reification to which Bloch refers in his review when he speaks of the 'exclusively sociological homogenisation of the process' of history. Herein lies an element of continuity in Lukács' work since, even in *History and Class Consciousness*, the critique of alienation remains trapped within an idealist framework in so far as its critique of capitalist society continually takes its orientation from the culture of that society whilst ignoring, for instance, the process of ideological production.

Secondly, both Lukács' earlier writings and his analysis of reification and class consciousness, present and attempt to solve many of the problems subsequently raised in the sociology of knowledge. This is most apparent in his treatment of the critique of ideology, and the relativist problematic. Indeed, his statement of such central problems in the sociology of knowledge within the German tradition predates their being taken up by Scheler or Mannheim or other writers.

In a similar manner, one can argue that, especially in *History and Class Consciousness*, Lukács presents the most forceful contemporary statement of the need for a critique of ideology. Since the major figures in the sociology of knowledge tradition in Germany also saw a central practical problem of their time as the cultural and ideological crisis — albeit from very different standpoints — this tradition too had to confront these crises. Finally, although this is necessarily an *ex post* judgement, Lukács' work unwittingly provided a critique of some of the ways in which central aspects of the sociology of knowledge were taken up. Again, this is especially true of the manner in which Mannheim developed many of the strands of the sociology of knowledge which he almost certainly felt compelled to confront as a result of his extensive knowledge of Lukács' treatment of ideology, history and the relativist problem. At times, it is almost as if Lukács is providing a critique of the central problems in a tradition that had not yet been developed.

That such a critique was possible can only be understood in the light of Lukács' critical confrontation with German sociology and philosophy, which had already raised some of the issues that were faced by the sociology of knowledge in Weimar Germany. The distinctive interpretation of Marx's work must also be viewed partly within this context. As Lukács himself suggested — his study of Marx commenced around 1908 — 'it was Marx the "sociologist" that attracted me — and I saw him *through spectacles tinged by Simmel and Max Weber* [italics added, D.F.]. I resumed my studies during World War I, but this time I was led to do so by my general philosophical interests and under the influence of Hegel *rather than any contemporary thinkers* [italics added, D.F.].'³

Elsewhere, Lukács specifically testifies to the importance of Simmel for his understanding of Marx, at least during his early acquaintance with his works. In a Hungarian introduction to some of his selected writings, published in 1968, Lukács writes: 'A properly scholarly use of my knowledge of Marx was greatly influenced by the philosophy and sociology of Simmel, who was experimenting with the fitting in of certain aspects of Marxism into the German *Geisteswissenschaft* [en] which [were] then in [their] early stages'.⁴ In a later preface to another collection of writings published in Budapest in 1970, and again commenting on his early interest in German philosophy, Lukács states that

> . . . when I looked for the perspectives, foundations and methods of application of philosophic generalisation, I found a theoretical guide in the German philosopher Simmel, not the least of reasons being that this approach brought me closer to Marx in certain respects, though in a distorted way.⁵

Again, in retrospect, Lukács states that he did 'not at all regret today that I took my first lessons in social science from Simmel and Max Weber and not from Kautsky. I don't know whether one cannot even say today that this was a fortunate circumstance for my own development.'⁶

In the Hungarian preface referred to above, Lukács recalls his meeting with Ernst Bloch: 'The experience of meeting Bloch (1910) convinced me that philosophy in the classical sense was nevertheless possible'.⁷ This classical sense of philosophy was revived by his intensive study of Hegel to which he alludes in his 1962 preface to *The Theory of the Novel* — completed in the winter of 1914–15 — by which time he 'had become a Hegelian'.⁸ Indeed, Lukács claims that this work 'was the first work belonging to the *Geisteswissenschaften* school in which the findings of Hegelian philosophy were concretely applied to aesthetic problems', even though 'the author . . . was not an exclusive or orthodox Hegelian'.⁹

In his writings on aesthetics in this period one should also recall the importance of Max Weber's methodological writings and especially his notion of ideal types. As Hanak argues, works such as *The Theory of the Novel* 'would be inconceivable without the influence of Max Weber. Weber's "ideal types" permeate Lukács' aesthetic thought'.[10] Kettler, Markus and Löwy have all pointed to the centrality of culture and cultural renewal in Lukács' early writings up to and including the period of his transition to Marxism. Markus, for example, argues that 'since the beginnings of his development as a thinker, the question of culture meant for Lukács the question of the *possibility of a life free from alienation*'.[11] The analysis of alienation that Lukács utilized was not that of Marx but of the *Lebensphilosophie* tradition, and especially Simmel. This analysis already contained a critique of bourgeois culture but was itself caught up in other contradictions. Lukács' 'road to Marx' lay in increasingly distancing himself from this *Lebensphilosophie*, in a dirction which, as Markus argues, brought him closer to Kant.[12] This is especially true of the work which Lukács was considering for submission as a *Habilitationschrift* in Heidelberg, as late as May 1918, with Rickert and Maier as assessors.[13] This did not in fact take place, but it still testifies to the centrality of Lukács' philosophical concerns in Germany as late as May 1918.

This very brief outline of Lukács' connections with important strands of German sociology and philosophy is not meant to suggest that there exists some break in Lukács' work which enables us to speak of a young and a mature Lukács, a non-Marxist and a Marxist Lukács. As Breines argues,

> while Lukács' turn to Marxism in 1918–19 stands as a watershed of his career, the pre-Marxist phase that preceded it is inextricably linked to the Marxism that followed. It can also be argued . . . that the whole matter can be looked at in the other direction, which reveals that Lukács' Marxism, is organically bound up with the pre-Marxist phase of his work.[14]

Indeed, we might suggest that this continuation of his earlier concerns and modes of formulation of problems gives Lukács' *History and Class Consciousness*, in part, its distinctive character and, in its fusion of these concerns with an attempt to understand and interpret Marx, presents him with the difficulties that are evident in his analysis.

On the other hand, it should not be forgotten that the context of this assimilation was not only study in Berlin under Simmel, or with Weber, Rickert and Lask in Heidelberg, but also the cultural milieu in Budapest in the periods before and during the First World War. This context has been particularly well illuminated by Kettler's study which shows both Lukács' concerns in Budapest and his significance for Mannheim's later development.[15] Kettler clearly illustrates the continuity of Lukács' concern with culture: how, in 1919, during the Hungarian Revolution,

Lukács could still argue that 'politics is merely a means, culture is the goal', and the political standpoint 'may only be a filter but not the sole source.'[16] He also shows that there was no complete, radical break with the past when Lukács entered the Communist Party in December 1918. One should also add that specifically Hungarian influences were important to Lukács, especially his relationship with Ady, Szabo and Balázs.[17]

But this is not our main concern. Rather, we must return to the central question as to whether the major figures in the sociology of knowledge such as Mannheim felt compelled to confront Lukács' work. One answer might be that the sociology of knowledge itself grows out of the critique of ideology. This is certainly the assumption that lies behind Mannheim's account of the transition from the study of ideology to the sociology of knowledge, from an engaged critique to a neutral academic discipline, from an evaluative to a non-evaluative concept of ideology. But it is doubtful whether the sociology of knowledge grew out of the critique of ideology in any simple manner. As Lenk correctly remarks, it is only the most complete misunderstanding of Marx's theory that could have led contemporaries to argue that Mannheim's sociology of knowledge was 'Marx's theory in the guise of bourgeois science'.[18]

Thus, it is incorrect to state that the critique of ideology has or should have nothing to do with the sociology of knowledge, or that the latter simply grew out of the former. In Lukács' case, there is considerable doubt as to whether his orientation to the problems raised in the sociology of knowledge was taken up, in the positive sense of developing that tradition. Lieber argues that Lukács' work, apart from its reception by Marxist writers, hardly had any effect upon the sociology of knowledge in Weimar Germany. He suggests that if

> one examines . . . the controversies surrounding the sociology of knowledge in the nineteen-twenties as to its relation to Lukács and its capacity to make his contributions to the problem of reified consciousness and class consciousness fruitful for the discussion of the problem of ideology, then one must state that such a confrontation with Lukács was reduced to a few references, mostly only in footnotes. This means that Lukács' work was hardly of importance for the discussion of the sociology of knowledge. The understanding of Marxism remained fixed in what was taken to be, and what had gained influence as — mostly in a vulgar Marxist guise — the historical-materialistic or Marxist 'world-view'.[19]

Lieber's view, however, is not unchallenged. It is certainly true that references to Lukács' work by contributors to the sociology of knowledge remain few and often only in footnotes. However, it has been argued by Huaco that Mannheim's discussion of ideology has affinities to that presented by Lukács.[20] Huaco states that 'it is fairly easy for anyone to verify that, at least at a formal level, the argument presented by Mannheim is almost a mirror image of the earlier argument developed by Lukács'.[21] Kettler, in a more detailed article, suggested that Lukács' *Geschichte und Klassenbewusstsein* was 'a work of decisive importance for Mannheim's development . . . for its influential argument that the cultural "solution" of the moral philosophic problems presupposes a social frame of reference and action, and for its provision of such a framework'.[22] Kettler, referring to a then unpublished essay by Mannheim, suggests that 'it represents Mannheim's effort to meet the challenge of Lukács' *History and Class Consciousness*' and concludes that 'after 1923, and at least until 1930, Mannheim no longer claimed a confident superiority to Marxism'.[23] Even though Mannheim's references to Lukács may only be in note form they are usually positive, as when in his 'Historismus' article published in 1924 he refers to the attempts to construct a rational dialectic and states that 'the most profound and significant of all these attempts is probably that of George Lukács'.[24]

Yet in order to show that the themes and problems raised by Lukács' account of class consciousness, reification and the critique of ideology are relevant for the sociology of knowledge, it is clearly necessary to develop Lukács' own position. Lukács' own intentions were not to develop a sociology of knowledge but to reconstruct Marx's dialectical method of understanding society. Even though the present study is concerned with the development of the sociology of knowledge and, in this instance, with Lukács' relationship to it, it must not be forgotten that Lukács' work stands in its own right as a Marxist attempt to reconstruct the dialectical method and to combat the very same vulgar Marxism that was the focus of attention in the sociology of knowledge. Lukács' work stands as a detailed attempt to extend the critique of ideology to Marxism itself.[25] Arato argues that whereas Marx's central concern was the critique of political economy, Lukács' was

> the critique of sociology, i.e. the critique of the totality of capitalist society and the self-critique of Marxism. The critique of sociology attempted to take the double form of *Anerkennung* (recognition) and *Aufhebung* (overcoming) . . . The self-critique of Marxism was a more difficult task for Lukács, and the incompleteness of this self-critique is a clue to many of the theoretical failures of *History and Class Consciousness*.[26]

Arato seems to imply that the critique of sociology was more successful than the self-critique of Marxism. Yet it can be argued that Lukács did not 'overcome' that tradition which was the object of his critique but remained within many of its basic assumptions. For this reason alone, Lukács' relationship to German sociology is an ambiguous one.

In the simplest terms, then, what were the themes which Lukács developed that are relevant for the sociology of knowledge? At the centre of Lukács' *History and Class Consciousness* lies the problem of how it is that we are able to grasp, to know and to understand social reality. For

Lukács social reality is not some objectively given body of facts to which forms of thought may be related, but rather is itself mediated by forms of consciousness. That is, the immediate apprehension of social reality in no way implies the apprehension of some 'true' reality but, on the contrary, usually implies false consciousness, an illusory apprehension of that reality. Stated simply, then, Lukács' problem is how to examine this reified reality and this false consciousness and how to overcome it.

This necessarily leads Lukács to examine the process of the generation of ideologies, false consciousness, class consciousness and reification. It also prompts him to attempt to delineate that process which we already know from Marx's writings to be the critique of ideology, but not merely a critique of ideology as a mode of apprehension of the world and its relationship to human engagement in the world but a critique of that reality which ideology purports to comprehend. In Marx's work, for instance, the critique of political economy is not merely a critique of the theories of political economists but, at the same time, a critique of that reality which their theories purport to explain. So, too, in Lukács' work we must investigate what it is that he criticises and what is the nature of the reality that is subjected to critique. In other words, 'Is Lukács' notion of capitalism and his conception of the bourgeoisie and the proletariat identical with those of Marx?' Do philosophy and sociology play the same role in Lukács' critique of ideology that political economy plays in Marx's critique?

In the course of his critique of bourgeois ideology, Lukács confronts the problem of how social classes perceive social reality. Specifically, he examines how social reality manifests itself in the class consciousness of the bourgeoisie and the proletariat. This investigation brings Lukács to discuss how we may study class consciousness and through which central relationships in these groups social reality is grasped and transmitted. If the immediate identity of the subject and object of consciousness is rejected, as is the case in Lukács' work, then the critique of ideology must examine how limitations and illusions emerge in various modes of grasping social reality. Do specific modes and methods of apprehending social reality provide objective knowledge of society? For Lukács this question involves an examination of the origins and relationship between alienation, reification and ideology. The task of any critique of ideology, however, must be directed towards more than just an account of how that ideology comes about; it must address itself to how human beings are able to be emancipated from such ideology. For Lukács this emancipation can only take place within the context of conscious political activity.

Themes similar to these are dealt with, but in a very different manner, by writers in the sociology of knowledge, especially where that discipline concerns itself with an examination of ideology. Yet, other writers did not conceive this discussion within such an explicitly political dimension, although, as an examination of Scheler's and Mannheim's writings reveals, the political dimension is not totally absent from their work. What is distinctive about Lukács' work is the mode of conceptualising the problems he faces. This can only be understood in the light of his earlier writings.

Lukács' early writings were concerned with the problem of the interpretation and critique of cultural forms, and they have a direct bearing upon an understanding and interpretation of *History and Class Consciousness*. That work may be read as a Marxist study of ideology, in order to retrace the Marxist standpoint inherent in Lukács' earlier writings on the problems of culture. Conversely, his early writings may be used to show that the non-Marxist elements are retained in Lukács' later work, especially in *History and Class Consciousness*. In the former case, we see Lukács pressing beyond the interpretations of, say, Weber and Simmel, whilst in the latter, the basic flaws in Lukács' major work in this period are traced back to *Lebensphilosophie* and to Simmel. The first interpretation is characteristic of Goldmann,[27] Breines,[28] and Arato[29], the second of Coletti[30] and Steadman-Jones.[31] For both positions, however, the understanding of Lukács' early writings is central to their subsequent overall interpretation of *History and Class Consciousness*. This is also true of Löwy's recent examination of Lukacs' earlier work, which contains a critique of the second interpretation and provides much more detailed information on the early Budapest years.[32]

There are, of course, other pitfalls associated with readings of the 'early' and the 'later' Lukács. As a recent commentator suggests,

> there is a tendency to view Lukács' relationship to his neo-Kantian past either in terms of a complete break or in terms of a continuance of a 'romantic Marxism' throughout his life. Both fail to appreciate the specific contribution which Lukács makes, the former by neglecting the way in which his later position is a refinement of an already critical attitude towards bourgeois society . . . devouring the latter by subsuming both Lukács and neo-Kantianism under the ready-made terms 'romanticism' or 'historicism' and by drowning the specific theoretical achievements of both in a sea of superficial parallels.[33]

But in order to follow through the implications of this argument we must first of all turn to Lukács' early writings

II

What were Lukacs' central concerns in his early writings? Kammler argues that we may discern three intentions in Lukács' writings on aesthetics and his early Marxist writings on culture. Lukács' early work, Kammler says, is oriented towards 'a historical-sociological analysis, especially of literary forms and problems'.[34] This sociological analysis is most evident in the essay 'Zur Soziologie des modernen Dramas' which, though published in 1914 in German, was Lukács' own translation of a study in Hungarian that had been completed in the winter of 1908-9.[35] This orientation can be seen, more briefly, in Lukács' review of a volume in a series edited by Alfred Weber. There, in 'Zum Wesen und zur Methode der Kultursoziologie', Lukács discusses some aspects of a sociology of culture.[36] It is also apparent in an early article on the methodology of the study of literature, now recently translated into German.[37]

But the most concrete version of this sociological-historical intention is *The Theory of the Novel*, written in 1914-15 and published in book form in 1920.[38]

A second fundamental intention in Lukács' early writings is the development of the 'basic structures of a philosophy of art with the aim of securing a philosophy of life, a world view'.[39] This interest is manifested in *The Soul and its Forms*,[40] in Lukács' then unpublished Heidelberg writings on aesthetics[41] and in the important article 'Die Subjekt-Objekt-Beziehung in der Aesthetik'.[42]

The third interest, and one which cannot be separated from the other two orientations, is Lukács' concern for a cultural renewal in bourgeois society. This problem is at the centre of the 1917-18 discussion in the Szellemkek group in Budapest of which Lukács was a member.[43] This interest is continued in Lukács' early Marxist writings and is typified by his article 'Old Culture and New Culture' published in 1920.[44] It is these three intentions, or interests, that will be examined in turn, to throw light upon the development of Lukács' thought and its central categories.

At the very start of 'Zur Soziologie des modernen Dramas' Lukács recognizes that, 'all that is sociological in the dramatic form only determines the possibility of the realization of the aesthetic value but not this value itself. How value and value realization are connected and how far historical-sociological phenomena are important for the structure of value itself'[45] Lukács says, he hopes to consider in other works. This neo-Kantian separation of the social-historical sphere from the sphere of spiritual ideal values is characteristic of Lukács early works and reflects the persistent influence of writers like Simmel and the neo-Kantian tradition. Lukács takes modern drama to be a 'symbol of the whole of bourgeois culture' and its crisis: 'every drama is bourgeois because the forms of culture in modern life are bourgeois and because the forms of every expression of life are today determined by these cultural forms'.[46] This crisis lies in the powerlessness of the individual and his values against the pure facticity of what exists. Kammler, in this context, points to a certain affinity with Scheler's view that the 'ideal factors' are fundamentally powerless against the 'real factors' once this dualism accepts no possibility of mediation.[47] With reference to this power of what exists Lukács argues that it is 'not only that every idea and every theory is powerless when confronted with its power; rather, they immediately come under the domination of this unformulable law . . . from the moment when they are expressed'.[48] This separation and alienation of ideas and values when confronted with the existent, this separation of man and history, of theory and practice, are all embodied in the dominant values of bourgeois culture — individualism and historicism. These values reflect this dualism, the one by emphasizing an individualism that cannot be realized, the other by emphasizing the unrealizability of individualism. More concretely expressed, this crisis, this 'problem of life' arises out of the relationship between the individual and his culture and the economic structure of a capitalist society. In the following passage, Lukács highlights the way in which individualism has become a 'problem of life'. This problematic lies in forms of alienation:

> This 'new life' of modern capitalism has made everything 'uniform' — clothing, transport, 'the diverse forms of activity' viewed from the workers' standpoint' have become 'increasingly similar' (bureaucracy, industrial machine labour); education, the experiences of childhood become increasingly similar (the influence and ever increasing importance of the metropolis) etc.[49]

Lukács, like Simmel, also refers to the uniformity of the soldier's occupation compared with earlier times. Along with this uniformity, and parallel to it, is the 'objectification of life' (*Versachlichung des Lebens*):

> From the standpoint of the individual, the essence of the modern division of labour is perhaps that it makes work independent of the always irrational, thus only qualitatively determinable, capacities of the workers and places it under objective, goal-oriented criteria that lie outside his personality and have no relationship to it. The major economic tendency of capitalism is this same objectification of production, its separation from the personality of the producers. By means of the capitalist economy, an objective abstraction — capital — becomes the real producer even though it hardly stands in an organic connection to the personality of those who happen to own it; indeed, it becomes increasingly superfluous whether the owners are persons at all (joint stock companies).[50]

This loss of relationship between the individual and his activity also applies to modern scientific methods, which become 'increasingly objective and impersonal'. This is said to be true of work as a whole, which 'takes on a specific, objective life over against the individual character of the human being, so that he is forced to express himself in some form other than in what he does'.[51]

A further consequence is that the relationship between people becomes increasingly impersonal. Commenting on part of the passage just quoted, Breines writes that 'the links between Lukács' standpoint here and the theory of alienation developed by Marx . . . are striking'.[52]

What is, in fact, more striking is that the whole of this passage can be drawn from sections of Simmel's *Philosophy of Money*,[53] a book whose political economy has its origins not in Marx but in writers like Schmoller, on the one hand, and marginal utility theorists on the other.[54] Thus, one should not be surprised, as Breines is, that Lukács 'saw absolutely no revolutionary prospects in the objectification of labour in capitalist society'. If there is an anticipation of Lukács' later Marxism in these passages on modern drama, then it may well be derived from Simmel. The quoted passages testify to the profound influence which Simmel's *Philosophy of Money*, with its theory of reification and alienation, had upon Lukács. Simmel's influence is also manifested in Lukács' treatment of forms of life and culture.

The second intention manifested in Lukács' early writings — the search for a new world-view, a philosophy of life — is closely connected with the themes raised in the discussion of modern drama. In his other writings of the same period, Lukács seeks to show how the ideal spheres of values, the realm of the essential, can be identified in the work of art. Such values and such essentiality cannot, as we have seen, arise out of the act of material production. Nor can they arise out of the reified, uniform life of modern society. For Lukács, as for Simmel, that life is fragmentary.[55]

> life is an anarchy of light and dark: nothing is ever completely fulfilled in life, nothing ever quite ends; new confusing voices always mingle with the chorus of those that have been heard before. Everything flows, everything merges into another thing, and the mixture is uncontrolled and impure; everything is destroyed, everything is smashed, nothing ever flowers into real life.[56]

The problem, then, is how 'true life' and structures of meaning can emerge out of this chaos. Lukács' answer is in terms of the 'form' of a work of art: 'Form is the highest judge of life . . . Form is the only pure revelation of pure experience, but just for that reason it will always stubbornly refuse to be imposed on anything that is oppressive or unclear'.[57] This pure manifestation of life-experience, of *Erlebnisse*, is also the bearer of values: 'Form is the highest judge of life. Form-giving is a judging force, an ethic; there is a value-judgement in everything that has been given form. Every kind of form-giving, every literary form, is a step in the hierarchy of life-possibilities'.[58] This metaphysic of forms is conceived of as lying quite outside historical, social reality. Its basis lies in a 'Kantianism that has been reworked by *Lebensphilosophie*'. Form and ideal values can only be realised over, against, and in opposition to, an objective reality; they remain, as Kammler argues, an 'abstraction of the subject from reality'.[59] Such a position led Lukács to espouse various forms of mysticism in the period around 1912.

But, as Kammler argues, Lukács' way out of this mysticism and, in part, his retreat from *Lebensphilosophie* lay in his study of Hegel, a study that, on a more concrete level, produced *The Theory of the Novel* and, at the abstract level, 'Die Subjekt-Objekt-Beziehung in der Aesthetik'. *The Theory of the Novel* enabled Lukács to develop a historical perspective and, at least in terms of this historical-philosophical conception, to relate forms dialectically to history. The notion of form also moves further away from that developed by Simmel, and from its relationship to the metaphysics of *Lebensphilosophie*, towards a methodologically more secure development of Weber's concept of ideal type.

In *The Theory of the Novel*, the themes that Lukács raised in his early work again appear, but with a heightened degree of concretion. Lukács contrasts the epic and the novel as two representative forms of very different societies. Whereas the epic is able to conceive of the individual and society as a totality, this is no longer possible in the novel, in an age of total alienation. Instead, the novel is an expression of 'the transcendental homelessness of man'. Again, the conception of the tragic separations of the individual and society comes to the fore but now in a more historical form. In modern society it is no longer possible to posit an immediate totality of the individual and society. Alienation takes on the form of alienation from nature as a result of man's being alienated from second nature, that is the society he has created. Thus, 'estrangement from nature (the first nature) . . . is only a projection of man's experience of his self-made environment as a prison instead of as a parental home'.[60] This second nature is

> the world of convention, a world from whose all-embracing power only the innermost recesses of the soul are exempt, a world which is present everywhere in a multiplicity of forms too complex for understanding . . . It is a second nature, and, like first nature, it is determinable only as the embodiment of recognised but senseless necessities and therefore it is incomprehensible, unknowable in its real substance.[61]

The function of Hegelian conceptualization of a first and second nature is altered by Lukács. Kammler argues that

> for Hegel, the 'second nature' of societal forms is not, as is the first nature, a conceptless necessity estranged from meaning but rather it is ultimately realised reason, objective spirit. Lukács certainly revises the Hegelian reconciliation of subject and object, man and society, but he does not yet connect it with Marx's transformation of the problem into one of the social praxis of human beings.[62]

Indeed, Lukács' revision of Hegel's notions is in the direction of a return to a Kantian conception of the unknowable 'thing-in-itself' — itself the subject of a detailed critique in the chapter on reification in *Geschichte und Klassenbewusstein*. Furthermore, the problem of alienation as conceived by Lukács is not yet the social conception of estrangement rooted in labour that is found in Hegel's *Phenomenology of*

Mind in his discussion of the master-slave dialectic and the unhappy consciousness.

The typology of novel forms which constitutes the second part of *The Theory of the Novel* not only recalls the Weberian use of ideal types — and, of all Lukács' work, Weber saw this as the embodiment of what could be achieved by the human sciences — but also, in its basis in diverse worldviews, it recalls the abstract typology of world views used by Dilthey to characterize diverse metaphysical positions. Lukács himself later characterized the work as a product of his 'youthful enthusiasm for the work of Dilthey, Simmel and Max Weber'.[63] The work does, however, point to the introduction of the Hegelian notion of totality and 'the historicization of aesthetic categories'.[64]

It is in Lukács' later essay, 'Die Subjekt-Objekt-Beziehung in der Aesthetik', that the notion of totality first comes to the fore. This article, Lukács states in a note to its title, 'presupposes a phenomenology of creative and receptive behaviour' but the notion of phenomenology it uses 'should be understood more in the sense of that of Hegel rather than Husserl'.[65] Lukács here constructs an aesthetic model in which the artist shapes and creates an autonomous world microcosm with its own laws, and the work of art generates a harmony of subject and object, form and content. The eternal shaping of the unending creative process of the artist reaches its highest manifestations in the subject-object relationship. In the strict sense, that is, in the sense in which in a subject-object relationship neither pole is negated, a subject-object relationship only exists in the aesthetic sphere: 'the aesthetic subject merely stands, in the strict sense of this sphere, over against an object, the work of art: the subject himself is, in the same strict sense, a pure and immediately experiencing subject'.[66] Only the work of art is adequate to this subject and the work of art is 'a microcosm'; it possesses a 'cosmic character'; it is 'a totality that is autonomous, complete and self-sufficient'.[67]

One important implication of this article is that this microcosm, this totality that is the work of art, is only possible for a subject that is also a totality. However ahistorical and abstract this conception may be, it constitutes an important aesthetic model that Lukács transposes into the political sphere in *History and Class Consciousness* when he seeks to identify the identical subject and object of history, the identity of which secures autonomy for its standpoint. In this earlier work, it is the artist and the work of art that constitute a totality. The affinities with Hegel's conception of totality are well illustrated by Pascal's characterization of Hegel's notion of totality in his *Ästhetik*. There,

> Hegel distinguishes art from science, from rational understanding, by saying that art does not analyse, but grasps reality 'in its living existence in the particular'; art dwells 'in the substantial entity' that analysis has not broken up. This complex entity of the work of art he calls a 'Totalität', an

essential feature of which is its completedness, so that he repeatedly speaks of it as a 'total and free whole', with the 'independence', or self-sufficiency, that characterises the work of art. And Hegel relates this self-sufficient totality of the work of art to a basic ontological characteristic of man, his 'interest and need to be a real individual totality and living independent being . . .' Totality appears in Hegel (as in Lukács) both as the fulfilment of life and as the essential characteristic of art.[68]

For Lukács, in his later work the identical-subject-object of history is no longer the artist or the work of art but the proletariat, and later, as Ludz argues, the partisan.[69] In his later work, Lukács also provides an account of why this totality has been lost.

The third motif in Lukács' work, that of the problem of cultural renewal, brings us to the period prior to the formulation of the major chapters of *History and Class Consciousness*. This motif relates to Lukács' position in Hungary after his final return to Budapest in 1917. The nature of Lukács' participation in the Free School for the *Geisteswissenschaften*, and in the *Szellemkek*, along with Mannheim and others, is open to some debate. Looking back upon that group many decades later, Lukács said that 'the basic binding element amongst the participants was an opposition to capitalism in the name of idealist philosophy. What held the group together was this opposition to positivism'.[70] Lukács also suggests that the discussions were no longer important to him:

> Towards the end of the war a group gathered around Béla Balázs and myself which soon grew into the 'Free School of *Geisteswissenschaften*'. My earlier work no doubt played a certain role in its formation. It became important later thanks to the role played abroad by some of its members (Karl Mannheim, Arnold Hauser, Frigyes Antal, Károly Tolnay); its influence in Hungary is often overestimated today for the same reason. It did not really mean anything important to me since it was essentially linked to a way of thinking and acting that I had already got over.[71]

The persistence of themes from Lukács' earlier commitments and, as Kammler points out, the continued importance of his distinction between the sociological and historical philosophical perspectives for his early Marxist work suggest, however, that he had not 'got over' the topics of these discussions. Yet, in another sense, Lukács was changing course in the period 1916–18 since this signalled his renewed interest in Marx's work, 'but this time it was a Marx seen through Hegel's glasses and no longer through those of Simmel . . . I sought, basically on a Hegelian foundation, to synthesise Hegel and Marx in a "philosophy of history" '.[72] This change of course was further signposted by Lukács' entry into the Hungarian Communist Party in December 1918.

In his early essays on Marxism, Lukács retains the distinction that was already apparent in his early writings on aesthetics, namely the separation of sociology from a historical-philosophical standpoint. This distinction is clear from a passage in Lukács' early Marxist essay

'Bolshevism as a moral problem', which originally appeared only in Hungarian.[73] There, the problem of the relationship between theory and practice comes to the fore but within the context of this earlier distinction. Thus, Lukács writes:

> Unfortunately, Marx's philosophy of history has seldom been consciously separated from his sociology and thus many people have not noticed that the two cardinal elements — namely, the class struggle and the socialist social order — do not emerge out of the same concept formation, even though they are still closely connected with one another. The first element represents the fundamental assertion of Marx's sociology: society has always existed and so too has its driving force;. . . The second element represents the utopian postulate of Marx's philosophy of history: the *moral purpose* for a coming world order.[74]

This separation of sociology from the philosophy of history in Marx's work, a separation of theory and practice, is resolved by the taking up of a revolutionary ethics that is related to the revolutionary class and the concrete individual. The proletariat must press beyond the sociologically-determined facticity, towards the generation of a genuine freedom in society. Lukács sees a structural identity between the purposive action of 'the historical subject — the revolutionary proletariat — and that of the ethical subject — the moral individual', but this identity remains a purely formal and abstract identity. This abstract identity, between the moral and historical or political spheres, is supported by the maintenance of the ideal of 'classical harmony' that Lukács retains from his aesthetics. In the same article Lukács asks: 'Is it possible to achieve the good through bad means, freedom through repression; can a new world order come into existence if the means of its generation are only distinguished in a technical sense from the means of the old system that have been rightly exposed and condemned?'[75] In quoting this passage, Kammler argues that 'the ethical question is immediately transformed into a political one', that is, the ethical judgement is transferred into the political realm without any mediation whatsoever'.[76]

This very same separation between sociology and a philosophy of history is retained in a slightly later work, 'Tactics and Ethics'[77], in which the centrality of the moral dimension is again asserted, and in which Lukács discusses 'the decisive criterion of socialist tactics: the philosophy of history. The *fact* of the class struggle is nothing other than a sociological description and an elevation of events into laws which are effective in social reality; yet the *significance* of the proletariat goes beyond this fact'.[78] In this work, and later, the gulf between these two spheres is resolved by the notion of 'objective possibility' in relation to class consciousness. This notion of objective possibility is applied by Lukács to both individual and collective action. However, in the context of the dual spheres outlined above, the first prerequisite for this objective possibility

... is the formation of class consciousness. In order for correct action to become an authentic, correct regulator, class consciousness must raise itself above the level of the merely given; it must remember its world-historical mission and its sense of responsibility. For the class interest, the attainment of which makes up the content of class-conscious action, coincides neither with the sum of the personal interests of the individuals belonging to the class nor with the immediate short-term interest of the class as a collective entity.[79]

It is this class consciousness which goes beyond the sociologically existent whilst taking it into account and unifying it with the historical-philosophical standpoint.

In 'Tactics and Ethics', Lukács is already arguing against the naive belief in a scientific Marxism that has already predicted historical inevitabilities. Rather, for Lukács, 'science, knowledge, can indicate only possibilities — and it is only in the realm of the possible that moral, responsible action, truly human action, is itself possible'.[80] Indeed, Kammler argues that, for Lukács, the concept of objective possibility is 'the decisive instrument for the mediation of a philosophy of history and a theory of society relevant for praxis on the one hand, and individual praxis on the other'.[81] Kammler goes on to suggest that, despite the affinity between some of Lukács' formulations and his earlier works, 'Tactics and Ethics' represents a decisive break with the past since 'Lukács not only unambiguously asserts the priority of the historical-philosophical perspective, but also for the first time relates — albeit at first only programmatically — the determination of the direction of praxis to the "material" of his philosophy of history' — concrete society'.[82]

This same transitional character of the retention of earlier formulations and their re-working within a new context is also apparent in Lukács' early Marxist discussion of the problem of culture. In an article entitled 'Alte Kultur und neue Kultur' published in *Kommunismus* in 1920,[83] it is possible to see how far Lukács has moved from a 'sociological' to a Marxist account of culture. Earlier, in a review article, 'Zum Wesen und zur Methode der Kultursoziologie' (1915)[84] — in which Lukács praised Töinnes' *Gemeinschaft und Gesellschaft* and Simmel's *Philosophie des Geldes* as isolated examples of a sociology of culture — Lukács criticized several aspects of attempts by Alfred Weber and others to ground a sociology of culture. What he did not criticize, however, and what is significant in this specifically Marxist account of culture, is Weber's distinction between culture and civilization as a basis for the discussion of the social determination of culture. Lukács still speaks here of 'the concept of culture (in contrast to civilization)'[85] and argues that it 'comprises numerous valuable products and capacities that can be dispensed with in reference to the immediate maintenance of life'. In this sense, culture is the product of an economic surplus, of an independence from the basic necessities of life.

Lukács argues that 'just as culture is the inner domination of human beings over their environment, so civilization means its external domination over their environment'.[86] This external domination is manifested primarily in the economy. Under capitalism, not only is everyone, including the dominant class, subordinate to the productive process but capitalism itself implies 'the domination of the economy'. This insufficient determination of capitalism is evident in Lukács' presentation of the process of alienation under capitalism, which he sees as being based merely on the relationship of the producer to his product. The analysis of the expropriation of labour power and the whole dimension of exploitation is missing in Lukács' account of the alienation process. The alienation of the producer from his product, in the form of commodity production, is contrasted with an earlier harmonious relationship between culture, ideology and society in the same manner as Lukács previously contrasted the novel as a disjointed art form with the earlier harmony of art and society that produced the epic as a literary form.

Lukács even takes as his example of the consequences of market production, the phenomenon of fashion that is found, not in Marx, but in Simmel's *Philosophy of Money*. Echoes of Simmel's sociological analysis of capitalism are also found elsewhere in this article. Lukács here advances the argument that is later central to his conception of a critique of ideology in *History and Class Consciousness*, namely that the bourgeoisie necessarily creates a disjunction, or contradiction, between its ideology — that of individual freedom — and 'the system of production, of society' which necessarily cannot grant freedom to the working class. At the level of cultural phenomena, this contradiction expresses itself as a contradiction between their form and their content, in a manner similar to that analysed — at a somewhat more abstract level — by Simmel in *The Philosophy of Money*. The culture-civilization dichotomy, which also informs the form-content distinction, forces Lukács to accept a concept of the capitalist production process that necessarily leads to culture and technical industrial production as simple oppositions.

Ultimately, then, Lukács believes that by destroying 'the autonomy of the economy' through 'the socialist organization of the economy', the form of alienation which he has outlined will be transcended. This abstract standpoint, which is totally without reference to the process of exploitation and is based upon a hypostatization of 'the economy', has another important consequence for 'the new culture'. The culture-civilization dichotomy and the hypostatization of the economy combine to produce a further dualism between the sociological analysis of the framework with which culture is created and the creative individual.

Lukács argues with reference to a socialist society that 'culture is the form of the idea of the human essence of man. Culture will therefore be created by people not by circumstances. Such a transformation of society thus forms only the boundaries, only the possibility for free self-creativity, for the human spontaneous creative force[87] We thus return once more to the distinction between sociological determinations and the philosophy of history. The new society will realise what classical idealism was unable to bring about 'for the idea of humanity as an independent goal, the basic idea of the new culture, is the legacy of the classical idealism of the nineteenth century'.[88]

It would appear that Lukács' notion of 'the new culture' in fact recreates the problem of the relationship between theory and praxis rather than solves it. It also assumes a specifically Hegelian reinterpretation of Marx's theory in which an autonomous, and no longer 'unhappy', consciousness will generate the new culture. The weakness of this 'messianic utopianism' — as Lukács was later to refer to his work in this period — lies, as Kammler persuasively argues, in the fact that

> Lukács . . . is not able to mediate between the theoretically postulated necessity of the revolutionary process and actual revolutionary praxis. His theory cannot suffice to realise his implicit claim, the practical realisation of the unity of theory and praxis through the existing concretisation of theory, because it all too inclusively subsumes the constructive idea of the substratum of theory, the historical society and the constituted specific forms of social praxis.[89]

This failure led Lukács, ultimately, into the examination of the problems of the organisation of social and political praxis that forms the final chapter of *History and Class Consciousness*.

III

As the title of Lukács' major work in this period indicates, one of his central concerns was the elucidation of the notion of class consciousness. This is carried out at a number of levels that are not always clearly distinguished. For example, class consciousness is important for Lukács as one of the crucial phenomena in which the category of totality is embodied. At another level, class consciousness is significant for Lukács because it is embodied in a particular institutional and organization form, the analysis of which constitutes the later chapters of *History and Class Consciousness*. Thus, Lukács argues that 'the form taken by the class consciousness of the proletariat is the Party.'[90] More specifically, Lukacs sets out to locate class consciousness within the class structure of capitalist society. But this class consciousness is not an immediate empirical phenomenon but one that must be imputed to particular classes. In order to understand these various levels of analysis of class consciousness we must relate them both to the actual context within which Lukács was developing his theory,[91] and to the continuing centrality of certain themes which persist in *History and Class Consciousness*.[92]

In his pre-Marxist writings, Lukács had already developed a subject-object dialectic in the realm of aesthetics (one which relied heavily on Lask as well as Hegel[93]) and this continued to be important in *History and Class Consciousness*, albeit on a different level and within a different context.[94] Similarly, Kammler has pointed to the hiatus in Lukács' earlier writings between a philosophy of history and a sociology of culture which attempts to be concrete. We may also bear in mind the centrality in Lukács' 'Heidelberg aesthetics' of the problem of timelessness and historicity, a problem which, in a different form, becomes acute in *History and Class Consciousness*.[95] In short, it is impossible to examine Lukacs' central arguments in this work without being aware that not only are many of these essays reformulations of earlier pieces but that certain central themes from Lukács' earlier work reappear here.

The central political themes of Lukács' work in the early 1920s are that the fate of the revolution depended upon the ideological maturity of the working class, and that a fundamental concern should be with the decisive barriers standing in the way of the formation of a revolutionary ideology. The crucial concepts of class consciousness and objective possibility had already appeared in *Taktika és ethika* in 1919,[96] where Lukács argues that,

> morally correct action is related fundamentally to the correct perception of the given historico-philosophical situation, which is in turn only feasible through the efforts of every individual to make this self-consciousness conscious for himself. The first unavoidable prerequisite for this is the formation of class consciousness. In order for correct action to become an authentic, correct regulator, class consciousness must raise itself above the level of the merely given; it must remember its world-historical mission and its sense of responsibility. For the class interest, the attainment of which makes up the content of class-conscious action, coincides neither with the sum of the personal interests of the individuals belonging to the class nor with the immediate short-term interests of the class as a collective entity.[97]

Here, the difference between the conceptual form of the philosophical-historical dimension of class consciousness and the actual empirical form does not appear unbridgeable, even though Lukacs is loath to identify class interests with the concrete empirical interests of a social class.

However, after 1920, that is, after the failure of the 1918/19 revolutions in Hungary and Germany, Lukács' essays are no longer permeated by a utopian anticipation of the revolution. Rather, they are increasingly concerned with the gap between the notion of a revolutionary class consciousness capable of grasping society as a totality and the actual level of working class consciousness. This is made evident where earlier essays are reworked for inclusion in *History and Class Consciousness*, for example, the essay 'Class Consciousness', first published in 1920. Grunenberg specifically relates the change in Lukács' position to his hopes for and the failure of the March offensive in Germany in 1921. Henceforth, she argues, 'Lukács took up the ideological crisis of the proletariat as *the* fundamental problem and, in contrast, placed the analysis of *objective* factors in the background', and sought 'to confront the daily struggles of the working class with the *idea* of the pure class struggle'[98]. Lukács' interpretation of the defeats of the revolutionary movement in this period was not in terms of the uneven power struggles between the bourgeoisie and the working class but 'was exclusively the result of a false consciousness on the part of the working class and falsely applied tactics on the part of the VKPD'.[99]

Hence, in the reworked article on class consciousness, 'Lukács had emphasized the crucial role of class consciousness in the decisive phase of the struggle for power. Yet, at the same time, he had characterized the actual empirical consciousness of the working class as completely incapable of taking over this role'.[100] It is not surprising then that 'at the centre of *History and Class Consciousness* there stands therefore not the everyday consciousness of the worker from the standpoint of its revolutionary transformation but a theoretical, historico-philosophical clarification of the question: what might revolutionary consciousness look like?'[101] Within such a context we are able to see why Lukács does not take up empirical class consciousness as the starting point of his analysis and why imputed class consciousness and the notion of objective possibility play a central role in his theory of class consciousness. Once more we are confronted, as Kammler suggests, with 'the danger of an unmediated dualism of speculative concept and socially related factors, of idea and reality'.[102]

Lukács argues against the 'belief that the concrete can be located in the empirical individual of history (''individual'' here can refer to an individual person, class or people) and in his empirically given (and hence psychological or mass psychological) consciousness' since for him concrete analysis means 'the relation to society *as a whole*'.[103] This rejection of any psychological dimension is in keeping with Lukács' critique of psychology, as when he maintains that

> all previous psychology, Freudian included, suffers from the systemic weakness that it starts out from artificially isolated — through the capitalist mode of production and society — solitary human beings. It treats their qualities — also produced by capitalism — as unchangeable qualities that are actually 'natural necessities' for human beings . . . In this manner, psychology turns the nature of things upon its head. It attempts to explain a human being's social relationships in terms of their individual consciousness

(or unconsciousness) instead of exploring the social foundations of their separated existence from the totality and the associated problem of their relationship to fellow human beings.[104]

This rejection of any psychological analysis of class consciousness is associated with a rejection of any analysis of class consciousness at the level of empirical immediacy. However, the two arguments are not identical since Reich's analysis of class consciousness and some of the work of the Frankfurt School in the 1930s would suggest that a social-psychological approach need not remain confined to the level of empirical immediacy. Nonetheless, it does remain true that most attempts at an empirical analysis of class consciousness have either concentrated on immediate levels of awareness of class (consciousness of class) or have been compelled to reduce class consciousness to some empirical indices such as trade union membership and participation.

Lukács' equation of any attempt to examine class consciousness at the level of its immediate existence (leaving aside, for the moment, the question of whether it is necessary to remain at this level) with opportunism only serves to heighten the need for an alternative notion of class consciousness. On the basis of the arguments so far advanced, the philosophical-historical rejection of an analysis at the level of immediacy, a methodological rejection of a social-psychological account of class consciousness and a political identification of 'the actual, psychological state of consciousness of the proletariat' with opportunism, leaves Lukács with no alternative but to argue for a sharp differentiation of the empirical consciousness of the proletariat from true class consciousness.

However, this non-empirical notion of class consciousness is also predicated upon an abstract notion of the proletariat as the identical subject-object of the historical process. Lukács had already argued that only an historical subject which is itself a totality is capable of apprehending history and society as a totality. This central category of totality is also 'the bearer of the revolutionary principle in science' and, as such, is the crucial category which Marx took over from Hegel. Hence, Marx's theory of society and history enables those who understand it to comprehend society as a totality. It is clear that, at any particular point in time, the majority of the working class are not amongst this group who understand Marx's theory. As we shall see from Lukács' analysis of the process of reification, the illusions created by the commodity structure of a capitalist society are all-pervasive, affecting the bourgeoisie and the proletariat alike. Therefore, it must be shown how the proletariat is able to break out of this reified world-view and how it is possible for it to develop a true class consciousness. At any time, this class consciousness (which at times seems to be coterminous not merely with a *comprehension* of Marx's theory of society but actually *identical* to it) can only be *imputed* to the working class. The nature of the working class's position in the production process — at a philosophical-historical level, almost identical with the position of the slave in Hegel's master–slave dialectic — guarantees that the development of such a class consciousness is, at least, *objectively possible*.

Lukács' philosophical-historical standpoint is clearly indebted to Hegel in several ways. We have already seen that the category of totality, though having its origins in Simmel's philosophy,[105] was transformed by Lukács into a Hegelian notion of methodological significance. At the epistemological level, Lukács also sought to make concrete Hegel's concept of reality. As Kammler puts it, 'the true reality — in contrast to *Dasein*, *Realität* and *Existenz* — was for Hegel the existence of the idea as the "unity of the concept and objectivity" '.[106] At the level of a philosophy of history, the subject-object dialectic which Lukács had already developed in relation to aesthetics becomes a Hegelian, dialectical philosophy of history. This has important consequences for Lukács' interpretation of Marx. Fetscher suggests that, on Lukács' interpretation, 'Marx's supersession of Hegel results not from a materialist critique (in Feuerbach's sense) but . . . makes it possible for Marx to show that the proletariat actually is the real subject-object of history, the "we" whose actions history actually is'.[107]

For Lukács, then, the notion of the proletariat is very close to that of the slave in Hegel's master–slave dialectic. This is reinforced by the central role which Lukács ascribes to the process by which the proletariat comes to full consciousness of its position, just as the slave, for Hegel, must achieve full recognition of his position. Similarly, slave-consciousness for Hegel, as with empirical proletarian consciousness for Lukács, remains trapped at the level of immediacy. There is even some support for the view that Lukács at times would subscribe to Hegel's belief in this context that *Anerkennung* is *Aufhebung*, that 'recognition' *is* 'transcendence'. This Hegelian philosophy of history serves to reinforce Lukács' lack of concern with — and even lack of faith in — actual working-class consciousness. As Grunenberg argues 'empirical consciousness is viewed by him as a form of expression, as a shallow reflection of reified social relationships'.[108]

Instead, Lukács utilizes and develops a notion of class consciousness that can be imputed to a social class, one which

> consists in the fact of the appropriate and rational reactions 'imputed' [zugerechnet] to a particular typical position in the process of production. This consciousness is, therefore, neither the sum nor the average of what is thought or felt by the single individuals who make up the class.[109]

The first part of this definition, with its emphasis on the 'appropriate', the 'rational' and the 'typical' is a completely Weberian formulation of class consciousness.[110] Lukács argues that it is possible to infer 'the thoughts and feelings which men would have in a particular situation if they were *able* to assess both it and the interests arising from it in their impact on immediate action and on the whole structure of society'.[111] This inference is made possible 'by relating consciousness to the whole of society'. What Lukács does not point out is that since this relation between consciousness and the whole of society does not exist, our knowledge of the existence of this 'true' class consciousness can only be established *ex post*.[112]

Nonetheless, Lukács does consider the difficulties involved in the use of this notion of objective possibility. We need to know whether the distance between this class consciousness and the empirically given is the same for all classes in society and to examine 'the *practical* significance of these different possible relations between the objective economic totality, the imputed class consciousness and the real, psychological thoughts of men about their lives'.[113] Later, Lukács also makes clear that there are probably different levels of empirical consciousness within the working class which need to be examined. Yet, as he suggests, 'the stratification of the problems and economic interests *within* the proletariat is, unfortunately, almost wholly unexplored, but research would undoubtedly lead to discoveries of the very first importance'.[114] Thus, Lukács is at least aware of some of the problems involved in his use of a dualistic notion of consciousness.

With regard to this notion of 'objective possibility', Lukács suggests that we must examine 'how far is it *in fact* possible to discern the whole economy of a society from inside it?' The notion must enable us to transcend individual immediate awareness whilst at the same time recognizing the extent to which this awareness is constrained by 'the economic structure of society'. By arguing that concrete analysis is knowledge of society as a totality, and imputing to social classes a class consciousness that is based upon that knowledge as an objective possibility, Lukács is able to introduce his version of the notion of *false* consciousness. Immediate consciousness appears

> as something which is *subjectively* justified in the social and historical situation. . . At the same time, *objectively*, it bypasses the essence of the evolution of society and fails to pinpoint it and express it adequately. That is to say, objectively, it appears as a 'false consciousness'. On the other hand, we may see the same consciousness as something which fails *subjectively* to reach its self-appointed goals, while furthering and realising the objective aims of a society of which it is ignorant and which it did not choose.[115]

It is quite clear from this passage that we can only recognise false consciousness if we are aware of the objective possibility of a class position in relation to the whole of society. Only by positing this 'objective possibility' can 'falsity' be ascribed to consciousness.

It is also apparent that Lukács applies the notion of class consciousness in two ways — as 'true' class consciousness and as 'false' class consciousness. The transition from false to true consciousness is made possible by utilizing the notion of 'objective possibility'. This false consciousness is, in the last resort, determined by the economic structure of society — a determination of which one is not aware since

> class consciousness implies a class-conditioned *unconsciousness* of one's own socio-historical and economic condition. This condition is given as a definite structural relation, a definite formal nexus which appears to govern the whole of life. The 'falseness', the illusion implicit in this situation is in no sense arbitrary; it is simply the intellectual reflex of the objective economic structure.[116]

Hence, until it is possible to recognise these determinations emanating from the economic structure false consciousness will be a permanent state. Lukács gives as an example a common illusion that the price of labour power is in fact the price of labour and then goes on to suggest that 'it requires the most painstaking *historical analysis* (italics added, D.F.) to use the category of objective possibility so as to isolate the conditions in which this illusion can be exposed and a real connection with the totality established'.[117] What Lukács is implying here is that Marx himself used this notion of objective possibility. Even if this were true, it would still suggest that false consciousness is removed by ex-post *analysis* which, in all probability, would not be undertaken by the subjects of that analysis but would appear from a source external to them.

Since these concepts of objective possibility and imputed class consciousness are of central importance to Lukács' theory of class consciousness it is worthwhile investigating their origins. Lukács' attempt to bridge the gulf between a speculative concept and empirical immediacy almost certainly has its roots in Max Weber's methodology, though Lukács' use of 'objective possibility' and 'imputation' (*Zurechnung*) differs from that of Weber in several important respects. Weber himself points out that he took the concept from 'the works of the outstanding physiologist v. Kries' and from the legal writings and critique of Radbruch.[118]

According to Fetscher, 'Max Weber introduced the concept of objective possibility into the methodology of the social sciences in order to gain a criterion for the standard of the *choice* of historically relevant facts out of the vast, heterogeneous continuum of reality'.[119] Weber argues that the social scientist seeks such facts as have a causal effect. The historian, for example, makes use of a thought experiment (*Gedanken-experiment*) when he takes over the thought process from the legal context of apportioning blame for certain events. Weber suggests that when one asks 'Under what circumstances can one assert that someone, through their action has "brought about" (*'verursacht'*) a definite external consequence?' then this is 'purely a question of causality — and is clearly of the same logical structure as the historical question of causality'.[120] Weber takes this mode of procedure as being applicable to individual action, whether of the historical individual or of the private person. The social scientist must impute objectively-possible consequences of action from the myriad of possible factors. This involves the act of selection, which is itself based upon our cognitive interests. Hence, Weber argues, 'the possibility of a selection from amongst the infinity of determinants is determined first of all by the nature of our historical *interest*'.[121] This concept of objective possibility must commence from a *rational* reconstruction of alternative development possibilities, but can also take account of irrationality since rationality is only a tendency within the necessarily heterogeneous continuum of reality and can never be complete.[122]

However, Fetscher argues that there are two crucial limitations in the use of the notion of objective possibility in Weber's work, both of which Lukács, in turn, seeks to overcome. The first is that the rational, calculating individual is the sole basis of objective possibilities. Fetscher argues that Weber fails to examine the historical development of such a bourgeois individual. It might be said, further, that this individual remains a crucial ideal-typical construct in the social sciences and especially in political economy. Secondly, Fetscher argues that for Weber the actions of collectivities are either left out of account or are reduced to instances of individual action: 'community action and social action are merely specific forms of the action of individuals'.[123]

Lukács is one of the first writers within the Marxist tradition both to apply Weber's notions of objective possibility and imputation in a new direction and to attempt to solve the weaknesses of these concepts. Lukács acknowledges that the notion of imputation is borrowed from Weber and that the notion of the ideal type occurs in Marxism, for example, as 'the very important category of the "economic persona" '. However, he suggests that he cannot at present take up 'the relation of historical materialism to comparable trends in bourgeois thought (such as Max Weber's ideal types)'[124] Nonetheless, Lukács, like Weber, is involved with theoretical constructs, with the construction of an adequate proletarian class consciousness, just as Weber is concerned with the construction of ideal types of rational action. Lukács, however, relates the concrete class situation and 'objective' class interest to the objective structures of capitalist society as a totality, whereas, for Weber, the notion of society as a totality plays no role whatsoever. Similarly, Lukács gives a historical dimension to the notion of objective possibility. A social class as an acting subject of history not only construes the past but also the future objective possibilities. Hence, Lukács' use of objective possibility extends far beyond that of Weber, since he

1. not only construes past but also future 'objective possibilities' of class action and

2. seeks to demonstrate that political action on the basis of adequate proletarian class consciousness is the only conceivable way to overcome the antagonistic contradictions in the capitalist mode of production. The concept of 'objective possibility' thereby takes on a radically different character and gains, as it were, an ontological and normative dignity.[125]

Thus, Lukács' notion of imputed class consciousness is certainly not that of a sum of individuals, but the action of a social class as a totality. In this and other respects it diverges sharply from Weber's use of the theory of objective possibility.

Even within *History and Class Consciousness* Lukács' treatment of the *realization* of the objective possibility of proletarian class consciousness changes as the work progresses. In the original essay (1920) on class consciousness, the influence of Rosa Luxemburg is still much in evidence and the degree of autonomous development of class consciousness appears to be much greater than in the essay on reification (1922) where the latter's effects are seen to be all-pervasive. This would imply that the development of class consciousness must be stimulated from outside. Hence, we find that in the essay on organizational problems (1922), Lenin's theory of organization of the Communist party comes to the fore. Fetscher, in fact, argues that the party takes on the form of objective possibility of proletarian class consciousness. In this respect it replaces Weber's rational personality, except that, whereas Weber's rationality of the bourgeois individual is limited, for Lukács the party's perfect rationality is limited only by the objective historical process.[126]

Be that as it may, Lukács' argument as to the objective possibility of the development of true class consciousness on the part of the working class remains extremely abstract. Lukács was altogether unaware of all the concrete problems involved in the development of class consciousness. For instance, he remarks, albeit as an aside, that 'status consciousness — a real historical factor — masks class consciousness; in fact it prevents it from appearing at all'.[127] Still, Arato's comment on Lukács' theory of class consciousness is apposite: 'not having thoroughly analysed e.g., the stratifications of the working class, the social reproduction of the worker in the family, and in schools, and the political legitimation of the capitalist system of domination, Lukács never faced most of the constraints that interfere with the possibilities of class consciousness'.[128] But this is not surprising in view of his reluctance to confront 'empirical' class consciousness.

IV

For Lukács, the crucial constraint upon the development of class consciousness is reification. What are the central features of his theory of reification? Apitzsch argues that Lukács is not concerned with an attempt 'as Gramsci expresses it — to comprehend the "material structure of ideology" — but rather one might formulate it conversely, that he seeks to grasp the structuring function of ideology in the base process itself'.[129] This is most obvious in Lukács treatment of reification, where he moves away from a simple base–superstructure dichotomy:

> thought and existence are not identical in the sense that they 'correspond' to each other, or 'reflect' each other, that they 'run parallel' to each other or 'coincide' with each other (all these expressions are only concealed forms of a rigid duality). Rather their identity lies in the fact that they are moments of one and the same real-historical dialectical process.[130]

Apitzsch argues, however, that a version of the base–superstructure model is retained in Lukács' work in that

> on the one hand, we have the 'true structure of society . . . in the independent rationalised and formal partial laws' which, however, rest upon an irrational interpretation of the total process; on the other, we have the logic of the praxis of the proletariat, its 'intention towards totality', whose substance is in no way immediately given to it but rather only in relation to the reifications produced by the bourgeoisie.[131]

Certainly, in the reification article, there is a subjective–objective dialectical process which pushes Lukács' analysis back in the direction of a base–superstructure model.

The analysis of the process of reification is one which points towards a new version of the sociology of knowledge in its widest sense, insofar as it takes the medium of communication in capitalist societies to be that of commodity production and holds the commodity to be the universal category of the whole of social existence under capitalism. Lukács argues that the problem of commodities appears as 'the central, structural problem of capitalist society in all its manifestations in life'.[132] The essence of the commodity structure is 'that a relation between people takes on the character of a thing and thus acquires a "spectral objectivity", an autonomy that seems so strictly rational and all-embracing as to conceal every trace of its fundamental nature: the relation between people'.[133] He assumes that his own analysis is based on 'the *presupposition* of Marx's economic analysis' and that this analysis will provide us with a 'clear insight into the ideological problems of capitalism and its decline'. Thus, from the very outset, Lukács makes a number of questionable assumptions. He had earlier assumed that reification was the central barrier to the development of proletarian consciousness and that 'the ideological crisis of the proletariat' was the crucial problem to be faced: '*Only the consciousness of the proletariat can point to the way that leads out of the impasse of capitalism.* As long as this consciousness is lacking, the crisis remains permanent.'[134] This 'permanent' crisis is, in fact, reinforced in Lukács' own analysis by the all-embracing process of reification. How this comes about must be central to our analysis of Lukács' account of reification. Secondly, Lukács assumes that his account of reification is predicated upon Marx's analysis. This raises two issues: whether in fact the theory of reification does rest upon Marx's analysis of the commodity structure and whether, in merely predicating this analysis, Lukács confines himself to an account of the 'phenomenon' of capitalism and not its 'essence'.

Marx himself uses the concept of reification (*Verdinglichung*) only once in his work, at the very end of volume three of *Capital*.[135] In this passage, part of which is quoted by Lukács (though not, strangely enough, the reference to reification), Marx describes 'the mystification of the capitalist mode of production, the reification (*Verdinglichung*) of social relations'[136] and 'the enchanted, perverted, topsy-turvy world, in which Monsieur le Capital and Madame La Terre do their ghost-walking as social characters and at the same time as mere things'.[137] All this is presented within the context of a critique of vulgar economy and a three-factors-of-production account of the capitalist mode of production which Marx refers to as 'the trinity formula'. It is perhaps ironic that Lukács should cite this passage in which Marx castigates vulgar economists' evasion of the relationship between the three kinds of revenue — wages, rent, interest — and their origin in the extraction of surplus value through exploitation since Lukács himself consistently avoids the theory of surplus value and exploitation in his own analysis of capitalism.

The concept of reification also appears in the work of Nietzsche and, more significantly, on several occasions in Georg Simmel's *Philosophy of Money*, a book which, as Lukács himself subsequently acknowledged, had greatly influenced his earlier development.[138] Hence, there must arise in any analysis of Lukács' discussion of the reification process the question of how far Simmel's own theory of reification finds echoes in Lukács' Marxist work. Significantly, Lukács' like Simmel, makes no distinction between reification and objectification. Thus, even at a preliminary glance, the question as to whether Lukács' account of reification 'presupposes' Marx's analysis has many more ramifications than a mere clarification of the 'faithfulness' of Lukács' account in relation to Marx would suggest.

This whole issue must be placed within the context of Lukács' analysis of capitalist society and its 'ideological problems', since the decisive determining factor in social consciousness under capitalism is not the contradiction between labour and capital, between the relations and forces of production, but the reified nature of the commodity structure.[139] The reification produced by commodity relations is seen by Lukács to be all-pervasive; indeed capitalism itself seems to take on the character of a hermetic totality of reification, in which the material forces of production combine with the capitalist relations of production into a negative homogeneity, whereas Marx saw the decisive dynamics of capitalist society which ultimately necessarily were revolutionary as being based upon this increasingly explosive contradiction between productive forces and the capitalist relations of production.[140]

We may question the automatic nature of this contradiction, but the central point which Kammler makes is important, namely, that Lukács removes this dimension from his analysis of capitalism.

Recent studies have argued that Lukács' analysis of capitalism is indeed almost consistently at variance with Marx's own.[141] Grunenberg, for example, demonstrates that Lukács' account of the emergence of reification differs markedly from Marx's account of the development of capitalism in important respects. Lukács argues that reification emerges with the transition from simple to capitalist commodity production and implies a qualitative distinction between the two types of commodity production: 'The distinction between a society where this form [commodity form, D.F.] is dominant, permeating every expression of life, and a society where it only makes an episodic appearance is essentially one of quality.'[142] Grunenberg argues that in Lukács' working out of this distinction there lie two erroneous assessments of simple commodity production. On the one hand, Lukács romanticizes simple commodity production and speaks of 'an organic process within a community'. On the other, he argues that only under capitalism does the mode of production determine social life whereas in pre-capitalist societies it was determined by 'state-legal forms'.[143] Neither view can be traced back to Marx. Once the commodity has become 'the universal category of society',

> a man's own activity, his own labour becomes something objective and independent of him, something that controls him by virtue of an autonomy alien to man. There is both an objective and a subjective side to this phenomenon. Objectively a world of objects and relations between things springs into being. . . . Subjectively . . . a man's activity becomes estranged from himself, it turns into a commodity which, subject to the non-human objectivity of the natural laws of society, must go its own way independently of man just like any consumer article.'[144]

Grunenberg rightly remarks that, whereas Marx speaks of the relationship of producers to the total societal labour and hence of the dual nature of the commodity of labour as labour and as labour power, 'Lukács explains the *same problem* in items of the distancing of the worker from the product of his labour, as the confrontation of producer and product', and in this respect his analysis remains at the level of 'the superficialities of the phenomena of capitalist commodity production'.[145]

However, what Grunenberg fails to point out is both the close relationship between this analysis and Lukacs' earlier accounts of estrangement and the similarities between his accounts and Simmel's theory of reification.[146] It is almost as if Lukács retained Simmel's theory of cultural reification and sought to justify it in terms of Marx's account of commodity fetishism — which is certainly a dimension that is absent from Simmel's theory of reification. Nonetheless, Simmel's theory of reification also rests upon the separation of the product from its producer and goes on to emphasize the ramifications of this process in the division of labour.

At a different level, Lukács' 'tragic' description of the situation of the bourgeoisie, trapped in the reified world which they created, clearly echoes not merely his own earlier writings — and perhaps his own situation — but also the tragic consciousness of Simmel. Simmel, too, sees the precarious position of the individual threatened by the processes of reification as profoundly tragic. At the level of everyday consciousness and with the universalization of the reification process. Lukács' argument is also pessimistic. All social groups are trapped in this reified totality. This is, in fact, a constituent element of what Fehér has termed Lukács' 'romantic anti-capitalism' which was evident in his response to the First World War and explains his relationship to other 'romantics' such as Paul Ernst.[147] What saves Lukács from offering a totally pessimistic picture is his messianic postulate of an abstract proletariat (or an equally abstract party) as the potential identical subject–object of history. That is, the pessimism which one could ascribe to the empirical world is cancelled out by the ungrounded optimism of a messianic philosophy of history.

Lukács argues that only when the commodity is 'the universal category of society as a whole' does it 'become crucial for the subjugation of men's consciousness to the forms in which this reification finds expression and for their attempts to comprehend the process or to rebel against its disastrous effects and liberate themselves from servitude to the "second nature" so created'.[148] This 'subjugation' to 'the forms in which this reification finds expression' derives ultimately from the labour process. More specifically, it derives from the progessive rationalisation of the division of labour. The transition to machine industry exhibits

> a continuous trend towards greater rationalisation, an increasingly intensified elimination of the qualitative, human-individual qualities of the worker. On the one hand, the labour process is progressively broken down into abstract, rational, specialised operations, so that the relationship of the worker to the product as a whole is broken and his work is reduced to a specific function that is mechanically repeated. On the other hand, socially necessary labour time, the basis for rational calculation, is converted, as mechanisation and rationalisation of the labour process, from a merely

empirically perceivable average labour time to an objectively calculable work-stint that confronts the worker as a fixed and autonomous objectivity. With the modern, 'psychological' analysis of the work process (the Taylor system) this rational mechanisation is projected right into the worker's 'soul': even his psychological attributes are separated from his total personality and placed in opposition to it so as to facilitate their integration into specialised rational systems and their reduction to statistically viable concepts.[149]

The analysis of the progressive rationalisation of the division of labour within the factory and its progressive calculability is then extended, without further argument, to the functioning of the social division of labour as a whole. Yet, Marx established a basic distinction between the division of labour within the factory and within society as a whole in order to demonstrate the contradiction between the seemingly planned nature of the division of labour within the factory and its totally unplanned nature in society as a whole, between the concentration of the means of production in the hands of capitalists and the fragmentation of these means as far as workers are concerned.[150] Lukács, in contrast, argues that the internal organization of the factory contains 'in a concentrated form the whole structure of capitalist society'.[151]

Not surprisingly, therefore, Lukács' account is concerned with 'the *principle* at work here: the principle of rationalization, based on what is and *can be calculated*'.[152] This Weberian grounding of the nature of capitalism moves further and further away from the capitalist process of accumulation, the theory of surplus value and exploitation, thereby removing from the analysis of capitalism many of those contradictions which Marx held to constitute the dynamic of capitalist societies. Instead, Lukács proceeds to examine two crucial changes brought about by rationalization. Firstly, this increased calculability of the work process becomes 'the objective synthesis of rationalized special systems whose unity is determined by pure calculation'. Hence this results in the 'fragmentation of the object of production'. Secondly, the subject of production, the worker, also becomes fragmented; he becomes 'a mechanical part incorporated into a mechanical system', a system which functions independently of him so that 'his activity becomes less and less active and more and more *contemplative*'.[153] This contemplative stance, induced by the workers' confrontation with the mechanical fixed laws of the machine process, 'must likewise transform the basic categories of man's immediate attitude to the world: it reduces space and time to a common denominator and degrades time to the dimension of space'.[154] Confronted with this reification, 'the personality can do no more than look on helplessly while its own existence is reduced to an isolated particle and fed into an alien system'.[155] But 'this isolation and fragmentation is only apparent'. It is merely 'the reflex in consciousness of the fact that the "natural laws" of capitalist production have been extended to cover every manifestation of life in society'.[156]

The all-pervasive 'principle of rational mechanization and calculability', and its attendant reification, leads Lukács to view the modern division of labour 'exclusively from the aspect of an increasingly more total inhumanity',[157] providing his analysis with a tragic conception of the possibilities of overcoming this fate. The structural contradiction in capitalist society cannot be overcome by means of any changes in that society's structure. Lukács has provided us with an account of a one-dimensional process of reification which has affinities not merely with Weber's but also with Simmel's analyses. It also anticipates the central argument of Marcuse's *One Dimensional Man*. As Grunenberg argues, 'it is apparent in Lukacs' analysis of the division of labour, which he conceives solely as a "question of organization", that for him his concern is not with a materialist analysis of the capitalist mode of production but rather with an earlier cultural-critical description'.[158] Grunenberg goes on to ascribe this to Lukács' increasing reliance upon Weber's account of capitalism and his attempt to fuse this analysis with that of Marx, but it could equally well be derived from Simmel's account in *The Philosophy of Money*.[159] Even the manner in which Lukacs presents us with the contradiction between a determined totality of reified existence and the necessity of generating 'true' consciousness outside this totality has some affinity between Simmel's opposition between objective and subjective culture. In both cases, one can only be pessimistic with regard to the objective structures and optimistic (messianic) with regard to the possibilities for human consciousness. Of course, in Simmel's case, it is the autonomous individual who must be preserved; for Lukács, it is revolutionary proletarian class consciousness and later the revolutionary party that is the motor for change.

The increasing reliance upon Max Weber's analysis of capitalism is also evident. Lukács, like Weber, emphasises rational calculability as a crucial feature of capitalism, indeed as the basic principle generating reification. Yet, as Grunenberg points out, 'the principle of rational calculation was . . . for Weber, not only applicable to the developed capitalist mode of production but in his view determined the whole course of development since the middle ages'.[160] Similarly, Maretsky has argued that Lukács takes over Weber's notion of the hierarchical organization of the labour process without realizing that its consequence is that 'the opposition between property and lack of property, capital and wage labour is thereby no longer a specific social determination . . . but a natural quality of the labour process itself'.[161] Maretsky also claims, though with less justification, that the discrepancy between part and whole upon which Lukács places great emphasis is merely the other side of Weber's distinction between formal and substantive rationality.[162] He also concludes, like Kammler and Grunenberg, that Lukács' identification of the development of reification ensures that revolutionary possibilities are absent within the capitalist mode of production and that hence a revolutionary proletarian consciousness has to be developed outside this process.

What are the consequences, then, for Lukács' theory of reification? There exists a contradiction between Lukács' avowed aim of understanding Marx's work and his actual analysis of capitalist society, which diverges sharply from that of Marx. This means that it becomes difficult to see Lukács' analysis of reification as an extension of Marx's critique of ideology, even though it may have been intended as such. Rather, a case can be made for saying that it is an extension of the critique of culture — already begun by Lukács — that has its origins in the work of Weber and Simmel as well as that of Marx. Of course, Lukács' critique is more radical and in many respects takes up a Marxist position. Had it not done so, it would not have proved such an irritating work for so many orthodox Marxists. At the other end of this spectrum — and unlike Lenk, for example, who tends to draw a sharp demarcation line between the sociology of knowledge in Germany (especially that of Scheler and Mannheim) — it is possible to argue that not only does Lukacs' theory of reification share many elements in the German sociological tradition but also that the distance between the two is not necessarily as great as has been assumed.

But Lukács' theory of reification did not terminate with an analysis of the origins of reification in the division of labour and the universalisation of the principle of rational calculation. Lukács went on to show why two avenues of escape from reification did not in fact exist — namely, science and philosophy. Unlike many subsequent theorists who have sought to preserve at least one of these avenues by a sharp demarcation between science and ideology, Lukács saw science — and philosophy — as being trapped within the reified consciousness that had permeated every other area of life. In the course of presenting this argument, Lukács provided a sustained critique of German philosophy. Part of this critique involved — probably unwittingly — a severe attack upon a position in the sociology of knowledge that was subsequently taken up by Mannheim.

Even in removing science as a possible candidate for providing a view of the totality, Lukács developed an argument that was later to be central to Mannheim's concerns, if only in relation to the social sciences. Lukács argues that the increased specialization that is attendant upon a more advanced division of labour 'leads to the destruction of every image of the whole'. This is no less true of modern science since

> the more intricate a modern science becomes and the better it understands itself methodologically, the more resolutely it will turn its back on the

ontological problems of its own sphere of influence and eliminate them from the realm where it has achieved some insight. The more highly developed it becomes and the more scientific, the more it will become a formally closed system of partial laws. It will then find that the world lying beyond its confines, and in particular the material base which it is its task to understand, *its own concrete underlying reality*, lies, methodologically and in principle, *beyond its grasp*.[163]

The position stated here seems akin to Mannheim's avowed intention of providing a sociology of knowledge that will form the basis for the social sciences. However, this is not the direction taken by Lukács, who goes on to argue that in the social sciences, and especially in bourgeois political economy, 'it is the very success with which the economy is totally rationalized and transformed into an abstract and mathematically orientated system of formal "laws" that creates the methodological barrier to understanding the phenomenon of crisis'.[164] Both modern economics and law are permeated by formal rationality so that, for example, law becomes merely 'a formal calculus' and its substantive basis and the basis for its transformation is lost from view.

This same critique is extended to philosophy, which has also succumbed to the formalized reifications of the special sciences. Lukács is aware that there is a desire for philosophy to synthesize, to achieve a grasp of 'that overall knowledge which the particular sciences have so conspicuously renounced,' but argues that such a synthesis would have to do more than 'unite the special sciences mechanically: they would have to be transformed inwardly by an inwardly synthesizing method'.[165] However, it is not possible for philosophy to perform this task, since

> philosophy stands in the same relation to the special sciences as they do with respect to empirical reality. The formalistic conceptualisation of the special sciences becomes for philosophy an immutably given substratum and this signals the final and despairing renunciation of every attempt to cast light on the reification that lies at the root of this formalism.[166]

Hence, neither science nor philosophy provides a way out of the reified structures and formalism that have been established by the universalization of the commodity form. Lukács once more, sets out a problematic — the impossibility of a traditional philosophical synthesis — which provides a starting point for Mannheim's subsequent attempt to provide a dynamic synthesis of perspectives. Once more, the logic of Lukács' argument blocks any path towards Mannheim's solution of this problem.

In his analysis of classical philosophy, which can be understood in part as a philosophical-sociological critique of the development of modern philosophy, Lukács argues that it was bourgeois society itself — its structure and its organization — which prevented modern philosophy from solving the 'antinomies of bourgeois thought'. It is a philosophy which 'springs from the reified structure of consciousness' and ultimately remains within its confines since

> it did not manage to do more than provide a complete intellectual reproduction and a priori deduction of bourgeois society. It is only the *manner* of this deduction, namely the dialectical method, that points beyond bourgeois society. And even in classical philosophy this is only expressed in the form of an unsolved and insoluble antinomy.[167]

Even at its most critical moments philosophy was unable 'to break out of the limits imposed on formal and rationalistic (bourgeois, reified) thought'.

In the course of his analysis of the antinomies of bourgeois thought, Lukács also makes other connections between consciousness and society. Reference has already been made to Lukács' argument concerning the increasing control of society by the bourgeoisie. At one point he even seems to suggest that it is 'the thought of bourgeois society' which 'acquires increasing control over the details of its social existence subjecting them to its needs. On the other hand, it loses — likewise progressively — the possibility of gaining control of society as a whole'.[168] There is thus no simple mechanistic base-superstructure dichotomy at this level of Lukács' analysis. Instead, there is an attempt to argue that when consciousness has permeated the material basis of society (division of labour, commodity structure) this material basis, in turn, reacts back upon consciousness. This is presumably Lukács' view of the role of the natural sciences, since he argues that

> all human relations (viewed as the objects of social activity) assume increasingly the objective forms of the abstract elements of the conceptual systems of natural science and of the abstract substrata of the laws of nature.[169]

Lukács here, as elsewhere, is prone to obscure the material nature of scientific activity and, to ascribe to its intellectual content (its theories and laws) a determining function which it would be difficult to substantiate. Nowhere does Lukács attempt to answer the question as to why it is, even within the framework of his own views, that the natural sciences can exert such a decisive influence. Presumably, this could only be because they are central to the reproduction of surplus value and capital accumulation, as Marx argues in the *Grundrisse* and in *Capital*. However, as with the roots of reification, this dimension of his analysis is absent.

In the final section of his essay on reification, Lukács elaborates the problem of mediation in greater detail than in his essays on class consciousness and orthodox Marxism. He continues to assert that 'the objective reality of social existence is *in its immediacy* "the same" for both proletariat and bourgeoisie'. But he goes on to argue that the '*specific categories of mediation*' through which this immediacy becomes 'the authentically objective reality' are 'fundamentally different'[170] and that this is related to their different positions in the economic process.

In a critique of the neo-Kantian standpoint on historical knowledge and its reliance — at least in Rickert's work — upon 'cultural values' as an index of its objectivity, Lukács argues that the bourgeoisie is unable to advance beyond the level of immediacy; it remains trapped in the givenness of its existence. The proletariat, however, is able to advance beyond the level of immediacy, as far as Lukács is concerned, because 'once this immediacy turns out to be the consequence of a multiplicity of mediations', the worker's consciousness 'is the self-consciousness of the commodity; or in other words it is the self-knowledge, the self-revelation of the capitalist society founded upon the production and exchange of commodities'.[171] And it is not merely a question of becoming conscious since '*this knowledge brings about an objective structural change in the object of knowledge*'.[172] For the working class this implies that the awareness that its commodity — labour power — is a use value which generates surplus value 'becomes *social reality*'.

Lukács is therefore again confronted with the radical disjunction between a level of empirical immediacy and objective possibility, between the 'given' consciousness of the proletariat and a philosophy of history in which only proletarian class consciousness yields a knowledge of the totality of society, though here the problem is raised a stage further along the path to class consciousness. Nowhere does Lukács specify to any degree of concreteness how this class consciousness emerges. Instead, he takes up the implications of the situation in which it has emerged and leaves obscure the process by which workers become aware of their position within the commodity structure. This in turn, opens up the possibility of stimulating this process from outside — by the intervention of the revolutionary party. In other respects, the view of capitalist society remains the same as that found in the essay on class consciousness. Thus, for example, Lukács argues that with regard to commodity production 'interrupted abruptly now and again by "irrational" catastrophes, the way is opened up for an infinite progression leading to the thorough-going capitalist rationalization of society as a whole'.[173]

It is by removing this reified veil from the world produced by this rationalization that we are able to recognize that history is a process which is made by human beings. When this occurs, the 'image of a frozen reality that nevertheless is caught up in an unremitting, ghostly movement at once becomes meaningful'.[174] However, to take human beings as the measure of all things can lead to a relativist standpoint. Lukács seeks to distinguish this relativism from his own position which attempts to expose the historical function and meaning of particular truths. To do this he argues that it is one thing to relativise the truth about an individual or a species in an ultimately static world . . . And it is quite another matter when the *concrete, historical function and meaning* of the various 'truths' is revealed within a unique, concretized historical process. Only in the former case can we accurately speak of relativism.[175]

All relativism rests ultimately on the assertion of some absolute and in its present-day versions represents merely a symptom of the crisis in contemporary society. In a passage that is central to his understanding of relativism and unwittingly offers a critique of the positions of both Scheler and Mannheim, Lukács asserts that what modern relativists do is

to take the present philosophy of man with its social and historical limits and to allow these to ossify into an 'eternal' limit of a biological or pragmatic sort. Actuated either by doubt or despair they thus stand revealed as a *decadent version* of the very rationalism or religiosity they mean to oppose. Hence they may sometimes be a not unimportant *symptom* of the inner weakness of the society which produced the rationalism they are 'combating'. But they are significant only as symptoms.[176]

Indeed, Lukács goes further and argues that at the present time 'the only possible function of truth is to establish the various possible attitudes to an essentially uncomprehended world in accordance with man's needs in the struggle to master his environment'. In this reified world, truth can only be objective 'relative to the standpoint of the individual classes and the objective realities corresponding to it'.[177] In other words, within this context, truth can only be relative in Lukács' second sense of the term and he maintains that once mankind has understood and changed 'the foundations of its existence' then the notion of truth will take on its true form as the '(societal) *self-knowledge of man*'. This is because the grounds for the existence of the relative and the absolute will have disappeared in the process of de-reification, a process which commences 'when the proletariat becomes conscious of its own class point of view'.

What Lukács seems to be arguing here is that truth is not relative to a static historical process which is posited as an absolute, but that certain groups are at given periods of time capable of transforming this historical process of which they are a part. In present circumstances, this is represented by the proletariat. Hence, the importance of the transformation of its consciousness in order for it to transform capitalist society. As we have seen, this does not, in turn, imply that the actual working class is capable at any time of effecting this transformation. Rather it means for Lukács that there exists an objective possibility for its role as the transformer of society. Unfortunately, we also know that Lukács' argument for stating that the proletariat is the identical subject–object of history rests very uneasily beside his notion of the concrete situation of the proletariat and that the links between the two are not presented convincingly.

Lukács adopts a theory of reality as an emergent process, so that his criterion of truth is not a simple correspondence theory. He argues that 'the criterion of truth is provided by relevance to reality. This reality is by no means identical with empirical existence. This reality is not, it becomes'.[178] However, the dominant stance adopted towards 'reality' by a reified consciousness is a contemplative one — subject and object are always separate entities. Lukács argues that thought itself must be conceived of as a form of reality that is also in the process of changing.

This notion of reality as process also has an important implication for historical knowledge. Lukács asserts that 'as long as man concentrates his interest contemplatively upon the past *or* future, both ossify into an alien existence. And between the subject and the object lies the unbridgeable "pernicious chasm" of the present.'[179] It is possible to see this specific problem of historical knowledge as lying at the heart of Mannheim's discussion of ideology and utopia where he too conceives of a 'total coincidence between existence and consciousness in a universe which has ceased being in a state of becoming'.[180]

Lukács' rejection of a correspondence theory of truth is most evident when he suggests that

> thought and existence are not identical in the sense that they 'correspond' to each other, or 'reflect' each other, that they 'run parallel' to each other or 'coincide' with each other (all expressions that conceal a rigid duality). Their identity is that they are aspects of one and the same real historical and dialectical process.[181]

In a sense, what Lukács is asserting here is, so far from a correspondence theory of truth, an identity theory of truth, in which the problem is shifted further back to one of how to grasp the 'real historical and dialectical process'. And we know that for Lukács this is not produced through reflection, through the mere recognition of the process of becoming, but through the realization of such insights in practice. It is for this reason that Lukács asserts that 'proletarian thought is in the first place merely a *theory of praxis* which only gradually (and indeed often spasmodically) transforms itself into a *practical theory* that overturns the real world'.[187] This not merely highlights once more 'the crisis of proletarian consciousness' and its importance but also points towards a necessary component of any theory and critique of ideology: namely, that a theory of ideology which asserts that ideological thought is contemplative, and therefore unable to grasp (i.e. transform) reality, must presuppose a theory of action. In Lukacs' theory of reification we have an account of why the process of reification is a barrier to praxis, of why the frozen categories of a reified world merely cause people to reproduce the illusions of that world and prevent them from understanding its real basis. A critique of ideology therefore necessarily presupposes not merely the hermeneutic problem of understanding but also a theory of action.

4 Karl Mannheim: From the Critique of Ideology to the Sociology of Knowledge

I

Mannheim shares with Scheler and Lukács an early concern for a theory of culture and an emphasis upon the cultural crisis. This much is evident from Mannheim's earlier writings such as the 1917 lecture 'Lelek és Kultura' ('Soul and Culture'),[1] his review of Lukács' *Theory of the Novel* (1920),[2] his essay on the interpretation of world views (1923),[3] and the important unpublished essay 'Über das Eigenart kultursoziologischer Erkenntnis' (1922).[4] Indeed the similarity goes further than this. Not only is Lukács' work important for Mannheim's early formulations of the problems of the sociology of culture, as Markus has recently shown[5] but, as Kettler's study of the relationship between Mannheim and Lukács in Hungary has demonstrated, the influence of Lukács' views as a whole was central to the young Mannheim.[6]

Mannheim's connections with Scheler are not so close. His early writings do betray a heavy reliance upon a phenomenological standpoint which, in some respects at least, brings Mannheim closer to Scheler, but the phenomenology is that of Heidegger and Husserl, rather than Scheler. Of course, Mannheim's phenomenological position is also fused with Dilthey's hermeneutics as well as Lukács' own early amalgam of these two traditions. One may also detect, sometimes very clearly as in 'Soul and Culture', the fascination which Simmel's theory of cultural alienation had for Mannheim, as indeed it had for the early Lukács. In another direction, the neo-Kantian philosophy of Rickert and Lask is evident in Mannheim's doctoral thesis 'The Structural Analysis of Epistemology' (1922, Hungarian original 1918).[7]

However, it would be a mistake to assume that these early formulations of a sociology of culture are concerned only with a theory of culture. On the contrary, they often contain the rudiments of certain central problems which Mannheim later developed into his sociology of knowledge. There thus seems little point in making the claim, as Remmling does, that 'Mannheim made the transition from philosophy to sociology in 1925, when he published his article, "The problem of a sociology of knowledge".[8] By this time Mannheim had already developed not only a sociology of culture but also a number of themes central to his sociology of knowledge.

In what follows, in the first systematic section of this chapter, an attempt is made to highlight the major themes of Mannheim's early work and to demonstrate their relevance not just for a sociology of culture but also for a sociology of knowledge. Attention is paid to Mannheim's unpublished essays since, as Kettler rightly points out, Mannheim 'took greater intellectual risks in the essays written for self-clarification and these are, accordingly, more self-revealing.'[9]

In the second part, we focus, attention upon Mannheim's explicit confrontation with problems associated with the development of a sociology of knowledge and his attempts to apply such a sociology of knowledge to specific areas. Within the context of the first of these endeavours belongs the essay 'Historismus' (1924),[10] followed by 'Das Problem einer Soziologie des Wissens' (1925),[11] 'Ideologische und soziologische Interpretation der geistigen Gebilde' (1926)[12] and the important unpublished essay *Eine soziologische Theorie der Kultur und ihrer Erkennbarkeit. (Konjunktives und kommunikatives Denken)*[13] (undated but, from the references cited, probably written in 1924 or 1925).

Mannheim's two unpublished essays are important since they both provide the meta-theoretical basis for an understanding of his contemporary published works. The attempts to apply the sociology of knowledge in this period comprise Mannheim's *Habilitationsschrift* 'Das Konservative Denken' (written 1925, published 1927),[14] 'Die Bedeutung der Konkurrenz im Gebiete des Geistigen' (paper delivered in 1928, published 1929)[15] and 'Das Problem der Generationen' (published 1928).[16] The examination of these essays is not intended to imply that Mannheim had now turned his attention exclusively towards a sociology of knowledge since the continued significance of problems associated with a sociology of culture are still much in evidence. Rather, the explicit taking up of a sociology of knowledge grows out of his earlier concerns and develops new themes.

Such interests must necessarily lead to a re-examination of what is usually acknowledged to be Mannheim's major German work *Ideologie und Utopie* (1929) which is, in many respects, a very different book from *Ideology and Utopia* which was introduced to the English speaking world in 1936.[17] Only by a detailed analysis of *Ideologie und Utopie* will it be possible to account for the impact of this work in Germany, an impact which can hardly be comprehended by a study of the English translation.

In his post-1929 writings, Mannheim assumed that, along with others, he had successfully established the sociology of knowledge as a recognized discipline. The role of the sociology of knowledge within sociology and the social sciences as a whole is a major theme of both his article 'Wissenssoziologie' (1931)[18] and his lecture, *Die Gegenwartsaufgaben der Soziologie* (delivered and published in 1932).[19] Between about 1928 and 1932 Mannheim also intended publication of not only a substantial study of Max Weber's sociology but also a collection of essays *Soziologie des Geistes* (outline written 1930), as well as a briefer study of contemporary social thought — Weber, Troeltsch, Scheler — under the title *Zur Denklage der Gegenwart*.[20] Unfortunately, his intentions were not fulfilled.

II

Kettler's investigation of the relationship between Mannheim and Lukács in Budapest prior to and, in part, during the Hungarian Revolution has shown that Mannheim was very much under the influence of Lukács at this time. Many years later, Lukács himself suggested that 'I stood in a close relationship to Mannheim when he was a student and he was, one might say, my unofficial academic pupil'.[21] Mannheim took part in the regular weekly discussions of the *Szellemkek* group organised by Lukács and others between 1915 and 1918. This group of intellectuals, cut off from contact with the mass of the population, were concerned with the cultural renewal of Hungarian society. As one of the group's founders relates,

> Amongst its founder members belonged the intimate friends of Georg Lukács: Béla Balázs, Lajos Fülep and Anna Lesznai . . . Those who also came along were the younger people ('the children'), Béla Fogarasi, Karl Mannheim and Arnold Hauser . . . Generally, these Sunday discussions were organised and dominated by Lukács; he put forward some topic for discussion which would be thoroughly discussed by the group. Typically it was concerned with a moral and/or literary problem in which one concentrated especially upon Dostoyevsky and German mystics like Eckart. One could crudely characterise the political leanings of the group as 'left orientated'; however, it is more accurate to point out how unpolitical they all were. In fact the group had more in common with a religious gathering than with a political club.[22]

The unpolitical and unsociological nature of these discussions is confirmed by Arnold Hauser who suggests that,

> In 1917 Karl Mannheim was uninterested in politics as were all the members of the group. The main responsibility for this lay with Lukács who was concerned with Lask, Weber and Jaspers and interested in philosophy and religion ever since he had returned from Heidelberg as a kind of mystic. . . . We never discussed politics but rather literature, philosophy and religion. At that time no one was yet interested in sociology.[23]

However, in 1912 Mannheim studied in Berlin for a year and attended courses by Simmel as well as later studying at Freiburg and Heidelberg before returning to Budapest shortly before the First World War. In 1917, again probably under Lukács' stimulus, members of the Sunday discussion group, *Szellemkek*, founded a 'Free School for the *Geisteswissenschaften*' which was to propagate the cultural-philosophical world-view of those who, in Lukács' words, constituted 'an opposition to capitalism in the name of idealist philosophy. What they had in common was the negation of positivism.'[24] This 'opposition to capitalism' was not always of an overt political nature but lay rather in its idealistic, often spiritualistic rejection. Amongst those who gave lectures in this 'school' were Lukács, Mannheim, Fogarasi, Szabó, Hauser, Kodály, and Bartok. Only Erwin Szabó offered a directly political lecture: 'On the Basic Questions of Marxism'. Lukács lectured on aesthetics, Fogarasi on the methods of intellectual history, Hauser on dilettantism in art, Kodály on the Hungarian folk song and Bartok on folk and modern music.

Mannheim's lecture 'Soul and Culture' — delivered in the autumn of 1917 and published in 1918 — was intended as a programmatic statement of the group's intentions. Its general tenor, as Márkus comments, 'originates in Simmel and in Lukács' essays, that is, in the *Philosophie der Kunst* conceived in the spirit of these essays, although the *Lebensphilosophie* tendencies emerge in Mannheim significantly more strongly than in the Lukács manuscripts of 1912-14'.[25] The Lukács works referred to here by Márkus are part of his then unpublished writings on aesthetics completed between 1912 and 1916[26] and are often referred to by Mannheim in his later writings. The central theme of his lecture is undoubtedly drawn from Simmel.

As in Lukács' writings from this period, Mannheim conceives of the contemporary crisis as a cultural one. He argues that 'the greatest danger in contemporary culture is that it grows beyond our grasp and makes our relationship to it increasingly precarious'.[27] Mannheim develops this theme in a manner which mirrors Simmel's theory of cultural alienation and the opposition between subjective and objective culture.

> It is the mutual dependency of objective and subjective culture which makes impossible the existence of the one or the other. Objective culture envelops us like an independent leviathan, yet it cannot continue to develop and maintain its own existence without the assistance and co-operation of individuals. On the other hand, the individual denies his own fulfilment if he fails to regenerate the objective culture and constantly appropriate it.[28]

In the course of the lecture, Mannheim expands upon this growing separation of objective and subjective culture, again within the framework of a theory of culture which is reminiscent of Simmel. Mannheim maintains that objective culture is

> the totality of objectivations of the mind which, in their historical development, have become a human legacy. They comprise religion, science, art, the state and forms of life. In contrast, we speak of subjective culture when — as Simmel correctly observed — the soul strives for fulfilment not through itself, through an inward movement but indirectly through these cultural objectivations, that is, through their appropriation.[29]

Mannheim develops this theory of cultural estrangement with reference to the work of art which, though having its origin in its creator, becomes separated from him when it becomes a cultural object, such that 'insofar as the work becomes a cultural object and an independent reality, it distances itself from the soul'.[30] This process of separation is apparent at every stage in the creation of an artistic work. One general attribute of culture, for example, is that it makes possible continuity not merely between generations but also with regard to style. At the same time, however, the continuity of technique and common meaning structure, for example, do not always coincide. In such instances, Mannheim argues, this is the source of 'the tragedy of culture'. Within this context, Markus has argued that Mannheim explicitly takes over Lukács' arguments from his 1912–14 *Philosophie der Kunst* as, for example, when he writes that

> Man is certainly capable of making the objectification of culture — when it has completely estranged itself from the soul — remain alive as form, of allowing it to be observed and even of making it mean something even though in an inadequate manner. . . . The aesthetic mode of interpretation is just such an inadequate interpretation and Lukács, the originator of this whole theory of inadequate contemplation, constructs the whole of aesthetics as a system of inadequate contemplation.[31]

Again, however, this reference to Lukács is also closely bound up with Simmel's theory of cultural alienation. Mannheim argues that 'the whole dynamic of culture' is a 'process of cultural over-development and false development' and that 'it was Simmel who recognized this tendency towards cultural hypertrophy'.[32] This 'alienation process' extends to every cultural sphere and is acute in the present period in which 'the old forms are no longer immediately relevant and their contemporaneousness has been lost. We feel that, at the present time, we are living in such an epoch.'[33] In such a period and as a result of this process of estrangement, form and content also become alienated from one another, a process which 'reaches its highest point in impressionism'. Both Lukács (in his 1918 obituary of Simmel)[34] and Mannheim (in his obituary of Simmel and in the unpublished 1922 essay)[35] recognized very early the impressionistic stance of Simmel's own world view and approach to reality. In another respect, however, the characterisation of cultural alienation as, in part, the increasing irrelevance of older cultural forms points forward to Mannheim's later use of this notion in his typification of ideologies as being modes of relating to reality whose relevance has now passed.

This fragmentation of culture is echoed in contemporary philosophy. Mannheim is quite explicit in stating that 'our world view is idealistic'. But it is also a world view which has rejected philosophical Marxism as 'unfruitful' and has replaced it with a mode of research 'inclined towards pluralism', a 'methodological pluralism' that recognizes the fundamental diversity of reality. This 'methodological pluralism' and a pluralist notion of reality constitute the central core of Mannheim's subsequent analysis of cultural objectifications, including — much later — his analysis of ideology.

However, Mannheim is not concerned in this lecture with the analysis of ideology. Indeed, one of the potential sources of such a theory — Marx's writings — is seen to have been partly superseded. Amongst the 'superseded influences' to which the group's world view nonetheless still owes something are 'naturalism and impressionism in art and Marxism in sociology'.[36] In more general terms, Mannheim also lists the work of several others 'whose path is also our path': Dostoyevsky's world-view, Kierkegaard's aesthetics, Lask, Zalai, the works of Ernst and Riegl, modern French lyrical poetry, especially that of the Nouvelle Revue Française, Bartok, Ady and the Thalia theatre movement, many of which are also central figures in Lukács' own early development and were the subject of discussions in the *Szellemkek* group.

In the course of his summary of the themes and contents of the group's lectures, Mannheim is more explicit about his own, and the group's, social and philosophical concerns. He asks 'whether cultural objectivations, such as, for example, the forms of art, have some kind of relationship to the social situations, social classes for instance, in which they emerge'. At this point, Mannheim explicitly refers to Marx's work and also to that of Lukács. He states that,

> Marx was the first to see clearly the relationship between the objectification of culture and the social structure and his starting point will not be superseded here at all. Certainly, our interpretation of this relationship is not that of Marx. We reject the theory of superstructure but the problem it throws up — over and above Marx's solution — is also acute for us. . . . That such a starting point can be fruitful, with its question of the penetration of societal forms in art, is shown by Lukács' *Geschichte des Dramas*.[37]

In 1917 the whole normative basis of this essay was an optimistic theory of cultural renewal, a call to break down the alienation of subjective and objective culture.

Mannheim's own contribution to this series of lectures was clearly the draft for his *Structural Analysis of Epistemology*, his doctoral dissertation awarded in November 1918 by the University of Budapest. A version of this dissertation appeared in Hungarian in 1918, and a fuller version in German in 1922,[38] by which time Mannheim had moved to Heidelberg as a private scholar supported financially by his parents. The later version of *Structural Analysis of Epistemology* makes considerable use of the work of Emil Lask, Rickert and Lukács' early works.[39]

In this work, Mannheim attempts a logic of philosophy in the sense of a systematization of philosophical problems and levels of analysis. It is an attempt to understand and synthesize the structural diversity of intellectual endeavours since 'every mental, intellectual or cultural field has a structure of its own'.[40] Mannheim argues that, in the past, such an analysis would have proceeded in a Cartesian or Hobbesian manner and explained complex structures in terms of simpler ones. The present trend, exemplified by an increasing interest in the theory of judgement, aims at explaining simpler structures in terms of more complex ones. In the course of his examination of the structure of particular disciplines in relation to philosophy, Mannheim produces an argument that is reminiscent of a problem later raised by Kuhn:

> the special sciences, as long as they deal with their own topics and do not transcend their proper fields, are always concerned only with answerable 'questions' (no matter how complicated the answers might be), rather than with 'problems' properly so called. If a real 'problem' does come up in a special science, it always has to do with marginal methodological aspects of that science — with a difficulty of procedure which makes the investigator stop and reflect. And that already amounts to philosophy: the philosophy of the science concerned.[41]

Unfortunately, here, as elsewhere, Mannheim does not take up the problem of the development of science but favours the kind of search for typologies of structures advanced, for example, by Dilthey. However, he refuses to take up the relationship between a particular structure and the empirical world on the grounds that

> The historical interpretation of a meaningful whole is a possible and necessary task, but all too often the mistake is made of trying to explain the meaning itself with reference to the temporal features of the work in question — with reference to empirical, real factors. If we seek to validate or invalidate meanings by means of such factors, we shall inescapably fall into relativism. The temporal as such contains only the conditions for the realisation of the meanings, but not the meanings themselves; they can only be represented by means of a structural analysis.[42]

Such a view contrasts markedly with Mannheim's essay 'Historicism' and with some of his subsequent writings. Here, however, Mannheim sharply demarcates his own position from that of historicism since

> historical factors determine only the materialization of the mental content in question. The mere fact that history brings to light various types of systems

of thought (and amongst them theories of knowledge) by no means entails a historicist, relativist philosophy of truth.[43]

Nonetheless, Mannheim concedes that at the present time many are concerned with finding 'the solution to the problem of historicity and timeless validity'. One of these many was indeed Lukács who, in his *Heidelberger Philosophie*, specifically devoted a whole chapter to precisely this problem — though within the realm of aesthetics.[44] Mannheim, for his part, holds to a strict separation of genesis and validity. Indeed, he advances a criticism of historicism which is crucial to the weakness of his own later analysis of ideologies when he argues that historicism 'flounders helplessly as soon as it treats all historical solutions as equivalent, and allows the notion of validity to lapse'.[45] In *Ideologie und Utopie*, on the other hand, Mannheim provides precisely such an account of competing ideologies.

In the latter parts of this work, Mannheim sets out to develop a systematization of epistemologies and ontologies. With respect to epistemologies, he argues that 'the specific subject-object correlation is constitutive, and any epistemological theory is concerned with the determination and resolution of this correlation'. The work as a whole testifies to Mannheim's early concern for synthesizing pluralities of structures and to his belief that *'the presuppositions of knowledge are always capable of becoming in their turn objects of knowledge'*.[46]

On balance, however, it can be argued that Mannheim's thesis on epistemology does not lead us to the core of his sociology of knowledge. In some respects, it leads firmly away from many of the problems which he subsequently took to be central to his sociology of knowledge. Against this interpretation, it could be argued that the work is concerned with the plurality of epistemologies, a typology of epistemologies and an examination of the meta-theoretical presuppositions of knowledge — all, in their way, potential themes for a sociology of knowledge as conceived by Mannheim. But the focus of his research in this period moves in the direction of a theory of culture and world-views, and a sociology of culture, that in fact establishes some of the major problematics for his sociology of knowledge.

The continued concern with a theory of culture can be seen, briefly, in Mannheim's review of Lukács' *Theory of the Novel* (1920) — in fact, Mannheim's first work to appear in Germany. In this review, Mannheim is not yet primarily concerned with a sociology of cultural forms. That is, he does not extract the sociological significance of this work for a sociology of the novel as did Lucien Goldmann.[47] Rather, he is concerned to outline the plurality of perspectives through which we come to understand a work and the attendant problem of interpretation.

Mannheim takes up the diversity of contexts within which cultural forms can be understood — psychologically, sociologically, technically, stylistically, etc. All perspectives emerge out of the same object but take up different sides of it. As such, they are to be sharply distinguished from one another since

> all these diverse modes of explanation correspond to diverse *logical* objects. Just as the individual natural sciences first create their logical object by means of method, so also the object of the respective human science emerges first in and through its method, through its viewpoint, through its approach and however this subjective-functional correlate of the changing object may be termed. The work of art 'as an experiential complex', 'as a sociological product', 'as a form of art', etc., are inadequate characterizations of these possible fundamentally divergent logical objects.[48]

This logically grounded perspectivism, and Mannheim's insistence on the separation of these approaches, not merely foreshadows his later preoccupation with relating diverse modes of interpretation but is also at the root of his problem of reconciling diverse ideologies, once this perspectivism has been translated onto a societal level. Mannheim goes on to treat the distinctions between academic disciplines as absolute and is then inclined to argue that, within these 'diverse logical objects of the diverse disciplines there exists a hierarchy' of perspectives. In this way, he is led to argue that aesthetic objects should be explained from above and not from below — namely, on the basis of a metaphysics and philosophy of history rather than psychologically or sociologically. This provides the possibility for a 'deeper kind of explanation'. It is within this context that Mannheim praises Lukács' *Theory of the Novel* for its interpretation of the novel in terms of 'a higher standpoint', that of the philosophy of history. The review as a whole is not merely a justification of this hierarchical perspectivism, but is also a reworking of the problem of the relation between accounts of cultural forms in sociological terms and in terms of a philosophy of history. We have already encountered this as a central problem of Lukács' early work where he conceives of 'the synthesis of literary history in a new organic unity' as 'a unification of sociology and aesthetics'.[49] But in Mannheim's review, the central feature of 'a possible new culture' was, as Apitzsch has rightly argued, 'not the contradictory objectivity itself but that phenomenon derived from it as a "generation with affinities to its sense of life", which saw itself in a position "to represent objective culture in a unified cross-section" '.[50]

In the same year as this review appeared, Mannheim moved to Heidelberg, where he studied with, amongst others, Alfred Weber whose interest at that time centred around the development of a sociology of culture. Weber in fact published his influential article 'Prinzipielles zur Kultursoziologie' in 1920.[51] It is instructive to note here how much Mannheim's early formulations of a sociology of culture were indebted to Alfred Weber who, as Weber explains in the preliminary remarks to his 1920 article, had been concerned with the sociology of culture since about 1909.[52] In 1915, Alfred Weber published a reply to a review by Lukács on the nature and method of the sociology of culture in which he briefly advanced some basic themes of a sociology of culture which were taken over by Mannheim.[53] Weber argued that the sociology of culture must commence with the concept of culture itself and ensure that the uniqueness of cultural phenomena is not destroyed by a subsequent sociological analysis. With reference to the relationship between cultural phenomena and 'social aspects of life', Weber maintained that the analysis must remain at the level of 'a mutual functional dependency' such that the sociology of culture will 'remain not a *causal* discipline but an *intuitive* discipline [*Evidenzwissenschaft*].' He cited as his example here, Lukács' sociology of drama. Weber also refers to the '*plurality of world-views*' in a manner which Mannheim himself takes up in his 1922 essay. Finally, Weber argued that a sociology of culture should be concerned with the core of cultural phenomena, with the central 'sense of life' of a period, but not forgetting that its qualitative content is not fully open to sociological analysis.

In the course of the six years before his appointment, in 1926, as a *Privatdozent* at the University of Heidelberg, Mannheim set out to develop his own sociology of culture and, in the later part of this period, his sociology of knowledge. His longest work on the sociology of culture — *Über die Eigenart kultursoziologischer Erkenntnis* ('On the Nature of Knowledge in the Sociology of Culture'), a manuscript of 183 pages — remained unpublished. The work was begun in September 1922 and was probably completed early in 1923, before the publication of his essay 'Beiträge zur Theorie der Weltanschauungsinterpretation'. It is an important study for several reasons. Firstly, it allowed Mannheim to outline more freely than in his published works his attempt to develop a sociology of culture. Secondly, it is the source of several of his works in this period. It contains, for example, an outline of many of the themes of his later 'Ideologische und soziologische Interpretation der geistigen Gebilde', not published until 1926, as well as some of the issues raised in the essay on world-views mentioned above. Thirdly, it provides us with a quite detailed perspective upon Mannheim's sociological orientation, especially his relationship to phenomenology.

Mannheim's essay on knowledge in the sociology of culture examines 'what it means to submit culture to a sociological investigation'. From the very outset, Mannheim seeks to provide a phenomenological description of cultural phenomena. If we take an actual world-view, then it is not, viewed sociologically, a theoretical structure which stands at its centre,

> rather, at the centre, there stands that substratum of the life-structure which is evaluated in 'lived life' as precisely the ultimate substratum. That is, one does not merely think on the basis of one's intellectual composition, rather

one also *experiences* hierarchically, i.e. there is constantly at hand a largely unreflected 'system' of inner-worldly and environmental objects to which one is orientated in action, life and experience.⁵⁴

Within this order of things, some aspect or sphere is evaluated as the most important and the other spheres of life are organized around it. There is thus a historically changeable 'hierarchical structure of experience'. Whereas in the Middle Ages this 'ultimate value emphasis' was a transcendental one which, as a world-view, constituted a relatively stable closed structure, we are today faced with '*a struggle of cultural spheres*' in which that stable, central world view has been rendered problematic and is increasingly threatened. We are thus confronted with a competition between scientific, aesthetic and ethical culture in which no one of them alone is capable of regrouping the elements of our world-view. Individuals are unable to relate the various elements of their world-view to a stable centre. Instead, they experience the movement and dynamic of the historical process.

This historical change in our world-view has important consequences for the modern conception of culture. Mannheim highlights six factors which characterize this new conception:

1. The relativization of individual cultural spheres *vis-à-vis* one another, such that the value-emphasis upon the whole is absent.
2. Consciousness of the relativity and transitoriness of every historical manifestation of cultural phenomena.
3. Consciousness of the basically processual character of culture.
4. The formative nature of experience of cultural phenomena as such, the educational ideal [*Bildungsideal*].
5. The opposition between the concept of culture and the concept of nature.
6. Consciousness of the social character of cultural phenomena.⁵⁵

Each factor, in its own manner, is a persistent theme of Mannheim's work in Germany. This characterization of the changes in our worldview represents some of the central themes of Mannheim's sociology of culture and his sociology of knowledge: the relativization of cultural areas (social group experiences, later, political ideologies); awareness of the transition of historical phenomena (the constant search for a 'dynamic' standpoint); the attempt to grasp social diversity as a totality (often as a synthesis); the quasi-independent role of culture and a concern with the didactic potential of the discipline which not only investigates that cultural sphere, but is, at the same time, a part of it; an assertion of the differences between natural and cultural scientific knowledge (even, later, the exclusion of natural scientific knowledge from social determination); and, finally, a consistent attempt to establish connections (relational, determined, functional, causal etc.) between various cultural phenomena and the social milieux.

With respect to the last two factors, Mannheim reveals the basis for his distinction between culture and nature and utilizes a concept of nature that is not dissimilar to Scheler's notion of 'real factors'. Nature, for Mannheim, is 'something that is completely free of meaning and of value, something that is merely the substratum of possible meaning'. It is something which is 'impenetrable by the intellect' and 'value-indifferent'.[56] However, the more human beings become conscious of their historical determination, the less stable is their conception of what is natural and permanent so that

> in its extension, the concept of culture increasingly absorbs more and more and as a residue there remains merely . . . our impulsive life and our sensuousness, which is now termed nature, not as a result of its valuation but rather as a result of its estrangement from meaning and its ahistorical nature.[57]

However, unlike Scheler, Mannheim does not take up this residual natural element as a decisive determining factor upon culture. Rather, it often remains implicit in his early analysis of culture. In contrast, the cultural form 'is experienced as valuable and not merely as something existent (*Da-seiend*). Through the phenomenological subject's intentionality, the cultural form is experienced as valuable and 'culture becomes a value'.[58] Thus, Mannheim's notion of culture is here grounded in the phenomenological notion of intentionality and experience (*Erlebnis*), though the latter concept is just as easily derivable from Dilthey as it is from, say, Husserl.

This recognition of the historical nature of culture and its social determination coincides with our awareness of social processes themselves. Marx and his followers were the first 'to locate society in the economic sphere, to see the forms of sociation as having their genesis in the economic sphere, whereas more recently attempts have been made by Simmel, Kistiakowski and Max Weber to conceive of the social as a possible independent conceptual apparatus'. Hence, with the emergence of sociology as the study of society, it is possible to conceive of a 'sociogenetic' theory of culture and thus to interpret cultural changes 'from below to above' rather than from above to below (Mannheim having earlier praised Lukács' *Theory of the Novel* for successfully performing the latter).

However, Mannheim points to a number of methodological difficulties which must be faced in the establishment of a sociology of culture. He rejects a 'purely logical-methodological' analysis of the basis of a study of culture since it completely overlooks two factors:

> *Firstly*, the fact (and its methodological consequences) that the cultural sciences are themselves a part of this process which they describe, that therefore, in this case, the *subject and object of this science* in a certain sense coincide. *Secondly*, the fact (and its methodological consequences) that the subject of

cultural scientific knowledge is not merely the epistemological subject, but the '*whole human being*'[59]

Mannheim sees the first factor as deriving from Hegel, the second from Dilthey. If we accept the implications of these two factors then we should not falsify cultural phenomena by interpreting them in a reified manner, by applying a methodology analogous to that of the natural sciences. Not only do such methodological reflections clearly relate back to Hegel and Dilthey, as well as to the early Lukács, but they point forward to concerns that are present in the attempt to construct a dialectical-hermeneutical social science by Habermas and Apel.[60] However, Mannheim does not develop these reflections in this direction.

Instead, he suggests that neither are cultural phenomena to be conceived of as something rigid, nor is knowledge of them to be viewed as being static. In contrast, new cultural realities are always emerging and with them our conceptions of them change. Mannheim's plea is therefore for a dynamic sociology of culture. Any attempt to investigate the constitution of cultural-scientific knowledge must ask 'in what *attitude* [*Einstellung*] the total subject approaches the intellectual reality it wishes to investigate scientifically'.[61] For Mannheim this requires that we attend to the second factor outlined above, namely, that the subject of this knowledge is not the epistemological subject but the whole human being. It follows from this that cultural phenomena are '*not reified*' but emerge within the cultural process, and that, furthermore, they are constituted '*in the process of being experienced [Erlebtwerden] and that thereby in their inner structure they are projected into the attitude of the experiencing human subject.*'[62] This is true not only for the creative human subject but also for the person who seeks to understand cultural phenomena.

In the latter form, as 'receptive human subjects' we can see the diversity of the process of reception and interpretation. A phenomenological typology of receptive human subjects has, Mannheim suggests, already been outlined by Lukács with regard to naive reception, the essayist, the aesthetician and the historian.[63] Such a typology necessarily involves a typification of concrete human subjects since

> These types are not to be taken in an empirical-psychological sense, because they never describe a real existing human subject in his empirical-psychological disposition but rather they describe the constitutive, typical possibilities of conscious access to intellectual realities according to their structural nature.[64]

Mannheim does not remain content with 'a mere analysis of the phenomenological subject of cultural-sociological interpretation' but also calls for an explanation of cultural phenomena 'since the sociology of culture is not merely a pure *understanding* of intellectual forms but is, at the same time, a *knowledge* of these forms on the basis of this interpretative approach'.⁶⁵ At this level, Mannheim appears to favour a neo-Kantian analysis of the methodological problems of concept-formation and specifically alludes to Rickert's work. This leads Mannheim to the second stage of his analysis, to the study of 'the immanent and sociological observation of cultural phenomea' — one which prefigures in many ways his later article 'Ideologische und soziologische Interpretation der geistigen Gebilde' (1926).

Mannheim conceives of sociology as the study of either the development and organization of social life (*Gesellschaftslehre*) or of the embeddedness of cultural forms in social life: the sociology of culture. Society is a culture-forming factor whose 'forms and forms of sociation one can even view, in a certain sense, as cultural forms'. Another task of sociology — and especially the sociology of culture — is the investigation of the role which ' "social-historical reality" (Dilthey) plays in the constitution of cultural forms'.⁶⁶ But both aspects of a sociological study of culture are closely connected with one another since 'cultural forms emerge out of social life and return to it; they are one of the functions of society; at the same time, however, it is one of their functions to operate as sociation.'⁶⁷ Yet for Mannheim these two types of sociology are not of equivalent status and a distinction between them is to be made.

> As the study of society, sociology is a foundational science [*Grundwissenschaft*]; as the sociology of culture it is a method, a vantage point for the observation of a phenomenon which to a certain extent lies outside its own genuine sphere.'⁶⁸

The implication of this argument is that the concept of culture is constituted outside the realm of sociology — in fact, by philosophy and not a scientific methodology.

The objects of the sociology of culture can therefore only be grounded outside 'a merely methodological approach'; they can only be grounded phenomenologically. Mannheim argues that 'we must have a pre-scientific (experiential) access to these basic phenomena' which are capable of being checked by theoretical study. Thus, the conceptual constitution of a science is not merely 'a reflection of "reality" but is instead co-determined,' since we possess 'a completely atheoretical access' to cultural phenomena insofar as we are part of the cultural process which we experience. However, our knowledge of these phenomena is dependent upon our conceptual system, upon concepts which are conditioned not merely by the pre-theoretical phenomena but also by 'the state of the whole conceptual systematic' and problematic we have developed. Hence, for Mannheim, not only is a pure phenomenological description inadequate — however essential it may be as a starting point — but the progress of the human sciences themselves depends not merely upon an 'increasing or declining pre-theoretical *sensibility*' towards the phenomenon under investigation but also upon 'the *state* of conceptual systematization'.[69]

Hence, the sociology of culture views its object from the level of sociological concepts. Furthermore, the normative aspect of cultural phenomena is 'bracketed' and treated as a factual entity. Whereas the 'immanent study' of a phenomenon occurs on the experiential level, a fuller investigation requires distance or detachment so that the phenomenon can, for example, be viewed within the context of 'the totality of life and experience'. Within the framework of this distinction between the immanent and non-immanent study of an object, Mannheim suggests that a philosophical study of an object expresses its 'theoretical-immanent' investigation whereas a sociological study is 'non-immanent'.

This sociological 'non-immanent' investigation of cultural phenomena represents an 'approach to the social functionality of cultural forms', but one which is pre-theoretical. Hence

> the subject of social knowledge is not only the theoretical (e.g. aesthetic, etc.) subject but, as Dilthey termed it, the 'whole human being' or, as we shall later state it more specifically, the social human being.[70]

This functionality, Mannheim emphasizes, is far from being identical with a notion of organic functionality. Rather, it is the task of an interpretative sociology to grasp the functionality of cultural objectivations, not in relation to individual inner experiences but in relation to the social process. This, in turn, means relating the cultural form to the communal experiential context from which it arose. The experiences of the individual cannot be conceived of as merely part of a stream of individual life. Rather,

> A large part of their total experiences are shared with other individuals. These experiences which are, as it were, at hand and which are the experiences of individuals within the same society and community must, however, be structurally related to one another in the same way as in the case of the strands of experience within an individual stream of experience.[71]

Indeed, we are only fully socialized to the extent that we have 'common strands of experience' that we share with others. What this implies for the functionality of cultural forms is that 'such a functionality can only exist in relation to *experiential contexts*'[72] which are not merely individual, but also social. An interpretative sociology is therefore concerned with exploring 'the functionality of an intellectual form in relation to a *communal stream of experience*'[73] and not merely, as in Max Weber's version, with the understanding of individual social actions. Implicitly, Mannheim also rejects the individual biography as the model of hermeneutic understanding (Dilthey).

Interpretative sociology will aim towards a 'social structure of consciousness', since 'by far and away the major part of the experiential constellation of the individual (even when apparently isolated) moves within a direction that is perfectly typical for a group or for an epoch.'[74] Within such limits, 'only *relatively* new experiences' can be incorporated into the constellation of the individual's experience, and within a given common life-structure only a limited amount of deviation can be tolerated. Yet this does not mean that the individual must be conscious of the functional relationship between his actions and his cultural objectifications, on the one hand, and the 'social stream of consciousness', on the other. On the contrary, a state of naive unreflection is the most common attitude. Recognition of this functional relationship is, indeed, only likely to occur 'when groups (e.g. strata, classes and races as entities) confront one another'.[75] The notion that awareness of social determination only emerges when confronted with another group is one that is central to Mannheim's sociology of knowledge and, indeed, to his theory of ideology.

At this stage of his analysis, Mannheim seeks to draw a number of conclusions from this analysis of the functional relationship between cultural objectivations and social experiences. Firstly, he reiterates the view that 'not only the *object* but also the *knowing subject* of sociology is the socialized individual'.[76] Secondly, that 'the socio-genetic observation of cultural forms is really only an extension, a consequent resultant attitude of "everyday life-experience", that it cannot and should not readily leave this basis'.[77] Mannheim notes here that 'Dilthey has made everyday or "general experience of the world" a problem for philosophy. We see in it one of the most important tasks which one could set it'.[78] Not only is Mannheim hostile to all positivistic attempts to free the social sciences from the attitude of the everyday world, but he argues that a sociology of culture should especially attend to 'the phenomenon of so-called "pre-scientific experience" ', to 'everyday life-experience'. Futhermore, 'sociology need not be ashamed, therefore, of this origin and of this permanent connection with the pre-scientific, with the "whole human being" but should rather take up both of them in its *presuppositions*'[79] The final conclusion which Mannheim draws from this analysis is that 'this pre-theoretical origin of socio-genetic knowledge in no way implies an invitation to be inexact'.

Mannheim's discussion of the differences between intrinsic and extrinsic interpretations of cultural phenomena foreshadows the analysis subsequently published in article form in 1926 (except that the ideological dimension — although present in this early version — receives little attention). Mannheim takes as intrinsic interpretations those which are concerned with an internal interpretation of a work, an interpretation on the basis of an author's ideas and an interpretation of one text in terms of another. Genetic interpretations of a work may take the form of a history-of-ideas interpretation, an individual psychological interpretation and a psychological interpretation. What particularly concerns Mannheim here is the socio-genetic interpretation of thought, since

> not only may law, morality, life-forms, art, religion, etc. be investigated in relation to their socio-genetic functionality but also the process of thought and cognition, the structure of thought forms as well as the concrete intellectual content of an epoch can be comprehended in relation to its socio-genetic function and even in relation to a functionality oriented towards several directions: on the one hand, as the function of comprehensive internal constellations, as the function of the world view of respective individuals and, on the other, as a function of the striving of groups for economic and social power.[80]

However, such genetic interpretations contain a potential contradiction which Mannheim highlights with reference to Marx's argument that the ideas of specific groups in the production process are historically transitory products of the relations of production. Mannheim argues that such a statement proclaiming the relativity of all knowledge must also refer back to itself, i.e. that this statement must itself be relative. Yet, Mannheim goes on to suggest that analogous statements must be made in the sociology of knowledge 'even though one may not wish to trace the ideological moment in the last instance back to the relations of production as Marx does'.[81] That is, the sociology of knowledge must make some statement about the derivation of 'theoretical contexts from extra-theoretical constellations'. It is worth noting here that a common feature of the sociology of knowledge advanced by Mannheim and Scheler is that the extra-theoretical is not itself theoretically apprehendable and therefore acquires an ultimate validity beyond which theoretical argument cannot go. But Mannheim is at pains to separate genesis and validity since

> the truth or falsity of a statement or of a whole theoretical sphere can never be reinforced or weakened by a sociological or other genetic explanation. How something has emerged, what functionality it may possess in certain contexts is irrelevant for its immanent validity. At the same time, this means that one can never construct a sociological critique of knowledge or, as has recently been asserted, a *sociological critique of human reason*.[82]

This is an explicit criticism of Jerusalem's positivist attempt to provide such a critique.[83] Thus, at this stage, Mannheim holds firmly to the separation of the spheres of genesis and validity and makes no bold claims for a sociology of knowledge.

Mannheim is at pains to preserve both the immanent and the genetic interpretation of cultural phenomena. The structures of meaning in cultural forms are not merely comprehended but also experienced. This means that 'apart from their meaning content, the experiential context from which they emerge is also more or less given as well'.[84] Mannheim argues that cultural forms cannot be reduced merely to the one or the other; both moments of comprehension and experiencing must be taken into account. Although he does not see this relationship as explicitly dialectical, and although these moments are conceived phenomenologically, this is nonetheless not too far removed from recent discussions by Apel, for example, on the dialectical relationship between reflection and engagement.[85] Mannheim is at least attempting to grasp this process of acquisition of knowledge in a more sophisticated form than many of his opponents managed to do and more sensitively than he himself, subsequently, often did.

Turning from the intuitive and phenomenological aspect of cultural knowledge, Mannheim examines the conceptual apparatus of the sociology of knowledge, and draws upon his discussion of world-views which was about to appear during or after the writing of this manuscript. As an example of the methodological problems involved in the sociology of culture, Mannheim takes up the concept of style, as an aesthetic and as a sociological concept. In this example, he draws heavily once more upon the early writings of Lukács and specifically upon his essay 'On the Theory of Literary History' published in Hungarian in 1910.[86] This deals with the concept of style and the relationship between a literary aesthetic and a sociology of literature.

Mannheim argues that we may characterize an explanation of a cultural object as sociological if it 'moves back from the work to the experiential context that lies "behind" it'. More precisely, this experiential context must be shown to have a specific social character, as when one refers to 'Impressionism as being derived from a self-disintegration of late-bourgeois individualism'.[87] That is, the genesis of cultural objectivations is traced back to 'the general structural forms of human sociation' (Weber). But Mannheim sees a problem in relating these 'two worlds' of cultural objectivations and life experiences. There must be some mediating factor between the two spheres. This is

> the world of the psyche which creates the bond between meaning and 'social reality'. It is a humanistic psychology which forms a bridge between the sphere of validity of cultural structures and the forms of sociation.[88]

This has important implications for the socio-genetic grounding of cultural objectivations. Mannheim provides the following example:

> If one speaks of bourgeois existence [*Bürgerlichkeit*], then one no longer means by this merely the role of a social class in the production and distribution process of the social product but rather the *experiential contexts* [*Erlebniszusammenhänge*] which result from this economic, social and historically specifically determinable position. The social categories referred to

do not imply human groups or concrete individuals but rather, for their part, experiential contexts.[89]

Here, Mannheim makes explicit the grounding of his theory of the functionality of cultural objectivations. Their genesis can be traced back not to social groups as such, but to the constellation of their life experiences. In other words, cultural forms have their social genesis in structured human experiences and the relationship between their meaning and this social reality is mediated by the human psyche. Such a theory has the advantage of not reducing cultural forms immediately to social groups and their position in the productive process. However, it should be clear from the use which Mannheim makes of the notion of experiential context that this is no essential mediating category but is itself, as it were, the basis or the grounding of cultural objectivations.

Yet, Mannheim is more specific about the mediating element between the social and the intellectual spheres. This mediating factor is the world-view [*Weltanschauung*].

> The world-view (of an epoch, a group, etc.) is a structurally connected series of experiential contexts which form, as it were, for a larger number of individuals, the common basis of their life experience and their penetration of life.[90]

Such a notion presupposes that the basic experiences cannot emerge in isolation as the individual's living core (*Lebenssubstrat*), but rather the contents of these experiences are shared with other members of the same group. Secondly, the concept of world-view presupposes that individual strands of life experience do not exist side-by-side in isolation but 'possess an inner coherence and thereby constitute, as it were, a "life-system" '.

However, this basic form is never directly describable; it can only be apprehended through the 'group formations' in which it is manifest. This, in turn, means that the world-view is itself apprehendable within the most diverse spheres of objectification so that 'one and the same world-view of an epoch can be apprehended through its art, religion, morality, politics, economic structure, etc.'.[91] Each of these spheres reveals a different aspect of the same world-view. The social scientist must, of course, attempt to show the coherence of the different manifestations of the world-view; in other words, 'attempt to penetrate the spheres of experiential contexts, which appear as completely untheorizable, in accordance with their structure'.[92] Ultimately, then, the sociologist of culture is not concerned with the analysis of cultural forms as such, or with social formations, but with the analysis of the structure of individual world-views and the particular experiential contexts which provide them with their coherence.

Yet, the potentially mediating category of the world-view ceases to perform this function and becomes, instead, 'the common basis' of individuals' life experience. As a cluster of life experiences, the world-view is certainly not a completely idealist construct; yet Mannheim constantly refuses to relate these experiential contexts back to particular types of social relationships. Rather, they constitute an oscillating basis of cultural formations, since Mannheim is unsure of their exact location. World-views are both a coherent *manifestation* of clusters of life experience and, at the same time, they *are* these clusters. At this stage of Mannheim's development, world-views constitute totalities. The sociology of culture is not concerned with an explanation of individual facts in terms of other individual facts but with an explanation derived from 'the totality (which one can term, amongst other things, a world-view) that lies behind them'. Already Mannheim is inclined to reduce the concept of totality to that of a world-view. Within an historical dimension, Mannheim distinguishes between history and the analysis of world-views on the grounds that 'history searches for *causes* whilst an analysis of world-views searches for the *preconditions* under which causes can be effective'.[93]

A causal analysis is only one possible type of analysis appropriate to the sociology of culture since 'either one applies the category of *causality*, or the relationship *of the whole and the parts*, or that of *function* or that of "correspondence" '.[94] At the level of concrete analysis, Marxism utilizes a causal analysis which reduces the social sphere, in the widest sense, to the economic, whereas as a philosophy of history, it operates with the category of function so that

> Ideology is then the function of a stage of development of the process of production. The one-sidedness of *Marxism* lies in the fact that it replaces other forms of social aggregation by socio-economic forms and in so doing it is not clear why the remaining social formative factors cannot also be co-ordinated with ideologies.[95]

If the social sphere is reduced to a narrow definition of the economic then this will lead to many experiential clusters being ignored. In contrast, the analysis of correspondence is applied to the analysis of world-views.

The various types of contemporary sociology — of which Marxism is only one variant — have to confront the problem of historicism when they venture into the cultural sphere since,

> Historicism has broken down people's feeling of static permanency and has set in motion the once stable world-view in which each thing and each living entity had its specific place accorded by divine plan. Our feeling for life tells us: everything could also be different. Everything has become historical . . . The spot from which we previously viewed the world as if from a stable standpoint has been broken down, our whole self is abandoned; we seem, as it were, to be suspended above ourselves. In thousands of forms we find ourselves again . . .'[96]

This 'fundamental homelessness of our human existence' cannot be comprehended fully by a general sociology of culture. One can, like Dilthey, provide a general typology of world-views but they can never be fully appropriate to historically-changing circumstances. History never repeats itself in an identical manner.

Therefore, Mannheim favours a dynamic sociology of culture, one which will relate cultural forms to a dynamic totality and to historically specific groups (e.g., rather than abstract social agents such as 'negatively privileged strata', historically specific social subjects such as the 'proletariat in high capitalism').[97] Such a sociology of culture is concerned with the 'total situation' of social positions and world-views. It will recognize that 'within a single historical body *not merely one* world-view *is alive*', but several; it will recognize that 'human beings within an epoch do not live in the same time'. Thus, at the end of his analysis, Mannheim is already moving towards a concern not merely with the analysis of world-views but also towards an attempt to explain their historical dynamic. This is taken up both in 'Historicism' (1924) and 'The Problem of a Sociology of Knowledge' (1925).

Central to his theory of cultural knowledge are the notions of life, experience and world-view. History is viewed as a dynamic stream of life, as a sequence of similar and opposing standpoints. The notion of existential boundedness (*Seinsverbundenheit*) that is so important in Mannheim's later work has its roots here in the theory of culture. Within it, the notion of cultural objectification becomes, in Mannheim's work, the general concept denoting superstructural phenomena as a whole. As Neusüss argues,

> The relationship between 'inner' and 'outer', experience and the expression of experience that Dilthey dealt with as a theoretical problem in the foundation of an autonomous human scientific method, is no longer directly under discussion in the sociology of knowledge; it takes over, to a certain extent, Dilthey's considerations as it finds them without itself making them problematic.[98]

Similarly, whereas Dilthey's concept of life only applies to the intellectual world, it applies in Mannheim's work to the whole world of objects. As Neusüss suggests, the danger then exists that 'material existence becomes a "massive" *Geist*'[99] The mediation between nature and thought, that in Marx's work is located in labour, is missing in Mannheim's theory of culture. The natural world as 'life' becomes immediately a cultural phenomenon. The mediation between life and thought is borne by the world-view. Systems of life within the historical stream of life are given expression in different systems of world views. These world-views, in turn, are competing with one another in such a manner that there is no stable location within the stream of life. Instead, as

Mannheim puts it, there is only a 'fundamental homelessness' — one that is later to become 'the homelessness of the mind.'

III

Clearly, a central theme of Mannheim's work in this period is not merely the need for a theory of culture that will incorporate the sociological element but also the centrality of a historical perspective — and this, for Mannheim, is a historicist perspective. Mannheim was attempting to come to terms with and work out the consequences of Troeltsch's monumental survey *Der Historismus und seine Probleme*, which appeared in 1922.[100] The incorporation of the historically dynamic element within his sociology is completed in the essay 'Historismus', published in 1924.[101] However, it is not only here that Troeltsch exercised an important influence upon Mannheim's formulation of a sociology of knowledge. Although he never published it, Mannheim intended to produce a work entitled *Zur Denklage der Gegenwart* which was, in fact, advertised in the original edition of *ideologie und Utopie* in 1929 and was still under discussion with Mohr Verlag at the end of 1930.[102]

This survey of contemporary thought was to deal with the three thinkers, Max Weber, Max Scheler and Ernst Troeltsch, whom Mannheim took to be crucial to the formation of contemporary social thought. Elsewhere, Mannheim also argues that his approach to the central problems of *Ideologie und Utopie* are 'directly affiliated with the approaches of Max Weber, Troeltsch and Scheler'.[103] All this is, of course, not to suggest that Troeltsch is the sole source of the historicist problematic. From his early writings onwards, it is also apparent that Dilthey is a central figure in Mannheim's formulation of historically located world views and a historicist perspective. Nonetheless, Troeltsch's major work brought together the key figures in the German philosophy of history.

In his own essay on historicism, Mannheim was concerned with working out not the historical origins and development of the historicist problematic but its implications for his sociology of culture and knowledge. The historicist perspective is

> an intellectual force of extraordinary significance; it is the real agent of our world-view, a principle which not only organizes like an invisible hand, the whole of the work of the human sciences but also permeates everyday life. . . . Our view of life has already become thoroughly sociological and sociology is just one of these spheres which, increasingly dominated by the principle of historicism, discloses most fully our new orientation to life.[104]

As such it is 'the very basis on which we view the socio-cultural reality'. Whereas Mannheim here sees historicism as the agent (*Träger*) of our world-view, he shortly afterwards argues that it '*is* a world-view' and that 'it not only dominates our external and internal life but . . . also our thought'.[105] In a strikingly idealist and contradictory manner, Mannheim sees historicism as the agent of our world-view and as itself a world-view which dominates us internally and externally, an ambiguity that is well expressed by Lieber who suggests that, for Mannheim,

> The historical process is a dynamic unity which encompasses spirit and life; since, however, both — spirit and life — are historical there exists no pure autonomy (*Ansichsein*) for the mind, no thought that remains undisturbed by the development and change in the real historical process. And since, for Mannheim, on the basis of the presupposition of a dynamic-historical *Lebensphilosophie*, there exists no development of the mind separated from existence, so also there can be no non-intellectual, purely natural occurrences that are historically significant. The relationship of superstructure to base and vice-versa is reciprocal.[106]

Hence, one looks in vain for the location of this historicist world-view — it permeates our thought *and* our life. As a 'mode of thought and living' we confront it through our 'ability to experience every segment of the spiritual–intellectual world as in a state of flux, in the process of emergence'.[107] But then we learn that it is not merely an all-pervasive world-view but also a theory (*Lehre*) that is able 'to derive an *ordering principle*' within this flux by penetrating 'the *innermost structure* of this all-pervading change'.[108] Historicism is, then, both history and a philosophy of history.

As a philosophy of history, however, historicism is confronted with several problems. Mannheim views it as, in part, a philosophy of the history of philosophies which incorporates 'old insights' into the new more comprehensive one. Philosophy, too, is part of this flux, and the old formal categories of reason (represented by Kantianism) must give way to historicism since they no longer accord with the present 'real historical substratum of psychic and intellectual reality'. What historicism attempts in various spheres is a synthesis of elements that accords with 'the changed world situation'. These various spheres are located within the context of totalities. In this respect, there is a correspondence between historicism and the changing social structure:

> If the atomizing, sectionalizing mode of thought may be regarded as corresponding to a social structure which allowed a maximum dissolution of social bonds and produced an economy of liberalistic, independent, atomized individual forces, then the present trend towards synthesis, towards the investigation of totalities, may be regarded as the emergence, at the level of reflection, of a force which is pushing our social existence into more collectivistic channels.[109]

This motif of atomization giving way to synthesis is one which constantly recurs later in Mannheim's sociology of knowledge both in his essay on competition and in *Ideologie und Utopie*. Here, however, historicism, too, is 'bound to the historico-philosophical position and its corresponding "life basis" '. Yet this 'bond' is no more than one of 'correspondence'. Indeed, the relationship is even weaker since historicism is a part of the 'dynamically developing totality of the whole psychic and intellectual life' which permeates actual life as well. It is both everywhere and nowhere. It is, in fact, 'a kind of philosophy which goes even beyond epistemology and tries to secure a basis for it. Thus, its systematic place corresponds to that of the "metaphysics" of earlier times'.[110] At the root of this 'dynamically developing totality', which is the historical process, there lies 'the self-unfolding substratum of life itself'. This substratum of life is, in a sense, the 'thing-in-itself' which the historicist must penetrate. But as a '*self-unfolding* substratum' it has presumably not been permeated by historicism. If this is the case, then it fundamentally contradicts Mannheim's original assertions concerning historicism as a world-view.

At a different level, Mannheim openly proclaims a theory of 'perspectivism', which only applies to the human sciences since

> It is because the exact sciences can, in fact, make statements into whose content the historical and local setting of the knowing subject and his value orientation do not enter, that one may here legitimately construct a correspondingly abstract subject (free from historical determination).[111]

In the human sciences, one must take account of Troeltsch's arguments that the knowing subject is not contemplative and that historical knowledge necessitates an evaluative standpoint. Along with Troeltsch Mannheim argues that

> historical knowledge is only possible from an ascertainable intellectual location [*Standort*], that it presupposes a subject harbouring definite aspirations regarding the future and actively striving to achieve them. Only out of the interest which the present acting subject has in the pattern of the future, does the observation of the past become possible.[112]

This leads Mannheim to insist upon our examination of not merely the 'historical-philosophical (sociological) *positional determination*' of historical knowledge but also the '*practical extra-theoretical aspirations*' of the 'inner *circle between aspiration and cognition*'. Mannheim's statement of this relationship is still grounded in a *Lebensphilosophie* ontology, in a notion of the extra-theoretical as irrational. At the same time, however, he is aware of the hermeneutic problem of historical understanding even though it is located within a historicist framework. Within a historical epoch, 'the concrete values which serve as a standard have *developed* in their fullness of meaning *organically out of the same historical* process which they have to help interpret'.[113] These standards, then, are rooted in 'the interpreter's own "psychic-cultural" situation'. The mediating function of tradition and other features of the hermeneutic circle, elucidated by Gadamer, for example, do not figure in Mannheim's analysis at all.[114]

Instead, perceiving the potentially relativistic impasse of perspectivism, Mannheim seeks to preserve a non-relativistic notion of truth by locating it within the dynamic of the historical process itself. Here, historicism as a world-view enables one to grasp 'the overall inner meaning of the historical transformation process with the help of the category of "totality" '.[115] Though this conception may appear to have affinities with that of Lukács, it differs in at least two important respects. Firstly, the category of totality is reduced in Mannheim's work to that of a synthesis of perspectives and trends. Secondly, Mannheim maintains that 'no one social stratum, no one class is the bearer of the total movement; nor is it legitimate to assess this global process merely in terms of the contributions of one class'.[116] However, as Kettler has argued, the confrontation with Lukács' work also plays a role in Mannheim's unpublished *Eine soziologische Theorie der Kultur und ihrer Erkennbarkeit*,[117] which he saw as a contribution to the sociology of thought (*Soziologie des Denkens*). This important study is worthy of detailed exposition and commentary.

In the first section on the sociological determination of methodological reflection — Mannheim's 'historical-philosophical and sociological self-orientation'[118] — he seeks to establish not merely the difference between the human and natural sciences but also the wider social origins of these differences. In contrast to the neo-Kantian distinction between the natural and the human sciences that is established at the level of the results of knowledge, Mannheim introduces an ontological distinction by asking whether 'the *object* of the natural sciences and that of history differ in their *mode of existence*'[119] Secondly, one might utilize the 'ontic distinction between the world of nature free of meaning and that of structures of meaning (culture)'. Finally, one might place 'a further ontic, pre-methodological question, whether or not the cognitive subject stands in a completely different relationship to the objects of the cultural sciences than in the law-seeking natural sciences'.[120] In fact, Mannheim seeks to ground cultural scientific knowledge in 'pre-scientific modes of cognition' which are effective in everyday life — a largely phenomenological grounding for this knowledge.

But the reasons why these two different types of knowledge should emerge historically has very different roots. Whereas the new philosophy and methodology of the natural sciences was symbolized by Cartesian philosophy, the cultural sciences have their roots in 'the romantic consciousness'. In practical terms, the philosophy of the natural sciences was rooted in 'a technically orientated interest in nature', in 'a technical domination of nature' which sought to remove 'qualitatively conditioned thought' from the realm of science and developed 'a mistrust of all anthropomorphically associated sources of knowledge'.[121] In the course of the establishment of this new ideal of knowledge, the rational was seen as a guarantee for the objectivity of knowledge as opposed to the subjectivism of anthropomorphic knowledge. This points towards 'the striving for a societalization of knowledge' in the natural-scientific cognitive ideal which favours the 'depersonalization and decommunalization of knowledge', the 'linking of universal validity and truth'.[122]

Insofar as natural-scientific rationalism may be 'imputed' to the 'capitalistic spirit', to 'the spirit of the emergent bourgeoisie', there are strong affinities between the rationalism of the modern natural sciences and the structure and rationality of central aspects of an emergent capitalist society. Mannheim acknowledges that such links have already been suggested by Simmel, Sombart, Weber and Lukács, but argues that all these writers, with the exception of Lukács, have failed to be sufficiently historically-specific.[123] Weber and Sombart, although recognizing that rationalism and money calculation existed prior to capitalism, failed to recognize that 'it is precisely in modern capitalism and only here that the category of commodity becomes a universal category which structures the whole world view'.[124] This and other passages in this section testify not only to Mannheim's assertion of the need for historical analysis but also to his largely Marxist account of the relationship between natural scientific rationality and modern capitalism — an account that he derives from Lukács. Furthermore, Mannheim accepts Lukács' account of the emergence of reification through commodity fetishism and its manifestation in increasing rational calculation and in the development of modern science.

Rational calculation and quantification through commodity production and exchange have important consequences for the dominant group in a capitalist society. The bourgeoisie, having created this system of commodity exchange and rational calculation, transpose these relationships onto all other relations in society. In particular, any other mode of experiencing the world that does not conform to this calculable, quantifiable rationality is reduced to a subjective, pre-scientific status. The communal subject of knowledge in pre-capitalism is replaced by 'on the one hand, the isolated individual and, on the other, the "consciousness as such" that resides in him'.[125] Thus, the emergent bourgeoisie 'makes one sphere of knowledge into the paradigm of knowledge as such' and thereby overlooks the fact that other 'methods of thought and modes of knowledge exist which differ from these structural forms'.[126]

This intellectual process is part of a wider one under capitalism of reducing all relationships to impersonal abstract ones, and concrete individuals to abstract individuals or functions of general processes. Hence

> the possibility of the reduction of all organic relationships to the contractual form, the possibility of depersonalized wealth and capital and the possibility of enterprises in the form of stock companies is only attainable through this new relationship which eliminates all that is qualitatively distinctive.[127]

Through such an analysis Mannheim hopes to have shown 'how a specific rationalism as a form of thought belonged to the "reifying" life structure of capitalism as a form of existence'.[128]

In contrast to this dominant form of rationality and its associated epistemology, Mannheim posits the existence of a complementary counter-current that has been maintained by social strata 'not incorporated in the capitalist process of rationalization or at least having no functional role (*Trägerrolle*) within it', and within the private spheres of life by those who are engaged within the capitalist process of rationalization, but are excluded 'from the foreground of *public* and *official* life'.[129] Mannheim recognizes, however, that the 'irrational' sphere of life — 'the more basic relationship of human beings to one another and to things' — has been pushed to the "periphery" of individual life' and is to be located in traditional strata which are now more marginal to the new, predominantly bourgeois world. It is in this context that Mannheim argues for the importance of the romantic reaction against the Enlightenment. This provides us with a different way of viewing Mannheim's concern with the romantic movement, which he was to take up in his *Habilitationschrift* on conservative thought.

Because diverse tendencies of bourgeois rationalist, anti-rationalist (bourgeois), and proletarian thought exist historically, and Mannheim is intent upon providing a perspective that will be able to grasp historical tendencies, he feels compelled to call for a synthesis of these opposing currents. Having rejected any notion of a single truth, Mannheim commences his analysis with the problem of relativism, which 'has become for us today a question of life'. Mannheim argues that 'each epoch has its truth' which is

> only possible from standpoints which are formed in history, which emerge as functions of history. However, since each direction of thought is partial (as are the social currents and their basic intentions which they bear), the totality can only be grasped in a synthesis.[130]

Hence, this totality is to be grasped 'not through a "leap" out of history but through an even deeper engagement in it'. Mannheim, on the one hand, recognizes that there can be no knowledge of the totality outside of history (and that includes all positivistic abstractions from it) and that knowledge must come from greater engagement within it but, on the other hand, he is unprepared to push the contradictory world-views any further (a task made impossible by his lack of commitment to any of them), and can therefore only call for their synthesis.

But Mannheim did not pursue this synthesis at this stage. Instead, he develops in some detail his sociological theory of understanding. Whereas the positivistic, quantitative tradition culminated in 'the de-anthropomorphizing of the results of knowledge', in 'a societalization of these results of knowledge', the qualitative tradition is anthropomorphic and culminated in 'the communalization of the results of knowledge'.[131] On the basis of this distinction, Mannheim seeks to revise part of the methodology of historical cognition, namely the theory of interpretation as it affects the historian or sociologist of culture who

> either seeks to understand concrete cultural objectivations or individual characters or who makes it his task to ascertain the contexts of intelligible relationships between individual objectivations and the totalities of world-views associated with them, between social strata and their ideologies or is concerned with the elaboration of the continuities of ideas and their changes in function.[132]

Thus Mannheim sees the study of ideology as part of a wider process of interpretation of cultural phenomena and not yet as clashing with a sociology of knowledge. Indeed, when he speaks of the existence of 'concrete interpretation in a specific form as the investigation of ideology, as the sociology of culture', it is almost as if he ascribes to them an equal status within a theory of interpretation.

Mannheim reiterates his critique of positivism — which he equates with natural scientific methodology — on the grounds that it 'hypostatizes one form of knowledge into knowledge as such'. It is rooted in 'a specific type of existential relationship' and 'implies a specific form not only of the depersonalization and dehumanization of knowledge, and as such alienates its objects, but it also presupposes such "estrangement" '.[133] This calculatory knowledge not only assumes a change in human relationships but a change that accords with a capitalist society. Such a narrow definition of what legitimately constitutes knowledge — one which excludes much of human knowledge — is symbolized in the separation of theoretical and practical activity. This view of the natural scientific mode of cognition not only reiterates, in many respects, Lukács' critique of the natural scientific model but also, like Lukács, equates one of its modes — positivism — with natural scientific knowledge as such.

Within the framework of his more comprehensive social theory of knowledge, Mannheim's central thesis is that

> every cognitive act is merely a dependent part of an existential relationship between subject and object, an existential relationship which, in each case, establishes a different kind of communality and a correspondingly specific unity between the two.[134]

Whereas Kantian philosophy is unable to examine the subject-object relationship since it rules out the ontological dimension and seeks to assert that knowledge commences with conceptualizations, Mannheim suggests that what is to be known involves the whole of consciousness, not merely its theoretical side. This existentially grounded knowledge Mannheim terms 'conjunctive knowledge'. Conjunctive knowledge is knowledge for interacting human subjects located in the same existential community. It is perspectival knowledge which is 'completely *one-sided*', thereby limiting its sphere of validity to those with whom one has an existential relationship.

Such a theory of knowledge escapes the individual solipsism of much traditional epistemology for, Mannheim argues, 'the precondition for self-knowledge is social existence' and not the isolated self. The starting point of a social theory of knowledge must be — as in Scheler's sociology of knowledge — the 'we' relationship which can be enlarged from two people to a whole experiential community. Mannheim contrasts this conjunctive knowledge with what he terms 'communicative knowledge', which he says, is the aim of natural scientific methodology. Whereas conjunctive knowledge is located in, and bounded by, an existential community, communicative knowledge is societalized knowledge, that is, it aims to be universal knowledge that is unbounded by experiential communities and perspectives.

Mannheim speaks of 'the functional anchoredness of concepts and thought at the existential level'. But the function of concepts in conjunctive knowledge is different from that in natural scientific knowledge, in that

> life and, in particular, life in the conjunctive realm of experience, creates ... concepts not for the purposes of theoretical contemplation ... but rather in order to *continue to exist in them and with them*. They are the organ of the ongoing current of life and, at the same time, living activity.[135]

The function of language within this sphere, then, consists in the articulation of this experience and its fixing within specific phases of the flow of conjunctive experience. Therefore, in order to understand conjunctively conditioned concepts, one needs to master 'the totality of this world and not the totality of an abstract conceptual realm'.[136] Whereas general concepts are potentially valid for all, conjunctive, historical concepts are valid only for members of a particular sphere of experience and hence 'the accumulated experience in a historical, conjunctive concept is and remains perspectival'. Mannheim sees this conceptual distinction as expressing the parallel sociological distinctions made by Töinnes between *Gemeinschaft* and *Gesellschaft*, and by Alfred Weber between *Kultur* and *Zivilization*.

Where we are concerned with historical knowledge, the cognitive subject is 'the collective communal subject in ourselves'.[137] Within this conjunctive realm, there exist as many 'spheres of significance' as there are spheres of conjunctive experience, and 'hence each specific conjunctive experience is tied to a specific context of significance which can only be realized in a specific community of individual and collective experience'.[138] This dimension of Mannheim's argument prefigures the later phenomenological account by Schutz of what he terms 'structures of significance'.[139]

Mannheim introduces a central distinction between knowledge within the natural scientific realm and knowledge within the historical sphere. Whereas the cognitive subject of natural science is a supra-temporal subject, the subject of historical modes of thought — since it is rooted in communal experiences — is ultimately dynamic. Mannheim's erroneous view of the natural sciences (for example, he ignores what is today a post-Kuhnian commonplace, that this sphere of knowledge is also grounded in communal experience either empirically, in the form of the scientific community, as in Kuhn or Popper, or transcendentally, as in Apel's theory) leads him to argue that changes in meaning can only occur in the cultural sphere, within 'the sphere of the conjunctively bounded community of experience'. This view certainly strengthens his conception of historical knowledge as dynamic, but it leads him to overemphasize the subjective dimension of knowledge in this sphere and, correspondingly, to underemphasize this dimension in natural scientific knowledge (e.g., the community of scientists). Thus, he argues that, in the conjunctive realm, 'change in the meaning of concepts is anchored in change in the collective phenomenon itself'.[140]

The actual tempo of change in conjunctive knowledge is quite varied and depends upon several factors. For instance, the process of stereotyping 'dams up' or blocks the flow of conjunctive experience. Similarly, the perspectives from which the communal subject views the institutions and norms of the society are likewise 'dammed up' or blocked by the process of stereotyping, and the flow of collective representations is likewise retarded. This notion of the stereotyping process, which Mannheim derives from Weber's concept of 'magical stereotyping', is significant in the light of his later characterization of ideologies as a barrier to genuine experience of a historical situation.

This discussion of stereotyping leads Mannheim to take up the notion of collective representations and to argue that society's institutions are not merely existent entities but also reflected notions shared by the communal subject. Economic structures and forms of the state, for example, are not, for Mannheim, natural structures but must be understood in terms of the totality of the relationships which constitute them. Likewise, Mannheim agrees with Max Adler in considering 'the economic sphere not as a material, natural sphere but already as a cultural-intellectual one'.[141] That is, we do not experience our existence in a purely nominalistic manner but within a particular cultural context.

Mannheim specifically counters Weber's excessive nominalism with the argument that it presupposes 'that only the individual subject exists and that contexts and structures of meaning only exist insofar as individual subjects conceive of them or are in some manner consciously orientated towards them'.[142] In contrast, Mannheim claims that the historian and sociologist are interested in supra-individual structures that extend beyond individual consciousness, structures that constitute 'inter-human constellations of meaning', which should not, as nominalism would have it, be treated as methodological constructs of the observing subject. Rather, there exist 'extremely interesting existential relationships between the intellectual realities of an age and the reflexive, conjunctive experiences of them'. The former exist, as it were, 'behind the reflexive consciousness of the single individual'. These realities, as 'global' realities, are perceived from within conjunctive communities so that knowledge of them is perspectival and bounded by particular standpoints. Thus, there exists an interaction between intellectual realities and reflection upon them from within a community in which

> Each aspect of conjunctive knowledge of the historical sphere is not only bound up in its emergence to the social sphere of experience and to the intellectual realities that absorb it, but also each new aspect of knowledge is again returned back to ongoing life and transforms the formation and thereby the intellectual state of these intellectual realities.[143]

Concepts and the intellectual realities which they express are not identical. It is, therefore, Mannheim's task to examine 'the dynamic of intellectual realities' and 'the dynamic of the conceptual level'.

Mannheim seeks to distinguish three types of intellectual reality: what Durkheim termed institutions; structures of meaning that comprehend both the natural environment and the inner world, and, finally, the individual 'work'. There exist also collective creations such as language and morality that are neither fully characterized as institutions nor 'works'. Each of these intellectual realities has a particular mode of existence that cannot be identified with or reduced to the reified existence of individual psychological existence. The social realm is thus full of collective creations of the life-community. Each of them changes, but not in isolation: 'the transformation of one sphere is co-determined by change in the others'.[144] In itself, this would suggest a mutual interaction of intellectual realities which gave prominence to no single one of them. It also suggests a notion of reality as an interrelated network, which is often found in Simmel's work. However, Mannheim argues that objective tendencies can be extracted from within this flux, at least within the totality of a single intellectual totality. Any structure may contain several objective tendencies. Yet,

> which of these tendencies is adopted by the total intention (*Gesamtwollen*) is only explicable from the existence of the living community and not solely from the structure of the objective form.[145]

In this way, Mannheim argues against those types of interpretation which see a work solely in terms of its own structure. Nonetheless, the existence of a wide diversity of cultural communities can only lead back to the possibility of asserting the dependency of perspectives upon different communities in which the individual participates. Within his total existence, the individual participates in 'various stages and circles of communities'. Which one is important to him can only be derived from a historical analysis.

It is this diversity of perspectives which raises special problems for the social and human sciences. The immanent or intrinsic level within these sciences is small compared with the natural sciences; their total problematic grows out of the social process and 'especially out of social struggles'. Similarly, intellectual realities, though historically specific, have something global and total about them, compared with perspectives, with 'particular reflexive knowledge'. Hence, in the social sciences, there is a specific problem of interpretation since every structure possesses 'an intended meaning and an objective meaning'. The former belongs to the conjunctive sphere, the latter to the communicative. Mannheim maintains that we need to take account of the conjunctive sphere in the social sciences. It is doubtful, however, whether he shows clearly how the two spheres relate to one another, though he does, at least, state the problem he is faced with:

> Intellectual structures of the most diverse type fill the communal sphere of experience; they are objectivities confronting human subjects. . . . First of all, in pre-reflexive intellectual intentionality in which one simply realizes them (one also terms this 'living in the structures'). And secondly, in that one is orientated theoretically and reflexively towards them. One can only be orientated perspectivally towards intellectual spheres . . .[146]

Any epoch of a cultural community is confronted with a series of competing 'intentions towards the world' [*Weltwollungen*] that also express diverse intellectual intentions. Historical knowledge must therefore bring some order to this diversity. In other words, 'historical knowledge — insofar as it constitutes an interpretation — is the ordering of intellectual realities of heterogeneous origin within the historical realm of our life and experience'.[147]

This distinction between pre-reflexive knowledge located within the community of experience and theoretical reflexive knowledge has important implications for the problem of interpretation. Understanding involves two elements: understanding as empathy, which is an inner capacity of the individual, and understanding in terms of locating something within a life-context, which is an intellectual capacity:

> hence we distinguish *understanding of existence* (existential, inner contagion) and *understanding of meaningful entities* (comprehension of meaning, intellectual understanding).[148]

In our ongoing life-experience, the two are clearly connected but in the case of

> the understanding of intellectual realities which belong to a particular sphere of experience, we apprehend the particular existentially-bounded perspectival meanings only when we somehow investigate the sphere and structure of experience that lies behind them.[149]

This distinction remains central to Mannheim's later analysis of ideology, not only in the sense that intellectual understanding must somehow rise above pre-reflexive acceptance of ideologies in order for us to engage in a critique of ideology, but also in that, for the 'relatively unattached intelligentsia', their experience of diverse conjunctive communities assists their intellectual understanding of the knowledge (ideologies) that are derived from them. At this stage of his analysis, Mannheim wishes to designate supra-conjunctive understanding (*Verstehen*) by another term, that of comprehension (*Begreifen*). This theoretically reflexive comprehension Mannheim terms 'interpretation', in contrast to understanding, which he defines as 'the penetration of a communally bounded sphere of experience, of its structures of meaning and of the existential bases of these structures'.[150]

The perspectival nature of both simple understanding and the interpretation of intellectual structures is manifested

> not only for reflexive comprehension in interpretation but already for the existential relationship of the human subject to the forms of alien subjects and alien world which, in a historical tradition, can confront him as a 'pre-world' [*Vorwelt*].[151]

In other words, Mannheim recognizes here the central mediating function of tradition in hermeneutic understanding. There exists no pure interpretation by the human subject of his object; rather, this relationship is mediated by the pre-existing location of the objects within a specific historical tradition.

However, the relationship between the knowing subject and his object is mediated not merely by a historical tradition that is already given to the human subject but also by utopia, a utopia which

> contains a direction, standpoint, perspective and problematic from which the existent and the emergent first become graspable at all. The investigation of the structure of utopia is therefore one of the most essential tasks in the sociology of thought.[152]

Thus, in his first systematic reference to utopia, its function lies within the context of a sociological theory of interpretation. But, even at this early stage, Mannheim also argues for its political significance too. He views pure utopianism as pre-scientific and perspectival, emerging out of the 'tension between existence and desire'. Even at the scientific level, concepts remain political, since

> historical-sociological knowledge is also perspectival and each concept in such a dynamic reflection contains a dynamic perspectivity: the general *tensio* lives within it. In the words 'capitalism', 'proletariat' and 'culture' a compilation is not contained and intended but rather a directional movement viewed from a standpoint embedded in the historical flux. Of course, it is in their concrete specificity that these concepts are determined by a direction and not as abstract *destillata*.[153]

This prompts Mannheim to ask, 'Which of sociology's concepts are clearly not complicated and constituted by some political *tensio*?' Once more he comes to question Max Weber's nominalism and theory of value-freedom. The understanding and interpretation of intellectual realities in earlier epochs implies their injection into our own realm of experience. We can understand and interpret them naively or dynamically. We can also interpret them from within their own perspective — 'immanent understanding and interpretation'. But there is the problem of the location of this perspective. Mannheim argues that there exist several realms of experience within the same epoch. For instance, those who experience social mobility move from one milieu to another, and this means that the milieux lose their absolute character. Again, this is essential to Mannheim's later attempt to escape from the relativist problematic by positing the existence of an intelligentsia whose members possess socially-diverse origins. It also presupposes that no-one is necessarily rooted in any one of them; it presupposes a universe of possibilities like that outlined by Musil in his novel, *The Man Without Qualities*.

These aspects of conjunctive knowledge give rise to two specific problems. The first is the nature of evidence in conjunctive knowledge. Evidence is derived from the existential community and is qualitative. It is not guaranteed by formal methods that lie outside the community. Rather, the apprehension of the qualitative 'is *not the result* of the application of these methods but is the *precondition* for the fact that they can be applied at all'.[154] Mannheim seeks in 'the phenomenon of genuineness' (*Echtheit*) an ontological criterion of truth, indeed a criterion that is close to Heidegger's notion of authenticity (*Eigentlichkeit*) in *Being and Time*.[155] It is summed up in the following passage:

> Where the inherent perspectivity of some particular conjunctive knowledge is given, then there exists within this perspectivity genuine and ungenuine existences and also genuine and ungenuine participation in experiences. An

existence is genuine which exists on the basis of its ontological principle [*Seinsprinzip*]; an experience is genuine whose perspectivity is determined only through the perspectivity of the standpoint.[156]

In this way, genuineness becomes 'merely an expression of the search for such an ontological criterion of truth'. Truth thus resides within 'a conjunctive experiential community of authorities (*Kennern*)', within a community that is usually conservative and bounded by tradition. It is these ontological roots of knowledge (including ideology) that later give rise to the sheer density of competing ideologies.

The second related problem is that of the consequences of a stratified society for conjunctive knowledge. Where relationships of subordination and domination exist, the same cultural reality is experienced and interpreted differently — from above and below. However, institutional structures such as language give a stratified society a communicative sphere not restricted by conjunctive perspectivism. At the same time, the exclusiveness of class communities leads to the autonomous dynamic of their cultures so that we can speak, for example, of 'bourgeois art'. At the level of the naïve experiencing of the world, communicative exact knowledge is pushed aside and we participate almost entirely in the conjunctive community of experience and knowledge. The individual's consciousness is 'to be seen as a petrifaction of previous epochs of the history of consciousness' whose layers and strata have to be reconstructed by a sociology of knowledge. However, there exists in stratified societies a 'relatively independent' intellectual culture (*Bildungskultur*). Here, the continuation and development of the cultural process 'does not result immediately from the life-community'; rather, tendencies and world intentions are experienced at one remove from the primary conjunctive communities. None the less, 'the intellectual culture is not free-floating since it can only exist primarily out of the comprehension of such cultural communities',[157] and because its participants come from diverse existential communities which thereby provide it with its competing tendencies.

Within the intellectual community at any one time, 'several standpoints for reflexive knowledge of the cultural sphere' are available. Mannheim concludes that 'the investigation and development of these standpoints proves to be the most essential task of any sociology of culture and thought',[158] not least because, faced with the diversity of standpoints, it is essential to grasp the fundamental movement and relationship of these standpoints, to group them around the basic dynamic direction, within the cultural process. This basic dynamic is focused around the development of the economic and social forms of capitalism and the groups that lie behind them. Thus, the conclusion to this section of Mannheim's manuscript already anticipates the problematic of *Ideologie und Utopie* — the competing ideological standpoints rooted in specific social existence; the need to grasp the totality of these standpoints, or at least what is valuable in them, and the crucial role of an intellectual stratum in performing this synthesis.

In the final, unfinished section of his treatise, Mannheim commences an analysis of the sociological genesis of a sociology of culture, but unlike his earlier attempt to deal with this problem, this one is much more preoccupied with the theory of ideology, which is presented in a more sympathetic and sophisticated manner. Mannheim views 'the ultimate goal of an investigation of ideology' as being 'to grasp the total ideological superstructure with regard to its sociological determination'. Such an analysis must examine, for example,

> how a specific type of methodology in its systematic points of origin is the expression of a specific intellectual intention (*Denkwollen*), the latter a part of a specific world intention (*Weltwollen*) and how this world intention directly coincides — through a certain *tensio* — with a specific stratum in a determinate constellation of the social process. If one wishes to make more of the sociology of culture and the analysis of ideology than a collection of convenient observations upon interest-determined thought, then this latter method must be applied. For this purpose, we must introduce the concept of 'immediate interestedness' and that of 'mediated engagement' (*mittelbaren Engagiertsein*). It would also be a travesty of the economic theory of history to interpret the whole superstructure in all its parts as being linked by immediate interests to the social base.[159]

Mannheim here reveals his conception of the analysis of ideology as one which moves from the intellectual structure, through an intellectual intention which is itself linked to a particular orientation towards the world. This, in turn, coincides with a specific stratum in society. At the level of his own methodology, Mannheim still maintains that it is possible to remove what is false from the 'inherent perspectivity' of world views in order to finish up with a valid historical construct. Whereas Lukács argues that access to the totality of society is limited to the proletariat, Mannheim maintains that certain aspects of history are only accessible from certain 'centres of life' and that the whole historical process may only be graspable from a particular standpoint from which we can unify all existing methods and a view of 'the totality of the historical process'. The nature of this totality, however, is very differently constituted from that of Lukács, since it is derived from a synthesis of perspectives. What Mannheim does retain from Lukács, though again within a very different context, is the notion of mediation. A sociological theory of culture is not to be one that is merely concerned with 'the investigation of the *immediate interest* of certain strata in specific contents but with *mediated engaged existence*'.[160] This concern should include not just 'the partial interest of groups that confront other interested groups' but also the fact that 'worlds struggle against worlds'.

Furthermore, Mannheim rejects working exclusively with the category of the ends–means relationship that is often implied both in the notion of 'interestedness' and in the direct study of interests on the grounds that this would only be possible were one to treat the cultural sphere as a natural process. He argues that

> Were human history merely the struggle for life, a vital process, then it would not be necessary that struggling strata should fight one another with world views, it would suffice . . . that, apart from the means of brutal struggle, they also possessed political ideologies. However, it is as a result of the supra-natural sphere of human beings that it also possesses world-views in which these ideologies are embedded and also that, hence, ideologies are only effective as ideologies because they possess such a deep anchorage. Conversely, however, this cultural world-view sphere is not so free-floating that in its point of departure it is not connected with the natural and social side of social life: not in the sense of immediate determination but in the sense of a mediated anchored existence.[161]

Thus, for Mannheim ideologies are subordinate to the more comprehensive world-views in which they are embedded and from which they derive their effectiveness. It also follows from this conception of the sociology of culture and the analysis of ideology that it

> represents a combination, a connection of natural scientific and human scientific methods. It connects a natural-scientific study of the social process with an interpretation of the whole cultural superstructure that runs in a specific direction.[162]

Though Mannheim does not continue this line of thought, he does at least raise the problem of the relationship between the scientistic and hermeneutic moments in a critique of ideology. To discover how Mannheim seeks to apply these two methods, however, we have to turn to his other writings.

The three attempts by Mannheim to apply the sociology of knowledge to specific areas are the studies of conservative thought, competition and generations. The first two are probably of greater significance than the third. What has been handed down to us as 'Das konservative Denken' and, in English, as 'Conservative Thought' are two versions of Mannheim's *Habilitationschrift* which he wrote in 1925 and was accepted by Heidelberg University on 12 June 1926 after giving his required public lecture.[163]

The theme of 'Conservative Thought' is the development of a specific '*conservative style of thought*' and the analysis of it seeks

> to determine the specific morphology of this style of thought, to reconstruct its *historical and social roots*, to pursue the *change in form* (*Gestaltwandel*) of this style of thought *in association* with the social fates of the groups that bear it, to demonstrate its extension and its sphere of emanation in the whole of German intellectual life up to the present day.[164]

We have here some of the central features of Mannheim's programme for a sociology of knowledge. The object of analysis remains rooted in the earlier framework of the analysis of world-views, namely, as a 'style of thought'. The changes in its *Gestalt* are to be examined in the light of the 'social fates' of the groups who produce such styles of thought. As so often in Mannheim's later work, the sociological analysis is to conclude with some reflections upon the relevance of this analysis for the present period — a 'diagnosis of the times' that is evident not merely in the book of that title but also in *Ideologie und Utopie*.

The analysis of world-views is confronted with the problem of the mediation between particular cultural styles and specific social tendencies. This mediation is not necessarily clarified by a hermeneutic interpretation which sees all works, however far removed they may be from 'the battlegrounds of life', as 'part' of a 'comprehensive context of experience'. This context or these constellations of experience (*Erfahrungszusammen*hänge) also include 'everyday life-experience'. The kind of knowledge that is to be investigated, however, does not possess this comprehensive quality. The conservative style of thought is also a form of political knowledge which is 'excessive', 'perspectival' and 'one-sided'. But if we confront this 'one-sidedness' and expose it, we can counter its 'propagandistic excesses'.[165] Thus, Mannheim introduces a distinction between the political dimension of a style of thought or world-view and that world-view as a whole. If the 'one-sidedness' of this political dimension is revealed as only a 'perspective' and its absolutist claims are undermined, then the style of thought may well remain valuable for human knowledge. In concrete terms, this means that the conservative style of thought is part of a stream of thought that lies at the roots of the philosophy of life of present times.

This conservatism is 'an objective-intellectual structural constellation'. In order to examine its specific 'mode of existence' (*Seinsart*), one must 'first of all strictly separate timelessness and objectivity from one another'. This structural constellation is '*a special connectedness of forms of the soul and intellect*' which survives its individual bearers. In opposition to both nominalism (Weber) and realism, which he views as being unable to cope with the mode of existence of such a structural constellation, Mannheim seeks to advance a third alternative, that of a '*historical-dynamic structural constellation*' that possess 'an objectivity that uniquely commences in time, whose fate is contained within it and which finishes with it'.[166] At the root of this structural constellation there is '*a principle of style (Stilprinzip)*' that is also historically dynamic and which changes 'with the concrete fates of living human beings'. This 'principle of style' is, in turn, the reflection of the life experience of a particular group.

Mannheim examines the development of German conservatism in the first half of the nineteenth century both in terms of its 'unity of style', its 'inner principle of development' and in relation to changes in

German society. It becomes a systematic political style of thought only in reaction to other styles of thought (e.g. bourgeois liberalism). At the root of these styles lie different modes of experiencing the world; for instance, the 'conservative experiencing of *property*'. What is at issue is not the nature of property relationships but always, for Mannheim, the mode of experiencing them. Hence, when comparing progressive and conservative thought, Mannheim insists that

> here we have before us, ultimately, two original types of *experience*, of things and the environment, from which only subsequently two currents of *thought* result.[167]

Here, Mannheim clearly reveals his belief in 'experience' as something prior to 'thought', which appears 'only subsequently'.

If we follow through this distinction to its conclusion, then we are faced with the problem of how to analyse this non-rational experience, this *ens realissimum*. Presumably, it can only be approached indirectly throught its manifestations in thought or other cultural complexes. Mannheim sees the unity of the conservative style of thought as being rooted in the modes of experiencing property, freedom and time, which also includes the experiencing of history, All form part of a *Grunderleben*. Conservative thought is thus 'embedded in this form of experience of the environment and inner world'.[168] As 'modern structural forms of social existence' develop, so too does conservative thought become more reflexive and distanced from its original basic experience.

This analysis of the conservative style of thought as a comprehensive *Gestalt* is only the first part of Mannheim's sociological study. He goes on to examine the 'concrete-historical emergence' of this style of thought from the standpoint of 'stratification and development'. Thus, 'the phenomenological — logical analysis of style' must be complemented by a sociological analysis of the 'social agents' of this style of thought. At the root of the concrete-historical emergence of the conservative style of thought in Prussia lies a conflict between 'feudal-traditionalistic intentions (*Wollungen*) and bureaucratic-absolutist rationalism'. The romantic irrationalist reaction to the Enlightenment is given expression primarily by 'socially *free-floating intellectuals*'. In a remarkable footnote at this point, Mannheim speculates as to 'from which social standpoint a philosophy of history, hence an interest in the totality of the historical process, is likely to arise'.[169] Mannheim suggests as an answer to this very Lukácsian question that, despite the free-floating intelligentsia's tendency to develop 'empty speculation',

> the best chance for the achievement of comprehensive views (*Gesamtanschauungen*) of history nonetheless exists when intellectuals, gifted with an instinct for what is concrete, and who are, to start with, free-floating, ally themselves with the aims of real existing social forces.[170]

At this point, Mannheim already substitutes the free-floating intellectuals for the proletariat in answer to the question originally posed by Lukács. But there is another important difference. Where Mannheim speaks of these strata in relation to specific historical situations, he argues that they provide a comprehensive perspective that is both valuable and, at the same time, falsified. He suggests that,

> Their own social position does not bind them to any cause, but they have an extraordinarily refined sense for all the political and social currents around them . . . [which allows] them to take up and identify themselves with someone else's interests — they will know them better, really better, than those for whom these interests are laid down by the nature of things, by their social condition. . . . Their virtue is not thoroughness but a flair for events in the spiritual and intellectual life of their society. Their constructions are therefore always false or even deliberately falsified. But there is always something that is astutely observed.[171]

Later, in *Ideologie und Utopie*, Mannheim suggests that, armed with the sociology of knowledge, they can provide a historical synthesis of perspectives. But even in the earlier work Mannheim argues that they are an essential element of modern society

> If . . . there were no such stratum of socially free and unattached intellectuals, it might easily happen that all spiritual content would disappear from our increasingly capitalistic society and *leave nothing but naked interests. For it is indeed the latter that are the agents of both ideas and ideologies* [italics added, D.F.].[172]

Despite this correlation between 'naked interests' and ideologies, and, presumably, their central importance, the notion of social interests plays a marginal role in Mannheim's sociology of knowledge.

Instead, Mannheim proceeds with an examination of the social thought of the central figures in the German romantic conservative tradition. We find that the 'older stratum of experience and thought' came to life with its contact and association with 'the romantic orientation to the world'.[173] In reaction to the bureaucratic rationalism of the Prussian state, conservative thought emphasized life against conceptualization. Mannheim views the polarities in nineteenth-century philosophy between 'being' and 'thought', 'concept' and 'idea', 'speculation' and 'praxis', as an expression of 'the political polarities of liberal and conservative world orientations'.[174] However, he argues that it is not enough to explain these different streams of thought in terms of their contrary intellectual positions. Rather, the analysis must have recourse to 'the ultimate presuppositions' of these styles of thought, 'their *existential* premises'[175] and the relationship between theory and practice that is manifested in them. In this romantic conservatism 'thought is . . . a function of life and praxis' and 'knowledge is action'. This is the source, Mannheim argues, of the modern concept of 'life': real 'existence' was no longer to be found in the empirical or everyday sphere but in 'pure experience'. Mannheim presents this later concept of life, embodied in the phenomenological school on the one hand, and Dilthey's historicism on the other, and analyses its roots in a manner reminiscent of Lukács. The philosophy of life points out that this rationalized world, 'this world of alleged reality is merely the world of capitalist rationalization which, as such, conceals behind it a world of "pure experiences" '.[176]

Mannheim concludes his study, as he began it, with the emphasis upon experience. The analysis of the differences between conservative and progressive style of thought has shown that 'the social differentiation of experience and thought extends into the *ontological*' sphere. The task of the sociology of knowledge in this respect is, by the refinement of 'the methods of social analysis, on the one hand, and the phenomenological analysis of meaning, on the other',[177] to make the emergence of historical consciousness itself a problem that can be successfully studied. But, again, it can be pointed out that the programme that Mannheim establishes for the sociology of knowledge seldom confronts the relationship between the two forms of analysis. In part, this is because his political intention — the diagnosis of the times, the interpretation of historical phenomena within a universal context — often leads to false syntheses and false juxtapositions of structures of meaning whose origins themselves remain unanalysed. In another passage, Mannheim anticipates a central theme of *Ideologie und Utopie*

> Whereas conservative thought is thus directed towards the past, insofar as it lives in the present, and bourgeois thought, in contrast, since it is the agent of the present, lives from what is new now, proletarian thought seeks to grasp the elements of the future that also exist in the present by concentrating upon those present factors in which the future structural forms of social life can already be seen.[178]

Neither ideology (conservative thought) nor Utopia (proletarian thought) are appropriate for the present. The crisis of bourgeois thought lies in the difficulty of diagnosing the present.

Mannheim's second 'application' of his sociology of knowledge, his paper on competition,[179] highlights the permanent tension, in his programme for a sociology of knowledge, between a sociological analysis of the determination of knowledge and a social theory of knowledge that will constitute a *Zentralwissenschaft* or *Grundwissenschaft* (both are Mannheim's terms). In the essay on competition, this dual task is posed in terms of its confrontation with

> two comprehensive groups of problems (which are closely related to one another). . . . First of all it is intended to make more concrete the problem of *competition* and secondly it is intended as a contribution to a *sociological theory of the mind*.[180]

This concern for the development of a sociology of the mind was a constant theme in Mannheim's work until his emigration.[181] His paper is concerned with the necessity of examining intellectual life from the sociological standpoint. Social scientific knowledge is taken to be an instance of 'existentially bounded cognition and knowledge', some of whose characteristics are the problem of *Verstehen*. Within the context of the process of competition in social life, modern thought is seen to exhibit the following processes:

A *Contrary thought*
  (a) The social division of the centre of the will (*Willenszentrum*) that lies behind thought
  (b) The social division of sensibility (sphere of intuition)
  (c) The social differentiation of the statement of the problem . . .
  (d) The social division of methods and categories of thought: axiomatics
  (e) The social division of 'historical experience of time'
  (f) The social division of the ontological experience of reality
  (g) The social division of the hierarchy of values

B *Mutual thought (synthetic tendencies)*
  (a) The orientation of competitors with one another
  (b) Mutual enhancement
  (c) The opponent as the ground for self-knowledge. Emergent reflexivity
  (d) Learning from one another
  (e) The phenomenon of 'transcendence'.[182]

Though Mannheim by no means deals with these and the other topics he outlines in his paper on competition, the programmatic outline provides some interesting insights into his sociology of knowledge. However unclearly formulated, this programme indicates a sequence of determination from the will, via the world-view, to social thought. Both the will that lies behind the world-view and 'social sensibility' constitute the limits of existentially-bounded knowledge. They are the sources of creativity and, at first sight, would appear not to be existentially bounded. However, it is clear that Mannheim also speaks of their social differentiation. Indeed, this differentiation is an essential feature of his conception of society as consisting of opposing, stratified systems of life and the conflict of competing world-views.

Such considerations lead us to the heart of his paper on competition. Competition is a central feature of 'social life as a whole' that 'enters as a constituent element into the form and content of cultural objectivation and into the concrete form of cultural movement'.[183] Competition plays 'a *co-constitutive* role' in social life. Indeed, in accepting a dialectical view of 'the form of development and change in intellectual life', Mannheim argues that competition along with generations constitute two 'structural determinations of social life'. This emphasis upon competition as a determinant of social thought introduces, in an ahistorical manner, a market model of society and social change that can be applied to social groups, world-views and, later, ideologies. Competition is 'a general social relationship' that also permeates economic life: hence it must be universal and not historically specific. Since Mannheim emphatically excludes the questions of truth and validity in this analysis, these world-views can be seen to have equal value.

This lack of evaluation of world-views is paralleled in Mannheim's delimitation of the sphere of 'existentially bounded thought'. Not only is natural scientific knowledge excluded but the social knowledge that is existentially bounded is lumped together as an undifferentiated whole. This comprises

> historical thought (the mode and manner in which one conceives of history and represents it for others), political thought, human and social scientific thought and also everyday thought.[184]

Mannheim thus implicitly maintains that these forms of knowledge are all existentially bounded in the same manner, and includes social scientific thought that is itself concerned with everyday thought or political thought. In all instances, the thinking subject is crucial to the results of thought. All these forms of knowledge are perspectival, which means that 'only specific historical-social structures of consciousness can open up specific qualitative features in the historically living object'.[185]

This does not lead to relativism but to relationism since, Mannheim argues, 'specific (qualitative) truths are not apprehendable or formulable other than as existentially relative'. These structures of consciousness and world-views, though rooted in group experience, come together in the process of competition. More specifically, parties compete for what Heidegger terms the 'public interpretation of reality', for 'possession of the correct (social) view'. In the humanities and social sciences there exists a similar attempt to secure the 'correct' interpretation in a particular field. Neusüss suggests that Mannheim's competition of world-views can be seen as a counterpart to Popper's notion of competing theories in the progress of science, except that, for Mannheim, objective knowledge is not possible.[186]

However, Mannheim's main concern here is with competition for the 'public interpretation of reality'. This arises because

> every historical world-view, and sociological aspect of knowledge . . . is embedded in and borne by the desire for power and recognition by specific concrete groups who seek to make *their* interpretation of the world the public one.[187]

Again, we are never presented with the possible parameters of this struggle for power except in the notion of competition. This is evident from Mannheim's typology of the various forms in which the public interpretation of reality emerges — through consensus, monopoly, atomized competition and concentration (in economic categories, oligopoly or duopoly). Atomized competition, for example, comes about through the challenge to the monopolitic position of the church's public interpretation of reality. It is also part of the process of the democratization of the mind. Ironically, having earlier (in his second unpublished essay) questioned Simmel's analysis of money on the grounds of its lack of historical specificity and failure to locate its particular capitalistic features, Mannheim here provides an analysis of competition that suffers from exactly the same weakness.

After analysing the concentration of competition, Mannheim poses the question as to whether competition produces a synthesis as well as polarization. Mannheim's reply is that synthesis and polarization spring from 'the same social process' — 'the simple law of "competition on the basis of achievement" '[188] in the sense that one party borrows from its opponent and vice versa. Not only are there many instances of syntheses in social thought but, most significantly, the sociology of knowledge itself can synthesize viewpoints since it

> provides just such a viewpoint pushed further back, from which purely theoretical–philosophical differences, that can no longer be reconciled immanently, can be revealed to be partial and thereby can be apprehended from a synthetic standpoint.[189]

This synthesis is facilitated by the process of distancing from social competition and conflict and is a constituent element of Mannheim's later theory of an intelligentsia armed with the insights of the sociology of knowledge.

However, Mannheim points to a central problem of the process of achieving a synthesis. Syntheses involve selection, and necessarily raises the question of the standards for such selection. For Mannheim, the principle of selection is 'that which is the most applicable, thus the most useful for the living world-orientation of *all* parties in an epoch.'[190] But Mannheim is aware that this introduces a merely pragmatic criterion of truth. He argues that, at this point, the question of the criterion for truth cannot be answered by the sociology of knowledge, since it is concerned with *quaestio facti*, but must be answered by epistemology, which is concerned with *quaestio juris*. However, the sociology of knowledge would suggest that epistemologies are also existentially bounded since each epistemology 'exists only as the justification of a mode of thought that already exists or is just emerging' and 'in the historical-social context, epistemologies are only advanced posts in the struggle between styles of thought'.[191] At this point, of course, such reflections on the part of the sociology of knowledge would suggest that it has replaced the 'structural analysis of epistemologies' as a more comprehensive discipline.

By the end of the paper on competition, Mannheim had sketched out not merely his contribution to the 'sociology of the mind' but also two central problematics in *Ideologie und Utopie*. The first is the problem of competing world-views and ideologies in a period of increasing concentration of ideologies and political positions. The second problem, associated with a 'sociology of the mind', is that of truth and validity claims of ideologies within a market model of ideologies and worldviews. Both problems were brought together in *Ideologie und Utopie*.

IV

Mannheim's *Ideologie und Utopie* (1929) is in many ways a different book from the one we know as *Ideology and Utopia*.[192] It comprises only three chapters: 'Ideologie und Utopie', 'Ist Politik als Wissenschaft möglich?' and 'Das utopische Bewusstsein', and contains a brief introduction to the first chapter that is omitted from the English edition. It is therefore important to return to the original text of *Ideologie und Utopie* and attempt to reconstruct its context.

One essential part of that context is contained in the untranslated introductory remarks, where Mannheim argues that, though the sociology of knowledge is too new 'to make possible a systematic and architectonic' treatise, nonetheless the themes it examines signify a 'new orientation to the world'. As a new approach, it is not confined to 'a rigid organizational schema'. Instead,

> Thought, viewed from the total context, is never an end in itself but rather a permanently self-reconstituting living organon that forms itself anew with the changes in historical events: an emergent structure in whose elements the new anthropogenesis also takes place.[193]

Hence, Mannheim intends that his study will not be lifted out of 'this living stream' in which things are rendered problematic but will remain sensitive to the 'immediate existential situation and the "predicament of life"' that must be approached through interpretation and empathetic understanding (*Nacherleben*).

At the substantive level, the problem of ideology is to be systematically examined within the context of 'the decisive currents of contemporary thought', particularly since within specific problem areas such as the relation of theory to practice, the determination of concepts themselves varies 'according to the social standpoint of the observer'. Furthermore, whereas 'the present utopian and ideological rootedness of thought has been seen up till now largely in party terms (i.e. only in the opponents' thought),' Mannheim will examine this rootedness for all thought. Only when this 'unavoidable radicalization' of the problem of ideology and utopia has been carried out will it be possible to ask 'how at this level of thought it can still be recognized as such, how at this level of being intellectual existence is still possible'. Thus, from the very outset, Mannheim is posing the question of the possible alienation and powerlessness of the mind. Mannheim directs his analysis at the 'totality' of the present 'crisis situation of thought', but in the knowledge that 'no premature solutions' are possible. By revealing the contradictions that exist within the various possibilities open to us, Mannheim hopes to make the reader more aware of the crisis.

But this crisis is not merely an abstract intellectual one. Ideology and Utopia do not represent two isolated phenomena. Rather,

> The words ideology and Utopia do not simply signify the historical emergence of two new facts but, rather, the serious emergence of a fundamentally new theme. Through them, the whole world has become a theme in a new sense, because in their medium the meaning relevances which actually transform what exists into the world, confronts us in a new manner.[194]

This new mode of encounter with the world and ourselves arises because 'whereas the earlier, naïve person lived confined within "contents of ideas", we experience these ideas in the light of this tendency increasingly as ideologies and utopias'. We now live out these ideas as ideology and utopia not as ideas in themselves. Indeed 'what is common and ultimately decisive in ideological and utopian thought is that in them one experiences the possibility of *false consciousness*.'[195] This is the starting point of the original analysis of ideology and utopia. Thus, for Mannheim, the crucial issue is alienation from our own thought which has been transformed into ideology or utopia. Further, it places his analysis potentially much closer to that of Lukács than is evident in the English translation.

In the first chapter, Mannheim aims to develop further Marx's study of ideology and to render it scientific (value-free) in order to develop a new theory of ideology. Mannheim's notion of ideology is both a heuristic concept and a process that permeates all human thought in all historical periods. In proceeding to his value-free concept of ideology and to the sociology of knowledge, Mannheim starts out by separating the particular and total concepts of ideology. The particular concept refers to the rejection of ' "*specific*" ideas and "representations" ' of one's opponent, which are seen as 'more or less conscious disguises (*Verhüllungen*) of a situation whose true recognition does not lie in the interests of the opponent'. In contrast, the '*radical, total* concept of ideology' refers to 'the *total structure of consciousness*' of an age or concrete social group. What both have in common is that the intended content of the ideas is not apprehended directly, but indirectly through an understanding of a particular 'collective or individual subject' and the 'existential situation of the subject'. That is, the ideas are 'interpreted as functions of this existential situation'. Hence, 'the concrete constitution, the existential situation of the subject, is of co-constitutive significance for these opinions, assertions and knowledge'.[196]

But there are significant differences between the two concepts. The particular concept referred to 'only a *part of the assertions* of the opponent' and even then only to their content, whereas the total concept 'places in question the whole world-view of the opponent (including the categorial apparatus) and also seeks to understand these categories from out of the collective subject'. Secondly, the particular concept engages in '*functionalization* only at the *psychological* level'. In contrast, the total concept 'functionalizes the noological level' — the contents, form and conceptual apparatus of thought. Thirdly, the particular concept operates with

> a *psychology of interests*; the total concept, in contrast, with a much more formalized concept of function, where possible a concept of function that is intended towards objective structural connections.[197]

Furthermore, this implies that the particular concept is associated with a causal analysis, the total concept with a notion of correspondence. Finally, whereas the particular notion refers to 'a psychological, real' functionalization, the total concept functionalizes thought in terms of 'an *"imputed subject"* ' — though this is not identical with Lukács' notion of imputed class consciousness.

Mannheim cites Marx's conception as an instance of the total concept of ideology. But, in subsequently asserting that ideology is universal, Mannheim removes it from Marx's more specific formulations. Ideology becomes a concept that refers to a general connection between thought and existence; it becomes existentially-bounded thought.

The total conception of ideology involves a much more 'radical doubt' and 'destruction' of thought, an attempt to destroy 'the intellectual basis' of one's opponents thought. This is only possible in a world subject to fundamental transformation, a world of 'decisive social polarities'. Such a world emerged out of the bourgeoisie's 'new approach to the world' (*Weltwollen*) which developed a new economic system and 'a new *style of thought*'. The most important stage in the development of the total concept, indeed 'the *last and most important* step' was its association with social classes so that styles of thought could be seen to vary with class divisions. But this very attempt to question the structure of consciousness of a whole group in its totality brings with it the problem of the possibility of false consciousness. At this point in the English text, 'The Problem of "False Consciousness" ' becomes 'Objectivity and Bias' and a new definition of false consciousness is added which is not in the original. It is defined as 'the problem of the totally distorted mind which falsifies everything which comes within its range'[198] — a truly individualistic, psychologistic definition!

After tracing the recent development of the concept of ideology, Mannheim suggests that the concept has retained its relation to political praxis to such an extent that ' "pragmatism" in specific spheres of life belongs, as it were, to the natural world-view of modern man.'[199] Today, the concept has become the weapon of 'strata who find themselves in opposition, above all the proletariat'. But it 'cannot permanently be the intellectual privilege of a single class'. Rather, it can be and is applied by all groups in society. However, 'through this general expansion of the ideological conception a fundamentally new state of consciousness is constituted' and 'the problem of false consciousness, the problem of reality etc., receive a new meaning' which 'transforms our whole axiomatic, our ontology and epistemology'.[200] As soon as we move beyond a specific sociological analysis of ideology and recognize that our own standpoint is ideological, we move to 'a *general* conception of the *total* concept of ideology'. Indeed, 'This *general conception of the total concept of ideology* whereby human thought of all parties and in all epochs is ideological, is difficult to avoid.'[201]

But it is at this very point of generalization of the total conception of ideology that the sociology of knowledge emerges and it is here that the existential boundedness of thought (its *Seinsgebundenheit*) becomes the theme of 'intellectual-historical research'.

This 'modern historical-sociological insight into the factual standpoint-boundedness of all historical thought' raises, in turn, the problem of relativism. Mannheim argues that relativism emerges out of the conflict between this insight and adherence to a traditional 'static paradigm of thought' that rejects any knowledge that is bounded by its standpoint as merely relative and overlooks the fact that 'epistemology is just as much embedded in the historical stream (*Werdestrom*) as is our whole thought'.[202] There exist 'areas of thought in which standpoint-free, unrelated knowledge is inconceivable'. In particular, historical knowledge is 'essentially relational' and only formulable in terms of its relation to a standpoint. If this is the case then, Mannheim argues, we must ask 'which standpoint has the greatest chances of an optimum of truth'.

In relation to the general and total conceptions of ideology, Mannheim conceives of two possibilities: a '*value-free*' approach and an '*evaluative (epistemological–metaphysical)*' approach. The value-free, total and general concept of ideology is to be found in historical research, where the question of the 'correctness' of the ideas studied is not raised, only the question of 'how particular socially structured existential situations press for particular forms of interpretation of existence'.[203] But the very awareness of the permeation of ideology in all thought is itself only possible in a period of 'rapid and radical social and intellectual transformation'. In such a period — and it is clear from the context that Mannheim is thinking of contemporary Germany — 'there exist too many positions of *equal value* and intellectually of *equal force* that mutually relativize one another'[204] for one to take up a single position. It is a 'twilight in which all things and positions reveal their relativity'. In this sense, it is a privilege of the present times to be in a position to see 'all things suddenly become transparent', by stepping out of 'the fortuitous existence of the everyday world (*das zufällige Sosein des Alltags*) where today romanticized notions ("myths") belong'.[205]

This implies, in turn, operating within 'an evaluative, epistemological and, ultimately, in an ontological–metaphysical evaluation' and 'assenting to a particular world-view'. It is, in fact, 'an unavoidable ex-post ontology'; it '*is* our horizon which no ideological destruction can destroy', and points to a possible solution to the problem of ideology, in that

> the unmasking of ideology and utopia can only expose entities [*Gehalte*] with which we are not identical and it raises the question as to whether or not, in particular circumstances, the constructive lies already in the destruction itself, whether the new will and the new human being are already present in the direction of exposure to questioning.[206]

Although this is extremely vague, and Mannheim — as he himself admits — never returns to this issue, it serves to illuminate his belief in an ontology that lies deeper than ideological and utopian distortions.

Yet Mannheim's solution to the problem of ideology does not lie in this direction. He argues that historical research must examine historical factors in terms of an 'emergent totality'. The study of ideology undertaken along these lines represents a 'sociological diagnosis of the times' in which 'the concept of ideology itself can be applied in the diagnosis of the contemporary intellectual situation'.[207]

In moving to an evaluative concept of ideology, impelled by 'the historical dialectic', the problem of false consciousness recurs since the evaluative conception seeks

> to distinguish from amongst norms, modes of thought and schemes of orientation *at one and the same time*, the true and untrue, the genuine and ingenuine.[208]

False consciousness therefore prevents us from grasping the newly formed existence that makes up our present time. Its recognition is only made possible by a dynamic concept of ideology:

> Accordingly, in the ethical sphere a consciousness is false when it is oriented towards norms that, even with the best will, are incapable of dealing with a given stage of existence, when therefore the individual's failure cannot be interpreted as an individual violation but rather the erroneous action arises from the compulsion of a falsely grounded moral axiomatic. In moral self-interpretation, a consciousness is false if, through the customary sources of meaning (life-forms, forms of experience, interpretation of the world and humanity), it obscures and hinders new moral reactions and new human activity. A theoretical consciousness is false if, in 'worldly' orientation to life

it thinks in categories which, if taken seriously, would lead to one being unable to cope with a given stage of existence. Hence, it is primarily redundant and outmoded norms and forms of thought, as well as modes of interpreting the world, that can degenerate into this 'ideological' function.[209]

This new concept of ideology is both evaluative and dynamic; evaluative because it makes judgements concerning 'the reality of contents of thought and structures of consciousness', and dynamic because 'these judgements are measured against a reality that is always in constant flux'. This new concept recognizes that 'diversely situated false structures of consciousness can exist in the same historical-social realm', structures that refer to a form of existence that is either past or not yet in existence. These false structures of consciousness, in turn, can only be measured against 'a "reality" that only reveals itself in praxis'.[210]

In arguing that ideological and utopian thought is striving for, and is to be measured against, reality, we are confronted with the nature of this reality. This is important for two reasons. The first is that Mannheim's criterion of truth appears to be its pragmatic appropriateness for the present reality, since 'thought should contain neither less nor more than the reality in whose medium it operates'. This criterion, however, would rule out not merely ideological and utopian thought but also any critical stance that refused to take reality as an existent given. Secondly, and more importantly, Mannheim argues that our notion of reality has also been called into question since 'precisely upon the multiple forms of this concept depends the multiple forms of our whole thought'. The implication of this for a diagnosis of the times is that

> only when the investigating individual has assimilated all the decisive, important series of motivations that have developed historically and socially and characterize in their actual tension the contemporary situation — only then can it be possible to conceive of finding a solution appropriate to the present life-situation.[211]

But Mannheim argues that the problem here lies in the appropriation of the relevant material since 'facts' themselves are constituted in 'an intellectual and life-context' and concepts have their 'perspectivity'. Therefore, one cannot appeal to a single standpoint since 'the intellectual crisis is not the crisis of a *single* standpoint but the crisis of a world which has reached a certain stage in its intellectual development'.[212] Mannheim's solution is to search for the totality that is arrived at by taking up particular viewpoints which are also intent upon grasping the whole of reality and achieving 'the maximum possible enlargement of our horizon of vision'. The situational analysis of the sociology of knowledge is thus to be directed towards knowledge of the totality.

In outlining Mannheim's new theory of ideology, there is a tendency to assume that the particular and total concepts of ideology are those of Marx. However, neither the psychologistic aspects of the particular concept nor the total negation of thought in the total concept are to be found in Marx. But perhaps most significantly of all, false consciousness for Marx is one which is a true representation of a false reality. That is, the accent falls upon the object and not the subject. The reverse is true for Mannheim. This inversion is formulated by Neusüss as follows:

> Whereas Mannheim reproaches thought for not being at all autonomous but rather existentially bounded and hence ideological, Marx reproaches 'existentially bounded' thought for being ideological insofar as it takes itself to be autonomous. . . . The connection between being and consciousness which, where it is not reflected upon, becomes the characteristic of ideologies for Marx, appears for Mannheim to be itself the index of what is ideological.[213]

Further, whereas the problem of ideology for Marx (and Lukács) is a consequence of alienation and reification, for Mannheim it is the result of an abstract existential boundedness. Even if we accept the significance of social dependency in Mannheim's argument, there remains the problem of what exactly this social dependency is based upon.

The definition of reality (*Sein*) is an amalgamation of being and meaning, i.e. it is the meaningful experiencing of what is there or at hand. Thus, whereas one can find apparently concrete references to social processes and entities, there remains at the meta-theoretical level a more fundamental, phenomenological, *Lebensphilosophie* identity of being and meaning, of life systems and social theories.[214] For instance, to take an example central to Marx and Lukács, social classes do not derive from a material process of reproduction but from their association with world-views. Reference to such relationships as the production process and systems of domination that can be found in Mannheim's work are usually seen as part of a centre of experience. Indeed, at the heart of Mannheim's analysis is the human individual who mediates the spheres of existence and meaning.

For all Mannheim's emphasis upon praxis, the theory of action that is implied in his notion of ideology and utopia (both prevent adjustment to the present) is extremely passive ('adjustment', coping, etc.), and ultimately is not a theory of action at all. At its roots lies a phenomenological notion of human beings not primarily as *actors* but as *experiencing* human subjects of history. Being and consciousness are not mediated through a concrete process *of human intervention* but are unified in experience. In turn, the individual and his experience are embedded in a dynamic stream of life that is constituted by the sequence of similar and opposing standpoints, life-systems, world-views and structures of experience. The individual is, therefore, not a point of observation of this process but a part of this process itself. This reflexivity is, of course, quite valid except that the individual does not constitute this process, he merely experiences it. Theories are merely a stream within a stream;

Marxism, for example, is no longer a practical social theory but a metaphysics or a world-view.

Yet the central chapter of *Ideologie und Utopie* in fact examines the relationship between theory and practice. Indeed, when discussing the English translation with his publishers, Mannheim originally suggested that this should be the first chapter.[215] Though this suggestion was not followed up even by Mannheim himself, it is interesting to note that this is the largest chapter of the book.

Mannheim argues that with regard to the study of political action we need to ask, 'Is there a science of what is in flux, what is becoming, a science of the creative act?'[216] This, in turn, depends upon the existence of areas of society not already brought under the process of rationalization and administration. For Mannheim, 'the most important areas of our social sphere are even now still anchored in *the irrational* [italics added, D.F.]'.[217] These include the economy and the class structure. But the problem of acquiring knowledge of this sphere is that it is in a state of permanent flux. More importantly, the observer himself is a participant in 'the conflicting forces', which means not merely that he takes up a position within this conflict, but that 'the form of stating the problem, the most general form of his mode of thought and even his categorial apparatus' are bound up with 'vital political undercurrents'. This then, in an acute form, is part of the problem of the relationship of theory to practice.

When Mannheim examines these 'vital political undercurrents' — the bureaucratic conservatism, conservative historicism, liberal-democratic bourgeois thought, the socialist-communist conception and the fascist versions of the relationship between theory and practice — he not only accords them equal status but searches for a synthesis of them. As with the discussion of ideologies earlier, Mannheim's response is to argue that their content is dependent upon the social standpoint from which they emerged:

> not only the ultimate orientations, evaluations, contents but also the manner of stating the problem, the type and mode of observation and even the categories in which one subsumes, collects and orders experience vary according to the standpoint.[218]

One way out of this apparent impasse is the formation of party schools that will examine their own world-views, but this would encourage the suppression of 'the problem of the whole' and prevent the emergence of a conception of politics and society as a totality.

A more promising possibility lies in the very fact of recognizing 'the partisan boundedness of knowledge of politics and world-views'. Like Simmel, Mannheim argues that all knowledge is fragmentary but he sees in the complementary nature of these partial perspectives of the totality the possibility of attaining knowledge of the totality.

the different vantage points (standpoints) as they emerge in the stream of social life enable each one from its particular point in the stream to recognize the stream itself . . .

All political viewpoints are merely partial because the historical totality is always too comprehensive to be grasped by any one of the individual points of view that emerge out of it. But precisely because all these points of view emerge out of the same historical and social stream, because therefore their partiality is constituted in the elements of an emergent totality, it is possible to see them in juxtaposition and their synthesis (*Zusammenschau*) becomes a task that must be continually reformulated and resolved.[219]

This synthesis of world views must be dynamic and cover not merely the contents of thought but also their basis. At no point does Mannheim suggest that 'the same historical and social stream' might also be the subject of analysis, perhaps because it is precisely this present reality that is totally problematic.

The agent of this synthesis is the intelligentsia. Mannheim also recognizes, however, that historically the desire for a synthesis of perspectives has usually come from 'those middle classes who feel themselves threatened from above and below and who, from the outset and out of social instinct, seek a mediation between extremes'. This synthesis can be static — 'the arithmetic average' of viewpoints — or dynamic. In the latter case, it must be based upon a political position

> that affords a progressive development of history in such a manner that it will retain as much as possible of the accumulated cultural acquisitions and social energies.[220]

Such a position is not likely to be the middle stratum but that of 'a relatively classless stratum that is not too firmly anchored in the social order' — 'the *socially free-floating intelligentsia*'. This intelligentsia cannot be simply located in social class categories, even though 'our intelligentsia is, to a considerable extent, a *rentier* intelligentsia that lives from industrial loan capital' and contains state officials and members of the liberal professions. But in all these instances, it is the case that they are 'less clearly identified with one class than those strata who directly participate in the economic process'. This is the first criterion of their suitability for performing a synthesis of political viewpoints. Here, there is, of course, an implicit assumption that the degree of political commitment also varies in proportion to the degree of direct participation in the economic process.

The second criterion is 'a unifying sociological bond between intellectual groups, namely education'. This is because

> participation in a common educational heritage tends increasingly to suppress differences of birth, status, occupation and ownership and unites individual educated people on the basis of this education.[221]

Thirdly, this 'modern education' is 'a living struggle, a microcosm of the conflicting purposes and tendencies in the social sphere'. The individual is thus subjected to the opposing tendencies of social life, unlike someone directly participating in the production process who 'tends to take up the world-view of the specific life-circle and act exclusively on the basis of the determination of his specific situation'. Intellectuals are therefore determined in their outlook by both their social background and their education.

As a free-floating intelligentsia, they have two courses of action open to them: either attachment to one of the antagonistic social classes, or 'the *concrete conscious recognition of their own social position* and the mission that emerges out of it'. Though not playing an independent politically-active role, they can none the less seek the position 'out of which a total orientation to events is possible'; they can choose 'to be nightwatchmen in an otherwise all too dark night'. Here, we come across the fourth criterion for intellectuals' role as synthesizers, namely, their ability to choose a position, 'to create a forum outside the party schools that secures the perspective of and interest in the particular totality'.[222]

The political knowledge of the totality gained by the intelligentsia, and — by implication — political science, is a form of situationally determined knowledge that is not secured merely by 'observation' but by 'active participation'. It is, Mannheim argues, a new form of knowledge 'for which *decision and viewpoint* are inseparably bound together' and in which 'one must never separate impulse of the will, evaluation and world-view from the result of thought'.[223] Mannheim is assuming here that only political knowledge is the result of engagement as well as reflection, and not the whole of human knowledge. Ironically, the form of engagement he has in mind is itself the product of the intelligentsia's detachment: the role of the night watchman is, of course, to 'watch', to observe. In other words, his role is to search for a synthesis of 'the one-sidedness' of knowledge derived from particular social positions.

What options are open to the sociology of knowledge in achieving this synthesis? One can argue that its existential boundedness makes any true knowledge and understanding of politics impossible. This is presumably a strictly scientific viewpoint. Secondly, Mannheim suggests that the sociology of knowledge's task could be that of

> disentangling the evaluative, standpoint bounded and impulsive element from every concrete, existing 'knowledge', eliminating it as a source of error and doing so in order to arrive at a 'value-free', 'supra-social', 'supra-historical' realm of 'objectively' valid knowledge.[224]

This is presumably a *positivistic* strategy, not unlike that recommended by Geiger.[225] Mannheim sees it as the strategy employed by Max Weber and 'formal sociology' and it is one which he regards as legitimate for certain spheres of knowledge.

Mannheim himself, however, adopts a third strategy which argues that, although in the case of political knowledge the evaluative element cannot be easily separated from the non-evaluative, there exists a *consensus ex post*. Mannheim's strategy involves a 'decision' in favour of a dynamic synthesis. But his own strategy also contains a strong positivist element since he argues that the advances in the sociological analysis of ideologies will enable us 'to *calculate* more precisely the collectively bounded wills and their corresponding thought and to *predict* approximately the ideological reactions of social strata [italics added, D.F.].'[226]

At no point does Mannheim examine the *ends* to which these predictions and calculations will be put, other than that they will rest upon an ethics of responsibility (*Verantwortungsethik*). Again echoing Weber, Mannheim argues that this kind of knowledge is part of the increasing rationalization of the world in which politics is replaced by administration insofar as the irrational realm — for Mannheim the root of political activity — becomes correspondingly narrower.

Mannheim's search for a synthesis of one-sided, political perspectives can be seen as an extension of his earlier argument for the synthesis of ideologies in the broadest sense. The cultural synthesis has become a political synthesis that mediates class and political conflicts. As such, it is an extension of the search for a synthesis that Mannheim had been postulating ever since his essay on historicism. As Lenk argues, 'thinking through historicism to its ultimate limits also implies, at the same time, thinking through ideologies to their limits'.[227] Hence, one should not regard Mannheim's theory of intellectuals merely as a response to a sociological problem since 'Mannheim's theory of the "free-floating intelligentsia" does not spring from a sociological problematic but a cultural and philosophy of history postulate.'[228] Mannheim assumes that this intelligentsia is distanced from the historical process and that this very distance and its social lack of attachment gives it the best chance of revealing the synthesis of historical, political standpoints.

Mannheim sees the harmonization of conflicting class positions and polarized political ideologies as a possibility even in the later period of the Weimar Republic. Perhaps nowhere more clearly than in the theory of the relatively detached intelligentsia can one see the practical, political intention behind Mannheim's sociology of knowledge as the mediation of political conflict. Within a different context, Lukács, only three years previously, had pointed to this notion of a detached intelligentsia when he argued that

> This belief in being suspended above all class antagonism, all egoistic human interests is the typical standpoint of intellectuals who do not directly participate in the process of production, whose existential basis, both material and intellectual, seems to be the 'whole' society, without class differences.[229]

It is possible to state Mannheim's position more forcefully. In a world in which all ideologies and political positions have been reduced to equal status — rather like the equivalent exchange-value of commodities — and all seem to be competing with one another on an equal basis — as in the notion of a free-market model of society — the liberal response is to search for some commanding position above these ideologies and conflicting parties from which it will be possible to regulate them or, at least, extract from each what is valuable in them. With some exaggeration, one could say that Mannheim's free-floating intelligentsia in late Weimar Germany play a not dissimilar role to Hobbes' Leviathan in a mid-seventeenth-century England that had been disrupted by civil war.[230]

Though Mannheim's free-floating intelligentsia form a necessary part of his contemporary diagnosis of society and his attempt to construct a sociology of the modern world in a period of crisis, the search for a cultural synthesis was a common theme amongst many sections of the intelligentsia in Weimar Germany. As Ringer suggests, the disintegration of German society, and especially the crumbling status of the *Gelehrtenstand*, prompted more urgent searches for cultural syntheses.[231] Perhaps part of the appeal of Mannheim's *Ideologie und Utopie* lay in the forceful manner in which the author drew the political parallel between the need for a cultural synthesis and a period of increasing social and political crisis. That is the context, for example, within which Neusüss comments on Mannheim's political intentions when he suggests that

> In Mannheim, a typical member of that German late-liberal learned world is evident which saw itself hemmed in between the fronts of a situation of rapid social upheaval that it conceived of as a 'cultural crisis' and in danger of being destroyed.
> Mannheim's path of confronting this danger through a 'cultural synthesis' and thereby at the same time of raising himself above the social and political struggle of his time, in fact therefore implied an attempted escape. It finished-up in the fictitious position of a 'free-floating intelligentsia' that, more a wishful image than reality, was to synthesize everything with everything else, whereas in fact it was the expression of social, political and intellectual hopelessness.[232]

Although this may be an accurate judgement of Mannheim's position at this point, the intelligentsia also plays an important role in producing utopias. 'Utopian Consciousness' is the third and final chapter of *Ideologie und Utopie*.

In the only detailed study of Mannheim's notion of utopia, Neusüss argues that its contradictory definitions can only be understood in the light of his meta-theoretical intentions.[233] Mannheim certainly does not provide us with a fixed definition of utopia. It appears as a form of consciousness similar to ideological consciousness, as the revolutionary principle of history and as fictional thought. Mannheim starts out by defining utopian consciousness as one that 'does *not* find itself covered by the "reality" [*Sein*] that surrounds it'. This incongruity arises from the fact that 'such a consciousness is oriented in experience, thought and action towards factors that are unrealized in this "reality" '.[234] Yet this definition is identical with one of the definitions of ideology. However, Mannheim goes on to argue that

> Only those orientations that 'transcend reality' will be referred to by us as utopian which, transformed into action, tend to shatter, partly or wholly, the prevailing order of existence.[235]

To be utopian, consciousness must not merely conceive of states of affairs beyond the status quo but must also be realized. All historical periods have had states of consciousness that transcended their reality but they did not operate as utopias but as ideologies, as

> appropriate ideologies to this stage of existence, as long as they were 'organically' (i.e. without revolutionary effectiveness) integrated into the world-view of the period.[236]

Mannheim himself suggests that what is crucial to such definitions of utopia is the notion of existence or reality which utopias transcend. For Mannheim, this is a reality or existence that is 'concretely valid', 'a *functioning* and, in this sense a *real* determinate social order', one which contains not merely economic and political structures but 'all forms of human interaction'. It is also 'enmeshed by notions that are therefore to be designated as "transcendent of existence," as "unreal" ' because they cannot be lived out in that society. In an illuminating passage, Mannheim states the motive for a sociology of knowledge. He suggests that

> all those ideas which do not fit into the current order of life are 'existentially transcendent' or unreal. Ideas which correspond to the concretely existing and *de facto* functioning present order of existence, we term 'adequate', existentially congruent ideas. They are relatively rare and only a *consciousness fully clarified by sociology* [italics added, D.F.] [*soziologisch völlig geklärtes Bewusstsein*] operates through existentially congruent ideas and motives.[237]

Once more, Mannheim points to the sociology of knowledge's role as ensuring that consciousness is congruent with *present* existence. This is why a diagnosis of the present time is so significant. In both ideologies and utopias, the present is precisely what is absent.

Though utopias are also existentially transcendent, they are not ideologies 'insofar and to the extent that they succeed through counter-activity in transforming the existing historical existential reality in the direction of their own notion.'[238]

What is ideological and what is utopian depends upon 'at what stage of *existential reality* one applies the standard'. This, in turn, implies that the standard is determined by the human subject's position and perspective. For instance, 'the representatives of a specific existential reality will term utopian all those notions that *from their point of view* can, in principle, never be realized.'[239] They will conceive of them as '*absolutely utopian*'. In contrast, Mannheim argues that he will speak of a 'merely relative utopia, i.e., one that seems to be unrealizable only from the point of view of an existent stage' of history. Even here, however, the notion of utopia, like all other historical concepts, depends upon the perspective of the person using the term. But once more Mannheim is in search of the 'correct' concept of utopia — the one 'most adequate to our stage of thought'. This can only be in relation to the present existing social order. Therefore, as Mannheim himself argues, '*the utopias of today can become the realities of tomorrow*' and, presumably, the ideologies of the day after tomorrow.

The other implication of this 'historical' notion of ideologies and utopias ('historical' in that they are judged in terms of an absent present) is that dominant groups will determine what is utopian, and ascendant groups what is ideological. Despite these difficulties, however, when we look into the past we can see an unambiguous criterion for both forms of consciousness: 'The criterion for ideology and utopia is *realization*'.[240] It hardly need be pointed out here that this is an *ex post* criterion, which makes it impossible to recognize what is utopian *in the present*. Thus, when Mannheim proceeds to argue that what is utopian are 'all those existentially transcendent notions (hence not merely wish-projections) that in any way have a transforming effect upon historical-social existence',[241] we cannot know *whether* they will have a 'transforming effect' until that effect has been realized.

In the examination of utopias, what interests Mannheim specifically is 'the concrete analysis of the historical-social position from which they arose: from the structural situation of that stratum which at any time espouses them'.[242] Historically, utopias change their form in response to changing social circumstances and the 'constantly shifting total constellation'. So far, the analysis would be concerned with the 'socially bounded form of utopia' at a particular time. It is also possible, however, to investigate 'the problem of a transformation of "utopian *consciousness*" ', but

> only when the utopian element . . . tends to be completely infused into every aspect of the dominant consciousness of the time, when the form of experience, the form of action and mode of observation (perspective) are organized in accord with this utopian element, can one speak *fundamento in re* not only of diverse forms of utopia but, at the same time, also of diverse forms and levels of utopian consciousness.[243]

His notion of 'utopian consciousness' presumably corresponds here with the total conception of ideology, at least with regard to its comprehensiveness.

Mannheim, in fact, proceeds to develop four historical ideal types of utopian consciousness: the orgiastic chiliasm of the Anabaptists, the liberal humanitarian idea, the conservative idea and the socialist-communist utopia. From the examples Mannheim provides, it is obvious that he proceeds only with an immanent analysis of the concept of utopia. Each utopia can potentially be played off against the others. As with the instances of political ideologies, it is difficult to see any criterion for evaluating them. They are not related to substantive historical changes but are instead interpreted merely in terms of their immanent changes in form.

Mannheim concludes this chapter, as he did the first two, with an analysis of the contemporary situation with regard to utopian consciousness. Utopias in the modern world become 'guiding perspectives', 'heuristic principles' and 'possible points of view'. The disappearance of utopias is accompanied by the disappearance of a total perspective, which is now confined to the political left (Lukács) and right (Spann) — the only groups who still believe in a totality of historical development. Others, like Troeltsch, retain it as a working hypothesis or, like Alfred Weber, retain it as a *Gestalt*. In the middle are those like Max Weber who search for 'eternally valid structures of types'. In the modern period, with the disappearance of utopias, we experience the 'homogenization of events in which every fact loses its particular temporal index and its local colour' and 'all those elements of thought and perspective rooted in utopias are now relativized sceptically as ideologies.'[244]

This disappearance of reality transcendence — both ideological and utopian — has taken other forms. In a somewhat obscure passage, Mannheim seems to suggest that Marxism both reduced the intellectual sphere to the social-economic situation whilst at the same time was 'materialist only in name', since this economic sphere was 'a structural context of mental attitudes'. But this process of undermining the intellectual sphere was extended to its relativization, to an 'eternal human substratum of *drives*' by writers like Freud and Pareto. This 'process of the complete destruction of all spiritual elements' has also permeated the arts, sexual relations and sport as well as the political sphere, where politics has been reduced to economics, to the point at which 'all ideas have been discredited, all utopias destroyed.[245]

Faced with this pervasive reified and ahistorical *Sachlichkeit*, Mannheim asks whether all that we can hope for is the maintenance of 'integrity' (*Echtheit*) or genuineness in the ethical sphere. This was certainly an important category in his unpublished writings, but now Mannheim implies that it, too, has fallen prey to modern *Sachlichkeit*. He further suggests that there are, in fact, only two possible ways out of 'the contemporary lack of tension' between the existent and the transcendent. The first is socialism and communism, which retain 'at least one form of utopia'. If there is a peaceful evolution towards 'a later, more complete form of industrialism' then Mannheim suggests that the subordinate strata will also undergo the same kind of transformation that he has just outlined. If it can be achieved only through revolution, then the utopian and ideological elements will flare up anew. The 'fate of reality-transcendence' therefore rests, in part, upon this form of social opposition.

The second possibility for the maintenance of utopias and the intellectual sphere lies with 'a distinctive social-intellectual middle stratum'. This 'narrow stratum' (*Dünnschicht*) is smaller than the intelligentsia as a whole and comprises those critical elements within the intelligentsia — its 'free-floating intellectuality' — who remain out of accord with the existing situation. As a stratum, it is faced with four alternatives. The first is affiliation with 'the radical wing of the socialist–communist proletariat'. Mannheim suggests, however, that they live in 'an aproblematical situation.' For them, there still exists no conflict between intellectual and social allegiance. The second option (Max Weber, Pareto), having discarded utopias, 'becomes sceptical and, in the name of integrity, proceeds . . . to destroy ideology in science.' The third alternative is a retreat into the past. The fourth and final alternative shuts itself off from the historical process and returns to the 'ecstatic'.

Mannheim does not predict which of these alternatives will come to dominate the future, since 'because we are human beings and not things' much depends on our will.

> what one here opts for lies ultimately with each individual. What has been presented so far can only contribute towards helping them to see the significance of their option.[246]

In the last resort, therefore, all Mannheim's emphasis upon 'existential boundedness' falls away and one is left with the decisions of the individual will. As a final comment, Mannheim suggests that it is possible to conceive, in principle, of a world that is 'absolutely lacking in ideology and utopia'. But 'the most fundamental distinction between the two forms of transcendence of reality' would become apparent since

> Whereas the disappearance of the ideological represents a crisis only for specific strata and the objectivity (*Sachlichkeit*) that emerges from the unmasking of ideologies always implies self-clarification for the totality, the complete disappearance of the utopian would transform the structure of the whole of human nature. The disappearance of utopia brings about a static *Sachlichkeit* in which man himself becomes a thing (*Sache*).[247]

In such a state of affairs, the individual, 'with the relinquishing of diverse forms of utopia, loses the will to make history and thereby a vision of it'. Here, Mannheim makes explicit his belief that utopias supply the dynamic to history just as he argued earlier that competition and generational changes were the co-determinants of changes in forms of knowledge.

Yet it is also apparent that utopias are of a different order to competition and generations in Mannheim's metaphysics of history, since his analysis of utopias is orientated towards a dichotomous model of society insofar as utopias emerge from below and ideologies are seen to operate in the other direction. This contrasts with his more pluralistic model of society both in the essay on competition and in earlier chapters of *Ideologie und Utopie*. Similarly, the sociological concept of ideology employed in the earlier chapters is characterized by a closed partial standpoint that can be overcome through cultural synthesis. The concept of utopia, on the other hand, is ultimately to be located not in a sociological context — though Mannheim attempts this, somewhat unsuccessfully, in his analysis of historical examples of utopias — but within the context of an ontology of human history. Utopia, here, is to be seen at the end of the chapter as a kind of voluntaristic moment of human consciousness that is enlightened and dynamic.

However, if we accept this as being the case, then it is difficult to see what, precisely, is the role of the sociology of knowledge with regard to utopian consciousness. One role, of course, is the examination of the social foundations of historical utopias. But, with regard to Mannheim's ontological notion of utopia and in relation to his philosophy of history, the sociology of knowledge would appear to be robbed of its crucial role, for example, as synthesizer of perspectives. It can only point to the significance of utopia as the dynamic of history. The diagnosis of the present crisis then appears without any resolution — except the hope that utopian consciousness will be preserved in the future.

These kinds of ambiguities in the notion of utopia, however, form part of the wider context of the divergent conceptions of both ideology and utopia which Neusüss has usefully outlined. He argues that it is possible to distinguish in *Ideologie und Utopie* the following concepts of ideology and utopia:

1. *A general, total and value-free concept of ideology*. This concept concerns the existence of the 'existential boundedness' of all thought and knowledge. It is an uncritical concept that says nothing concerning the truth or falsity of thought.
2. *A general, total and evaluative concept of ideology*. Describes 'false consciousness in the sense of an "ingenuineness" [*Unechtheit*] that is grounded in a philosophy of history'.
   This concept, too, does not distinguish between ideology and utopia.
3. *A concept of reality incongruence or existentially inadequate consciousness*. This can also refer to both ideology and utopia.

3a *A pragmatic concept of ideology*. Refers to consciousness which 'hides social and political reality in favour of dominant interests'.
3b *A particular concept of ideology*. Refers to specific contents of thought.
3c *A total and special concept of ideology*. Refers to 'the total consciousness of a dominant strata' (*cant-consciousness*)
4 *A utopian consciousness*. A consciousness that 'transcends' existence and leaps out of reality.
4a *A revolutionary utopia*. The consciousness of subordinate strata and hence the complement to ideology as defined in 3b and 3c.
4b *A potential utopia*. Refers to ideologies that can become utopian.
4c *A dynamic concept of utopia*. The dynamic element of all human thought.
4d *A utopia that is adequate and immanent to existence*. The 'dynamic synthesis of existentially inadequate utopias', in fact, the sociology of knowledge itself.[248]

As Neusüss argues, such a diversity in the usage of the two concepts casts considerable doubt upon their fruitfulness for empirical sociological analysis, which is at least *one* of the intentions behind Mannheim's sociology of knowledge. Not only is the sociological dimension of the concepts fused with their ontological, philosophy-of-history dimension, but they change their significance and meaning in the course of *Ideologie und Utopie*. Their 'congruence, adequacy and transcendence' in relation to social and historical reality or existence also raises the question as to the nature of the reality against which consciousness is judged.

Furthermore, Neusüss is correct to point out that at least one of the concepts of utopia (4d) in fact denotes the sociology of knowledge itself. Its function as the synthesizer of inadequate utopias would suggest that, within the sociological dimension, it is a 'scientific' utopia and, within the philosophy of history and also ontologically, it is the form of consciousness most adequate to contemporary reality. But, once more, as Neusüss suggests, we are confronted with

> the core of the ontological problems of the sociology of knowledge . . . : can 'reality' [*Sein*] as such in terms of itself be 'adequate'? or, taken still further: Does not the adequacy of 'reality' [*Sein*] to itself not lie in precisely its being inadequate to itself, insofar as it constantly transcends itself?[249]

The sociology of knowledge and its consciousness is itself a part of that reality or existence against which consciousness is judged to be adequate. Adequacy, for Mannheim, *must* also include the possibility of transcendence.

Whereas many later commentators have identified the central problem of the sociology of knowledge at the epistemological level — as the relativist problematic — it would seem more reasonable to argue that it lies further back, in Mannheim's case, in its basic ontological presuppositions. Mannheim is not merely advancing a sociology of knowledge that possesses a sociological dimension but behind it, and often fused with it, are a series of meta-theoretical presuppositions grounded in a questionable philosophy of history and ontology.

V

In 1930, within a year of the publication of *Ideologie und Utopie*, Mannheim succeeded to Oppenheimer's chair of sociology and economics at Frankfurt University. Though Mannheim was still working on the sociology of knowledge until 1933, and had in hand a number of projects, little was published directly in this area.[250] Two brief pieces that did appear in this period are worthy of some discussion. The first is the contribution to Vierkandt's *Handwörterbuch der Soziologie* published in 1931.[251] The second is Mannheim's lecture on the contemporary tasks of sociology published in 1932.[252] Both illustrate the extent to which Mannheim by now regarded the sociology of knowledge as an established tradition within sociology, with its own distinctive history of development, and having achieved encyclopaedic if not textbook status. But in so doing, it lost its problematic status, its relationship to a diagnosis of the times and that sense of urgency which is apparent in *Ideologie und Utopie*.

In his article 'Wissenssoziologie', Mannheim views the sociology of knowledge as pursuing two aims: as a theory, it develops 'a doctrine of the so-called "existential boundedness" of knowledge' and as 'historical-sociological research' it traces the different forms which this 'existential boundedness' has taken in the past and the present. As a discipline that emerged with the 'contemporary intellectual crisis situation', it has sought to take as one of its central themes 'the social boundedness of theories and modes of thought', which requires 'an unreserved, radical thinking through to its limits of this problem' in order to arrive at 'a theory appropriate to the present situation'.

The sociology of knowledge, as a discipline, is closely related to the theory of ideology whose task has been 'to unmask the more or less conscious lies and disguises of human interest groups and especially of political parties'. The sociology of knowledge is not so much concerned with deliberate lies but with the way in which phenomena reveal themselves 'in a necessary manner' according to the social standpoint of the observer.

> Thus, it is not the intention to disguise that determines in all these instances the 'one-sidedness' and 'falseness' of statements, but the unavoidably diverse forms of structures of consciousness of diversely situated types of human subject in the historical-social sphere.[253]

The sociology of knowledge is aimed at achieving a total conception of ideology that does not raise the 'accusation of deception' (*Lügenverdacht*). Hence, in the sociology of knowledge, not only is the word 'ideology' 'no longer pejorative', but it will be increasingly replaced by the notion of 'an "existentially bounded — or standpoint-bounded — perspectival structure (*Aspektstruktur*)" of a thinker'.[254] We see here how quickly Mannheim distanced himself from the discussion of ideology in *Ideologie und Utopie* or, at least, how soon he moved over to a 'value-free' concept of ideology.

What is also new in this account of the role of the sociology of knowledge is Mannheim's more explicit concern for its relationship to epistemology. In particular, he takes up the phenomenon of the 'particularization' of thought where we are dealing with an instance in which

> a pure determination of a fact (the fact of the partiality (*Partikularität*) of a perspective that is confirmable in human assertions) may be relevant to its meaning (*Sinnrelevant*), *a genesis that may be relevant to the genesis of its meaning* and therefore at least makes the further construction of the sphere of validity as autonomous from its genesis very difficult.[255]

Unfortunately, Mannheim argues, the present dominant epistemology does not allow this to be taken into account since it would challenge its primacy over individual disciplines. But epistemology itself, though it is 'the fundamental science (*Grundwissenschaft*) of individual sciences (*Einzelwissenschaften*)' is itself '*based upon the state of existing cognitive situations*', upon a 'historically and socially pre-given substratum'. There is a further instance of the inversion of the supremacy of epistemology over individual disciplines in the development of knowledge itself, since

> New forms of knowledge emerge, ultimately, out of collective life-contexts and do not first emerge after a science of principles has demonstrated their possibility; hence they do not need to be first legitimated by an epistemology.[256]

Mannheim here anticipates some elements of Kuhn's argument concerning the development of scientific knowledge in that he argues that revolutions in epistemology succeed revolutions in science and not vice versa and, in that, he sees epistemology as a mode of legitimation of the existing state of science.

Yet, Mannheim views natural science as largely detached from 'the historical-social perspectival structure of the knowing subject', whereas in the case of historical knowledge its notion of truth is dependent upon what 'is realized' in a particular period. But the absence of any further discussion of the notion of historical period at this point leaves Mannheim with a thorough-going historicist stance in relation to truth. For him, the central problem in the historical and social sciences is that of their objectivity. In the case of 'existentially bounded thought', objectivity is only attainable 'by indirect means' in those instances where observers do not share the same perspective. It is attained through seeking out 'a formula for the conversion and translation of these diverse perspectival viewpoints with each other'.[257] The criterion here is the comprehensiveness of the various standpoints. A second possibility lies in the very recognition of the existential boundedness of thought and the neutralization of its partiality so that one can move to a higher level of abstraction. Mannheim suggests that this approach is pursued by formal sociology, which produces general categories through the 'neutralization' and 'formalization' of particular facts, but its weakness is that it is likely to overlook the qualitative contents and meanings of particular phenomena. In the end, Mannheim does not come down in favour of either approach to what he considers to be objectivity in the social sciences.

At the level of concrete analyses in the sociology of knowledge, Mannheim argues that the central methodological approach is not dissimilar from 'the methods of art history as the history of style'. In particular, the 'imputation of meaning' (*sinngemässe Zurechnung*) and the 'imputation of facticity' (*Faktizitätszurechnung*) are central to its approach. The first form of imputation constructs unities of styles of thought and perspectival structures by tracing the various elements back to a 'focal world-view and sense of life' (*Lebensgefühl*). These ideal types are then examined in relation to their actual appearance in society, i.e., to the composition of the groups and strata which expressed them. Mannheim's notion of imputation does not, therefore, proceed to a notion of 'objective possibility' but merely renders imputation a heuristic device that will produce valuable hypotheses for empirical research.

In the essay under consideration we can detect Mannheim's increasing distance from the problem of ideology and a firmer orientation towards an empirically orientated sociology of knowledge. At the same time, however, he retains an interest in the epistemological problems raised by his sociology of knowledge, though, as with his account in *Ideologie und Utopie*, he remains as far as ever from any solution to them. Possible solutions are still presented as tentative suggestions. In his later works, neither the problem of ideology nor the epistemological problems were substantially developed any further.

Die Gegenwartsaufgaben der Soziologie (The Contemporary Tasks of Sociology) is not specifically concerned with the sociology of knowledge but it does serve to highlight its role within sociology as a whole. Sociology itself, Mannheim says, 'can confront us in a dual form and function: as a particular discipline and as a foundational science [*Grundwissenschaft*].'[258] As a particular discipline (*Spezialwissenschaft*), sociology has its own thematic and methodology: 'the intellectual strategy that was applied in the conflict concerning sociology from Simmel to von Wiese was to legitimate our discipline as an individual discipline'. Since then, however, we have moved towards the total problematic of the *globus intellectualis* and our viewpoint has been extended towards sociology as a universalistic science. Mannheim argues that there are three basic constellations of sociology — as a special science (general sociology), as the sociology of individual disciplines (e.g., politics) and as the study of the social character of culture and its development.

Amongst the sociologies of individual disciplines, Mannheim singles out the sociology of knowledge, which, according to him, has two areas of research: the theory of ideology and the sociology of knowledge. As a theory of ideology it is concerned with all 'conscious and unconscious lies and illusory interpretations', since

> the everyday interpretation of the world is full of concepts, intellectual schema and myths that are either still so primitive that they can really only be understood as the rudiments of magical — mythical consciousness, or as conscious, ready-to-hand deceptive tales that can be interpreted as the suppression of an appropriate social orientation.[259]

In order to counter such illusions, sociology must have 'a critical and rational consciousness' and 'knowledge of social forces'. The study of ideology should achieve not the destruction but the 'exposure of reality, of real phenomena that surround us'. It is therefore an illusion to maintain that ideologies only exist within the political sphere. Rather they permeate 'the whole of our everyday reality'. Hence,

> In this sense, the purification of the basic concepts and erroneous interpretation of the everyday world, a revelation of the forces and interests that socially determine history, is an absolutely essential pedagogic mission of sociology and particularly of that branch which we have termed the theory of ideology.[260]

At a deeper level, this 'self-revision of thought' takes place through the sociology of knowledge in the more restricted sense of the term, which seeks,

> over and above the conscious and semi-conscious deceptions of the everyday world and party interests, to examine that constitutive false approach of thought which is evident in the sciences themselves . . . Its task therefore lies in the elimination of all those masks that emerge out of particular outlooks, out of particular outlooks which originate in the natural limitation and confinement of individual sciences, of spheres of life and historical situations.[261]

Our intellectual apparatus does not reveal every side, or the whole contents, of the world but overlooks certain perspectives and so masks the total situation. It is therefore sociology's task to reveal false perspectives not merely in everyday thought but also in other disciplines through its capacity to show 'from which social standpoint' different theories emerge.

The third sociological domain is that of the 'study of the total context of social-intellectual phenomena' and is concerned with 'the totality of cultural spheres in relation to social life'. Here culture is interpreted either as 'an *expression* of life' or as 'a *causal* or *mutual interactional* relationship' that exists between society and cultural spheres, or finally, as a '*dialectical* development' of the two. In this context of the sociology of culture, Mannheim — unlike in his earlier writings or in Scheler's major work — does not view the sociology of knowledge as part of this sphere of sociology.

When Mannheim turns to the principles governing the choice of subject-matter for sociology, he also sees the sociology of knowledge playing a significant role, especially in relation to the examination of values. Sociology itself should not espouse a political position since 'it would be the death of sociology if it became merely an instrument of agitation for one or several parties'. On the other hand, sociology should not shy away from examining 'the political and social themes of life' which should be examined within a value-free context.

> The very fruitful confrontation over the value-freedom of the social sciences has . . . shown the way in which politics can be taught without the suggestion of judgement and evaluation. And if too, in this context, the sociology of knowledge has pointed to some difficulties that remain with the complete abstention from evaluation, and that even with complete 'freedom from evaluation', a certain amount of standpoint-boundedness remains in this notion, then it did so precisely in the interests of a still more thorough-going self-control and objectivity but not in order to leave the door wide open to every possibility.[262]

The sociology of knowledge is here seen as functioning 'in the service of self-criticism and the distancing of existential boundedness'. On the other hand, Mannheim also insists that sociology emerged as an 'oppositional science' (*Oppositionswissenschaft*) and 'is born in conflict with the diverse, collectively pre-given attitudes to society'. As an attempt to group the various currents in society,

> 'sociology is the appropriate orientation to life by people in an industrial society . . . whether this society is organized on a capitalist or socialist basis.'[263]

Sociology provides an understanding of the total constellations out of which individual life situations can become intelligible. In this respect, therefore, what Mannheim earlier argued was a central feature of the sociology of knowledge has now become a task of sociology itself: namely, 'a deeper self-understanding and . . . an enlarged understanding of the world'. Indeed the tasks of the sociology of knowledge have become the tasks of sociology itself.

5 The Contemporary Controversy Surrounding the Sociology of Knowledge

I

An examination of the controversy surrounding the sociology of knowledge in Weimar Germany implies not merely an extension of the discussion of the tradition behind it but also, in a sense, a summary of the issues it raised. The various debates also illustrate the extent to which the sociology of knowledge questioned and sometimes challenged the foundations of sociology itself. Many contemporaries were in no doubt that this branch of sociology raised issues that lay at the very roots of the social sciences themselves.

There were three 'debates' surrounding the sociology of knowledge within this period as well as an earlier intervention by Max Scheler in the so-called *Wissenschaftsstreit* concerned with Max Weber's 'Wissenschaft als Beruf' lecture of 1919.[1] Scheler's paper 'Science and Social Structure' was the subject of debate at the Fourth German Sociological Congress of 1924.[2] A more heated controversy arose over Karl Mannheim's paper on competition at the Sixth German Sociological Congress, in 1928.[3] Finally, the range of the reception of Mannheim's *Ideologie und Utopie* testifies not just to the interest in the sociology of knowledge but also to the significance of Mannheim's work for the social sciences and philosophy. It was not merely that the sociology of knowledge, as Schelting puts it, 'today undoubtedly stands in the foreground of sociological cognitive interests',[4] but it was also treated seriously within several philosophical traditions. It is to these 'debates' that we now turn our attention.

The intervention of the sociology of knowledge in the methodological debates surrounding the social sciences commenced with Scheler's contribution to the *Wissenschaftsstreit*. The debate that succeeded Weber's 'Science as a Vocation' lecture of 1919 has been located within the context of the heightened tension between the belief in an autonomous, timeless reason and a 'unique' historical life that resulted from the experience of the World War.[5] However, this very emphasis upon the uniqueness and specificity of the historical world had already been stated by Dilthey, Windelband and others long before the war. Wittenberg suggests that the experience of the war, of a 'unique' historical event without any foundation in previous experience produced a profound shock to the belief in universal reason. In particular, he argues that this was felt specifically by the younger generation,

> for they found themselves at the end of the world war at the graveyard of their hopes; never before had a generation of youth experienced such a distinctive destruction of all values, sciences and arts; never before was the distance so great and unbridgable between the credulous hope with which the youth went onto the battlefield and the hard and cold reality.[6]

Kracauer too points to the 'hatred of science' felt by 'the best part of present-day academic youth'[7] as a result of science's apparent barrenness and inability to grasp basic experiences. In the human sciences, this constituted a reaction to conceptual formalism and the naïve collection of facts, to a relativism that arises out of and induces a profound scepticism.

Against this background, Wittenberg terms Weber's 'Science as a Vocation' 'a last high-point of a rational foundation' that recognizes the 'disenchantment of the world', whilst firmly asserting the objectivity of science and the goal of scientific progress against a notion of science as achieving the 'absolute' or 'true being'. Instead, the world of thought in the form of academic disciplines and the world of action are to be strictly separated and science is necessarily to be excluded from producing the ideals of life. Similarly, Weber 'requires of the politician exactly the same qualities' as those of the scientist: 'Politics is made with the head but not with other parts of the body and the soul'. The politician, too, should be concerned with the truth and factual objectivity by means of a systematic, unpartisan testing of facts. Both activities are to be based on purposive, rational action.

More specifically, Weber seeks to establish the separation of science and politics, personality and objects, and science and religion. Above all, he insists upon the separation of facts and standards, and science and world-views. From the standpoint of science, all value-decisions are relative and cannot be rationally grounded. It is here that the sociology of knowledge takes up Weber's position on science and politics from a number of directions. Both Scheler and Mannheim recognize the need for value-free science. Both apparently take up the social relativity of world-views but Scheler seeks to maintain essential values from social determination. Indeed, where Scheler explicitly concerns himself with Weber's central argument important differences emerge.

Scheler, like Weber, emphasizes the growing intellectualization, specialization and bureaucratization in the way that modern science is organized. But whereas Weber sees this as an unavoidable fate, Scheler sees 'in these symptoms evidence of a crisis of western culture that can no longer rest solely upon a scientific basis.'[8]

Scheler insists upon the existence of three forms of knowledge — salvational, educational and knowledge for domination — that exist in all periods including the present.

> Thus, according to Scheler's interpretation, Weber's concept of science encompasses only the small and restricted zone of purposive knowledge, but in no way provides a true picture of the reality of the situation of science in the past and the present.[9]

Indeed, in his sociology of knowledge, Scheler no longer holds knowledge of reality to be possible merely on the basis of science as such, since it too — as one form of knowledge amongst others — is also socially determined. Scheler departs even further from Weber here, since the 'human existence' that 'directs' this knowledge is not merely social but also psycho-biological.

At the practical level, Scheler insists upon the separation of research and vocational study and maintains that the gulf between the two is unbridgeable. His solution is to call for the foundation of *Bildungsakademien* in which the major synthesizers of knowledge will be the teachers. In contrast, *Volkshochschulen* will be reserved for the non-academic majority. Wittenberg summarizes the theoretical and practical consequences of Scheler's position as follows:

> with the triple division of all knowledge, Scheler breaks with the central claim of German idealism of the possibility, meaningfulness and value of a *single*, genuine knowledge. Scheler's doctrine of the sociological determination of all knowledge likewise arrives at the pronouncement of the end of science as such. Scheler's degradation of universities into pure technical schools would reduce academics to technicians, make science into a means of production and place the whole of knowledge in the service of external progress.[10]

What Wittenberg fails to grasp with regard to the last consequence of Scheler's position is that Scheler is unwittingly referring to changes that have taken place in higher education to which other writers such as Veblen had already referred.[11] 'Despite this, Wittenberg does indicate the extent to which Scheler's sociology of knowledge directly takes up key aspects of Weber's position in 'Science as a Vocation'.

Scheler's reduction of science to knowledge for domination, in one respect, has the same result as a positivist reduction of science to technique in which, as Habermas argues,

> The social potential of science is reduced to the powers of technical control — its potential for enlightened action is no longer considered. The empirical, analytical sciences produce technical recommendations, but they furnish no answers to practical questions.[12]

That is, the critical dimension of science is ignored. This further distances Scheler from Weber, who at least argues that the function of science is 'to render problematic what is given as conventionally self-evident'. In Weber's case, however, the separation of the 'completely *heterogeneous* problems' of securing facts and grounding normative judgements, together with the absence of a critique of ideology, makes it difficult for him to attain this goal.[13]

For Scheler, the problems are quite different, though he too accepts the plurality of values in 'relatively natural world-views', as well as the principle of value-freedom for the sociology of knowledge. In his earlier work, and especially in *Der Formalismus in der Ethik und die materiale Wertethik*, Scheler sought to show how values constituted the 'practical world'. Furthermore, as Bracht has shown, Scheler also sought to secure an objective order of values.[14] Since the human

> drive *is* value-determined, he *asserted* a . . . convergence between the human structure of drives and the objective order of values. The values which direct the drive, are objective even when they are in fact only found in human beings.[15]

But the values directing the drives are relative too. The values of life are also 'relative', and can only be 'objective' if they are grounded in higher values. There exists, then, for Scheler — in his ethics at least — a distinction between absolute intellectual values and relative values. The relevance of this for Scheler's sociology of knowledge is that the concept of value is the source of the separation of 'real' and 'cultural' sociology. Again, to cite Bracht,

> The separation between mind and reality, culture and nature, ideal factor and real factor, group spirit and group soul, value and drive in sociology are the result of the difference between relative and absolute values, that Scheler merely . . . juxtaposes with one another as immediated facts.[16]

That is, the concepts of value and value orders are transposed from his earlier ethics into the historical dimension of his sociology of knowledge.

But the sociology of knowledge is to deal with the plurality of values and world-views and the changes in corresponding forms of knowledge. The problem then becomes one of realizing these values since

> Scheler makes his concept of value into the interpretative model for historical change as such. The insoluble problem that thereby emerges is the problem of the realization of *diverse* types of value by means of an *identical* subject, whether it is the group or the individual; for the types of value contradict one another.[17]

As we have already seen, Scheler's sociology of knowledge rests upon his philosophical anthropology and metaphysics. The resolution of the problem of value, if indeed it can be resolved in the manner in which Scheler formulates it, cannot be found in his sociology of knowledge but in a metaphysics that ultimately secures the objectivity of values by positing the possibility of God as an *ens realissimum*. It is a symptom of a 'thorough eclectic' who, as Kracauer argued, can combine Catholicism and relativism.[18]

II

A significant feature of the debate surrounding Scheler's paper 'Science and Social Structure' at the Fourth Sociological Congress in 1924 is that it is the only occasion upon which a sociological standpoint (Scheler's) is confronted explicitly with a Marxist one (Adler's).[19] One might have expected greater public debate within the sociological tradition between supporters of both positions, especially in such an area as the sociology of knowledge where the disagreement seems so explicit. Less surprising is the fact that the 1924 confrontation was hardly productive in terms of the development of the sociology of knowledge. Scheler's discussion of science was taken up in his own later writings, expecially in *Die Wissensformen und die Gesellschaft*, but only Dunkmann's article 'Die soziologische Begründung der Wissenschaft' (1927) can in any way be traced back to this discussion. Much of Adler's reply to Scheler hardly addresses the issue of the relationship between science and social structure, though it does provide a clue to his own version of a sociology of knowledge. Yet Adler's approach was scarcely taken in at all within the German tradition. The subsequent major controversies surrounding the sociology of knowledge centred around Mannheim's work.

Adler's central argument against Scheler's paper was framed around whether it formed a contribution to sociology at all. Adler suggested that Scheler commenced with an 'intellectual-historical' approach that confused the intellectual-historical and social determination of thought. A sociological interpretation of forms of thought should commence when the 'whole intellectual historical process is investigated in terms of its social dependency and beyond its inner psychological and ideological determination.'[20] But it is the psychological dimension that most concerns Scheler. When Scheler's analysis moves on to his theory of drives (*Trieblehre*), Adler suggests that he can see

> neither a phenomenological nor a sociological advantage and [indeed believes that], wherever intellectual problems are traced back to a drive, a methodological error is present since, in so doing, an actual ideological problem is reduced to a biological one. The drive is always to some extent biological and we can never come from biology to sociology. In any case, these drives display, for Scheler, a very remarkable diversity such that one is inclined to believe that they are not genuine drives at all but rather are arbitrary characterizations of diverse currents of intellectual life.[21]

Adler suggests, in fact, that this theory of drives is a substitute for Marx's analysis of the material base, arguing that Scheler's confrontation with Marxism is misplaced. He both criticizes Scheler's position and, in much of the remainder of his reply, proceeds to outline his own, Marxist standpoint.

Adler accuses Scheler of a false notion of Marxism in that, 'like so many other opponents of Marxism, he believes that the materialist interpretation of history brings the whole of intellectual life and ideology into a one-sided causal dependency upon something non-intellectual, upon the so-called material relations of economic life so that, according to this interpretation, the intellectual sphere is directly derived from the economic'.[22] In contrast, Adler argues that Marxism is not primarily materialist in the single sense of material determination but is concerned with intellectual relations within material relations in that,

> economic relations are not something factual that confronts human beings as alien but rather they are their own, that is, *also intellectual* relations, their work and interaction relations under which they live. In this manner, Marxism represents social life as a system of *continuous intellectual activity*.[23]

Marxism, Adler argues, does not maintain a dualism of economy and ideology in which the former is alien to the intellect but rather asserts that 'the economic relations are themselves already intellectual relations'. This version of Marxism, although it is an implicit critique of the parody of Marxism in German sociology, can only be understood in the light of Adler's neo-Kantian Marxism, which he sees as providing the basis for a sociology of knowledge.

Adler argues that there are two senses in which one can speak of a sociology of knowledge (*Wissen*) and cognition (*Erkenntnis*). There is a sociology of knowledge that is concerned with the manner in which 'historically given knowledge is determined by the social structure of the group in which it arises'. In a very different sense, one can speak of a sociology of knowledge concerned with the fact that 'prior to all historically determined development of intellectual life, this life consists, in its very nature, entirely of socialized nature'. In the light of these two senses of a sociology of knowledge, Adler maintains that the former embodies 'merely a historical sociology whereas this latter provides the foundation for sociology'. Thus, he raises here the dual claims for a sociology of knowledge that have stood at the centre of the controversy which surrounds it: namely, the conception of the sociology of knowledge as a branch of the sociology of culture, or historical sociology, and a conception which sees it as a foundational discipline, (*Begründungswissenschaft*). This latter project is concerned with the fact that

> the cognitive process itself, although it takes place only within the individual, is nonetheless, in accordance with its transcendental preconditioning, thoroughly social and socialized. I have termed this cognitive-critical character the *transcendental-social aspect of experience* and shown that, as

a social apriori, it still also belongs to the forms of all experience in the same way as do space, time and categories.[24]

This version of a sociology of knowledge is developed elsewhere by Adler, not only in his early work *Kausalität und Teleologie im Streite um die Wissenschaft* but in his contemporary writings such as *Kant und der Marxismus* and his essay 'Soziologie und Erkenntniskritik'.[25] As a version of neo-Kantian Marxism, it was the subject of considerable criticism, for example, by Siegfried Marck[26] and Herbert Marcuse.[27] As such, it represents a Kantian foundation not just for Marxism but also for sociology with its 'concept of the transcendental social formation of the individual consciousness. With Kant and Marx, says Adler, 'we are erecting the structure of modern critical sociology'.[28] This critical sociology also appears to be one that is firmly rooted in German sociology. Adler concurs fully with Max Weber's insistence upon the 'value-freedom of all objective science. . . . Marxism, too, stands decisively on the basis of value-free science' and is not based upon 'arbitrarily or unconsciously presupposed evaluation.'[29]

However, when Adler addresses himself to the role of science he locates his remarks within the context of the first version of the sociology of knowledge, that concerned with the social determinants of modes of thought. Adler argues that there are two currents of science in the present period, which can be characterized as static and evolutionary or bourgeois and proletarian. Both 'are determined in the final instance, even though largely unconsciously, by class interests'.[30] He attempts to counter the hostility to his remarks at this point with an argument on the unitary nature of science. He claims that

> there are no Marxists who would consider asserting that scientific truth is one thing for the proletariat and another for the bourgeoisie but rather only that each class takes something different to be the truth. There exists only a single science but there are results of that science which do not possess the same significance and the same acceptability for everyone.[31]

Similarly, Adler rejects the dualism of the natural and social sciences most strongly asserted in neo-Kantian circles, since

> the social sciences too can only be constructed on the same epistemological and logical foundations as natural science, namely on the basis of a law-like conformity of *being* and causality. Social science, too, is a causal science of existence [*Seinswissenschaft*] and not a normative science of ends [*Zweckwissenschaft*]. Nonetheless, the distinction between natural and social science emerges in the type of existence and causality that exists in the sphere of social phenomena.[32]

Whereas nature stands estranged from man and quite outside man's 'socialized and goal-directed strivings', society consist precisely of the latter. Unfortunately, Adler does not develop this standpoint further in his reply but merely expands slightly upon his distinction between a static and an evolutionary science. The former remains 'confined to within bourgeois society' as a naturally-given milieu, the latter is able to go beyond it — though no satisfactory account of why this should be so is provided.

Even from our brief summary of Adler's reply to Scheler, it is clear that this 'debate' is yet another instance of opponents talking past one another. Yet Adler's reply does illustrate the extent to which, even in its early stages, the discussion of the nature of the sociology of knowledge very quickly took up the question of the nature of social scientific knowledge. This is not merely another instance of the extent to which the debate surrounding the sociology of knowledge can be seen as an extension of the *Methodenstreit*, and possibly also the *Werturteilsstreit*, within one sphere of sociology; it also testifies to the very restricted nature of the definition of what is to constitute 'knowledge' for a sociology of knowledge. That is, the field of study can very quickly become another kind of discussion of the nature of social scientific knowledge within some form of Kantian, neo-Kantian or post-Kantian parameters. In this way, one strand of the discipline can be seen as a sociological extension of the pre-war neo-Kantian discussion of the logical and philosophical foundations of the distinction between natural and social science.

Indeed, this ambiguity on the nature and aims of a sociology of knowledge was sensed by a number of the participants at the 1924 German Sociological Congress. It was taken up most dramatically and misleadingly by Dunckmann in the following manner when he argued that,

> If we claim that all science is somehow dependent upon the social structure then it is also certain that all science depends upon sociology. There then emerges the problem that, in my opinion, is the decisive one — and one that has not been dealt with here by either of the two speakers. How is sociology as a science possible if all science depends upon sociology? From whence does sociology take its standard as a science if all other sciences (i.e., art, religion, morality, law and even metaphysics and philosophy) depend upon the social structure, that is, are sociologically determined?'[33]

Were Dunckmann to develop this argument fully we would then be faced with a perfect example of sociologism. Like most of his contemporaries, Dunckmann goes on to exclude those disciplines 'science, mathematics, logic, or we can think of statistics, which are *not* dependent upon social structures'.[34] With regard to the two speakers, Dunckmann argues that Scheler's analysis is limited to a theory of drives and a notion of spiritual creators and Adler's analysis of bourgeois and proletarian science begs the question of how sociology as a science can exist in such a way as to transcend class distinctions.

On the problem of sociology as a science, another contributor, Sulzbach, argues that Scheler, though speaking of three interests in knowledge, fails to ask whether different types of understanding exist, and whether these differences derive from the social structure and hence may be understood by sociology. The possible diversity of sociological standpoints was also noticed by Salin. He suggests that both the papers and comments on them 'have shown us how impossible it has been up to now to speak of a unified science of sociology. What has been given to us is, at most, in so far as it was sociology at all, different sociologies: Max Scheler's sociology, that of Max Adler and that of the discussants as well.'[35]

The response to Marxism is significant in this discussion since it gives some indication as to why so little attention was subsequently paid to Adler's sociology of knowledge. Further, it shows how little was the influence of Lukács' *History and Class Consciousness* only a year after its publication. Alfred Weber, in his contribution, rejects both static and evolutionary, and bourgeois and proletarian modes of apprehension. More significantly, Weber states his case against Marxism as follows:

> what separates us from those who today call themselves Marxists, although they are perhaps best called quasi-Marxists, is that they are rationalists and, in fact, *pure* rationalists. They treat everything in this manner and in this sense they are 'progressives' and cannot be anything else. In this sense, they must be evolutionists; since for a rationalist there exists no historical movement other than progressive evolution. What separates us from their completely rational approach and the attempt to explain everything by this rationality is . . ., above all, a pre-war experience from the time when things were still going very well for us and one could still count us economically amongst the 'bourgeois' nations, and not primarily a war or post-war experience since when things have gone badly.[36]

Weber's comments here point to the abandonment of 'rationalism' and a recognition of the need for 'another way' and 'another perspective' since 'progress' can no longer be presupposed.

The other discussants exhibited a varied response to Marxism. Dunckmann suggests that he did not understand what a 'materialist interpretation of history' was. Michels, in his brief remarks, makes no reference to Marxism except to point out that Adler should not overlook that there exists 'not only a bourgeois but also a proletarian human type'. Of the discussants, only Alfred Meusel refers to specific Marxist works relating generally to the sociology of knowledge. Significantly, Meusel criticizes both Scheler's and Adler's papers on the grounds that,

> to show how a specific social group is impelled towards specific ways to knowledge and kinds of knowledge on the basis of its concrete set of interests but, over and above that, [it is necessary] to allude to the close affinity of form and structural identification between economic base and intellectual superstructure — in the very same manner, for instance, as Georg Lukács in *History and Class Consciousness*.[37]

At least in raising this kind of issue, Meusel argues that 'Professor Scheler has shown himself to be a better Marxist than Professor Adler.' On different grounds, Meusel also rejects Adler's discussion of a static and dynamic sociology.

Perhaps of greatest interest in the context of the reception of Marxism within the sociology of knowledge is the contribution by Arthur Salz who accepts that he has 'a "vulgar" interpretation of Marxism'. Salz attempts to locate the need to confront the Marxist standpoint in the changes that have taken place in German society. He argues that

> There seems to me to be no doubt that we have been drawn much closer to the materialist interpretation of history — which is the foundation of the Marxist philosophy of history — in recent decades than earlier, than in the decades before the war and that we experience the need for a confrontation with this doctrine and the questions it raises much more immediately, and in a completely different manner, than previously; in fact this is not the result, for instance, of an intellectual development that we have passed through in the meantime but, rather, the result of political and economic events which we have laid the course for in our own lives. Quite simply, it is the result of the fact that, to state it briefly, the *proletarian* prime experience has become *the national* consciousness for us Germans, that today the whole nation or large parts of it have internationalized their role in the social whole that previously only the proletarian class occupied, that this proletarian feeling is, in fact, 'socialized'. That polarization of society, of which Marx spoke, and which he saw as the basic fact of capitalist society, that disintegration of society into the exploiting wealthy and the exploited propertyless has taken possession of nations themselves and any sociological perspective on the present that does not start out from this fact — namely, that in this sense there exist today proletarianized, enslaved peoples — is doomed to failure.[38]

This sense of universal proletarianization and its extension from the proletariat to the whole of society is certainly a central theme of Max Scheler's wartime and post-war writings. The polarization within German society was also to become a central if implicit theme of Mannheim's analysis of society and its attendant conflicting ideologies.

But the core of Salz's contribution lies in a restatement of some of the issues raised by Lukács. Salz indeed refers to the dialectical method as having been developed 'from Hegel and Marx to Lukács'. It is this dialectical method which he sees as 'the core of the materialist interpretation of history' and, like Lukács, he criticizes orthodox Marxism for itself being undialectical. Salz, too, refers to the argument that commodity relations are the basis of forms of objectification and reification. However, he argues strongly against 'the mythologization of the proletariat'. Hence, Salz's contribution is the only one to refer in any detailed manner to Lukács' position and is the only instance of Lukács' central arguments in *History and Class Consciousness* being taken up at a sociology congress in this period. But although Salz takes up Lukács' arguments he does not develop or explore them further to see how fruitful they might be for a sociology of knowledge, or a critique of ideology.

In his closing remarks to this session, Adler again returns to his central thesis 'that the assumption of objective knowledge is itself class-determined in its possibility and totality'.[39] Adler rejects the view that 'progress never starts out from the masses but only always from individuals; that culture is something creative whereas the proletariat is not'. However, this should not be understood to mean that bourgeois or proletarian thought is that of 'the average thought of the individual bourgeois or proletarian'. Rather, it is a characterization of the 'motives, tasks and limits of thought'. In answer to Dunckmann's posing of the problem of the determination of sociology and science, Adler argues that he did not state that

> science is dependent upon sociology, which is certainly itself a science, but [that it] is dependent upon the social structure; and the presentation of this dependency is primarily the task of sociology. When Professor Dunckmann argues further, that there must certainly be a pure sociology that, like mathematics or mechanics, does not consist of a merely partisan truth, then I gladly concur fully with him.[40]

We know from his other writings that Adler has in mind as a basis for a pure sociology that of Georg Simmel, even though Adler's version is one which combines Kant and Marx.

In terms of the development of the sociology of knowledge, this first public debate points to a number of features of the discipline that are only properly pursued in later confrontations. Scheler's discussion of the relationship between science and social structure, for instance, is not taken up and developed in this period. Indeed, the development of natural scientific knowledge is seldom raised as a theme at all, except, as we have seen, in Mannheim's unpublished essays, and even there it seems to rest largely upon Lukács' earlier account. At the same time, the Scheler–Adler debate, which raises the question — particularly in Adler's contribution — of the foundations of sociology itself as a discipline, certainly remains a theme within the sociology of knowledge, even to the extent that we can see it as taking up earlier issues from the *Methodenstreit* and the *Werturteilsstreit*.

In short, the debate indicates the extent to which the Marxist perspective is ever-present as a background to the discussion of the sociology of knowledge. In the immediate context of the Scheler–Adler debate, it must also be pointed out that Adler's version of the sociology of knowledge found almost no resonance whatsoever amongst later writers. In subsequent sociological debates, it was to be Mannheim's presumed assimilation of the Marxist perspective that was to be the focus of attention. This was indeed the case at the Sixth German Sociological Congress held in Zürich in September, 1928.

III

Mannheim's paper 'The Significance of Competition in the Intellectual Sphere'[41] presented at the Sixth German Sociological Congress sparked off considerable discussion as well as stimulating two further papers on themes raised by the conference: one by Alexander von Schelting,[42] which was wide-ranging and sympathetic to Alfred Weber's position, and a much briefer discussion of the conference by Alfred Meusel.[43] Although unconnected with the actual theme of this session of the conference, Mannheim's comments on Sombart's paper *Das Verstehen* from the same congress are also worth examining briefly.[44] What particularly concerned the participants at the congress was the *Seinsverbundenheit* of knowledge. Mannheim himself provided a summary of the issues he was to deal with, together with some specific questions which he thought participants might wish to take up.[45] The questions Mannheim submitted for discussion were:

(a) Does the phenomenon of existentially bounded knowledge exist?
(b) Does the competition of strata asserted here have significance for our contemporary intellectual situation?
(c) Which areas of the humanities and social sciences (especially sociology) are *not* to be considered as existentially bounded knowledge?
(d) Can one draw an exact line between where existentially bounded knowledge ends and 'exact', timelessly valid knowledge commences?
(e) Must one unconditionally evaluate existentially bounded thought negatively? Is it not because of a too one-sided orientation of epistemology (predominantly on the basis of the paradigm of the exact natural scientific image of knowledge) that one does not deal justly with the innermost quality of this mode of thought?[46]

It is these kinds of questions rather than the discussion of competition between intellectual strata that formed the focal point of subsequent debate. In fact, this marked the first discussion at a sociology congress in Germany of those issues which lie at the heart of the German tradition in the sociology of knowledge.

Alfred Weber, the first speaker to comment on Mannheim's paper, agreed with what he took to be Mannheim's substantive theses, namely, that competition is a general sociological category, is apparent 'within the sphere of existentially bounded thought', and plays 'a co-constitutive role' there; that Mannheim's four categories of consensus, monopoly, atomized competition and concentration can be fruitfully applied there; and, finally, that Mannheim correctly characterized the present intellectual situation.

However, with regard to Mannheim's 'epistemological problematic',

Weber had major reservations. This is particularly true of the extent of the 'relationizing of thought'. On the one hand, Weber argues,

> I stand completely on the foundation of the existence of a thoroughgoing relationizing of thought. I believe that we still have hardly any idea as to how our thought is relationized, that probably . . . each of us who has worked on historical and sociological maternal and really attempted intellectually to enter into the spirit of strange historical phenomena is horrified at how relationized human thought in fact is.[47]

What Weber has in mind here seems to be different national traditions of thought (Greek, Indian etc.). On the other hand, he states

> I believe that it is really hardly necessary to express the fact that there exists a realm of thought and knowledge that is not relational, a universally compulsory mass of cognitions, at the same time a categorial element of a conceptual-intuitive identity that is followed by all human beings . . .[48]

This universal sphere of knowledge is quite separate from existentially determined thought. It is the sphere that is common to all human beings and appears to be similar to the Kantian a priori categories of thought, though this is by no means clear from Weber's statement. However, the fact that

> these categories, that have grown out of universal human positions *vis-à-vis* nature and the necessity to dominate nature, that are embodied, above all in natural science — though not solely in natural science — and are today in fact parts of human knowledge that are universally valid and necessary can indeed hardly be contested.[49]

Thus, once more, the problematic relationship between the natural and social sciences finds its resonance in the exclusion of natural scientific from social determination. Perhaps it is this aspect of the sociology of knowledge that continually required a confrontation with the natural–cultural sciences debate.

For Weber it is metaphysical thought that is the most existentially bounded form of knowledge since

> everything that we term metaphysically anchored concepts, cognitions and values associated with them, are all things of which we must immediately concede that, in accordance with their total *contents*, they possess their historically partial quality in the closest existential boundedness. Every sociologist must see this, otherwise he cannot carry out any historical sociology.[50]

Weber argues that, for Mannheim, there exists an 'intermediate area' between metaphysical, value-laden knowledge that is existentially determined and the sphere of universally valid knowledge. Within this intermediate area, Mannheim wishes to speak of styles of thought that give rise to different objects of cognition. What Weber objects to is the absence of a distinction between the contents of knowledge and their meaning since 'cognition is a processual concept. Style of thought is a formal concept. Knowledge is an ontological concept.' Weber sees Mannheim as advancing the position that styles of thought produce different objects, thereby presumably challenging the ontological foundation of knowledge as Weber understands it. Weber takes the example of class perspectives on capitalism and argues that

> Capitalism is a quite definite, unique, clear object. I simply assume its empirical, historical-positivistic reality here. In my opinion, there can only be a different approach to and a different illumination of the same object but it is impossible for there to be different objects and a different knowledge of it. Rather, there exists only *one* object and *one* complete knowledge.[51]

What is at issue here for Weber is not, for example, a critique of a phenomenological standpoint that can undoubtedly be found in Mannheim's work, but rather a critique of the kind of position Lukács puts forward in *History and Class Consciousness* with respect to class knowledge — a position which Weber presumably believes is also held by Mannheim.

This much becomes evident when Weber proceeds to what is 'perhaps the decisive' point in Mannheim's argument, namely

> that out of this different existentially bounded knowledge — or better cognitive or intellectual positions — you seem to wish to continually draw positions of the will (*Willens-positionen*). *We* would perhaps say — you call this another standpoint — the ideals of specific classes. You appear to identify them with interpretations of existence, as you indeed put it: a public statement concerning existence, a public interpretation of existence.[52]

Weber sees this position as raising the question of value-freedom, which arises out of the introduction of certain assumptions associated with the materialist interpretation of history. What Weber specifically misses in Mannheim's paper is

> the recognition of the intellectually creative as the foundation of action and of classes, for example. What I reject is the reduction of all these things ultimately to intellectual categories with the addition — if you will excuse me — of some of the sociological categories that belong to the old materialist interpretation of history. You have spoken of positions of social power, of intentions that flow from them, of a public interpretation of existence that is combined with these positions of power and intentions, of further factors in this context: What is this but a materialistic interpretation of history advanced once more with extraordinary refinement and brilliance?[53]

Weber concludes that this 'sublimated intellectualism' can only lead to the same results as 'the vulgarized intellectualism that is adhered to by the old materialist interpretation of history'.

In contrast, Werner Sombart — the next speaker — maintains that Mannheim

> is no longer influenced by the materialist interpretation of history . . . and indeed [is] so detached from it that he does not make the objectivity of

existence dependent upon the subjects of knowledge — this is what is decisive — and that, above all, he does not dispute the reality of the mind. For the materialist philosophy of history there is no reality of the mind; it is only a reflection of the economy. If I have correctly understood the referent, then he firmly maintains, in contrast to the materialist interpretation of history, firstly that there is an objectivity of existence and secondly that there exists a reality of the mind. Is that the case? (Dr. Mannheim agrees).[54]

But though Sombart broadly agrees with the *Seinsverbundenheit* argument he has reservations about the problem of the universal validity of knowledge. Indeed, he suggests that 'one of the most essential achievements of our age' is that 'it has separated the problem of objectivity and that of universal validity which in Kant were still bound together'. Sombart points to two attempts to solve the problem of universal validity in the present period. The first attempt, the philosophical one, starts out from the conviction that

> the world is knowable and that there exists an objective determinate entity, hence a specific object of knowledge, and is convinced that knowledge of this object — the world — can be approached from different sides. And these sides are the personal standpoint of the individual thinker.[55]

This accounts, Sombart argues, for the diversity of philosophical systems. The second attempt to solve the problem of universal validity occurs in the natural sciences, which 'do not seek to know the essence of things but rather . . . they seek to order phenomena . . . according to functional and, in part, fictional considerations'. Hence, they merely seek to create 'an ordering system'.

Sombart's main concern, however, is with the cultural sciences and his remaining argument concerns the role of values within them. He asserts that the cultural sciences must commence from the postulate of value-freedom since

> consideration of values is ultimately a personal matter. The postulate of value-freedom has nothing to do with a relativization of values. Values remain absolute, they are objective. Evaluations, however, are personal and hence socially and historically determined and lack universal validity.[56]

This does not mean, Sombart continues, that we should not recognize that the choice of problems is value-determined or that our object of study is value-laden. The relevance of this whole argument for Mannheim's paper is that, according to Sombart, Mannheim has contributed to the 'psychology of value-freedom' in so far as he asserted that 'the standpoint of value-freedom is ultimately an emanation of liberal convictions'. But Sombart argues that even when he himself earlier adopted a Marxist position he also took up a value-free position.

Similar themes were taken up by Wilbrandt, the next contributor, who said he was astonished to find Mannheim advancing an argument which increasingly replaced philosophy with the social sciences. Wilbrandt suggests that Mannheim's paper reminded him of Schmoller's contribution to the *Werturteilsstreit*. The struggle of values, one with another, was for Schmoller 'a kind of Darwinism on the intellectual level'. It occurred to Wilbrandt that Mannheim's arguments concerning competition between different world interpretations must refer to hostile and not to peaceful competition since the purpose is surely the hegemony of one world interpretation over another. Mannheim at this point objects that 'compromise situations' exist.

Secondly, Wilbrandt attempts to clarify Mannheim's relationship to historical materialism, pointing out that Mannheim had earlier 'spoken about this and stated that Marx has influenced him but, as he said, in association with Dilthey's spirit'.[57] Wilbrandt argues that what Mannheim shares with Marx is the notion that man does not think for himself alone but in a social situation and thinks differently according to the social situation.

Jerusalem — perhaps the most significant adherent of a positivist sociology of knowledge in Germany — is extremely brief in his remarks on Mannheim's paper. Arguing that Mannheim raised some of the most important issues affecting sociology as a discipline, he goes on to interpret what Mannheim has said in terms of his own perspective and, in particular, in contrast to von Wiese, in terms of his notion of a collectivity — 'that form of life where human beings as bearers of a collective mind are bound together mentally'. However illuminating this may be for Jerusalem's own position, it is hardly addressed to Mannheim's paper at all.

Emil Lederer, Mannheim's colleague in Heidelberg, defends him against Weber by arguing that Mannheim excluded the sphere of validity from his analysis and that the notion of creativity and its source has nothing to do with Mannheim's assertions. At the substantive level, Lederer argues that 'a certain competition amongst strata is the basis and precondition for intellectual productivity itself', which 'must have quite concrete preconditions for its existence and realization'.

The next three commentaries, by Adolf Löwe (a friend of Mannheim's), Alfred Meusel and Norbert Elias, all take up central issues in Mannheim's sociology of knowledge. Löwe argues that the existential boundedness of knowledge 'exists in all periods' but the recognition of this determination has taken on a distinctive form in our present age. Furthermore, one can be more specific and argue that it is 'the *sociological* boundedness of knowledge' which is not only peculiar to our present age but which, in its self-consciousness, constitutes 'revolutionary knowledge': 'through it, the real dynamics of social phenomena are grasped in the realm of knowledge, a social and political tension is carried out into the theoretical sphere'. Löwe goes so far as to suggest that it is revolutionary in a further sense, in that it 'restructures not only the theoretical world image but also social reality itself, whose tension has destroyed the time-honoured stasis of thought.'[58]

This sense of a revolutionary change in our approach to the social world also permeates Elias' contribution. He argues that Mannheim's thought is, 'in a quite specific manner, revolutionary, not in the sense of a socialist or social revolution but in the sense of an intellectual revolution. These thoughts are the expression of a shattering of that intellectual position which has hitherto been the dominant one.'[59] Mannheim's paper represents not merely a new theory but is the expression of a specific feeling of life (*Lebensgefühl*). Hence, Mannheim's notion of the 'consensus' of an age signifies that we experience nature, for example, in a distinctive way and cannot do otherwise.

A more critical contribution is provided by Alfred Meusel, who takes up Mannheim's relationship to Marx and the contradiction between Weber's and Sombart's views on that relationship. Meusel argues that one of the strengths of Mannheim's paper is precisely that it is influenced by Marx, but that Marx, unlike Mannheim, looked at the question of how 'correct, adequate knowledge of social existence' was possible given the social boundedness of thought, i.e., anything but an interest-free approach. Marx located this 'correct' and 'adequate' knowledge within a specific group in society whose subjective values and objective situation were identical. Nevertheless, Meusel concludes by praising Mannheim's paper and his other works in this area.

The two final contributions to the discussion, by Jonas and Eppstein, concentrate upon the philosophical and methodological aspects of Mannheim's paper. Jonas raises three problems associated with Mannheim's paper and the ensuing discussion. He asks whether Mannheim's position is, as Alfred Weber argues, one of intellectualism. In reply, Jonas maintains that

> The notion of *existentially* bounded knowledge, knowledge concerning the existential boundedness of intellectual positions as such, certainly implies the functionalization of knowledge in terms of the *totality* of human beings, of existence in the totality of their involvements with reality — indeed not solely in *material* reality . . . Functionalization in terms of the real situation thus implies, in fact, the replacement of the old concept of the 'theoretical subject', of the abstractness of 'consciousness as such' which is nothing other than a pure cognitive subject, with a completely new agent of knowledge which is, in contrast, the *whole, historical* human being and for whom the ideal of the absolute universal validity of knowledge — precisely in the sense in which Sombart has developed it — is no longer conceivable at all.[60]

Theoretical forms, as partial phenomena, are thus to be related back to the '*total facticity* of human beings'.

Jonas continues by questioning the relevance of this functionalization of thought for the validity of knowledge. A relativistic reductionism is possible, Jonas maintains,

> if the concern is with a one-sided functionalization in terms of the economic-material situation, ultimately in terms of the mere givenness of drives — and hence *estranged* from the mind — rather than in terms of the total situation: then, in fact, the actual truth claims of intellectual forms as mere 'ideological superstructure' are at the same time annulled by *this* relativization. But the concern is with the *total* situation, in which the *intellectual* cosmos itself, as a moment of the total facticity, is already associated with it as an *initial* precondition.[61]

Hence, rather than reducing intellectual phenomena to a material base, it is possible to view them as co-constituents of the totality. By means of their relativization to the total situation, their validity is not destroyed but rather their absolute claim to truth is qualified by the historical, social total context. With regard to the annulment of absolute truth claims, Jonas argued that

> This annulment, carried out in the form of the arrangement of one-sided partial aspects in a comprehensive synthesis that transcends their exclusiveness . . . is possible — this annulment of a necessarily 'false' absolutization through its functionalization in terms of a historical actual situation is thus, to a certain extent, in fact, a *preservation* of the truth content of a temporarily and socially conditioned theory and in no way its negation.[62]

This interpretation of the truth contents of a theory in terms of their relationship to a total synthesis is, of course, subsequently extended by Mannheim in *Ideologie und Utopie* to ideologies.

Thirdly, Jonas asks where the existential boundedness of a system of knowledge is particularly evident. He argues that there exists in any world-view an 'unavoidable excess' of assertions that go beyond what can be factually asserted. Here, he argues, we are confronted with the apriori assertions of metaphysics. A sociology of knowledge can, he believes, also annul the absolute nature of the dogmatic apriori by revealing its social basis. These aspects of the world view, thus 'purified', can be made fruitful by the researcher who 'belongs to the "free-floating" intellectual stratum that is not itself engaged in group conflicts.[63]

Jonas' contribution is significant in that, at least as far as the first two problems are concerned, he raises issues in the sociology of knowledge that have remained central to subsequent controversies surrounding its status. Though not specifically referring either to a mechanistic Marxism or to Scheler's sociology of knowledge, he does point to the reductionism that is evident in both positions and indeed to the implicit 'alienation of the mind' thesis. Again, in the second issue he raises, Jonas indicates a possible way out of this reductionism. However, with regard to his third problem, his conception of the sociology of knowledge as a neutral purifier of world views, whilst not dissimilar to that presented by Mannheim, retains positivist presuppositions about the relationship between fact and values that were incorporated into subsequent positivist critiques of ideology as advanced by such writers as Geiger.[64]

Finally, Eppstein summarizes Mannheim's method as one which 'combines phenomenological vision with dialectical method; his methodological position is a synthesis of phenomenological observation and dialectical-dynamic thought', which enables him to overcome the weakness of a '*statically* conceived phenomenology'.[65] Eppstein's major concern, however, is with the problem of attributing partiality to 'relativized (relationized) perspectives and standpoints' and then taking this partiality to be the constituent feature of the ideologization of thought. Eppstein argues that one does not need to take the partial aspect itself to be ideological.

In his concluding remarks to the discussion, Mannheim himself takes up the methodological issues associated with the sociology of knowledge as well as attempting to confront some of the controversy surrounding his paper. He suggests that the major questions which his paper raised became submerged in the ensuing discussion, but not because there was already a consensus surrounding them. Within the context of sociology itself, Mannheim argues that he tried to deal with strictly sociological issues for a specific reason.

> It is indeed to be recommended that the methodological, voluntaristic, evaluative, metaphysical and epistemological, on the one hand, be separated from the purely sociological on the other, not because they are separated in the objective world (in reality they are . . . connected) but because, in the clarification of problems, a provisional separation of these spheres is perhaps advisable.[66]

Nonetheless, these evaluative, metaphysical questions 'are today for us in fact perhaps the decisive ones'. As an instance, Mannheim attempts to answer the question as to whether his own position is basically a materialist or idealist one. It should be clear, Mannheim argues,

> that I hold the synthetic in a specific relationship to be the best of what occurs in the historical process, that I am of the opinion that precisely in the synthesis tensions will suddenly be relatively overcome that were still untranscendable for a previous epoch, i.e., that a third aspect is found where one suddenly realizes that, in fact, these distinctions: matter–spirit, freedom–determination etc., cannot be absolutized. This cannot imply that both parties and both aspects are in the right but rather that somewhere in the social process and intellectual system one can be free to realize certain synthetic insights. Perhaps you will be dissatisfied when I say: I am neither a materialist nor an idealist but rather I still believe in the creative freedom within the absolute sphere in an exclusively material determination.[67]

What concerns him as a sociologist of knowledge is why people should wish to view the world within these polarities. In order not to absolutize such polarities, Mannheim seeks a synthesis of what is valuable in a mechanistic and in an idealist model: 'The solution, which I have provisionally found, consists in the fact that each of the conflicting parties hypostatizes a partial aspect'. The mechanistic viewpoint hypostatizes an objective reality, the idealist viewpoint hypostatizes the subject of knowledge (perhaps in the form of a free moral decision).

This duality lies at the centre of the discussion of the relationship between the natural and human sciences, but here

> the justification of the duality (or plurality) of intellectual methods does not lie in the sphere of the object but rather in the fact that there already exists, for example, in the intellectual sphere itself, a specific sphere that is 'free', that is not apprehendable by 'mechanistic' models, but is another sphere that is still subject to a specific mechanism.[68]

However, for Mannheim, the deterministic and free elements that co-exist in the intellectual realm do not allow him 'to seek only understanding, only freedom in the intellectual realm and perhaps erect the comparisons: nature = necessity, mind = freedom'. Rather, the danger in the human sciences in Germany is that of reducing everything to interpretation, to a 'deeper meaning' — a danger existing in politics too. Methodologically, one must sometimes use formal concepts to deal with intellectual phenomena — even though they may not perfectly fit the phenomena as they appear to us — since 'there exists in intellectual things too, structures that are subject to a "mechanical apparatus" and, when it is a matter of apprehending them, then one must apply formalized concepts'. This is the source of the two major attacks upon the sociology of knowledge: that it is too formalized, and that it introduces the functionalization of ideas in terms of other mechanisms. But, Mannheim argues, 'if I wish to explain functional connections in the intellectual sphere then I must formalise; if I only wish to understand them then I can rest content with historical, individual, intuitive concepts.' This implies 'that understanding justifiably exists, in fact, in a specific sphere of the intellectual realm and represents a method *sui generis*, but that in the humanities it is not merely to be understood but also to be explained'.

Mannheim hopes the sociology of knowledge will synthesize the two approaches.

> what I have in mind is a synthetic situational analysis which . . ., viewed from the social and intellectual movement of forces, is at least as possible and necessary as the polarization itself. Thus, I aspire — to put it briefly — to give life once more to the basic desire for value-freedom. Not, however, in order to realize with a single blow scientific objectivity in the humanities and social science in the old all-too-intellectualized manner (which will not succeed) but rather in order gradually to bring this objectivity — on the basis

of an exact scientific analysis that focuses upon it and whose problems and methods we must first investigate step by step — closer to solution.[69]

Once more, Mannheim reveals both the close connection between his programme for a sociology of knowledge and the disputes surrounding methodology and value-judgments and a confidence that the sociology of knowledge will afford a solution to both disputes.

Though these are Mannheim's concluding remarks on the discussion of his paper, it is worthwhile pursuing his views on methodology a little further since, on the following day, he himself contributed to the discussion of Werner Sombart's paper *Das Verstehen*. His remarks there represent a continuation of some of the issues raised in his closing comments on his own paper.

Mannheim views the discussion of the problem of understanding to have been more fruitfully advanced by individual researchers in the humanities and social sciences than by philosophers, who, he argues, are thoroughly caught up in a pregiven system of thought. Hence, the value he attributes to the paper given by Sombart, as one who works on actual interpretative social research. However, Mannheim sees a number of difficulties arising from Sombart's presentation. The first is his apparently sharp distinction between 'motive' and 'idea'. Without going into Sombart's paper here, it is still instructive to follow Mannheim's critique at this point since he raises general issues concerning the problem of interpretation. The problem associated with the separation of 'idea' and 'motive' lies in the fact that,

> on the one hand, one provides an objectivated (which implies a desubjectivized) context of the creations of the mind that are to be understood through it and a principle resting upon it, a principle that develops out of itself, the 'idea'; on the other, however, purely subjective processes and an infinite number of subjective motivations. However, both of these two discrepant groups of phenomena are related to one another and yet nevertheless cannot be brought together in our theories.[70]

The reason for this persistent separation has been the 'completely diverse intellectual paradigms' for dealing with each of them. Max Weber, for example, attempted to throw out the 'idea' and operate only with 'subjectively intended meaning' ('motive' in Sombart's sense). Mannheim takes 'the spirit of capitalism' as an instance of an 'idea' in sociological research. The problem here is not, he argues, that such a 'spirit' exists but rather, 'what is its "specific *mode of existence*"?' An extreme nominalist like Max Weber only allows this spirit to exist in inverted commas; one cannot apprehend this 'spirit' if one starts out from 'subjectively intended meaning'. This spirit remains even though subjectively intended meanings change and even though it is manifested through them. On the other hand, one should not be tempted to accept the converse — precisely what Weber sought to avoid — that the 'idea' can be formulated as 'something pre-existent, pre-formed'. An undue emphasis upon either pole prevents us from adequately describing the relationships between 'the so-called "real" and "ideal" factors of history'. One may indeed be led to interpret new phenomena inadequately in a conservative manner, in the sense that they are always interpreted in terms of the past and not as the phenomena are actually experienced.

Mannheim offers a new paradigm for dealing with the 'idea', one that does not have to choose between 'psychologically apprehendable, subjectively intended meaning, on the one hand, and the existentially transcendent timeless "idea" that can be apprehended only in ideation', on the other. The predominant relationships must be examined so far as their genuine qualities are concerned until we can detect their relevance in subjectively intended meaning. At the same time, one must avoid any 'illusion as to pre-existence and pre-formation' of the 'idea' in order to preserve the genuine objectivity of the idea. Mannheim is quite clear that 'the objective "spirit" of an epoch cannot be reduced to the sum of the subjective intentions of isolated individuals'.[71] He bases his model of interpretation upon Fiedler's theory of art, in which the 'idea' that an artist works with is not pregiven but '*emerges* in the creative process', as the artist works upon his materials. Such a model for interpretation was already evident in Mannheim's unpublished essays.

What is the significance of these two discussions for the development of the sociology of knowledge in Germany? The 1928 debate constituted the major public sociological discussion of the sociology of knowledge in Weimar Germany. As in the earlier Scheler–Adler discussion, the relationship between the sociology of knowledge and Marxism is taken up by many participants and is the focal point of Alfred Weber's attack on Mannheim. But, interestingly, this aspect of the discussion does not take the form of a contrast between the sociology of knowledge and the Marxist critique of ideology. That only commenced in earnest after the publication of *Ideologie und Utopie* in the following year. Instead, the discussion on Marxism, as in 1924, takes the form of an attack on some naïve notion of historical materialism.

But the 1928 debate centres, more obviously than in the 1924 discussion, around the relationship between the sociology of knowledge and the *Methodenstreit* and, to a lesser extent, the *Werturteilsstreit*. This is, in part, the result of Mannheim's explicit attempt to illustrate the relevance of the *Seinsverbundenheit* thesis for the social sciences. However, as is clear from participants' comments, the sociology of knowledge was seen to be forging nothing less than an intellectual revolution in the human sciences. It was regarded as a new mode of interpretation of phenomena which relied upon not merely traditional hermeneutic methods but also empirical social science. In this respect, the sociology of knowledge could be seen as forming a significant bridge between the natural and cultural sciences as understood, for example, by neo-Kantian philosophers. It was thus clearly viewed by some as bringing about a paradigm shift in the humanities and social sciences. This is also made explicit in Mannheim's remarks on the problem of understanding.

The new and challenging significance of the sociology of knowledge is also the theme of an article published in 1929 by Alexander von Schelting, 'Zum Streit um die Wissenssoziologie' — [72] in part stimulated by the public debate. However, von Schelting's paper is largely concerned with an exposition of Alfred Weber's contribution to the sociology of knowledge, which is not our concern here. Indeed, although von Schelting makes out a case for the significance of Alfred Weber's sociology of culture, it is difficult to see how this played a major role in the sociology of knowledge in this period. Indirectly, we can see Weber's influence upon Mannheim's early Heidelberg writings, and von Schelting in fact argues that the basic categories in Mannheim's 'Historismus' article are grounded in Alfred Weber's work.[73]

Von Schelting maintains that Alfred Weber's sociology of culture provides a middle ground between the ahistorical, immanent interpretation of cultural phenomena and a deterministic sociologism. In particular, he highlights the dangers of the Marxist thesis of 'the ideological character of *all* intellectual forms', which results in an irreconcilable conflict between a 'bourgeois' and a 'proletarian' explanatory context. On the other hand, he takes the essence of the sociological standpoint as that of a 'concern with the "totality" of historical-social events, that it does not isolate historical phenomena but rather has to interpret them in their "location" or "embeddedness" in the total context of an age, a culture, the "living whole" of a society etc.'[74] However, the precise relationship to these totalities is most varied and sociology has hardly clarified it successfully. In this context, then, it is all the more surprising that von Schelting should go on to explicate Alfred Weber's contribution to this area since the vagueness of his categories of culture and civilization could themselves hardly illuminate this relationship.

The second article stimulated by Mannheim's paper, by Alfred Meusel, does explicitly discuss Mannheim's contribution.[75] Though Meusel agrees with Mannheim that, in the study of cultural phenomena, 'the interpretation cannot remain purely ideological, it must become a sociological one', he suggests that Mannheim did not extract all that he could from his theme since he starts out from problems of intellectual history or philosophy and not from economics or another social science. This would lead him, Meusel claims, into being concerned not merely with a sophisticated philosophical viewpoint but also with 'practical everyday life'. Since he cannot adequately deal with the latter he links the two spheres 'with the emergency bridge of a mere assertion concerning their inner connection'.[76]

Meusel, by contrast, argues that it is necessary to investigate why the competition between strata leads to competition between intellectual positions. Mannheim possesses too great a desire for synthesis, in that it is too easy to say that every intellectual direction provides us with a partial aspect of reality. Instead, we need to look at the wider context of competition and contrasting intellectual viewpoints. In the capitalist epoch, the economy forms an *ens realissimum* that sociology must examine. Mannheim is therefore correct in investigating the 'deep voluntaristic anchoredness of every theory' in the economy. But, Meusel contends, this requires us to think out the problem of value-freedom again, since

> Insight into the existential boundedness of thought indeed indicates that individual standpoints are not merely distinguished from one another in their programmatic intentions that are external in origin, but in fact in the manner in which things are approached. . . . The personal element, however, that the supporters of value-freedom saw as being located in value-judgements and that one could, as a rule, easily excude if one merely clearly distinguished the presentation of the existence (*Sein*) from that of the intention (*Sollen*) of particular wishes, penetrates knowledge in a much deeper, more basic, indeed more dangerous manner than was accepted at the time of the debate over value-judgements.[77]

This requires us to think beyond the confines of Max Weber's solution and requires 'a "demythologizing" cognitive sociology (the social scientific counterpart to Friedrich Nietzsche's "demythologizing" psychology)'. If this is accepted, then we need to deal with the problem that Mannheim merely raised, namely that of universal validity.

Meusel is highly critical of the attempts by Alfred Weber and Werner Sombart to deal with this question. He points to the inconsistency between Weber's acceptance of the *Seinsverbundenheit* thesis in relation to a contrast between Indian and European–American modes of thought, and its rejection when the issue of 'capitalism' as a single object is concerned. Similarly, Sombart, too, adopts a position which 'has led to the abandonment of existential determination and a return to the value-free position'.

In contrast, Meusel suggests that Marx's neglected contribution to cognitive sociology should be re-examined. This involves the recognition that those in a dominant position in society or with an interest in its preservation will seek to avoid recognizing the reality of its development and that 'divergent social classes have divergent cognitive chances'. Meusel, however, raises two problems associated with such a position: firstly, that Marx underestimated the strength of illusions within the subordinate class, and secondly that the notion of development presupposes the existence of a stratum that can anticipate this development from a non-existentially bounded position. Both these issues are, of course, raised in Lukács' *History and Class Consciousness*.

Hence, both von Schelting and Meusel attest to the widespread recognition that the *Seinsverbundenheit* thesis advanced by the sociology of knowledge must challenge the foundations of sociology itself. Further, Meusel's comments suggest that the sociology of knowledge must have as one of its central tasks the opening up of the methodological disputes which raged in Germany before the First World War. The fact that the sociology of knowledge rendered problematic the bases of social scientific thought, and that the sociology of knowledge itself held a problematic position within the social sciences, is apparent from the reception of Mannheim's *Ideologie und Utopie*.

IV

Despite the extensive nature of the reviews of Mannheim's *Ideologie und Utopie*, they possess a number of characteristics which suggests that certain groups were particularly interested in his work. Furthermore, despite the wide scope of many of the reviews, Mannheim himself only replied directly to one of the earlier and more hostile reviews, that of Curtius.

Between 1929 and 1932 no less than five articles appeared in *Die Gesellschaft* — a Social Democratic journal founded by Rudolf Hilferding — dealing with Mannheim's *Ideologie und Utopie*. Three were major reviews (those of Tillich[78], Arendt[79] and Marcuse[80], and two others (by Kleinberg[81] and Speier[82], took up certain aspects of his work. Two other reviews, by Wittfogel[83] and Fogarasi,[84] constituted the relativity orthodox Marxist response to *Ideologie und Utopie*, and a third Marxist review came from Ernst Lewalter.[85] The major sociology journals also contained reviews of *Ideologie und Utopie*, by Plessner[86] (*Kölner Vierteljahreshefte für Soziologie*), Fritz Stern[87] (*Archiv für Sozialwissenschaften*), Julius Kraft[88] (*Zeitschrift für Völkerpsychologie und Soziologie*) and Karl Dunckmann[89] (*Archiv für Angewandte Soziologie*). Other critiques included those of Siegfried Marck,[90] and Landshut in his *Kritik der Soziologie*.[91] The early Frankfurt School published an appraisal by Max Hokheimer[92] and Herbert Marcuse (though he was not, strictly speaking, a member of the group until later), whilst Theodor Adorno's critical comments on Mannheim are to be found scattered in his early works, for example his *Antrittsvorlesung* (1931)[93].

A consequence of the wide Marxist interest in Mannheim's work was that it ensured that one of the central issues taken up in relation to *Ideologie und Utopie* was the relationship between the sociology of knowledge and the critique of ideology — especially as Mannheim argued that the former had superseded the latter. This is true not merely, as one would expect, of critiques by authors like Horkheimer, but also of the penetrating review by Plessner. The relationship between the sociology of knowledge and the critique of ideology has remained one of the central areas of dispute surrounding the sociology of knowledge.

For the moment, it will be useful to examine one of the earliest reviews of *Ideologie und Utopie* — that by Ernst Curtius — since, it will be remembered, this was the only review to which Mannheim replied. Curtius' conservative critique, 'Sociology — and its Limits'[94], seeks to restrict sociology's intervention in the *Geisteswissenschaften*. Curtius hopes that German sociology will not play the same radical political and ideological role that it did in France during the Third Republic since it would be discredited as a legitimate individual discipline. However, what specifically concerns Curtius is that Mannheim seeks to transform this particular discipline into a universal science that will give a new meaning to the totality of historical events. *Ideologie und Utopie* raises 'nothing less than the question of the function of the mind in the present world'[95] since it asks how it is possible to think and live once the problem of ideology and utopia has been radically confronted. But, Curtius argues, this is merely 'a variant of . . . European nihilism, i.e., a state of mind of uprooted intellectual strata that has already been described by Nietzsche'.[96] Hence, rather than see Mannheim's work as something historically-specific and new, Curtius views it as merely 'a temporally bounded form of scepticism that belongs to the constants of intellectual history'.

Nevertheless, Curtius maintains that Mannheim's views must be challenged since 'in the wake of modern philosophies of life', he falsely evaluates change (as positive) and stasis (as negative). Mannheim's views are a danger to '*German* youth'; a critique of sociologism is essential to preserve German science and German universities. We must insist, Curtius argues, upon the importance of the '*unique person*' when we examine from various directions the 'essential determination of human beings'. Curtius in fact favours the development of a philosophical anthropology along the lines already advanced by Max Scheler — presumably because it, too, is concerned with essences and metaphysics. This is in contrast to Mannheim's position, which Curtius sees as resting upon the 'irrational experience' of Kierkegaard and mysticism. Ultimately, Curtius views Mannheim's argument as one that seeks to replace philosophy with sociology and to provide 'a theory and metaphysics of knowledge'.

But there is one area of *Ideology und Utopie* which particularly impresses Curtius, namely, its 'outstanding analysis of the sociological problem of the intelligentsia', even though it must return to an idealist standpoint:

The sociological analysis of the intellectual stratum must be completed by a philosophy of the mind. The mind can only recognize itself, however, in the collective display of its forms. Temporally, it is rooted in the past. Yet to the consciousness of the mind itself it is given as the eternal present. Hence it is neither ideological nor utopian to believe that the intellectual, if he understands himself, must experience this transcendence as reality and prove it in *this* existence.[97]

However one may judge Mannheim's account in *Ideologie und Utopie*, it is certainly directed against such intellectualist absolutization of the mind. But, as Ringer has shown, views such as those of Curtius were common among the German 'mandarins', especially in the *Geisteswissenschaften*.

Mannheim's reply to Curtius,[98] in a later issue of the same journal, is both an attempt to locate the problems of German sociology within a social and historical context and a detailed critique of Curtius' attack. Mannheim concedes that the sociology of knowledge is indeed concerned with the irrational since it seeks to show

> by means of *empirical research* those positions in all tendencies of thought in the humanities, social sciences, and in politics which have their roots in the irrational and, by means of conclusive analysis, of pursuing the question as to how taking such positions emerge even in the categorial apparatus.[99]

This irrational element is responsible for 'the inevitable nature of the element of *Weltanschauung* as, to a certain extent, a structural determinant of a particular area of thought: so-called "existence-related thinking" '. This 'existentially', in turn, is seen as 'a determinant stemming from irrationality and *Weltanschauung*'. Finally, these features taken together are presumably responsible for 'the one-sidedness of certain aspects of *all* points of view and of all parties', and this is what must be revealed by a sociology of knowledge.

Secondly, Mannheim counters Curtius' charge of nihilism by contrasting his own 'dynamic relationism' which 'invites *every* position for once to call itself in question and to suspend the self-hypostatization that is a habit of thought self-evident to everybody'.[100] As a result, the sociology of knowledge and the analysis of ideology will be able to demonstrate that 'the existentiality of almost all historical and social positions can be revealed'. This radical thinking through and Cartesian questioning is, Mannheim argues, neither the nihilism nor 'spiritual spinelessness' that Curtius claims it to be.

Finally, on the question of the relationship between sociology and philosophy, Mannheim quite specifically

> '[does] not wish to replace philosophy by sociology. . . . I am not only not against but expressly *for* metaphysics and ontology, and even teach their indispensability for an existence-related empiricism. . . . I am only opposed

to the presence of metaphysics which is not recognized and thus can serenely absolutize particulars.[101]

Indeed, Mannheim praises Heidegger's ontology as 'one of the most decisive achievements of contemporary philosophy'.

On no other occasion did Mannheim publicly reply to his critics. Had he done so, he would certainly have faced a more difficult task. However, Curtius' review does illustrate a by-no-means untypical response from conservatives in the humanities. Mannheim's reply is also significant, in that he again shows clearly the scientistic element of his programme for a sociology of knowledge that, by empirical analysis, will reveal and presumably correct 'irrationality', '*Weltanschauung*' and 'existentiality' in intellectual standpoints.

However, the present task is to investigate the various responses to *Ideologie und Utopie*. The philosophical, sociological and Marxist reception of *Ideologie und Utopie* will be broadly examined, even though the boundaries between these areas, particularly where the sociology of knowledge is concerned, are difficult to draw. The three 'philosophical' reviews examined are those of Hannah Arendt, Siegfried Marck and Paul Tillich, the three 'sociological' reviews those of Günther Stern, Julius Kraft and Helmuth Plessner, and the three 'Marxist' reviews are by Ernst Lewater, Adalbert Fogarasi and Karl Wittfogel. Finally, the 'neo-Marxist' reviews of Herbert Marcuse and Max Horkheimer will be discussed. Though this list is by no means exhaustive, hopefully it covers the most significant responses to Mannheim's *Ideologie und Utopie*.

The philosophical aspects of Mannheim's central thesis of the *Standortgebundenheit* of thought are critically examined by Hannah Arendt.[102] Mannheim's lack of commitment to any one of these *Standorten* immediately raises the question as to the possibility of a lack of standpoint (*Standortlosigkeit*). After destroying various philosophies' and world views' absolute claims to validity, Mannheim's sociology goes in search of reality, of what is useful for orientation towards the world (*Brauchbare zur Weltorientierung*). But, as Arendt points out,

> the striving for world orientation, however, signifies from the outset insight into the relevance of the intellectual sphere; a decision for lack of standpoint, knowledge about the possible fruitfulness of neutrality. In any case, this decisively distinguishes Mannheim's position from that of Georg Lukács who certainly also destroys the intellectual sphere's absolutist claim but from a particular standpoint, that of the proletariat and who thereby, unnoticed and without reflection, substitutes the concept of interest that is correctly valid there (and is very fruitful in concrete interpretation).[103]

Instead, what Mannheim does is to inquire into the reality that lies behind the intellectual sphere, into what Arendt calls 'the possible genuine origin of the intellectual sphere'. Secondly, he sees all standpoints and all 'interpretations of existence' as orientations to a specific, historically-given world. In other words, Mannheim is concerned at this level with the relationship between the ontic and the ontological — a concern that is also paramount in the contemporary philosophies of Heidegger (*das Sein des Seienden*) and Jaspers (*der Existenz*), except that Mannheim's sociology is concerned, Arendt says, 'with the emergent existence [*das Seiende*] that lies at the root of this "interpretation of existence" [*Seinsauslegung*]'.

However, Mannheim's approach destroys the absolute distinction between the ontic and the ontological; the destruction of the absolutization of thought takes place not merely through its relativization but through its refutation. This refutation, Arendt claims, is the demasking of consciousness derived from the unconditional as *ideology* (in the sense of "total ideology")'. This has an important implication for philosophy since,

> 'viewed sociologically, philosophy is thus no longer the reply to the question of the existence of the emergent [*Sein des Seienden*] but not only exists itself as enchained and confined to the world of the emergent and its possibilities for motivation, as one emergent entity amongst others. . . . its claim to unconditionality rests upon the fact that it has forgotten its historical rootedness.[104]

Such a sociology thus radically questions other philosophies that are also concerned with the search for 'reality' and 'existence'.

Indeed, sociology moves in the opposite direction to such philosophies. It is not concerned with 'Being-in-the-world' as 'a formal structure of human existence as such' but, according to Arendt, with 'the respective historically determinate world in which man lives at a certain time'. In itself, this distinction between philosophical and sociological concerns is 'apparently harmless' unless sociology claims that philosophy cannot or is unable to examine this 'formal structure of human existence'. But at this point we are confronted with a version of the 'powerlessness of the mind' thesis that Arendt sees as most evident in Scheler's work.

However, whereas Scheler was concerned with the *powerlessness* of the mind, Mannheim, Arendt says, is concerned with the *homelessness* of the mind.

> Everything intellectual is interpreted either as ideology or utopia. Both, ideology and utopia, equally 'transcend existence', both arise from a consciousness 'that does not find itself in accord with the existence that surrounds it'. The *mistrust* of the mind that is observable in sociology and its attempt at destruction is the source of the homelessness to which the mind is condemned in our society. This homelessness and apparent uprootedness ('free-floating intelligentsia') makes everything intellectual suspicious from the very outset; a reality is sought after that is more basic than the mind itself and all intellectual products are to be interpreted or debased in relation to it. Here, debasement [*Destruierung*] does not simply mean destruction

[*Zerstörung*] but the reduction of a claim to validity to that situation from which it has emerged.[105]

This unmasking of the intellectual sphere is not dissimilar to that undertaken in psychoanalysis except that Mannheim's sociology of knowledge still leaves the situationally-bounded validity of the spiritual intact to a certain extent and, what is more decisive, the reality to which the intellectual sphere is reduced is a historical one that has been created by humanity. But, both sociology and psychology

> require a fundamentally different mode of *understanding* recognized in the humanities: not a *direct* understanding that the interpreter takes to be what exists, not an immediate confrontation but a diversion via a reality that is taken by the interpreter to be *more fundamental*.[106]

Even though the reality to which psychoanalysis refers is more estranged from the mind than that which concerns sociology, both conceive of the mind as primarily 'secondary, estranged from reality'.

The reduction of the intellectual sphere to secondary status, and the tracing back of its objects to a prior historical reality, prompts Arendt to inquire into the nature of this reality and sociology's competence to carry out historical research. The reality back to which the mental sphere is traced is the 'concrete existent order of life' that is most clearly observable in particular types of 'economic-power structures'. Mannheim even sees in this existential boundedness a 'chance for knowledge' in that knowledge does not remain unlocated in some void. This reality to which the mind is reduced is a 'public existence' that its members take to be the world. But again, Mannheim's reduction of the mind to a historical reality can only lead to its alienation since,

> In that sociology destroys, it already takes the mind to be homeless, i.e., as living in a world that is fundamentally estranged from it. The mind transcends this strange world and becomes . . . *ideology* and *utopia*.[107]

Hence, the interpretation of the intellectual sphere as ideological or utopian assumes that '*Geist*, as such, first exists when consciousness is not identical with the existence in which it is created.' False consciousness therefore arises when the categories for orientation to the world are not appropriate; that is, ideology and utopia are distinguished by their relevance for reality. Hence, sociology is not concerned 'simply with reality but rather with the *reality that has power over the mind*'.[108]

The second question Arendt raises, that of sociology's status, can be viewed in the light of the preceding analysis. As she points out, 'sociology claims to be a "central science" (*Zentralwissenschaft*)' because it alone is in a position to disclose the determinants of thought. But this claim, paradoxically, gives it 'a remarkably marginal character' since the mind (as ideology and utopia) is, from the outset, given as something homeless in the world, and its possible freedom 'can only come to exist outside historical interaction', i.e., ahistorically. *Geist* therefore exists as an 'ultimate residue' that is transcendent and ahistorical since 'the reality of history is so understood that there remains no actual place for it within it'. From this, Arendt concludes that sociology too has

> its historically bounded place at which it could first of all emerge: namely where a legitimate mistrust of the mind was awakened out of the homelessless of the mind. Hence, as a historical science, there is a quite definite limit to its *historical competence*. The interpretation of the intellectual sphere as its destruction into ideology and utopia first justifiably emerges where the economic sphere has extended itself so far that the mind can and must *factually* become 'ideological superstructure'.[109]

The mind is rendered homeless when its position is secured not by tradition but by its reliance upon the economic sphere. As Arendt points out, Mannheim speaks specifically only of the homelessness of the mind in the modern world. In another brief review, Aaron Gurwitsch too recognized in the sociology of knowledge a 'mistrust of the mind' (*Mistrauen gegen den Geist*).[110]

In his review, Siegfried Marck[111] also starts out from the problem of the existential boundedness of thought, which implies both the dependency of thought upon some real existence and a kind of epistemological determinism. The problems associated with this thesis have been more radically stated in sociology with the introduction of the concept of ideology. Marck refers back to Mannheim's paper on competition and argues that his introduction of the particular and total concepts of ideology has deepened the understanding of the Marxist interpretation of history. Marck argues that what both Marxism and Mannheim's position have in common is:

> The thesis that specific knowledge and specific value-positions are to be functionalized in terms of a real human subject, that in a specific sphere social life is co-constitutive of knowledge, that the mutually-conflicting ideologies of a period compete for 'possession of the public interpretation of existence' — these are the common assertion of the most modern type of sociology and of Marxism.[112]

But Mannheim's analysis of ideologies is to be distinguished from a Marxist one in that his conception refers to a value-viewpoint (particular ideology) and to a world-view (total ideology). In the first case, we have a 'polemic against class- and domination-determined ethical and political value-standpoints', in the latter a 'more theoretical attempt at the causal derivation of knowledge and especially of culture from economically given phenomena'. Marxism's polemical stance, Marck argues, prevents it from reflecting upon its own ideology and applying its concept to itself. This Marck sees as having been performed by Mannheim to the extent of removing Marxism from its monopolistic position in relation to ideological critique. In another respect, too,

Mannheim's position differs from the Marxist standpoint, in that it is not concerned with natural scientific knowledge.

Nonetheless, 'close connections exist between the methodology of the sociology of knowledge and the problem of dialectics'.[113] Both seek to relativize absolutist claims through the relativization of the contents of knowledge as elements of a systematic totality. In the discussion of politics in *Ideologie und Utopie*, Mannheim sees the boundedness of standpoints as a source of creative insights but that they produce only partial truths that must be corrected in a dialectical synthesis; that is, they are only partial moments of truth and the totality. Hence, Marck characterizes the sociology of knowledge and culture as a 'dialectical perspectivism', but unlike for Hegel, the dialectical synthesis is not a fundamental law of the mind but is rather the attempt to search out chances of synthesis in the present social situation. Again, Marck sees this as particularly true of Mannheim's article on competition and, in a different way, in his attempt to secure 'a possible autonomy of the mind over against its socially manifested forms' via the intelligentsia.

In other words, Mannheim's affinity with a dialectical approach is only apparent. Despite his claims, Mannheim's theory of the existential boundedness of thought has affinities with sociologism as well as dialectics. In contrast, it is the case that

> the law of dialectics represents a *dynamic basic law*, that thereby the justification of ideal dialectics is asserted, that in this sphere there exists only a decision concerning the primacy of ideal and real dialectics. However, a real dialectics that does not recognize such a primacy, in fact no longer means a dialectics but transforms the dialectical law nto sociological causality.[114]

Marck takes this argument and the consequent acceptance of a powerlessness-of-the-mind thesis as applicable to both Mannheim and Scheler.

At a more substantive level, Marck is critical of Mannheim's distinction between ideology and utopia. This cannot be made merely in terms of a distinction between immanence and transcendence, Marck says, since, as far as their existential determination is concerned, both are taken into account and 'transcendence by consciousness is, in the sociological method, in fact related to immanent social existence'. If this is true, then utopia is

> not in fact characterized by its timelessness, its essential absolute character, its separation from existence. Hence, however, the distinction between ideology and utopia is relativized. If evolutionary ideology realistically orientates itself towards seizure of domination and power, then existing elements of opportunistic ideology are included in this utopia. The contrast between both structures, the criterion for their differentiation is then, in fact, merely abandoned to the future.[115]

This is indeed the option favoured by Mannheim, who states that 'the criterion for ideology and utopia is *realization*.' In this respect, his argument comes very close to that of Marx and Lukács and 'the future becomes the undisputed judge of the content of contemporary consciousness'.

Paul Tillich's review is a largely positive account of Mannheim's work.[116] Tillich sees the book as of fundamental importance to sociologists, philosophers and, above all socialists. Like Marck, however, he has serious reservations concerning Mannheim's distinction between ideology and utopia in terms of their transcendence of existence, since it 'is in both cases something so different that it is only the sound, and not the meaning, of the word which creates an identity'. On the other hand, Tillich finds the relationship between absolute and relative utopias a fruitful distinction. More problematic, however, is the notion of a total and general concept of ideology. The concept of ideology cannot be 'total' if one thesis is taken as being free from its rootedness in the ideological sphere, namely the thesis of a concrete dynamic truth. Nor can there be a 'general' concept of ideology if one stratum — the intelligentsia — is excluded from its existential boundedness.

However, Tillich is favourably impressed by Mannheim's overall problematic and suggests five areas where existing concepts or arguments might be improved or extended. His recommendations are: that the concept of ideology should retain 'its concrete, political conflict-laden character' and 'the particular and special concept of ideology should not be elevated into the general'; that one must ask how much ideology lies in one's own political theory, i.e., a plea for self-criticism; that the dynamic notion of truth should be developed further but this cannot be done without there being presupposed 'at one point an absolute standpoint in existence and hence in thought'; that the latter may be developed out of the concept of 'cognitive chance' though this may not necessarily, as in Mannheim's case, be the intelligentsia but might still be the social situation of the proletariat; and, finally, that one should not treat the ideological problem as something general and intellectual but as rooted in concrete social existence itself.

Of the three 'sociological' reviews of Mannheim's work to be examined, by Günter Stern, Julius Kraft and Helmuth Plessner, Kraft's article, entitled 'Sociology or Sociologism', is the most hostile.[117] Indeed, he starts out by asking whether the sociology of knowledge as a discipline is possible at all since 'sociology is certainly the (or, at least, a) theory of social phenomena, and knowledge is in and for itself not a social but a mental phenomenun'. On the basis of this remarkable argument, Kraft argues both that the distinction between sociological and psychological phenomena is crucial and that this is the source of the persistent danger of sociologism, of the reduction of social phenomena to social facts. Moreover, Kraft is uncertain in the case of the sociology of knowledge whether 'what is at issue is a new empirical science or a new philosophy'.

On the problem of ideology, Kraft suggests — without any grounds — that instead of a distinction between the particular and total concepts of ideology, Mannheim should 'distinguish between a psychological and an epistemological principle of ideology'. More seriously, he argues that Mannheim does not satisfactorily solve the problem of recognizing the ideological nature of all standpoints since Mannheim's relationism is also a form of relativism. Indeed Kraft sees this as emanating from Scheler's 'functionalization' of basic interpretations and agrees with Curtius that Mannheim's own standpoint here is a fundamentally nihilistic one. But Kraft goes even further, maintaining that Mannheim's position represents the 'dethroning of science and the enthroning of mysticism: What is real lies in the "extra-historical-ecstatic".'[118] Mannheim's position is said to be contradictory in that he wishes to proceed in a value-free manner whilst at the same time seeking to provide a 'sociological diagnosis of the times' that will ultimately lead to 'evaluation and to ontological decision'.

At the substantive level, Kraft vehemently denies that politics is not already a science, thereby rendering redundant the second chapter of *Ideologie und Utopie*. He also challenges the manner in which Mannheim draws up the various political positions in that chapter, calling Mannheim's attempt to synthesize political styles an instance of 'Kantian Marxism'. In short, at the end of his review, Kraft argues that there can be no sociology of knowledge either at a philosophical level or at the level of an empirical science — again, on the grounds of its inherent reductionism.

More rewarding as a critique of Mannheim's position is Günter Stern's review.[119] Stern seeks to extract some consequences of the existential boundedness-of-thought thesis that Mannheim has overlooked. For instance, if we assert the dependency of thought upon the social situation,

> then in so doing something is indirectly asserted about existence, about the situation. Now, from the outset, consciousness or self-interpretation etc. must conversely be taken into account as contributory factors in existence, in the situation, etc. This purely formal statement asserts: If consciousness is asserted to be a function of the existential situation, then it can no longer be compared with it or judged to be 'false' in the light of it — for the situation is nothing without this consciousness.[120]

Mannheim, Stern argues, does not see this consequence but instead operates with a dual notion of ideology, which, on the one hand, refers to the situational and relational dependency of thought and, on the other, refers to false consciousness. This prompts Stern to ask whether the concept of consciousness with which Mannheim operates, is inadequate for his problematic and whether the discrepancy between situation and consciousness actually represents a discrepancy between existence and consciousness. In part, the latter is a historical problem.

Stern suggests that, in itself, the examination of consciousness in the light of 'the basic situation and the specific existence of human beings' says nothing against historical method. However, historicism immediately becomes dangerous if it is the case that

> the existential concept of historicism — 'historical existence' — represents an *illegitimate absolutization*, that, despite the fundamental freedom of human beings in relation to history, it allows it to become *unhistorical*, hence a human existence that cannot be conceived of historically.[121]

If this is conceded, then we have here a fundamental philosophy of history thesis embedded in the sociology of knowledge. In other words, what Mannheim fails to examine is

> whether the existential base, to which one relativizes (in this case, in fact, history) is itself absolute; whether it is not . . . for its part, a *specific* situation and represents only a specific mode of human existence that is somehow fundamentally to be distinguished from the unhistorical existence of human beings.[122]

Stern examines this problem in the light of an analysis of the present(*heute*), the 'today' that is so important in Mannheim's 'diagnosis of the times'. For the historicity of human beings does not reside in their living in an 'unequivocal present' but rather in the fact that they appear 'to be with one foot already here and with another still there, i.e., to have an equivocal present'. What this implies is that the reduction of consciousness to a specific situation overlooks history itself since 'consciousness itself, *qua* existentially bounded consciousness, also represents an emergent or an existent factor that takes part in the making of the historical situation against which it is to be measured'.

Secondly, the problem of the plurality of present times in which people exist raises the question as to which one is 'genuine', which one is the norm for knowledge of the present for 'there exists many presents, many present existences "simultaneously" side-by-side and, because of the simultaneity of generations, in partial concealment'. This incongruity between consciousness and existence must therefore be viewed in a different light. It cannot be that consciousness is merely incongruent to a group of people, but that their existence is incongruent (Stern gives the example of the 'unhistorical' peasant threatened by emergent machine production and argues that it is not his consciousness that is incongruent but his existence). More significantly, this analysis of the 'present' reveals to us when it is that ideology emerges: in 'situations without a present', in situations in which forces or worlds with their own history confront other worlds in an ingenuine present. In such 'historically adverse' situations ideologies provide us with a false present. Again, what is false is 'not consciousness of the present . . . but the present "is false"', in so far as it makes a claim to historical dignity'. What Stern pinpoints here is a crucial feature of Mannheim's philosophy of history embodied in his theory of ideology and utopia — the philosophy of the absent present.

In the light of Stern's argument concerning the 'present', one can see that history itself becomes problematical. As Stern puts it,

> history — that appeared for Mannheim as the destroyer of every absolute truth-claim, as the genuine emergent, as the basis of destructions — *sub specie* the unhistorical situation, which in a real sense is not *one* situation and not being a single one is not in a real sense *emergent*, seems to be itself problematical, itself an absolutization.[123]

Thus, whilst the argument that Mannheim's position is nihilistic can be countered by the fact that it rests upon 'the secure basis of "history" whose existence he never doubts', Stern is correct to question history's status in Mannheim's doctrine since it is never clear 'in what existential medium history is realized'. Certainly, Mannheim sees a discrepancy between reality and history but Stern seriously doubts whether this justifies a new task for sociology. On the other hand, Stern is convinced that there exists in Mannheim's work

> the relativization of history itself or its claim to be the absolute medium of all that occurs. And the evidence that Mannheim's appeal to history, which originally had a viewpoint that merely relativized validity, must itself become the absolutization of history. More plausible than by means of the analysis of the ingenuine present is the legitimation of such relativizations by reference to positive unhistorical forms of existence.[124]

Ultimately, Stern views the study of ideology as based upon 'a metaphysics of history' that is itself rooted, paradoxically, in a vote of mistrust *against* history'. This metaphysics Stern formulates as follows:

> Although nothing exists other than history, history is its own history of concealment, it is the flight from its own existence, that moves in other modes of existence only located in the superstructure. In so far as it lives in other modes of existence, such as transcendence, validity, etc., then it is, despite itself, in the wrong.[125]

Here, then, perhaps lies an important clue to at least one of the sources of the radical historicist versions of the sociology of knowledge.

It is a different historical perspective that is taken up by Plessner in his article 'Modifications of the Notion of Ideology'.[126] He tries to show how the notion of ideology has been transformed from its inception in Marx's work, through its extension in historicism, to its restriction within the sociology of knowledge.

The first 'fateful metamorphosis' of the concept of ideology occurred, according to Plessner, with its historicist generalization. Whereas the original concept in Marx is both 'weapon and concept, political means and sociological reality' and refers to concrete historical class formations, its basic features can be taken out of this context and generalized. In other words, the notions of base and superstructure and their correspondence can be retained and extended in the direction of a 'universal comparative sociology' and a comparative history of culture. In so doing, however, Plessner argues that it loses

1. its unequivocal reference to a single development and becomes indifferent to the true and false or the genuine and ingenuine.
2. its unequivocal reference to the concept of social class and economic political interest. . . . Ideology becomes . . . a pure epiphenomenon of a vital lower stratum which ultimately can now appear merely as an irrational limiting sum without any kind of positive determination in the 'study of ideology'.[127]

The humanities and sociology have both sought to move away from the nineteenth-century concept of development (and indeed to view it as an ideology). Instead, Plessner says, they have sought to exclude their own value position by treating it as just as objective as any other, but with far-reaching consequences.

The levelling of one's own standpoint at the level of objectivity . . . is continued with a radical reserve in relation to the validity-claims of values in every particular value-sphere of every particular cultural circle.[128]

This methodological relativism is accompanied by a transformation of the concept of false consciousness into

consciousness that stands in relation to a specific human existence and standpoint. This consciousness is not false because it does not yet possess the truth that it can possess but because it cannot be detached from it and cannot secure a truth as an independent one. What is correct for one state of consciousness must be incorrect for another. Thus, consciousness stands indifferent to the true and the false in its particular relationally valid perspective.[129]

Hence, consciousness now becomes false precisely because it is derived from a specific existential basis, and this 'falseness' can no longer be corrected by human intervention since 'the possibility of measuring the particular "worlds" in which social forms live in terms of something is absent.'

The notions of superstructure and base are also transformed in this historicist generalization of the notion of ideology. The superstructure now confronts 'practical or natural vital "interests" ' or a 'psychophysical base' and in itself 'its claims have no basis. They are merely an expression of life that it needs in order to live'. The whole world becomes ideological and man himself 'an ideological animal'. Similarly, the base is no longer an economic situation, a social class or a historical subject but merely 'a piece of nature . . . life'. In other words, 'the base . . . declines to the level of the sub-human, the animal-like and ultimately . . . to the level of naked vitality'.

Against the background of this historicist enlargement and extension of the concept of ideology, and as a counter to charging one's own critique with being ideological (so that Marxism itself is explained as the ideology of the proletariat), a restricted concept of ideology leading to the sociology of knowledge emerged. Thus, Plessner argues, Mannheim seeks to introduce an evaluative concept of ideology in contrast to the historicist one. He wishes to move to a diagnosis of viewpoints through a correct understanding of them and hence returns to the notion of false consciousness as a critical concept and to an evaluative, dynamic concept of ideology. The concept of reality is also opened up once more and it seems as if Mannheim is returning to the original Marxist problematic.

But Plessner sees the sociology of knowledge's concept of ideology as lacking three of its original features:

1. For the sociology of knowledge there is no progressive development of history. There exists there only events taking place without reference to a comprehensive goal, also without an unequivocal gradation that results from dialectical constraint. . . . Ideology is here . . . the ever possible solidification in a state of consciousness that has been surpassed: the bad accord with the times of what has lagged behind.
2. Similarly, the sociology of knowledge's notion of ideology lacks unequivocal reference to class interest and hence political unequivocalness. In its place is the formalized 'group interest' . . . a category that was earlier characteristic of the historicist line of thought. It can be applied to the most diverse social forms . . .
3. Finally, this concept of ideology lacks the clear, specifiable criterion of true consciousness. . . . Thus, a consciousness is true which stands in existential accord or equilibrium with praxis. A criterion for this, especially in Mannheim's sense, does not exist. . . . We never know when and what the present [*heute*] is. It is the essence of the present (*Gegenwart*) to remain secret.[130]

In all these respects, the new concept of ideology is radically different from that of Marx. But these are not the only problems facing Mannheim's sociology of knowledge since he is also making other claims for it. Foremost amongst them is, that sociology can solve many of philosophy's problems. Plessner sees a tendency to identify philosophy with 'acceptance of absolutism and a fixation with transcendental questions', whilst ignoring the fact that the concept of ideology itself rests upon basic philosophical presuppositions concerning the historical nature of human existence.

In conclusion, Plessner argues that sociology should recognize that it differs substantially from Marxism, however important it has been in the past development of sociology.

> For neither research nor politics has an interest in the false peace between sociology and Marxism which, by means of more or less conscious change in the value and meaning of the concept of ideology, brings about its transformation into a category of empirical sociology. A decontaminated 'ideology', reduced to a category, to a principle of investigation, a 'tension between base and superstructure' that has been reduced to a general human mode of existence is contained in a Marxist orientated sociology and is eternalized in its particular 'revolutionary–materialist' thesis without burdening itself with the risks and consequences of Marxism.[131]

This false peace between sociology and Marxism is to the detriment of both, and Plessner detects a tendency to transform elements of Marxism into 'an eternal programme for sociology'. But the result is

> A semi-Marxist perspective in the social sciences and, precisely because of this, a gradual blindness to the social realities to which Marxist concepts actually give expression. *For there exist situations, for which the strategic instrumentarium, outlined by Marxism, in the sense of its revolutionary polemic, possesses an empirical, sociological truth value.* . . . But what is of concern here is in fact, specific situations and not, as fashion would have it, constants of every previous or even, over and above that, every possible human situation.[132]

Though Plessner does not refer to anyone specifically here, he pinpoints one of the central features of the sociology of knowledge's problematical relationship to Marxism and, especially, to the concept of ideology, regardless of whether it is a sociology of knowledge, advanced by Scheler or Mannheim.

Not surprisingly, Marxist reviews of *Ideology und Utopie* also concentrated upon the problematical relationship between Mannheim's sociology of knowledge and Marxism. This is certainly true of the reviews by Lewalter, Fogarasi and Wittfogel, but perhaps less true of the neo-Marxist critiques by Marcuse and Horkheimer.

Wittfogel's brief review is part of a more comprehensive survey of what at the time was recent literature on the sociology of knowledge.[133] The whole of this tradition — Wittfogel includes Troeltsch and Weber within it — is seen as part of a wider 'crypto-Marxist' movement which, though relying on Marx's work, has nothing to do with its political element and seeks to avoid in a scientific manner the 'one-sidedness' and 'exaggerations' of his work. Wittfogel does discern 'left' tendencies in *Ideologie und Utopie*, such as the emphasis on the crisis-ridden nature of the world, the play with Marxism and with the notion of a revolutionary solution to the crisis. But Mannheim's relativization of Marxism, results, Wittfogel says, merely 'from the standpoint of a formalistic eclecticism'. Similarly, despite his use of the notion of the class-boundedness of knowledge, Mannheim always falls back upon 'highly vulgar categories from the realm of parliamentarism and from the sphere of circulation' such as 'opposition' and 'competition'.[134] Indeed, in the latter case, Mannheim has no conception of class limits to knowledge and instead merely speaks of class competition.

In short, for Wittfogel, the destruction of the class basis of Marx's concept of ideology is manifested in Mannheim's reluctance to raise the question of 'which' standpoint is the basis for correct knowledge. Instead, with respect to both ideology and utopia, it is merely a question of 'when' they appear as to which determines their truth value. What this implies is that competition between ideologies, for example, takes place 'within the same cognitive level', while 'structural diverse cognitive processes' that take place on 'diverse social class levels' are ignored. Even where Mannheim refers to social classes his analysis is purely external, unconcerned with their roots in the production process.

Though Mannheim is reluctant to locate his own position, it is revealed in his notion of the free-floating intelligentsia, Wittfogel argues, in the evolutionary goals of the social democrats to which he subscribes and in his ultimate 'decision in favour of the dynamic centre'. In short, 'the great fashion of bourgeois social science, the sociology of knowledge', Wittfogel says, 'has *nothing at all* to say to Marxism'.[135] Yet behind all the invective, Wittfogel accurately points to the source of Mannheim's political and economic categories in parliamentarism (it will be recalled here that Scheler saw this as the social source of relativism) and the circulation process (competition).

A more interesting orthodox Marxist review of *Ideologie und Utopie* is provided by Adalbert Fogarasi in his essay, 'The Sociology of the Intelligentsia and the Sociological Intelligentsia'. Forgarasi argues that a fundamental critique of the sociology of knowledge is necessary 'since the issue is not merely an abstract methodological school, but a tendency that has a deep social and political significance'.[136]

The fundamental aim of *Ideologie und Utopie*, Fogarasi argues, is the transcendence of Marxism, in that its theory of ideology may be applied to itself. This prompts Fogarasi to ask what it means to apply a proposition to itself in both logical and dialectical terms, whether this problem was unknown to Marx and whether Marxism is itself an ideology. Formal logic, Fogarasi argues, has already refuted scepticism on the grounds that its assertion that all truths are open to doubt is itself not open to doubt. More interestingly, Fogarasi argues that the application of concepts and categories to themselves has led to the development of a 'philosophy of philosophy' (Croce or Bergson), or 'logic of philosophy' in the case of Emil Lask. What this represents, according to Fogarasi, is a kind of self-destruction of philosophy (e.g., Lask's logic of the 'logic of logic'), of which Mannheim himself is guilty both in his epistemology of epistemology ('Structural Analysis of Epistemology'), developed under the influence of Lask and Lukács, which 'relativizes all individual tendencies' and, more recently, in his sociology of sociology (presumably in *Ideologie und Utopie*).

> The consequence of this critique of epistemology was clear in its masters — Mannheim, Zalai, Lukács just as much as Lask. Zalai, Lukács and Lask strove to move from *epistemology* to metaphysics. They wished to transcend epistemology in order to replace it with metaphysics. Mannheim is less explicit on this but his tendency is nonetheless precisely the same. This must be asserted in order to clearly recognize the character of his critique of Marx.[137]

For Fogarasi, however, scepticism and idealism are not transcended by formal logic but by praxis. Instead, what Mannheim does is to engage in 'a tedious empty play with formulae' that are applied to Marx's arguments in order to refute them. But this universal application of formal logic and universalization of the social boundedness thesis does not confront Marx's theory at all. Its social boundedness is completely different from the social boundedness of bourgeois ideology. Thought becomes ideological in a capitalist society 'not because it is *determined* as such but because it is determined by the *antagonistic relations of production* in capitalist society' and by the fetishism of commodities and the illusions it creates. In contrast, Mannheim's analysis of ideology is that of a kind of 'critical critique' which treats all social boundedness alike. For instance,

> bourgeois ideology is not therefore false consciousness because it is a class standpoint as such but in fact because it is a *specific* class standpoint, the capitalist class standpoint and because from *this* standpoint reality necessarily appears inverted.[138]

Similarly, social classes have an interest in supporting or transcending certain forms of consciousness but Mannheim's analysis also excludes such interests.

Fogarasi maintains that Mannheim's work represents 'a kind of sociological intellectual history' that erroneously believes in some neutral position from which it can judge the whole, one which seeks to overcome the deep intellectual crisis of the times from 'the standpoint of eclecticism' by synthesizing the partial truths of all other standpoints. In other words, it seeks

> to overcome ideology purely ideologically. It interprets the crisis of bourgeois ideology as a purely intellectual crisis and does not see that this relativistic intellectual crisis is merely the reflection of the deeper crisis of the capitalist system itself. . . . The *first* fundamental illusion and self-illusion lies in the fact that one can overcome ideology through abstract considerations upon the relativity of all ideology. . . . The *second* fundamental error is the eclectic viewpoint that one can grasp a specific part of reality from *each* standpoint.[139]

But this procedure, Fogarasi argues, merely leads one to believe that what is wrong with ideology is merely its one-sidedness rather than its distortion of reality. Secondly, the synthesis derived from eclecticism, the *Zusammenschau*, is associated with the irrational, anti-intellectualism of modern bourgeois philosophy (e.g., the phenomenological school) and represents merely a mechanical addition of parts of knowledge and, ultimately, a renunciation of scientific knowledge. By this means, it is impossible to grasp the totality which is a dialectical, not a mechanistic, concept.

If, according to Mannheim, the guiding thread of *Ideology und Utopie* is the intellectual crisis, then, Fogarasi argues, this is in itself nothing new; it does not differ greatly from what Simmel saw as the 'crisis of modern culture'. But this crisis is really that of a specific capitalist society. The *weltfremd* manner in which philosophy takes up this crisis leaves room for Mannheim to see the crisis as capable of being solved scientifically by a sociology of the intelligentsia. But, Fogarasi suggests, if we examine the composition of this stratum then we can see that it does have a political significance. It is composed of the free professions, state officials (Fogarasi views this as significant for social fascism), those in the middle who do not constitute a class and are therefore not class-conscious but are nevertheless conscious of their task, and those engaged in partyless politics in universities and political schools. If a political decision has to be made then it will be 'a decision for the dynamic centre'. Fogarasi dismisses this theory of the 'Heidelberg sociological school' as a mask for bourgeois ideology, as linked with the social fascism of the social democrats.

In contrast, the most thorough attempt to analyse the relationship between Mannheim's sociology of knowledge and Marx's theory of ideology is Ernst Lewalter's article, 'The Sociology of Knowledge and Marxism'.[140] Lewalter sees German sociology as having changed its response to Marxism after the First World War, from one of 'ignoring' or 'refuting' Marxism to 'overcoming' it. This new position he sees as being best represented by Mannheim's work and especially his attempt to go beyond Marx's critique of ideology.

Lewalter maintains that whereas Marx's notion of ideology contains two elements — the extent and character of ideology is correlated with the particular stage of social existence and the possibility of the development of theory is largely limited to dominant classes in society — these are reduced in much modern sociology to the vulgar Marxist correlation of ideology with specific social classes. Mannheim, however, with his distinction between total and particular ideology comes close to Marx's distinction between concrete and ideological consciousness, but they differ in that, for Marx 'concrete consciousness' is, in principle, only possible after the 'communist revolution', for Mannheim it is . . . already contained in the individual's 'existential experience' and only requires, in some respects, prudent self-critical further development.[141]

Mannheim's notion of particular ideology also differs from Marx's in that the 'standpoint-boundedness' of thought has, for Mannheim, not merely a negative side (its limited validity), but a positive side (it contains a section of the total truth). Thus, Mannheim is rightly opposed to the absolutization of thought, but his 'brilliant analysis and deductions' are marred by erroneous assertions. For instance, how can historical materialism be imputed to the proletariat in the same manner as classical political economy is imputed to the bourgeoisie? The notion of imputation, Lewalter argues, is totally inappropriate here. In any case, Lewalter continues, a clear statement as to '*how far* Marxism is the "ideology of the proletariat" and hence only a "particular" truth is missing'. Perhaps part of the problem lies in Mannheim taking up elements that he erroneously imagines belong to Marx's concept of ideology, such as a presumed prevalence of praxis over theory, an economistic interpretation and a presumed determinism. Indeed, Lewalter suggests that Mannheim is much more deterministic than Marx, since

> The 'existential boundedness' of thought . . . contains a strong deterministic element. If 'I' am really bound up with my thought in my 'standpoint in the sociological sphere', then this thought appears, in fact, to be so determined that, to a certain extent, I can only think 'as a citizen', 'as a worker', 'as an academic', 'as a politician', etc. and the possibility of ideology-free thought in principle is not present so long as the 'sociological sphere' is not homogeneous, i.e., as long as classes are not transcended. The two claims that Mannheim provides — the proposition of class-boundedness as a social–psychological determinant of every system and the proposition of the 'striving for totality' — stand, as it were, directly in the way of access to his 'dynamic relationism'.[142]

One of the problems here, according to Lewalter, is that Mannheim tends to misinterpret the notion of existence determining consciousness as referring to 'the "social–vital" boundedness of the individual thinker to his "standpoint" '. But, as Lukács argued, Marx's theory cannot be psychologized in this manner. Lewalter concludes by suggesting that the existential boundedness thesis is one of correspondence for Marx and one of determination for Mannheim.

Lewalter goes on to argue that more than the concept of ideology seems to have been taken by Mannheim from Marxism. The second chapter of *Ideologie und Utopie* is concerned with praxis, with 'politics as political praxis' and 'action in a still-not-regulated situation'. But, when Mannheim outlines five major tendencies of political thought in relation to the notion of praxis, he fails to see that it is the Marxist one that comes closest to his notion of dynamic relationism. Instead, he moves on immediately to the question of synthesizing political perspectives through the intelligentsia, even though the assumption that the possession of education can lead to group solidarity is actually a hypostatization of intellectuals themselves. With regard to Mannheim's ultimate 'decision' for dynamic relationism, Lewalter sees it as 'a form of active resignation, a "diagnosis" of the present that is directed towards an, in principle, unrecognizable future, an extreme attempt to maintain as value-free what is necessarily value-laden'.[143]

One might imagine, Lewalter suggests, that moving on to the third chapter of *Ideologie und Utopie* we should encounter the most significant aspects of Marxism, having already been through the 'economistic' image in the first chapter and the 'theory–praxis philosophy' of Lenin and Lukács in the second. Indeed, discussion of utopia prompts Lewalter to ask whether it is historical materialism or dynamic relationism that has the deeper insight into the principles of historical development. Here there seem to be certain affinities, in that both are:

1. *Individualizing theories of history* . . . Hence both reject 'generalizing', 'causalistic' and 'deterministic' theories since they rob the specific present moment of its existential significance.

2. *Activistic theories of history* insofar as the study of its principles is to serve the 'therapeutic' via the 'diagnosis'. Hence both reject 'contemplative theories' (cf. for instance Marx against Feuerbach, Mannheim against Scheler's doctrine of the 'pre-existence of the superstructure').

3. *Ontic theories of history* insofar as they claim to reveal the 'essence' of historical development in 'historical time'. . . .

4. *Dialectical theories of history* insofar as they make the growth of theories out of existence . . . into an axiom.[144]

However, Lewalter points out that it is at the level of the determinants of historical ontics that the difference between Mannheim and Marx is greatest since, in Mannheim's case, there is almost no evidence to suggest what the basis of his theory is. Even if we concede that Mannheim's reservation about Marxism is 'a purely sceptical one', we are likely to argue either that his basic motives are Marxist or that his scepticism, clothed as perspectivism, does indeed lead beyond Marxism. Lewalter argues that the last section of Mannheim's book would lead one to believe that 'this scepticism is absolute'.

If we turn, finally, to the reception of Mannheim's *Ideologie und Utopie* by the Frankfurt School, then, as with the more orthodox Marxist reviews a common response is not at all evident.[145] The reviews of Herbert Marcuse and Max Horkheimer represented very different positions, not merely because Marcuse was not yet a member of the

Institut für Sozialforschung but because his Marxism was still mediated by Heidegger's philosophy, and therefore closer to that of Mannheim.

Marcuse sees the whole problematic of our present scientific situation (which is itself the problematic of present human existence)' as being presented in a dramatic fashion in *Ideologie und Utopie*, namely, 'the universal historicity of human existence and the questionable nature of the traditional separation of real and ideal being that springs from it.'[146] The sociological method of interpreting intellectual phenomena itself emerges out of the scientific knowledge of universal historicity. Mannheim presents a radical interpretation of this thesis with his notion of the existential boundedness and ideological nature of thought, including Marxism itself. Hence, for Mannheim, Marxism too is seen as the ideology of a particular social class — the proletariat. Marcuse sees a positive gain in this interpretation of Marxism since it views Marxism as a theory that relates back to the social existence of the proletariat and can only be understood in this manner. This is in contrast to both revisionism and Adler's transcendental–sociological interpretation of Marxism, both of which obscure this fact.

Furthermore, Mannheim's position recognizes Marxist theory as a concrete theory of political praxis which refers to the concrete actuality. This relativization of Marxism, Marcuse says, could be countered with the argument that 'the concrete historical determination of a theory . . . does not say anything at all about the truth and validity of this theory'. But, according to Marcuse, Mannheim shows that the question of the truth and validity of a historical theory cannot be solved by the traditional concept of truth that presupposes an 'ideal, universal, timeless system detached from history itself'. What Mannheim does is to raise the problem of the historical nature of theories that are a function of the social existence from which they emerge. He provides, Marcuse argues, two solutions to the problem of historical truth: that of 'true and false consciousness' and that of the 'dynamic totality'.

Mannheim's first solution is to suggest that consciousness is false when it is not in accord with its realization at a given stage of existence. But where, Marcuse asks, are the grounds for its realization? Sociology ignores two aspects of the existential nature of events. Mannheim 'takes the particular historical stage of existence as the ultimate datum that is irreducible and necessary for the sociological method'. But if one takes 'apparently stable, rigid, unequivocal stages of existence', such as feudalism or early capitalism, then it is clear that, in their concrete actuality and not merely as abstract conceptions, they are 'in themselves dynamic, fluctuating, equivocal'.

Secondly, the sociological method ignores the '*intentional* element of all events', in the sense that modes of existence are related to something; historical situations realize something that must already be given to them. Marcuse draws two implications for the problematic of historical truth from these considerations. Firstly, that 'the sociological method cannot take up the historical stage of existence (*Seinstufe*) as merely a given foundation and make it into the concrete instance for a decision as to truth' not least because the particular consciousness is itself a constituent of that existence. Secondly, and this is especially important for Marxism, 'the political-social stage of existence is itself not something ultimate but as a historical necessity can and must be transformed.'[147]

The second solution, that of a 'dynamic synthesis', maintains that each particular theory, as an existentially bounded theory, contains a partial aspect of the truth. Hence, a possible criterion for truth is the comprehensive synthesis that 'realizes the historically-possible optimum of the total view'. The concrete presuppositions for such a synthesis are, that

> the theories dealt with were historically prior and that the new standpoint was historically so situated that it made possible the comprehensive perspective. Both presuppositions again represent the given stage of existence as the ultimate decisive instance. The second approach therefore leads back to the first. Only by presupposing that the particular historical stage of existence is also *eo ipso* the historically 'true' stage of existence can such a synthesis guarantee the optimum of truth.[148]

In opposition, Marcuse argues that the historical stage of existence is not given as an ultimate foundation but also 'transcends itself'. However, this in turn implies that one cannot remain content merely with an evaluation of consciousness since, 'in the realm of history it is not only a consciousness, a line of thought, a theory, that is true or false, but also a concrete situation *itself* and its mode of life'. Thus, both consciousness and historical situations are not, with reference to truth or falsity, of 'equal value'. Valuations are already contained within a particular historical situation and its form of life that extend beyond what is immanent to it. Hence, we can never take a particular mode of organizing life as a mere facticity.

In contrast to Marcuse's critical but not unsympathetic review, Horkheimer's attack on Mannheim's concept of ideology leaves little that can be salvaged from *Ideologie und Utopie*.[149] Like Plessner, Horkheimer is concerned with the inversion and distortion of Marx's original concept of ideology. In Marx's case,

> the purpose of his science was not knowledge of a 'totality' or a total and absolute truth, but the transformation of specific social circumstances. In connection with this purpose, philosophy too was criticized, but without putting a new metaphysics in the place of the old.[150]

This, Horkheimer seeks to show, is precisely Mannheim's intention — though one may note in passing that the critique of the centrality of the totality is also an implicit criticism of Lukács.

Horkheimer argues that Mannheim radicalizes and generalizes the concept of ideology in the direction of a 'correspondence' between group situation and modes of cognition, evaluation and action (i.e., not merely the 'content' of thought). Similarly, whereas the original total concept of ideology was bound up with the political, particular concept, for Mannheim the concept of false consciousness is generalized. This new 'value-free' application of the concept of ideology leads to 'a new separation of intellectual systems with reference to their truth'. Their degree of agreement with the existing stage of reality is the norm for deciding their truth-value. Hence, the contemporary crisis lies in the fact that each competing 'system of life' is 'particular', even though each claims to represent the totality.

This 'new' concept of ideology operates within a totally different context when compared with Marx's concept. Whereas

> Marx wished to transform philosophy into a positive science and into praxis, the sociology of knowledge ultimately pursues a *philosophical* purpose. The problem of absolute truth, its form and its content, disturbs it; it sees its mission in its illumination. The ever-deeper insight into the change in all metaphysical decisions . . . itself becomes a metaphysical procedure.[151]

Hence, Mannheim's preoccupation with changes in intellectual forms as 'the essence of man' restores a metaphysical intention reminiscent of Dilthey's philosophy of history. But ultimately Mannheim has recourse to ahistorical elements such as 'ecstacy', to a metaphysics of history which his own theory of ideology would negate as being ideological. Marx's critique of ideology, on the other hand, was directed against metaphysics, against viewing the 'essence', human beings, as the subject of history and against viewing history as a harmonious totality. Instead, history was seen as the result of 'processes that grow out of the highly contradictory relationships in human society' (Horkheimer) and not as composed of competing world-views. In Mannheim's sociology of knowledge, however, there lies an 'idealist conviction' which results in the restoration of the metaphysics of history.

This is the context within which Mannheim's radicalization of the concept of ideology can be understood. Devoid of any specific content, it has been removed from the realm of political critique and no longer refers to 'individual theories and evaluations of opposing parties', Horkheimer says, 'but immediately to the whole of consciousness'. Mannheim's notion of ideology replaces any psychology of interests by a structural analysis. But what this analysis consists of is unclear. Systems of world-views are presumably seen as developing not, Horkheimer says, out of 'the life-situation of human beings' but as being bound-up with 'specific social strata'. In a similar vein, the system of world-views also includes a specific 'economic intention' (*Wirtschaftswollen*) but there is never any suggestion that social or economic processes determine the intellectual totality. Rather, Horkheimer believes, Mannheim is searching 'for the "correspondence of form" between the social situation and the world-view totality conceived roughly in the sense of an "ideal type" '. This notion of totality is also problematical since Mannheim conceives of it in the form of 'a superficial concept of *Gestalt*'. This implies that one can understand a world-view in terms of its intellectual form in an immanent and intuitive manner. This, Horkheimer argues, is an 'idealist illusion'.

This, in turn, raises the question of the nature of the existential boundedness of consciousness. Despite Mannheim's insistence that the intellectual sphere is closely bound up with social classes,

> still his idealist endeavour to conceive of intellectual processes as untarnished by the crude power struggles of real human beings is so strong that each indefinite connection between being and consciousness actually appears as merely an external juxaposition, even as fateful submission. For him there exists the crude struggles of the historical everyday world and *also alongside them* the conflicts between 'systems of world-views'.[152]

This can only be because Mannheim lacks a comprehensive theory of the concrete structuring of society that can locate this 'being' and these 'world-views'. Otherwise, 'without such a theory, the expression *Seinsgebunden* remains completely without content'. Even where Mannheim makes reference to specific groups in society, his account of their determination remains unclear.

Obviously, this has consequences for his notion of truth — the criterion can now only be whether thought is appropriate to its 'times'. But such a standard is completely arbitrary since there exists no means of deciding whether thought is appropriate to its times. This idea is all the more remarkable in view of Mannheim's intention of providing a 'diagnosis of the times' which, based as it is on idealist presuppositions,

> must provide a highly one-sided picture: it certainly advances the claim that from it 'our total existential and intellectual situation' will be grasped 'in a cross-section', but this cross-section leaves the most important parts of social reality undisturbed.[153]

Even where Mannheim takes up a specific mode of thought and attempts to locate it socially and historically, as in his essay on conservative thought,

> few indications are to be found as to the connections between intellectual group categories, such as 'conservative', and social reality. The historical circumstances of the agents of his thought, their relation to other social strata and the total political situation are only occasionally sketched out, as if the 'conservative' world image were intelligible at all without the most careful study of these states of affairs. The whole work limits itself almost exclusively to 'phenomenological–logical analysis of style', 'immanent analysis of world-views', analysis of 'experience', analysis of the common currents of

diverse intellectual styles and similar-sounding analyses of intellectual forms.[154]

In conclusion, Horkheimer argues that Mannheim's sociology of knowledge, whilst utilizing 'a highly "radical" language and Marxist intellectual means' ultimately leads to the transformation of 'existing contradictions into the oppositions of ideas, "intellectual styles" and systems of world views'.

It should be apparent from this brief overview of Marxist and neo-Marxist responses to *Ideologie und Utopie* that all the reviewers felt the necessity for a serious confrontation between Marxism and Mannheim's sociology of knowledge and especially his introduction of a 'new' concept of ideology. Perhaps more surprising is the fact that writers like Lewalter and Marcuse, despite substantial criticisms, should feel that the sociology of knowledge has something valuable to contribute to an understanding of problems already raised within the Marxist tradition. That is, some reviewers saw Mannheim's work as containing something more than a Marxist rhetoric.

Within the Marxist tradition itself, what is noticeable about these reviews is the relative absence of references to the work of Lukács and his critique of ideology. In the case of orthodox Marxist reviews this is less surprising since Lukács was not in favour in this period. Hence, from the standpoint of Fogarasi, for example, Lukács' work can be linked with the general problematic within which Mannheim himself operates. But there is hardly so much as a suggestion that a Marxist account of ideology might deal with the problem of reification and commodity fetishism, even within the neo-Marxist camp.

A key feature of these reviews must therefore remain the reluctance to take up the critique of ideology from Lukács' standpoint as a counter to, or alternative to the sociology of knowledge. Hence, when reviewers in the Marxist tradition appraised Mannheim's theory of ideology they compared it not with Lukács' account but with that of Marx. All of them, to a greater or lesser degree, found substantial differences between Mannheim's and Marx's accounts of ideology. Only an inadequate knowledge of Marx could therefore promp Otto Neurath to characterize Mannheim's work as 'bourgeois Marxism'[155] — an epithet subsequently applied to many other writers and sociology itself.

In examining the debates surrounding the sociology of knowledge and, in particular, the reception of Mannheim's *Ideologie und Utopie*, it is clear that contemporaries readily understood the theoretical and practical issues that this project confronted. To a greater or lesser extent, they shared its preoccupations or, at least, could conceive of them as real and also as urgent. Hence, as Neusüss argues in relation to Mannheim's work,

In terms of present-day awareness, the reaction to Mannheim's sociology of knowledge in the social sciences and humanities at the close of the Weimar Republic can . . . only be fully comprehended if the specific intellectual and political atmosphere is recalled in which the problems of relativism and historicism, of the autonomy of the human mind over against all political and social determinations and the independence of 'culture' over against a threatening 'mass civilization', were still burning existential questions for intellectual strata.[156]

All these issues were present, to a greater or lesser degree, in the sociology of knowledge of this period and especially in Mannheim's work which, Eisermann argues, is 'perhaps the most distinctive contribution that German sociology has made to the whole construction of this discipline'.[157] But the sociology of knowledge not only took up all these issues, it also presented them in a radical form as theoretical *and* practical problems. For instance, all the philosophies which the sociology of knowledge took up also raised the problem of relativism, but the fact that these competing philosophies were seen to exist within the same temporal sphere further heightened the sense of relativism. Moreover, in reducing these philosophies to the status of world-views (a project already commenced by Dilthey) and, in turn, in reducing world-views to systems of life, the sociology of knowledge transformed relativism into a *practical* issue that had to be resolved practically as well as theoretically. This task was particularly urgent if, at the same time, one had already called into question the possibility of 'theoretical' solutions by reducing the 'superstructure' of society to an epiphenomenon. The crisis of consciousness is at the root of the work of Lukács, Scheler and Mannheim. Whereas for Lukács the problem is that of the transformation of consciousness out of its reified state, for Scheler it is the 'powerlessness of the mind' and for Mannheim the 'homelessness of the mind' that are the central issues. In all three cases, albeit in very different contexts, one can speak of the central importance of the alienation of the mind.

Similarly, the historicist prolematic was not confined to questions relating to how one can interpret cultural phenomena, though the hermeneutic intention was particularly strong in both Lukács' and Mannheim's work. Rather, the presupposition of a historically-dynamic flux within which cultural objectification was located and understood, combined with the conflict between 'cultures' in the sense of systems of life, called forth a desire for synthesis. Again, this was not confined to the sociology of knowledge but was often to be found in traditions which the sociology of knowledge took up. Troeltsch, for example, saw *Der Historismus und seine Probleme* as being not merely concerned with the historical emergence of modern thought but as itself 'a historical-philosophical theme'. In the preface, he writes:

> My fundamental notion is . . . directed towards the formation of a *contemporary cultural synthesis* [italics added, D.F.] out of the historical inheritances, for which task it is unimportant whether one belongs to the emergent or declining branch of cultural development.[158]

For Mannheim, however, at least by the time of the publication of *Ideologie und Utopie*, the demand for a synthesis had become political as well as cultural. The sociology of culture had become the sociology of political ideologies. Furthermore, it now mattered for Mannheim where one was located within the totality of historical development: one had to be located in the progressive historical flux. The problem of historicism had taken on a practical and political urgency.

The immediate aspects of the philosophy of history within this tradition were significant, in that for Lukács, Mannheim and, to a lesser extent, Scheler — in their different ways — a 'philosophy of history with a practical intent' (Habermas) was of considerably urgency. Lukács saw the progressive decline of capitalism as not bringing about a revolutionary consciousness in the proletariat. His concern was to retain this consciousness as an 'objective possibility' and, later, to embody it within the political party. Lukács' orientation was still towards the *future*. Scheler, in contrast, viewed the disintegration of post-War society, and the threatening collapse of what he took to be essential values, with dismay. In this sense, his orientation is towards the *past*, in so far as his intention is the preservation of essential values. Mannheim, too, was preoccupied with social and political disintegration and the consequent lack of orientation. His response is to seek to develop a 'diagnosis of the times' — an orientation towards the *present*.

Conclusion

An account of the problems faced by a sociology of knowledge and a critique of ideology in the work of Scheler, Mannheim and Lukács, together with the debates surrounding the sociology of knowledge in Weimar Germany, should dispel any notion that the development of this field of discourse was unilinear. Its history is not that of the steady accretion and accumulation of knowledge. Nor does it resemble textbook histories in which victory is presented as inevitable for those who were victorious. No 'tacit consensus of great minds' emerged. Rather, it was a complex history of often unrealized but always disparate intentions. This partly accounts for the difficulty in according the whole project a place within sociology. The ease with which its epistemological interventions have been dismissed has often hidden a latent distaste for some of its other concerns — a philosophy of history, a theory of the crisis of modern culture, a plea for sociology as an analysis of the present, or an attempt to supersede a critique of ideology whilst seeking to retain its intention.

Aside from distancing oneself from the German tradition — a strategy adopted by Berger and Luckmann — a more common response until recently has been hostility towards the whole project and ignorance of its foundations. Surveying the American reception of this tradition, Kurt Wolff commenced with

> two tendencies that have characterized most, though not all, American writings in this field: *impatience with epistemology* and rejection of the idea that the sociology of knowledge occupy itself with it and, perhaps more than animosity, indifference toward Marxism and ignorance of it.[1]

Wolff goes on to suggest that in the United States two further tendencies are apparent in work on the sociology of knowledge: that it usually 'takes *an ahistorical-systematic, rather than a historical approach*'[2] to its subject matter; and its 'attention to *social psychology* and to G. H. Mead in particular'.[3]

This is an accurate summary of trends in this field in the USA at least until the late 1960s, and suggests why the German tradition would remain alien to American sociological consciousness. Berger and Luckmann argue that this was largely the result of its embeddedness in a distinctive socio-intellectual context, in

> a particular situation of German intellectual history and in a philosophical

context. When the new discipline was subsequently introduced into the sociological context proper, particularly in the English-speaking world, it continued to be marked by the problems of the particular intellectual situation from which it arose.[4]

They maintain that perhaps this accounts for its marginal position within contemporary sociology, since the original problems appeared no longer relevant. Indeed,

> the sociology of knowledge remained a peripheral concern among sociologists at large, who did not share the particular problems that troubled German thinkers in the 1920s.[5]

This 'peripheral concern' was later echoed by Mannheim himself when, towards the end of his life, he referred to the sociology of knowledge as 'this marginal field of human knowledge'.[6]

But this assessment confuses the problems raised by the sociology of knowledge with its reception as a branch of an academic discipline that became increasingly divided. The problems raised within the German tradition have remained troubling to sociology and have even resisted being confined to its periphery. Some of the issues, and even the mode of analysis, have continued to be pursued in recent years. The renewal of a phenomenological tradition in the sociology of knowledge has caused many of the starting points of Scheler's earlier analysis to be taken up. The stimulus for this direction most probably lies in Scheler's phenomenological accounts of *ressentiment* and sympathy rather than in his axiomatic programme for a sociology of knowledge.[7]

In Lukács' case, the centrality of the reification problematic was maintained not merely amongst his own students in the post Second World War period (and even more recently in an identifiable Budapest School) but also within an important tradition that, on many issues, remained hostile to Lukács' position, namely the Frankfurt School. Even though Horkheimer, for instance, announced his distance from Lukács' position in his key essay 'Traditional and Critical Theory', with the conviction that 'even the situation of the proletariat is, in this society, no guarantee of correct knowledge',[8] this did not prevent him, together with Adorno, from later presenting a pessimistic theory of reification and rationalisation in their *Dialectic of Enlightenment*,[9] a project that is impossible to conceive of outside the context of *History and Class Consciousness*. In other words, the pessimistic implication was of a dialectic of rationalisation advanced as a philosophy of history and based upon Lukács' amalgam of Marx, Weber and possibly Simmel, but lacking faith in the proletariat and rejecting Lukács' own philosophy of history assumptions. But within the Frankfurt School the actual analysis of the process of reification at a concrete historical level was to be found in the later work of Walter Benjamin whose *Passagen-*

werk, intended as a 'prehistory of modernity', represents a fundamental advance in Marxist cultural analysis. However, as his recently published notes for this project show, Lukács does not figure prominently.[10]

The Frankfurt School also retained Lukács' insistence upon the centrality of a critique of ideology, even to the extent of either identifying it with Marx's notion of science or of evading the issue of the relation between the two. The tradition of critical theory also maintained a hostility to the whole of Mannheim's project for a sociology of knowledge and insisted on the demarcation between the critique of ideology and the sociology of knowledge.[11] This was despite their own earlier tendency — evident in Horkheimer's work, as Apel has argued[12] — to bring their own analysis down to the level of sociologistic reductionism. And, in this context, one may suspect that their obsessive demarcationism with regard to Mannheim's work — however justified many of their criticisms may be — was sometimes due to uncomfortable similarities with their own work.

However, more recent developments in critical theory have resulted in the restoration of a number of dimensions of social theory that are also present in Mannheim's work though not originating there. In his study of Mannheim's German writings, Simonds has drawn attention to the significance of the hermeneutic tradition within Mannheim's sociology of knowledge.[13] Yet, however persuasive Simmonds' argument may be with respect to Mannheim's earlier writings — and especially the two unpublished essays — our analysis of *Ideologie und Utopie* suggests that this methodological aspect of Mannheim's work became increasingly less important.

Similarly, whatever judgment may be passed upon Mannheim's sociology of knowledge, his *Ideologie und Utopie* cannot be accused of being a purely academic project. Mannheim, like Lukács earlier, sought to provide the social sciences with what Habermas terms 'a philosophy of history with a practical intention'. Mannheim assumed that the sociology of knowledge would lay the foundations for a 'diagnosis of the times'. His own subsequent development after his emigration to England exhibits the reinforcement of this tendency and an ever-decreasing interest in the sociology of knowledge. Yet in Weimar Germany, the response to *Ideologie und Utopie* shows that Mannheim impressively raised both the case for sociology as an analysis of the present (*Gegenwartsanalyse*) and the wider problematic of the practical role of sociology. In so doing, he may have expressed this practical role in the context of what he took to be a dynamic philosophy of history (as Lukács had done earlier, more radically) that clashed with a theory of society incapable of unlocking the social existence (the *Sein*) that formed its counterpoint. The critical intention remained well in advance of the actual analysis of society. Here, and again with reference to the reviews of his *Ideologie und Utopie*, Mannheim's contemporaries scented the suggestiveness of the concept of the social boundedness (*Seinsverbundenheit*) of thought whilst, at the same time, realising the vagueness of the actual content of this *Sein*. Mannheim's use of the concept was undoubtedly greatly influenced by Heidegger's *Sein und Zeit* and pointed to the extent to which his sociology of knowledge was grounded in a phenomenological ontology that could not easily be translated into an empirical analysis of society.[14]

This deficiency is related to a further problem that remained more widespread in the sociology of knowledge. In the work of Scheler, Mannheim and Lukács, this field of discourse had its origins in a sociology and philosophy of culture. Some contemporaries detected with unease the extent to which society was often reduced to culture — a tendency already present in German sociology. In the sociology of knowledge this problem served only to compound the difficulties of clarifying the nature of the social existence with which knowledge was 'bounded'.

In a wider context, this raises the question as to the extent to which the sociology of knowledge and its critique of ideology not only rested upon but remained caught within a base-superstructure model. This is a consistent feature of Scheler's sociology of knowledge and, for most of the time, Mannheim's too. Lukács' location of the reification problematic within the context of the commodity structure of society moves in a different direction, though the base-superstructure model often reappears elsewhere in his work. This is not surprising given how widespread was the permeation of orthodox and mechanistic Marxism and much cultural sociology by this model; it provided an essential source of the alienated mind thesis in its various forms. The tendency to reduce ideology to a superstructure determined by a material base — whatever its content — was detected by many contemporaries, as the survey of the debate surrounding the sociology of knowledge has shown. Again, this problem has not disappeared from sociological discourse, as recent discussion illustrates.[15]

What the preceding comments suggest is that we need to look once more at the issues raised by the sociology of knowledge in Germany whilst retaining a critical stance in relation to its alienation of the mind thesis. For beyond its many weaknesses lies a body of issues that have returned to the centre of sociological debate. Furthermore, the theories of alienation, the contributions to the methodological disputes in the social sciences, and the whole domain of a critique of ideology, as well as the foundations for a sociology of knowledge and 'a philosophy of history with a practical intention', all have a history that goes beyond the German tradition in the sociology of knowledge. It was no mere aberration in the development of sociology, as its confinement to a marginal or totally historical contextual status would suggest. Nor was it a discourse upon issues that should be forgotten. Debates on the practical role of a critical sociology, even calls for a 'reflexive' sociology, suggest the opposite.

At the same time, the alienated mind thesis does permeate this tradition in various forms. Even with regard to the sociology of knowledge as a whole, one contemporary, Gurwitch, detected a 'mistrust of the mind' (*Mistrauen gegen den Geist*).[16] Scheler's life/spirit dichotomy, combined with the laws of the relationship between the two, leads to the 'powerlessness of the mind' and what Lenk termed a 'tragic consciousness'. For Lukács, the gap between actual reified consciousness (which also contains elements of a tragic consciousness, especially for the bourgeoisie)[17] and the 'objective possibility' of revolutionary consciousness was to be overcome through political activity and reflection. For Mannheim, the 'homelessness of the mind' is resolved by its relocation within the relatively detached intelligentsia and, by implication, within the sociology of knowledge itself. Each, in their different ways, was concerned with the alienation of consciousness.

References and Notes

1 The Sociology of Knowledge in Weimar Germany

1. An account of the historical antecedents of the theory of ideology on the one hand, and the sociology of knowledge on the other, is to be found in the following two studies: H. Barth, *Wahrheit und Ideologie*, Zürich 1945, and E. Grünwald, *Das Problem der Soziologie des Wissens*, Vienna 1934, especially pp. 1–51; and also, more briefly, in K. Lenk, *Ideologie*, Neuwied/Berlin 1967, 3rd ed., pp. 17–59.
2. E. Wittenberg, 'Die Wissenschaftskrise in Deutschland im Jahr 1919', *Theoria*, vol. 4, 1938, pp. 235–64; also S. Kracauer, 'Die Wissenschaftskrise', in *Das Ornament der Masse*, Frankfurt 1963.
3. G. Lukács, *Die Zerstörung der Vernunft*, Berlin 1954, ch. 4, part 5.
4. K. Mannheim, 'Wissenssoziologie' in A. Vierkandt (ed.) *Handwörterbuch der Soziologie*, Stuttgart 1931. Reprinted in K. Mannheim, *Ideologie und Utopie*, Frankfurt 1969, 5th ed., pp. 227–67. All references are to this reprint. See especially pp. 266–7.
5. E. Grünwald, *Das Problem der Soziologie des Wissens*, p. 184.
6. K. Mannheim, 'Diskussion uber "Die Konkurrenz" ' in *Verhandlungen des Sechsten Soziologentages* 1928, Tübingen 1929, p. 97.
7. L. Coser, 'Max Scheler: an Introduction', in M. Scheler, *Ressentiment*, New York 1961, p. 9.
8. H. Barth, *Wahrheit und Ideologie*, p. 294.
9. Ibid., pp. 295–6.
10. K. Lenk, *Marx in der Wissenssoziologie*, Neuwied/Berlin 1972, esp. pp. 199 ff. See also the critique by E.M. Lange in *Philosophische Rundschau*, vol. 21, 1975, pp. 129–38.
11. A. Wellmer, *Critical Theory of Society*, New York 1971.
12. D. Böhler, *Metakritik der Marxischen Ideologiekritik*, Frankfurt 1971.
13. K. Lenk, *Marx in der Wissenssoziologie*, pp. 199–200.
14. Ibid., pp. 202–3.
15. Ibid., p. 203.
16. A. Wellmer, 'Communications and Emancipation', in J. O'Neill (ed.), *On Critical Theory*, New York 1976/London 1977, p. 236.
17. H. Bosse, *Marx-Weber-Troeltsch*, Munich/Mainz, 1971, p. 90. See also pp. 90–9.
18. K. Löwith, 'Max Weber und Karl Marx', *Archiv für Sozialwissenschaften*, vol. 67, 1932, pp. 53–99; 175–214.
19. See G. Simmel, *Philosophie des Geldes*, Berlin 1900; English trans. T. Bottomore and D. Frisby, *The Philosophy of Money*, London/Boston 1978, esp. chs. 3–6.
20. See, H. Barth, *Wahrheit und Ideologie*, especially pp. 207–82; also, more recently, M. Funke, *Ideologiekritik und ihre Ideologie bei Nietzsche*, Stuttgart

1974. For Nietzsche's philosophy of history see also H. Schnädelbach, *Geschichtsphilosophie nach Hegel*, Freiburg/Munich 1974, pp. 76–87 and J. Habermas, *Knowledge and Human Interests*, (trans. J. Shapiro), Boston/London 1971, pp. 274–300.
21. K. Mannheim, 'Wissenssoziologie' loc. cit., p. 266.
22. Quoted in H. Barth, *Wahrheit und Ideologie*, p. 223.
23. *Ibid.*, p. 228.
24. J. Habermas, *Knowledge and Human Interests*, p. 295.
25. Quoted in J. Habermas, *Knowledge and Human Interests*, pp. 297–8.
26. H. Barth, *Wahrheit und Ideologie*, p. 245.
27. Ibid., p. 247.
28. See M. Scheler, *Von Umsturz der Werte*, 4th ed., Bern 1955.
29. On Nietzsche's philosophy of history, see H. Schnädelbach, *Geschichtsphilosophie nach Hegel*, pp. 76–87.
30. For a commentary on Dilthey's influence upon Mannheim's sociology of knowledge, see M. Horkheimer, 'Ein neuer Ideologiebegriff?', *Archiv für die Geschichte des Sozialismus und der Arbeiterbewegung*, vol. 15, 1930, pp. 33–56. Reprinted in K. Lenk (ed.), *Ideologie*, especially pp. 288–91.
31. E. Grünwald, *Das Problem der Soziologie des Wissens*, pp. 46–7.
32. There is a substantial literature on Dilthey and some translations of his works. These include: H.P. Rickman (ed.), *Dilthey Selected Writings*, Cambridge 1976; H.P. Rickman, *Meaning in History*, London 1961; H.A. Hodges, *Wilhelm Dilthey: An Introduction*, London 1944; W. Dilthey, *The Essence of Philosophy* (trans. S.A. and W.T. Amery), Chapel Hill 1954. For commentaries on Dilthey see H.A. Hodges, *The Philosophy of Wilhelm Dilthey*, London 1952; H. Holborn, 'Dilthey and the Critique of Historical Reason', *Journal of the History of Ideas*, vol. 11, 1950; H. Marcuse, 'Das Problem der geschichtliche Wirklichkeit', *Die Gesellschaft*, vol. 8, 1931; M. Horkheimer, 'The Relationship between Psychology and Sociology in the work of Dilthey', *Studies in Philosophy and Social Science*, Vol.8, 1940; H. Gadamer, *Truth and Method*, (trans. G. Barden and J. Cumming), London 1975; M. Riedel, 'Einleitung' to: W. Dilthey, *Der Aufbau der geschichtlichen Welt in den Geisteswissenschaften*, Frankfurt 1970; M. Riedel, 'Das Erkenntniskritische Motiv in Dilthey's Theorie der Geisteswissenschaften', in R. Bubner, et. al. (eds.), *Hermenentik und Dialektik*, Tübingen 1970. More recently, see also the valuable study by R.A. Makkreel, *Dilthey, Philosopher of the Human Studies*, Princeton 1975.
33. H. Schnädelbach, *Geschichtsphilosophie nach Hegel*, p. 124.
34. W. Dilthey, *Der Aufbau der geschichtlichen Welt in den Geisteswissenschaften*, (Gesammelte Schriften, vol. 7), Stuttgart/Tübingen 1958, p. 199 f.
35. H.J. Lieber, *Kulturkritik und Lebensphilosophie*, Darmstadt 1974, p. 60.
36. Ibid., p. 33.
37. W. Dilthey, *Gesammelte Schriften*, vol. 7, p. 232.
38. Ibid., p. 201.
39. Ibid., p. 202.
40. H.J. Lieber, *Kulturkritik und Lebensphilosophie*, p. 62.
41. See W. Dilthey, *Weltanschauungslehre. Abhandlungen zur Philosophie der Philosophie*, (Gesammelte Schriften, vol. 8), Stuttgart/Göttingen, 1960.
42. H.P. Rickman (ed.), *Dilthey Selected Writings*, p. 136.
43. Ibid., p. 137.
44. W. Dilthey, *The Essence of Philosophy*, p. 24.

45. H.J. Lieber, *Kulturkritik und Lebensphilosophie*, p. 57.
46. H.P. Rickman (ed.), *Dilthey Selected Writings*, p. 140.
47. Ibid., p. 135.
48. H.G. Gadamer, *Truth and Method*, p. 192f.
49. K. Lenk, *Marx in der Wissenssoziologie*, p. 46.
50. For a useful discussion of the various meanings of 'Historismus', see H. Schnädelbach, *Geschichtsphilosophie nach Hegel*, p. 19 f. See also K. Heussi, *Die Krisis des Historismus*, Tübingen 1932.
51. E. Troeltsch, 'Die Krisis des Historismus', *Die Neue Rundschau*, vol. 33, 1922, p. 573. See also Troeltsch's *Der Historismus und seine Probleme*, Tübingen 1922, and *Der Historismus und seine Überwindung*, Berlin 1924.
52. E. Troeltsch, 'Die Krisis des Historismus', *loc. cit.*, p. 576.
53. Ibid., p. 589.
54. K. Lenk, *Marx in der Wissenssoziologie*, pp. 9–41.
55. Ibid., p. 39.
56. G. Simmel, *Philosophie des Geldes*, 2nd ed., Berlin 1907. See also G. Simmel, *The Philosophy of Money*, (trans. T. Bottomore and D. Frisby), London/Boston 1978 and my introduction there. See also my *Sociological Impressionism*, London 1981, esp. chs. 4, 5.
57. G. Simmel, *The Philosophy of Money*.
58. Ibid., p. 454.
59. K. Lenk, *Marx in der Wissenssoziologie*, p. 17.
60. S. Kracauer, *George Simmel. Ein Beitrag zur Bedeutung des geistigen Lebens unserer Zeit*, unpublished ms., c. 1919–20, p. 89. See also my *Sociological Impressionism*.
61. See S. Kracauer, *George Simmel*, p. 90.
62. See G. Simmel, *Die Probleme der Geschichtsphilosophie*, 5th ed., Munich/Leipzig, 1923, p. 67 f.
63. L. Marcuse quoted in K. Gassen and M. Landmann (eds.), *Buch des Dankes an George Simmel*, Berlin 1958, p. 189.
64. G. Simmel, 'The Conflict in Modern Culture', in G. Simmel, *The Conflict in Modern Culture and Other Essays*, (trans. P. Etzkorn), New York 1968, p. 42.
65. M. Weber in a letter to R. Liefmann (1920). Quoted in W.J. Mommsen, 'Discussion on Max Weber and Power Politics' in O. Stammer, (ed.), *Max Weber and Sociology Today*, (trans. K. Morris), Oxford 1971, p. 115.
66. K. Lenk, *Marx in der Wissenssoziologie*, p. 25.
67. See W. Mommsen, 'Max Weber's Political Sociology and his Philosophy of World History' in D. Wrong (ed.), *Max Weber*, Englewood Cliffs, N.J. 1970, p. 191.
68. M. Scheler, *Die Wissensformen und die Gesellschaft*, Bern/Munich 1960, p. 432.
69. K. Lenk, *Marx in der Wissenssoziologie*, pp. 29–30.
70. M. Weber, 'Wissenschaft als Beruf', *Gesammelte Aufsätze zur Wissenschaftslehre*, 2nd ed., Tübingen 1951, p. 604.
71. Ibid., p. 605.
72. K. Mannheim, 'German Sociology (1918-1933)' in K. Mannheim, *Essays on Sociology and Social Psychology*, London 1953, p. 210.
73. Ibid., pp. 211-2.
74. K. Mannheim, 'Zur Problematik der Soziologie in Deutschland', *Neue Schweizer Rundschau*, vol. 22, 1929, pp. 820-9. English trans. by K. Wolff in K.H. Wolff (ed.), *From Karl Mannheim*, New York 1971, p. 263.

75. Ibid.
76. Ibid.
77. See the recent collection, E. Lederer, *Kapitalismus, Klassenstruktur und Probleme der Demokratie in Deutschland 1910-1940*, Göttingen 1979, and esp. H. Speier, 'Emil Lederer: Leben und Werk' in the same volume, p. 269.
78. M. Scheler, *Schriften aus dem Nachlass*, vol. 1, Bern 1957, p. 264.
79. M. Scheler, 'Prophetischer order Marxistischer Sozialismus?' in *Schriften zur Soziologie und Weltanschauungslehre*, Bern 1963, p. 260.
80. M. Scheler, 'Arbeit und Weltanschauung' in *Schriften zur Soziologie und Weltanschauungslehre* p. 273.
81. M. Scheler, *Die Wissensformen und die Gesellschaft*, p. 84.
82. M. Scheler, 'The Future of Man', (trans. O. Becker), *The Monthly Criterion*, Feb. 1928, p. 101.
83. Ibid., pp. 106-7.
84. Lukács' political writings in this period have recently appeared in German. See G. Lukács, *Taktik und Ethik. Politische Aufsätze I, 1918-1920*, Darmstadt/Neuwied 1975; G. Lukács, *Revolution und Gegenrevolution. Politische Aufsätze II, 1920-1921*, Darmstadt/Neuwied 1976; G. Lukács, *Organisation und Illusion. Politische Aufsätze III, 1921-1924*, Darmstadt/Neuwied 1977.
85. A. Grunenberg, *Bürger und Revolutionär*, Cologne/Frankfurt 1976, p. 185.
86. G. Lukács, *History and Class Consciousness*, (trans. R. Livingstone), London 1971, p. xlvii.
87. K. Mannheim, 'Problems of Sociology in Germany', *loc. cit.*, p. 263.
88. Ibid., pp. 263-4.
89. K. Mannheim, 'American Sociology', *American Journal of Sociology*, vol. 37, 1932, pp. 273-82; Reprinted in K. Mannheim *Essays on Sociology and Social Psychology*, pp. 192-3.
90. K. Mannheim, 'Problems of Sociology in Germany', *loc. cit.*, p. 263.
91. K. Lenk, *Marx in der Wissenssoziologie*, pp. 78-9.

2 Max Scheler

1. Max Scheler, 'Die positivistische Geschichtsphilosophie des Wissens und die Aufgabe einer Soziologie der Erkenntnis', *Kölner Vierteljahreshefte für Soziologie*, vol. 1, no. 1, 1921. Reprinted in M. Scheler, *Schriften zur Soziologie und Weltanschauungslehre*, Leipzig 1923/4; 2nd enlarged edition Bern 1963. English translation in J.E. Curtis and J.W. Petras (eds.), *The Sociology of Knowledge: A Reader*, London 1971. Also M. Scheler, 'Weltanschauungslehre und Wissenssoziologie', *Kölner Vierteljahreshefte für Soziologie*, vol. 2, no. 1, 1922. Reprinted in *Schriften zur Soziologie und Weltanschauungslehre*, op. cit. Scheler's use of italics, though often quite arbitrary, has been preserved in my translations of the passages quoted. Where I have added italics for emphasis this is indicated within the quotation.
2. W. Jerusalem, 'Soziologie des Erkennens', *Die Zukunft*, vol. 67, 1909, pp. 236-46.
3. M. Scheler, (ed.), *Versuche zu einer Soziologie des Wissens*, Munich 1924.
4. M. Scheler, *Schriften zur Soziologie und Weltanschauungslehre* op. cit.
5. See *Verhandlungen des 4. Deutschen Soziologentages 1924*, Tübingen 1925.
6. M. Scheler, *Die Wissensformen und die Gesellschaft*, Munich 1926, 2nd ed.

Bern/Munich 1960. All references are to this second edition. The first part of this work is now in translation. See M. Scheler, *Problems of a Sociology of Knowledge*, (trans. M.S. Frings and introd. K.W. Stikkers), London/Boston 1980; also my review in *Sociology*, May 1981.

7. This is pointed out in M. Bracht, *Voraussetzungen einer Soziologie des Wissens, erarbeitet am Beispiel Max Scheler*, Tübingen 1974, p. vii.
8. *Verhandlungen des 4. Deutschen Soziologentages 1924*, op cit. p. 183. (Also see Chapter 5 for a further examination of the discussion at this congress.)
9. E. Grünwald, *Das Problem der Soziologie des Wissens*, Vienna 1934, p. 159.
10. W. Bühl, 'Max Scheler' in D. Käsler (ed.), *Klassiker des soziologischen Denkens*, vol. 2, Munich 1978, p. 180.
11. K. Stikkers, 'Introduction' to M. Scheler, *Problems of a Sociology of Knowledge*, op. cit., pp. 3–4.
12. M. Scheler, *Die Wissensformen und die Gesellschaft*, op. cit. p. 11.
13. M. Bracht, *Voraussetzungen einer Soziologie des Wissens*, op. cit. p. 15.
14. *Die Wissensformen und die Gesellschaft*, op. cit., p. 11.
15. Ibid., p. 9. Unfortunately, Scheler's foreword is omitted from the recent translation.
16. K. Lenk, *Von der Ohnmacht des Geistes*, op. cit., p. 2.
17. E. Grünwald, *Das Problem der Soziologie des Wissens*, op. cit., p. 186.
18. H.J. Lieber, 'Bemerkungen zur Wissenssoziologie Max Schelers' in P. Good (ed.), *Max Scheler in Gegenwartsgeschehen der Philosophie*, Bern/Munich 1975, p. 228. In an earlier article, Lieber speaks of Scheler dealing with 'the old ontological and static dualism of spirit and life'; see H.J. Lieber, 'Zur Problematik der Wissenssoziologie bei Max Scheler', *Philosophische Studien*, vol. 1, 1949, p. 89.
19. M. Scheler, *Von Umsturz der Werte*, 4th ed., Bern 1955. This notion of the subversion of values is adapted from Nietzsche's analysis.
20. M. Scheler, *Philosophische Weltanschauung*, Munich/Bern 1954, p. 62.
21. K. Lenk, *Von der Ohnmacht des Geistes*, op. cit., p. 6.
22. M. Scheler, *Philosophical Perspectives* (trans. O.A. Haac), Boston 1958, p. 22.
23. K. Lenk, *Von der Ohnmacht des Geistes*, op. cit., p. 7.
24. Quoted in K. Lenk, op. cit., p. 7.
25. E. Cassirer, 'Spirit and Life in Contemporary Philosophy' in P.A. Schilpp (ed.), *The Philosophy of Ernest Cassirer*, New York 1958, p. 857 ff.
26. K. Lenk, *Von der Ohnmacht des Geistes*, op. cit., p. 11.
27. See for instance, H. Spiegelberg, *The Phenomenological Movement*, Hague 1965, vol. 1, pp. 228–68, which deals with Scheler's relations with Husserl.
28. K. Lenk, *Von der Ohnmacht des Geistes*, op. cit., p. 13.
29. M. Bracht, *Voraussetzungen einer Soziologie des Wissens*, op. cit., p. 55.
30. P. Honigsheim, 'Max Scheler als Soziolphilosoph', *Kölner Vierteljahreshefte fur Soziologie*, vol. 8, 1929, p. 106.
31. M. Scheler, *Ressentiment*, (trans. W. Holdheim and ed. L. Cosec), New York 1961, pp. 172, 174.
32. M. Scheler, 'Future of Man', (trans. H. Becker), *The Monthly Criterion*, vol. 7, no. 2, 1928, p. 111.
33. Ibid., p. 104.
34. M. Scheler, *Ressentiment*, op. cit., p. 166.

35. M. Scheler, 'Forms of Knowledge and Culture' in M. Scheler, *Philosophical Perspectives*, op. cit., p. 13.
36. E. Troeltsch, *Der Historismus und seine Probleme*, Tübingen 1922, p. 609.
37. E. Lenk, *Von der Ohnmacht des Geistes*, op. cit., p. 32.
38. This is remarked upon briefly and compared with Mannheim's notion of the homelessness of the mind in Hannah Arendt's review of Mannheim's *Ideologie und Utopie*. See H. Arendt, 'Philosophie und Soziologie', *Die Gesellschaft*, vol. 6, 1930.
39. M. Scheler, 'Der Bourgeois', *Abhandlungen und Aufsätze*, vol. 2, Leipzig 1915, pp. 295-334. Reprinted in M. Scheler, *Von Umsturz der Werte*, Bern 1955. M. Scheler, 'Die Zukunft des Kapitalismus', *Abhandlungen und Aufsätze*, vol. 2, Leipzig 1915, pp. 383-411. Also reprinted in M. Scheler, *Von Umsturz der Werte*, Bern 1955.
40. M. Scheler, 'Der Bourgeois', op. cit., p. 295.
41. Ibid.
42. M. Scheler, 'Die Zukunft des Kapitalismus', op. cit., p. 383.
43. Ibid., p. 404.
44. For a useful brief discussion of Scheler's wartime views see H. Lubbe, *Politische Philosophie in Deutschland*, Basel/Stuttgart 1963, pp. 221-7.
45. M. Scheler, *Die Wissensformen und die Gesellschaft*, Bern 1960 (2nd ed.), pp. 10-11. See also J.R. Staude, *Max Scheler*, Glencoe 1967.
46. Ibid., p. 11.
47. Ibid., p. 18 n.
48. Ibid., p. 17.
49. Ibid., p. 19.
50. Ibid., p. 20.
51. Ibid., p. 19.
52. Ibid., p. 20.
53. Ibid.
54. Ibid.
55. Ibid., p. 21.
56. Ibid.
57. Ibid., p. 23.
58. O. Hintze, 'Max Scheler's Ansichten über Geist und Gesellschaft', *Zeitschrift für die gesamte Staatswissenschaft*, vol. 81, 1926, p. 46.
59. M. Scheler, *Die Wissensformen und die Gesellschaft*, op. cit., p. 24.
60. Ibid., p. 25-6.
61. Ibid., p. 26.
62. M. Scheler, 'On the Positivistic Philosophy of the History of Knowledge', loc. cit., p. 164.
63. M. Scheler, *Die Wissensformen und die Gesellschaft*, op. cit., p. 29.
64. M. Scheler, 'On the Positivistic Philosophy of the History of Knowledge', loc. cit., p. 164.
65. Ibid., p. 165.
66. M. Scheler, *Die Wissensformen und die Gesellschaft*, op. cit., p. 32.
67. Ibid.
68. Most notably in G. Gurvitch, *The Social Frameworks of Knowledge*, (trans. E. and K. Thompson), Oxford 1972. A connection between Scheler and Gurvitch is suggested in W. Bühl, 'Max Scheler', op. cit., p. 221.
69. M. Scheler, *Die Wissensformen und die Gesellschaft*, op. cit., p. 39.
70. Ibid., p. 40.

71. Ibid., p. 42.
72. Ibid., p. 50.
73. See W. Jerusalem, 'Soziologie des Erkennens', *Kölner Viertejahrashefte für Soziologie*, vol. 1, no. 3., 1921, pp. 28–34. Scheler's reply is contained in M. Scheler, 'Zu W. Jerusalem's "Bermerkungen" ', *Kölner Vierteljahreshefte für Soziologie*, vol. 1, no. 3, 1921, pp. 35–9.
74. M. Scheler, 'Weltanschauungslehre, Soziologie und Weltanschauungssetzung', op. cit.
75. M. Scheler, *Schriften zur Soziologie und Weltanschauungslehre*, Leipzig 1923/4.
76. M. Scheler, (ed.) *Versuche zu einer Soziologie des Wissens*. Munich 1924.
77. *Verhandlungen des 4. Deutschen Soziologentages 1924*, op. cit. (See also Chapter 5 for a summary of the discussion surrounding Scheler's paper.)
78. M. Scheler, *Die Wissensformen und die Gesellschaft*, op. cit., p. 52.
79. P.A. Schilpp, 'The "Formal Problems" of Scheler's Sociology of Knowledge', *The Philosophical Review*, vol. 36, 1927, pp. 101–20. As far as can be discovered, this is the first review of Scheler's sociology of knowledge in English.
80. Quoted in P.A. Schilpp, 'The "Formal Problems" of Scheler's Sociology of Knowledge', op. cit., p. 104.
81. Ibid.
82. M. Scheler, *Die Wissensformen und die Gesellschaft*, op. cit., p. 53.
83. Ibid., p. 54.
84. Ibid.
85. Ibid., p. 55.
86. Ibid., pp. 55–6.
87. Ibid., p. 56.
88. Ibid.
89. Ibid., p. 58.
90. Ibid., p. 427.
91. Ibid., p. 58, n. 1.
92. Ibid., p. 426.
93. Ibid., p. 328.
94. Ibid., p. 425.
95. Ibid., p. 84.
96. M. Scheler, 'The Forms of Knowledge and Culture', in *Philosophical Perspectives*, op. cit., pp. 39–40.
97. 'Züsatze' in M. Scheler, *Die Wissensformen und die Gesellschaft*, op. cit., p. 427.
98. Ibid.
99. M. Scheler, *Schriften zur Soziologie und Weltanschauungslehre*, op. cit., p. 15.
100. M. Scheler, *Die Wissensformen und die Gesellschaft*, op. cit., p. 61.
101. Ibid.
102. Ibid., p. 63.
103. Ibid., p. 62.
104. Ibid., n .2.
105. W. Stark, *The Sociology of Knowledge*, London 1958, p. 118.
106. M. Scheler, *Die Wissensformen und die Gesellschaft*, op. cit., p. 63.
107. P.A. Schilpp, 'The "Formal Problems" of Scheler's Sociology of Knowledge', loc. cit., p. 115.
108. M. Scheler, *Die Wissensformen und die Gesellschaft*, op. cit., p. 65.

109. Ibid.
110. Ibid., p. 66.
111. Ibid., p. 67.
112. Ibid., p. 68.
113. Ibid.
114. H. Barth, *Wahrheit und Ideologie*, Zürich 1945, p. 347, n. 14.
115. M. Scheler, *Die Wissensformen und die Gesellschaft*, op. cit., p. 163.
116. Ibid., p. 170.
117. M. Scheler, *Schriften zur Soziologie und Weltanschauungslehre*, op. cit., p. 17.
118. M. Scheler, *Die Wissensformen und die Gesellschaft*, op. cit., pp. 170-1.
119. Ibid., p. 171.
120. T.W. Adorno and M. Horkheimer (eds.), *Aspects of Sociology* (trans. J. Cumming), Boston/London 1973.
121. M. Scheler, *Die Wissensformen und die Gesellschaft*, op. cit., p. 172.
122. Ibid.
123. Ibid., pp. 172-3.
124. M. Scheler, *Schriften zur Soziologie und Weltanschauungslehre*, op. cit., p. 26.
125. See the 'Einleitung' to H.J. Lieber (ed.), *Ideologienlehre und Wissenssoziologie*, Darmstadt 1974, p. 34, See also H.J. Lieber, 'Zur Problematik der Wissenssoziologie bei Max Scheler', *Philosophische Studien*, vol. 1, 1949, pp. 62-90 and H.J. Lieber, *Wissen und Gesellschaft*, Tübingen 1952, esp. ch. 2.
126. M. Scheler, *Die Wissensformen und die Gesellschaft*, op. cit., p. 129.
127. J.R. Staude, *Max Scheler*, op. cit., p. 180.
128. M. Scheler, *Schriften zur Soziologie und Weltanschauungslehre*, op. cit., p. 31.
129. M. Scheler, 'Wissenschaft und soziale Struktur' in *Verhandlungen des 4. Deutschen Soziologentages 1924*, op. cit., p. 119.
130. Ibid., p. 142.
131. Ibid., p. 142-3.
132. Ibid., p. 143.
133. Ibid., pp. 143-4.
134. Ibid., p. 144.
135. Ibid., p. 145.
136. Ibid., p. 153.
137. Ibid., p. 163.
138. Ibid., p. 165.
139. Ibid., p. 168.
140. 'Züsätze' to M. Scheler, *Die Wissensformen und die Gesellschaft*, op. cit., p. 447.
141. W. Bühl, 'Max Scheler', op. cit., p. 200.
142. See A. Schutz, *Collected Papers*, vol. 3, Hague 1966, and especially 'Max Scheler's Philosophy' and 'Max Scheler's Epistomology and Ethics', pp. 133-78.
143. O. Hintze, 'Max Scheler's Ansichten über Geist and Gesellschaft' loc. cit., p. 51.
144. A. Eleutheropulos, 'Sozialpsychologie und Wissenssoziologie', *Zeitschrift für Völkerpsychologie und Soziologie*, vol. 3, 1927.
145. R. Müller-Freienfels, 'Literaturbesprechung', *Kölner Vierteljahreshefte für Soziologie*, vol. 6, 1927, pp. 190-94.
146. K. Mannheim, 'Das Problem einer Soziologie des Wissens, *Archiv für*

Sozialwissenschaft, vol. 53. 1925. Translated in K. Mannheim, *Essays on the Sociology of Knowledge*, London 1952, pp. 154-79.
147. K. Mannheim, 'The Problem of a Sociology of Knowledge', op. cit., p. 164.
148. This is not to suggest that the sociology of knowledge perspective disappears completely, since it can still be found in his later works. See, for example, M. Scheler, *Die Stellung des Menschenim Kosmos*, Bern/Munich 1966, 7th ed., (first published 1928), esp. pp. 56 ff. But even here it is quite apparent that Scheler's own interests had shifted towards a universalistic philosophical anthropology. Similarly, Scheler still speaks here of the 'powerless mind' (p. 71).
149. O. Becker and H.O. Dehlke, 'Max Scheler's Sociology of Knowledge', op. cit., p. 322. On Scheler's reception in America, see K. Stikkers, 'Introduction', op. cit. On the possibility of developing a fruitful sociology of knowledge, largely on the basis of Scheler's other writings, see I. Srubar, 'Max Scheler: eine Wissenssoziologische Alternative in *Kölner Zeitschrift für Soziologie*, Sonderheft 22, 1980, pp. 343-59.
150. S. Marck, 'Zum Problem des "seinsverbundenen Denkens"', *Archiv für systematische Philosophie und Sociologie*, vol. 33, 1929, pp. 238-52. (The main content of this article is also discussed in Chapter 5.)
151. S. Marck, 'Zum Problem des "seinsverbundenen Denkens",' op. cit., p. 248.
152. Ibid., p. 249.
153. K. Lenk, *Von der Ohnmacht des Geistes*, op. cit., p. 63.

3 Georg Lukács

1. In fact *Geschichte und Klassenbewusstsein* is a collection of essays written between 1919 and 1922. They are dated as follows: 'Preface', Dec. 1922; 'What is Orthodox Marxism?', March 1919; 'Rosa Luxemburg as Marxist', January 1921; 'Class Consciousness', March 1920; 'Reification and Proletarian Consciousness', 1922; 'The Changing Function of Historical Materialism', June 1919; 'Legality and Illegality', July 1920; 'Critical Observations', January 1920; 'Methodology of Organisation', September 1922. G. Lukács, *Geschichte und Klassenbewusstsein*, Berlin 1923; reprinted with additional material, Neuwied/Berlin 1968; English translation R. Livingstone: G. Lukács, *History and Class Consciousness*, London 1971. References in the text are either to the 1968 German edition or to the English translation (which may have been amended in places).
2. S. Marck, cited in F. Cerutti, *et. al.*, *Geschichte und Klassenbewusstsein heute. Diskussion und Dokumentation*, Amsterdam 1971, p. 58.
3. E. Bloch, 'Aktualitaät und Utopie', *Der Neue Merkur*, Vol. 7, 1923/4, p. 474.
3. G. Lukács, 'Preface' (1967), *History and Class Consciousness*, op. cit., p. ix.
4. G. Lukács, 'Art and Society', *New Hungarian Quarterly*, vol. 13, No. 47, 1972, pp. 44-5.
5. Quoted in F. Tökei, 'Lukács and Hungarian Culture', *New Hungarian Quarterly*, op. cit., p. 110.
6. T. Pinkus (ed.) *Conversations with Lukács*, London 1974, p. 100.

7. Quoted in F. Tökei, 'Lukács and Hungarian Culture', op. cit., p. 14.
8. G. Lukács, *Die Theorie des Romans*, 3rd ed., Neuwied/Berlin 1965. (English trans. A. Bostock, *The Theory of the Novel*, London 1971.
9. G. Lukács, 'Preface', *The Theory of the Novel*, op. cit., p. 15.
10. T. Hanak, *Lukács war anders*, Meisenheim 1973, p. 27.
11. G. Markus, 'Die Seele und das Leben', *Revue Internationale de Philosophie*, vol. 27, No. 4, 1973, p. 412.
12. G. Markus, 'Die Seele und das Leben', op. cit., p. 421. The work referred to has now been published as G. Lukács, *Heidelberger Ästhetik (1916–18)*, Darmstadt/Neuwied 1974.
13. See G. Markus, 'Die Seele und das Leben', op. cit., p. 438. Lukács' curriculum vitae forwarded along with his request to submit his *Habilitationschrift* is reproduced in 'Georg Lukács' *Text und Kritik*, No. 39/40, 1974, pp. 5–7.
14. P. Breines, 'Lukács, Revolution and Marxism, 1885–1918', *Philosophical Forum*, vol. 3., 1972, p. 403.
15. D. Kettler, *Marxismus und Kultur, Mannheim und Lukács in den unganischen Revolutionen 1918/19*, Neuwied/Berlin 1967. An English version has appeared as D. Kettler, 'Culture and Revolution', *Telos*, No. 10, 1971, pp. 35–92. See also M. Löwy, *Georg Lukacs — From Romanticism to Bolshevism*, London 1979.
16. D. Kettler, *Marxismus und Kultur*, op. cit., pp. 43, 44.
17. See F. Tökei, loc. cit. See also the illuminating remarks by A. Hauser in A. Hauser, *Im Gespräch mit Georg Lukacs*, Munich 1978, esp. pp. 48–81.
18. K. Lenk, *Ideologie*, 3rd ed., Neuwied/Berlin, 1963, p. 53.
19. H.J. Lieber, 'Einleitung' to *Ideologienlehre und Wissenssoziologie*, Darmstadt 1975, p. 31.
20. G. Huaco, 'On Ideology', *Acta Sociologica*, vol. 14, 1971.
21. G. Huaco, 'On Ideology', loc. cit., p. 250.
22. D. Kettler, 'Sociology of Knowledge and Moral Philosophy: The Place of Traditional Problems in the Formation of Mannheim's Thought', *Political Science Quarterly*, vol. 82, 1967, pp. 399–426, esp. p. 407.
23. D. Kettler, 'Sociology of Knowledge and Moral Philosophy', *loc. cit.*, p. 420.
24. K. Mannheim, 'Historismus', *Archiv für Sozialwissenschaft*, vol. 52, 1924, p. 5.
25. See, for example, P. Breines, 'Praxis and its Theorists: The Impact of Lukács and Korsch in the 1920s', *Telos*, No. 11, 1972, pp. 67–103. Also A. Arato and P. Breines, *The Young Lukács and the Origins of Western Marxism*, New York/London 1979.
26. A. Arato, 'Notes on History and Class Consciousness', *Philosophical Forum*, vol. 3, 1972, p. 387.
27. L. Goldmann, 'Introduction aux premiers écrits de Georges Lukács', *Les Temps Modernes*, 1962, pp. 254–80.
28. P. Breines, 'Lukács, Revolution and Marxism, 1885–1918', op. cit.
29. A. Arato, 'Notes on History and Class Consciousness', op. cit. For both Breines and Arato now see A. Arato and P. Breines, op. cit.
30. L. Coletti, 'From Bergson to Lukács' in *From Marx to Hegel*, London 1975.
31. G. Stedman-Jones, 'The Marxism of the Early Lukács', *New Left Review*, no. 70, 1971, pp. 27–64.

32. M. Löwy, *Georg Lukacs — From Romanticism to Bolshevism*, op. cit.
33. J. Schmidt, 'The Concrete Totality and Lukács' Concept of Proletarian *Bildung*', *Telos*, no. 24, 1975, pp. 2–40, esp. p. 3.
34. J. Kammler, *Politische Theorie von George Lukács*, Darmstadt/ Neuwied, 1974, p. 15.
35. G. Lukács, 'Zur Soziologie des Modernen Dramas', *Archiv für Sozialwissenschaft*, vol. 38, 1914, pp. 303–45 and 662–706.
36. G. Lukács, 'Zum Wesen und zur Methode der Kultursoziologie', *Archiv für Sozialwissenschaft*, vol. 39, 1914–15.
37. G. Lukács, 'Zur Theorie der Literaturgeschichte', *Text und Kritik*, loc. cit., pp. 24–51. The Hungarian original was published in Budapest in 1910.
38. G. Lukács, *Die Theorie des Romans*, op. cit.
39. J. Kammler, *Politische Theorie von Georg Lukács*, op. cit., p. 15.
40. G. Lukács, *Soul and Form* (trans. A. Bostock), London 1974.
41. G. Lukács, *Heidelberger Ästhetik* (1916–1918), Darmstadt/Neuwied 1974.
42. G. Lukács, 'Die Subjekt-Objekt-Beziehung in der Aesthetik', *Logos*, vol. 7, 1917/18, pp. 1–39.
43. See D. Kettler, *Marxismus und Kultur*, op. cit.; J. Kammler, *Politische Theorie von Georg Lukács*, op. cit.; M. Löwy, *Georg Lukács*, op. cit.; A. Hauser, *Im Gespräch mit Georg Lukács*, op. cit.
44. G. Lukács, 'Alte Kultur und neue Kultur', *Kommunismus*, vol. 1, no. 43, 1920, pp. 1538–49.
45. G. Lukács, 'Zur Soziologie des modernen Dramas', loc. cit., p. 304.
46. Ibid., p. 663.
47. J. Kammler, *Politische Theorie von Georg Lukács*, op. cit., p. 19.
48. G. Lukács, 'Zur Soziologie des modernen Dramas', op. cit., p. 322.
49. Ibid., p. 665.
50. Ibid., pp. 665–6.
51. Ibid., p. 666.
52. P. Breines, 'Lukács, Revolution and Marxism, 1885–1918', loc. cit., p. 414.
53. G. Simmel, *The Philosophy of Money*, (trans. T. Bottomore and D. Frisby), London/Boston 1978, pp. 453 ff.
54. See my discussion in 'Introduction to the Translation', *The Philosophy of Money*, op. cit., p. 22 f.
55. Later, Simmel was to make fragmentation an essential feature of his metaphysics of life. See, for example, G. Simmel, 'Der Fragmentarcharakter des Lebens', *Logos*, vol. 6. 1917, pp. 29–40.
56. G. Lukács, 'The Metaphysics of Tragedy' in *Soul and Form* (trans. A. Bostock), London 1973, pp. 152–3.
57. Ibid., p. 172.
58. Ibid., p. 173.
59. J. Kammler, *Politische Theorie von Georg Lukács*, op. cit., p. 26.
60. G. Lukács, *The Theory of the Novel*, op. cit., p. 64.
61. Ibid., p. 62.
62. J. Kammler, *Politische Theorie von Georg Lukács*, op. cit., p. 33.
63. G. Lukács, *The Theory of the Novel*, op. cit., p. 12.
64. Ibid., p. 15.
65. G. Lukács, 'Die Subjekt-Objekt-Beziehung in der Aesthetik' loc. cit., p. 1.

66. Ibid., p. 7.
67. Ibid., p. 19.
68. R. Pascal, 'G. Lukács and the Concept of Totality', in G.H. Parkinson (ed.), *Georg Lukács*, London 1970, pp. 151-2.
69. P. Ludz, 'Der Begriff der "demokratischen Diktatur" in der politischen Philosophie von Georg Lukács', in Georg Lukács, *Schriften zur Ideologie und Politik*, Neuwied/Berlin 1967. Also, P. Ludz, 'Die philosophischen Grundlagen der Partisantheorie von Georg Lukács, *Praxis*, vol. 3, no. 3, 1967.
70. Quoted by D. Kettler, in *Marxismus und Kultur*, op. cit., p. 20.
71. Quoted in F. Tökei, 'Lukács and Hungarian Culture', loc. cit., pp. 114-5.
72. Quoted in J. Kammler, *Politische Theorie von Georg Lukács*, op. cit., p. 60.
73. Now translated into German as 'Der Bolschewismus als moralisches Problem' in G. Lukács, *Taktik und Ethik. Politische Aufsätze 1*, op. cit., pp. 27-33.
74. Ibid., pp. 28-9.
75. Ibid., p. 31.
76. J. Kammler, *Politische Theorie von Georg Lukács*, op. cit., p. 75.
77. G. Lukács, 'Tactics and Ethics' in G. Lukács, *Political Writings 1919-1929*, London 1974.
78. Ibid., p. 5.
79. Ibid., p. 9.
80. Ibid., p. 10.
81. J. Kammler, *Politische Theorie von Georg Lukács*, op. cit., p. 78.
82. Ibid., p. 81.
83. G. Lukács, 'Alte Kultur und neue Kultur', op. cit.
84. G. Lukács, 'Zum Wesen und zur Methode der Kultursoziologie', op. cit.
85. G. Lukács, 'Alte Kultur und neue Kultur', loc. cit., p. 1538.
86. Ibid., p. 1546.
87. Ibid., p. 1549.
88. Ibid.
89. J. Kammler, *Politische Theorie von Georg Lukács*, op. cit., pp. 101-2.
90. G. Lukács, *History and Class Consciousness*, op. cit., p. 41.
91. See J. Kammler, *Politische Theorie von Georg Lukács*, op. cit. and A. Grunenberg, *Burger und Revolutionär: Georg Lukács 1981-1928*, Cologne/Frankfurt 1976; M. Löwy, *Georg Lukács — From Romanticism to Bolshevism*, op. cit.
92. U. Apitzsch, *Gesellschaftstheorie und Ästhetik bei Georg Lukacs bis 1933*, Stuttgart 1977; a. Arato and P. Breines, *The Young Lukacs*, op. cit.
93. M. Rosshoff, *Der Gegenstandsbegriff bei Lask und Lukács*, Bonn 1976.
94. U. Apitzsch, *Gesellschaftstheorie und Ästhetik bei Georg Lukács bis 1933*, op. cit., p. 98.
95. Ibid., p. 41 f.
96. G. Lukács, 'Tactics and Ethics', loc. cit.
97. Ibid., p. 9.
98. A. Grunenberg, *Bürger und Revolutionär*, op. cit., p. 185.
99. Ibid., p. 187.
100. Ibid.
101. Ibid.

102. J. Kammler, *Politische Theorie von Georg Lukács*, op. cit., p. 172.
103. G. Lukács, *History and Class Consciousness*, op. cit., p. 50.
104. G. Lukács, 'Freuds Massenpsychologie', *Die Rote Fahne*, no. 235, 1922. Reprinted in G. Lukács, *Organisation und Illusion*. Darmstadt/ Neuwied 1977, pp. 135-9, esp. p. 135.
105. S. Rücker, 'Totalität als ethisches und ästhetisches Problem', loc. cit.
106. J. Kammler, *Politische Theorie von Georg Lukács*, op. cit., p. 174.
107. I. Fetscher, 'Das Verhältnis des Marxismus zu Hegel', loc. cit., p. 111.
108. A. Grunenberg, *Bürger und Revolutionär*, op. cit., p. 195.
109. G. Lukács, *History and Class Consciousness*, op. cit., p. 51.
110. See M. Weyembergh, 'M. Weber et G. Lukács', *Revue Internationale de Philosophie*, vol. 27, 1973, p. 480 f. See also I. Fetscher, 'Zum Begriff der "objektiven Moglichkeit" bei Max Weber und George Lukács', loc. cit.
111. G. Lukács, *History and Class Consciousness*, op. cit., p. 51.
112. As we shall see in the next chapter, Mannheim's conception of ideology and utopia, by evaluating them in relation to the present, also confronts the same difficulty.
113. G. Lukács, *History and Class Consciousness*, op. cit., p. 51.
114. Ibid., p. 79.
115. Ibid., p. 50.
116. Ibid., p. 52.
117. Ibid.
118. Max Weber, *Gesammelte Aufsätze zur Wissenschaftslehre*, 4th ed., Tübingen 1973, p. 269, esp. n. 1, 2 and 3 pp. 269-70. See also U. Apitzsch, *Gesellschaftstheorie und Ästhetik bei Georg Lukács, bis 1933*, op. cit., p. 77 f.
119. I. Fetscher, 'Zum Begriff der "objektiven Möglichkeit" bei Max Weber und Georg Lukács', loc. cit., p. 501.
120. Max Weber, *Gesammelte Aufsätze zur Wissenschaftslehre*, op. cit., p. 270.
121. Ibid., pp. 271-2.
122. See D. Henrich, *Die Einheit der Wissenschaftslehre Max Webers*, Tübingen 1952, p. 102 f.
123. I. Fetscher, 'Zum Begriff der "objektiven Möglichkeit" bei Max Weber und Georg Lukács, loc. cit., p. 506.
124. G. Lukács, *History and Class Consciousness*, op. cit., p. 81, n. 11.
125. I. Fetscher, 'Zum Begriff der "objektiven Möglichkeit" bei Max Weber und Georg Lukács, loc. cit., p. 509.
126. Ibid., p. 524.
127. G. Lukács, *History and Class Consciousness*, op. cit., p. 58.
128. A. Arato, 'Notes on History and Class Consciousness', *Philosophical Forum*, vol. 3, 1972, p. 393.
129. U. Apitzsch, *Gesellschaftstheorie und Ästhetik bei Georg Lukács bis 1933*, op. cit., p. 84.
130. G. Lukács, *History and Class Consciousness*, op. cit., p. 204. (Translation amended).
131. U. Apitzsch, *Gesellschafts: theorie und Ästhetik bei Georg Lukács bis 1933*, op. cit., p. 90.
132. G. Lukács, *History and Class Consciousness*, op. cit., p. 83.
133. Ibid.
134. Ibid., p. 76.

135. See K. Marx and F. Engels, *Werke*, vol. 25 (*Das Kapital*, vol. 3), Berlin 1972, pp. 838-9.
136. Ibid., p. 838. This is obscured in the English translation where the passage appears as 'the complete mystification of the capitalist mode of production, the conversion of social relations into things'. See K. Marx, *Capital*, vol. 3, Moscow 1962, p. 809.
137. Quoted by G. Lukács, *History and Class Consciousness*, op. cit., p. 95.
138. See my introduction to G. Simmel, *The Philosophy of Money*, op. cit.
139. This Lukács himself acknowledged in his 1967 'Foreword' to *History and Class Consciousness*.
140. J. Kammler, *Politische Theorie von George Lukács*, op. cit., p. 180.
141. See K. Maretsky, 'Industrialisierung und Kapitalismus — Probleme der Marxrezeption in Georg Lukács' Geschichte und Klassenbewusstsein', *Das Argument*, no. 65, 1971, pp. 289-312; J. Kammler, *Politische Theorie von George Lukacs*, op. cit; A. Grunenberg, *Bürger und Revolutionar*, op. cit.
142. G. Lukács, *History and Class Consciousness*, op. cit., p. 84.
143. A. Grunenberg, op. cit., p. 217.
144. G. Lukács, *History and Class Consciousness*, op. cit., p. 87.
145. A. Grunenberg, *Bürger und Revolutionär*, op. cit., p. 219.
146. See my introduction to G. Simmel, *The Philosophy of Money*, op. cit., esp. p. 15 f.
147. See F. Fehér, 'The Last Phase of Romantic Anti-Capitalism: Lukács' Response to the War', *New German Critique*, no. 10, 1977, pp. 139-54. On Ernst and Lukács, see the valuable collection K.A. Kutzback (ed.), *Paul Ernst und Georg Lukács: Dokumente einer Freundschaft*, Emsdetten 1974. Also Fehér's discussion in F. Fehér 'Am Scheideweg des romantischen Antikapitalismus', in H. Heller et. al., *Die Seele und das Leben*, op. cit., pp. 241-327. Some indication of Lukács' response to the war can be found in G. Lukács 'Die deutschen Intellektuellen und der Krieg', *Text und Kritik*, 39/40, pp. 65-9.
148. G. Lukács, *Geschichte und Klassenbewusstsein*, Berlin 1923, p. 86.
149. Ibid., p. 88. Translation amended.
150. A. Grunenberg, *Bürger und Revolutionär*, op. cit., p. 222.
151. G. Lukács, *Geschichte und Klassenbewusstsein*, op. cit., p. 90.
152. Ibid., p. 88.
153. Ibid., p. 89.
154. Ibid.
155. Ibid., p. 90.
156. Ibib., pp. 91-2.
157. J. Kammler, *Politische Theorie von George Lukács*, op. cit., p. 181.
158. A. Grunenberg, *Bürger und Revolutionär*, op. cit., p. 224.
159. See G. Simmel, *The Philosophy of Money*, op. cit., pp. 454-6.
160. A. Grunenberg, *Bürger und Revolutionär*, op. cit., p. 225.
161. K. Maretsky, 'Industrialisierung und Kapitalismus', loc. cit., p. 306.
162. Ibid., p. 311.
163. G. Lukács, *Geschichte und Klassenbewusstsein*, op. cit., p. 104.
164. Ibid., p. 105.
165. G. Lukács, *Geschichte und Klassenbewusstsein*, op. cit., p. 109.
166. Ibid., p. 110.
167. Ibid., p. 148.
168. Ibid., p. 121.

169. Ibid., p. 131.
170. Ibid., p. 150.
171. Ibid., p. 168.
172. Ibid., p. 169.
173. Ibid., p. 171.
174. Ibid., p. 181.
175. Ibid.
176. Ibid., p. 188.
177. Ibid., p. 189.
178. Ibid., p. 203.
179. Ibid., p. 204.
180. K. Mannheim, *Ideologie und Utopie*, Frankfurt 1969, p. 243.
181. G. Lukács, *Geschichte und Klassenbewusstsein*. Berlin 1923, p. 204.
182. Ibid., p. 205.

4 Karl Mannheim

1. Mannheim Károly, *Lélek és Kultura*, Budapest 1918, German translation E. Mannheim, 'Seele und Kultur', in K.H. Wolff (ed), K. Mannheim *Wissenssoziologie*, Neuwied/Berlin 1964, pp. 66–84.
2. K. Mannheim, 'Besprechung von G. Lukács, *Die Theorie des Romans*', *Logos*, vol. 9, 1920-1, pp. 298–302. For English translation, see K.H. Wolff in K.H. Wolff (ed), *From Karl Mannheim*, New York 1971, pp. 3–7.
3. K. Mannheim, 'Beiträge zur Theorie der Weltanschauungs-Interpretation', *Jahrbuch für Kunstgeschichte*, vol. 15, 1921-22, pp. 236–74. English translation by P. Kecskemeti in K. Mannheim, *Essays on the Sociology of Knowledge*, London 1952, pp. 33–83.
4. K. Mannheim, *Über das Eigenart Kultursoziologischer Erkenntnis*, unpublished ms, 1922.
5. G. Markus, 'Lukács' "erste" Ästhetik: Zur Entwicklungsgeschichte der Philosophie des jungen Lukács' in A. Heller, et. al., *Die Seele und das Leben*, Frankfurt 1977, pp. 192–240, especially 230-1.
6. D. Kettler, *Marxismus und Kultur*, op. cit.
7. K. Mannheim, 'Die Strukturanalyse der Erkenntnistheorie', *Kant-Studien. Ergänzungsheft*, no. 57, Berlin 1922. English translation E. Schwarzschild and P. Kecskemeti in K. Mannheim, *Essays on Sociology and Social Psychology*, London 1953, pp. 15–73.
8. G. Remmling, *Karl Mannheim*, London 1975, p. 13.
9. D. Kettler, 'Sociology of Knowledge and Moral Philosophy: Karl Mannheim', *Political Science Quarterly*, vol. 82, no. 3, 1967, p. 407, n. 10.
10. K. Mannheim, 'Historismus', *Archiv für Sozialwissenschaft*, vol. 52, 1924, pp. 1–60. English trans. by P. Kecskemeti in K. Mannheim, *Essays on the Sociology of Knowledge*, pp. 84–133.
11. K. Mannheim, 'Das Problem einer Soziologie des Wissens', *Archiv für Sozialwissenschaft*, vol. 53, 1925, pp. 577–652. English trans. by P. Kecskemeti in K. Mannheim, *Essays on the Sociology of Knowledge*, pp. 134–90.
12. K. Mannheim, 'Ideologische und soziologische Interpretation der geistigen Gebilde', *Jahrbuch für Soziologie*, vol. 2, 1926, pp. 424–40. English trans. by K.H. Wolff in *From Karl Mannheim*, pp. 116–31.
13. K. Mannheim, *Eine soziologische Theorie der Kultur under ihrer Erkennbarkeit*.

(*Konjunktives und kommunikatives Denken*), unpublished ms. c. 1925.
14. K. Mannheim, 'Das konservative Denken', *Archiv für Sozialwissenschaft*, vol. 57, 1927, pp. 68-142; 470-95. English translation by P. Kecskemeti, though based both on this article and the original *Habilitationschrift* in K. Mannheim, *Essays on Sociology and Social Psychology*, pp. 74-164.
15. K. Mannheim, 'Die Bedeutung der Konkurrenz in Gebiete des Geistigen', *Verhandlungen des 6. deutschen Soziologentages 1928*, Tübingen 1929, pp. 35-83. English trans. by P. Kecskemeti in K. Mannheim, *Essays on the Sociology of Knowledge*, pp. 191-229.
16. K. Mannheim, 'Das Problem der Generationen', *Kölner Vierteljahrshefte für Soziologie*, vol. 7, 1928, pp. 157-85; 309-30. English transl. by P. Kecskemeti in K. Mannheim, *Essays on the Sociology of Knowledge*, pp. 276-322.
17. K. Mannheim, *Ideologie und Utopie*, Bonn 1929. All references are to 5th ed., Frankfurt 1969. Compare K. Mannheim, *Ideology and Utopia*, London 1936.
18. K. Mannheim, 'Wissenssoziologie', in A. Vierkandt (ed.) *Handwörterbuch der Soziologie*, Stuttgart 1931, pp. 659-80. Reprinted in K. Mannheim, *Ideologie und Utopie*, Frankfurt 1969, pp. 227-67. It appears in translation as Ch. 5 of *Ideology and Utopia*.
19. K. Mannheim, *Die Gegenwartsaufgaben der Soziologie. Ihre Lehrgestalt*, Tübingen 1932.
20. See Karl Mannheim's correspondence with Dr. P. Siebeck, the director of Mohr Verlag in Tübingen. From correspondence in 1929 (27.3.29 and 2.10.29), it is clear that the volume on Max Weber was to have been a substantial study. Mannheim states that he had been working on it for several months before March 1929. In October Mannheim suggest that a monograph on Weber might also be a possibility. Work on the intended volume, *Zur Denklage der Gegenwart*, on Weber, Scheler and Troeltsch was, according to a letter of 6 November, 1930, postponed in view of Mannheim's move to Frankfurt and a change in themes on which he was working. In the same letter, he offers Mohr Verlag a collection of essays entitled *Soziologie des Geistes: Versuche* which, would contain, as well as five of his earlier essays, two new ones, 'Die Bedeutung der Intelligenzschichten für die Gestaltung der Politik und Kultur' and 'Die Demokratisierung des Geistes', and an introduction. None of these three volumes appeared in Germany and it has not been possible to trace the whereabouts of the manuscripts.
21. G. Lukacs in a letter to F. Bensler. Quoted in J. Kammler, *Politische Theorie von Georg Lukacs*, p. 105, n. 40.
22. Anna Lesznai cited in D. Kettler, *Marxismus und Kultur*, p. 19.
23. Arnold Hauser cited in D. Kettler, *Marxismus und Kultur*, p. 60, n. 36. See also A. Hauser, *Im Gesprach mit Georg Lukacs*, op. cit.
24. G. Lukács quoted in D. Kettler, *Marxismus und Kultur*, p. 20.
25. G. Markus, 'Lukács' "erste" Ästhetik' in A. Heller, et. al., *Die Seele und das Leben*, p. 230.
26. G. Lukács, *Heidelberger Philosophie der Kunst*, Darmstadt/Neuwied 1974 and G. Lukács, *Heidelberger Ästhetik*, Darmstadt/Neuwied 1974.
27. K. Mannheim, 'Seele und Kultur', *Wissenssoziologie*, p. 66.

28. Ibid., p. 84.
29. Ibid., p. 69.
30. Ibid., pp. 72-3.
31. Quoted in G. Markus, 'Lukács' "erste" Ästhetik', loc. cit., p. 230. This translation differs from the one by Ernst Mannheim.
32. K. Mannheim, 'Seele und Kultur', loc. cit., p. 75.
33. Ibid.
34. G. Lukács, 'Georg Simmel', *Pester Lloyd*, 2 October 1918, reprinted in K. Gassen and M. Landmann (eds.), *Buch des Dankes an Georg Simmel*, Berlin 1958, pp. 171-6, especially pp. 172-3.
35. K. Mannheim, *Über das Eigenart Kultursoziologischer Erkenntnis*, op. cit. See also Mannheim Karoly, 'Georg Simmel, mint filozöfus', *Huszadik Szazad*, 38, 1918, pp. 194-6.
36. K. Mannheim, 'Seele und Kultur', loc. cit., p. 68.
37. Ibid., p. 81.
38. See *Athenaeum*, 1918, nos. 5 and 6. In German, see K. Mannheim, *Die Strukturanalyse der Erkenntnistheorie*, op. cit.
39. Markus suggests that the original Hungarian version of the thesis makes explicit reference to Lukács *Aesthetik*. See G. Markus, 'Lukács' "erste" Ästhetik', op. cit., p. 230.
40. K. Mannheim, 'The Structural Analysis of Epistemology', loc. cit., p. 16.
41. Ibid., p. 35. In some respects, this is the reverse of, say, Popper's formulation of the importance of scientific 'problems'.
42. Ibid., p. 37.
43. Ibid., p. 39.
44. See G. Lukács, 'Geschichtlichkeit und Zeitlosigkeit des Kinstwerks', in *Heidelberger Philosophie der Kunst (1912-1914)*, pp. 153-232. Here Lukács argues that a sociology of art can offer only negative 'laws' or 'conditioning laws': 'it can only say something about the possibilities of realization but not about the realization itself'. (p. 183). Lukács also speaks of the material for a work of art as 'a form of experience' and of our attitude to it varying, phenomenological, according to our 'standpoint' (p. 186).
45. K. Mannheim, 'The Structural Analysis of Epistemology', loc. cit., pp. 40-1.
46. Ibid., p. 45.
47. See L. Goldmann, 'Introduction aux premiers écrits de Georges Lukács', *Les Temps Modernes*, 1962.
48. K. Mannheim, 'Besprechung von Georg Lukács, *Die Theorie des Romans*', Logos, ix, 1920-1, p. 298.
49. Georg Lukács, 'Zur Theorie der Literaturgeschichte', *Text und Kritik*, 39/40, pp. 24-51, especially p. 24.
50. U. Apitzsch, *Gesellschaftstheorie und Ästhetik bei Georg Lukács bis 1933*, Stuttgart 1977, p. 16.
51. A. Weber, 'Prinzipielles zur Kultursoziologie', *Archiv für Sozialwissenschaft*, vol. 47, 1920, pp. 1-49.
52. A. Weber, 'Prinzipielles zur Kultursoziologie, loc. cit., p. 1.
53. A. Weber, 'Entgegnung', *Archiv für Sozialwissenschaft*, vol. 39, 1914-15.
54. K. Mannheim, *Über die Eigenart Kultursoziologischer Erkenntnis*, ms. 1922, p. 3.

55. Ibid., p. 10.
56. Ibid., p. 16.
57. Ibid., p. 17.
58. Ibid., p. 15.
59. Ibid., p. 24.
60. For example, Habermas' contributions to T.W. Adorno, et. al., *The Positivist Dispute in German Sociology*. (trans. G. Adey and D. Frisby), London/New York 1976 and J. Habermas, *Knowledge and Human Interests* (trans. J. Shapiro), Boston/London 1971. Also, K-O. Apel, *Towards a Transformation of Philosophy*, (trans. G. Adey and D. Frisby), London/Boston, 1980.
61. K. Mannheim, *Über die Eigenart Kultursoziologischer Erkenntnis*, p. 27.
62. Ibid.
63. G. Lukács, 'Phänomenologische Skizze des schöpferischen und receptiven Verhaltens' in G. Lukács, *Heidelberger Philosophie der Kunst (1912-1914)*, Neuwied/Berlin 1974, pp. 45-150.
64. K. Mannheim, *Über die Eigenart Kultursoziologischer Erkenntnis*, p. 28.
65. Ibid., p. 29.
66. Ibid., p. 32.
67. Ibid.
68. Ibid., p. 34. This conception of sociology as a foundational science is retained by Mannheim through to his last published German work (See K. Mannheim, *Die Gegenwartsaufgabe der Soziologie*, Tübingen 1932, p. 4.)
69. K. Mannheim, *Über die Eigenart Kultursoziologischer Erkenntnis*, p. 38.
70. Ibid., p. 48.
71. Ibid., p. 58.
72. Ibid., p. 61.
73. Ibid., p. 62.
74. Ibid., p. 63.
75. Ibid., p. 65.
76. Ibid., p. 66.
77. Ibid., p. 67.
78. Ibid., p. 178, n. 67.
79. Ibid., p. 69.
80. Ibid., p. 77.
81. Ibid., p. 79.
82. Ibid., p. 80.
83. W. Jerusalem, 'Soziologie des Erkennens', *Kölner Vierteljahreshefte für Soziologie*, vol. 1, 1921.
84. K. Mannheim, *Über die Eigenart Kultursoziologischer Erkenntnis*, p. 82.
85. K-O. Apel, *Transformation der Philosophie*, vol. 2, Frankfurt 1974.
86. G. Lukács, 'Zur Theorie der Literaturgeschichte', *Text und Kritik*, loc. cit., pp. 24-51. The original is G. Lukács, 'Megjegyzések az irodaiomtortenet elmélchéz', in *Alexander-emlékkönyv*, Budapest 1910, pp. 380-421.
87. K. Mannheim, *Über die Eigenart Kultursoziologischer Erkenntnis*, p. 91.
88. Ibid., p. 94.
89. Ibid., p. 95.
90. Ibid., p. 96.
91. Ibid., p. 98.
92. Ibid., p. 101.

93. Ibid., p. 104.
94. Ibid., p. 103.
95. Ibid., p. 106.
96. Ibid., pp. 156-7, N.B. The numbering of the pages should not be taken to indicate that a whole section of the manuscript has gone astray. Rather, it merely means that the pagination is erratic.
97. Ibid., p. 165.
98. A. Neusüss, *Utopisches Bewusstsein und freischwebende Intelligenz*, Meisenheim 1968, p. 71.
99. Ibid.
100. E. Troeltsch, *Der Historismus und seine Probleme*, Tübingen 1922. See also E. Troeltsch, *Der Historismus und seine Überwindung*, Berlin 1924.
101. K. Mannheim, 'Historismus', loc. cit.
102. See the correspondence referred to in n. 20.
103. K. Mannheim, 'Problems of Sociology in Germany', in K.H. Wolff (ed.), *From Karl Mannheim*, p. 266, n. 3.
104. K. Mannheim, 'Historicism' in K. Mannheim, *Essays on the Sociology of Knowledge*, p. 84. Translation amended.
105. Ibid., p. 85. Translation amended.
106. H.-J. Lieber, 'Einleitung', to H.-J. Lieber (ed.), *Ideologienlehre und Wissenssoziologie*, Darmstadt 1974, p. 35.
107. K. Mannheim, 'Historicism', loc. cit., p. 86. Translation amended.
108. Ibid.
109. Ibid., p. 96.
110. Ibid., p. 127.
111. Ibid., p. 101.
112. Ibid., p. 102. Translation amended.
113. Ibid., p. 104.
114. See H.G. Gadamer, *Truth and Method* (trans. G. Burden and J. Cumming) London/New York 1975. For a recent discussion of Mannheim's hermeneutics see Z. Baumaun, *Hermeneutics and Social Science*, London 1978, especially pp. 89-110.
115. K. Mannheim, 'Historicism', loc. cit., p. 127.
116. Ibid., p. 125.
117. See D. Kettler, 'Social Science and Moral Philosophy', loc. cit. Also, K. Mannheim, *Eine soziologische Theorie der Kultur und ihrer Erkennbarkeit*, ms. p. 169. The manuscript is in three sections, with the pages numbered separately in each. Therefore, reference will be to the section number (1, 11 or 111) followed by the page number.
118. K. Mannheim, *Eine soziologische Theorie der Kultur und ihrer Erkennbarkeit*, I, p. 41.
119. Ibid., p. 18.
120. Ibid.
121. Ibid., pp. 5-6.
122. Ibid., p. 8.
123. Ibid., p. 9.
124. Ibid.
125. Ibid., p. 12.
126. Ibid., p. 13.
127. Ibid., p. 20.
128. Ibid., p. 21.

129. Ibid., p. 22.
130. Ibid., p. 47.
131. K. Mannheim, *Eine soziologische Theorie der Kultur und ihrer Erkennbarkeit*, II, p. 1.
132. Ibid., p. 5.
133. Ibid., p. 7.
134. Ibid., p. 8.
135. Ibid., p. 31.
136. Ibid., p. 38. This is almost the reverse of Wittgenstein statement that 'the limits of my language are the limits of my world'.
137. Ibid., p. 53.
138. Ibid., p. 56.
139. See A. Schutz, *Reflections on the Problem of Relevance*, Yale 1970.
140. K. Mannheim, *Eine soziologische Theorie der Kultur und ihrer Erkennbarkeit*, II, p. 60.
141. Ibid., p. 65.
142. Ibid.
143. Ibid., p. 70.
144. Ibid., p. 78.
145. Ibid., p. 80.
146. Ibid., pp. 91-2.
147. Ibid., p. 93.
148. Ibid., p. 94.
149. Ibid.
150. Ibid., p. 95.
151. Ibid., p. 97.
152. Ibid., p. 99.
153. Ibid., p. 100.
154. Ibid., p. 108.
155. M. Heidegger, *Sein und Zeit*, Tübingen 1926. For a critique of this notion of authenticity see T.W. Adorno, *Jargon der Eigentlichkeit*, Frankfurt 1959.
156. K. Mannheim, *Eine soziologische Theorie der Kultur und ihrer Erkennbarkeit*, II, p. 108.
157. Ibid., p. 130.
158. Ibid., p. 134.
159. K. Mannheim, *Eine soziologische Theorie der Kultur und ihrer Erkennbarkeit*, III, p. 2.
160. Ibid., p. 5.
161. Ibid., p. 7.
162. Ibid.
163. See K. Mannheim, 'Das Konservative Denken', *Archiv für Sozialwissenschaft*, vol. 57, 1927, pp. 68-142; 470-95, and K. Mannheim, 'Conservative Thought', in *Essays on Sociology and Social Psychology*, (translation P. Kecskemeti), London 1953, pp. 74-164. Unfortunately, the original thesis is not available, so reference will be made to the published German version.
164. K. Mannheim, 'Das Konservative Denken', loc. cit., p. 68.
165. Ibid., p. 71.
166. Ibid., p. 75.
167. Ibid., p. 95.
168. Ibid., p. 104.

169. Ibid., p. 115, n. 76.
170. Ibid., pp. 115-6.
171. K. Mannheim, 'Conservative Thought', loc. cit., p. 127.
172. Ibid., p. 128. Translation slightly changed.
173. K. Mannheim, 'Das Konservative Denken', loc. cit., p. 140.
174. Ibid., p. 471.
175. Ibid., p. 484.
176. Ibid., p. 491.
177. Ibid., p. 495.
178. Ibid., p. 102. In passing, it is worth examining some of the contemporary background to this work, especially since this was Mannheim's *Habilitationschrift*. It was submitted in Heidelberg late in 1925 and was examined by Emil Lederer, Alfred Weber and Carl Brinkmann. Of the three *Gutachten*, only Lederer's was substantial. It was also unequivocally positive. Lederer states that it investigated

> the sociological problem . . . the dependency of thought upon the period, its social structure and, within it, upon the position, the standpoint of the thinker . . . In so doing, the problem of reality and 'superstructure' is raised, but reality is understood here not merely in the sense of naked economic interests but also the social forms of appearance, the social structure of a period.

(See E. Lederer, 'Gutachten' (p. 12). *Archiv der Universität Heidelberg Akten*, 111 5a, nr. 195, 1925/6 (Habilitation Mannheim, no. 103 1925/6), p. 1.)

Lederer goes on to suggest that the sociology of knowledge raises the issue of the social basis of the *Geisteswissenschaften* themselves. He concludes that in Mannheim's study

> A new sphere of scientific work is outlined whose results must also be of the greatest fruitfulness for the investigation of intellectual-historical connections just as one may also expect from penetrating intuition for the analysis of economic-social problems and for knowledge of their cultural significance. (Ibid., p. 12.)

Alfred Weber's much briefer *Gutachten* holds Mannheim's study to be 'a significant achievement' though he does have some reservations since his

> personal viewpoint would have sometimes put forward other formulations and questions too. The superstructure-base-theory that Mannheim — although no historical materialist — has indeed not completely grown out of seems to me to play too great a role in the establishment of the study.

(A. Weber, 'Gutachten', *Habilitation Mannheim*, no. 103, loc. cit.)

Brinkmann's *Gutachten*, though very brief, was also positive. As an indication of Mannheim's interests at this time, we find him offering three possible themes for his *Fakultätsvorlesung* — 'On Max Weber's Sociology', 'The Sociological Problem of Generations' and 'The Sociological Problem of the Intelligentsia'. As his *Antrittsvorlesung* in the same letter of 4 January 1926, Mannheim offered 'The Contemporary Situation of Sociology in Germany', which he gave on 12 June 1926. After taking out

German citizenship, which was deemed to be essential for him to be awarded his thesis — and which was the subject of some opposition in the Württemberg Ministry of Education, though not, apparently, in Baden — Mannheim was appointed as *Privatdozent* for the winter semester of 1926-7 in Heidelberg, where he remained until 1930. In Heidelberg, he offered the following courses:

Winter Semester 1926/27	Introduction to problems in sociology and the history of ideas
	History and sociology of political thought in Germany (1) Conservatism
Summer Semester 1927	The political and social significance of philosophy in the nineteenth century
	Seminar on the economic and intellectual foundations of imperialism (with Emil Lederer)
Winter Semester 1927/28	Max Weber's sociology
Summer Semester 1928	Introduction to sociology
	Seminar on sociology
Winter Semester 1928/29	General sociology
	Sociology of the press and public opinion
	Seminars on the sociology of knowledge
Summer Semester 1929	Sociology of the press and public opinion
	Seminars on problems of sociology and modern phenomenology
Winter Semester 1929/30	Sociology of public opinion and the press
	Seminars on the history of modern ideas. Introduction to the sociological interpretation of sources

179. K. Mannheim, 'Die Bedeutung der Konkurrenz in Gebiet des Geistigen', in *Verhandlungen des sechsten Deutschen Soziologentages 1928*, Tübingen 1929, pp. 35-83.
180. Ibid., p. 38.
181. In October 1930 Mannheim was still offering Mohr Verlag a collection of essays on 'The Sociology of the Mind'. K. Mannheim in a letter dated 6. 10. 1930. The collection was never published.
182. These comments are presented at the beginning of the paper and were not translated into English. See K. Mannheim, 'Die Bedeutung der Konkurrenz in Gebiete des Geistigen', loc. cit., p. 37.
183. Ibid., p. 39.
184. Ibid., p. 41.
185. Ibid., p. 42.
186. A. Neusüss, *Utopisches Bewusstsein und freischwebende Intelligenz*, Meisenheim, 1968, p. 25.
187. K. Mannheim, 'Die Bedeutung der Konkurrenz in Gebiete des Geistigen', loc. cit., p. 45.
188. Ibid., p. 74.
189. Ibid., p 77-8.
190. Ibid., p. 80.
191. Ibid., p. 81.
192. K. Mannheim, *Ideologie und Utopie*, Bonn 1929. Recent German editions

of this work have incorporated the additional material from the English edition into the text. Since the new edition is more accessible, all references will be to K. Mannheim, *Ideologie und Utopie*, Frankfurt 1969, 5th ed. The English edition was first published in 1936 as K. Mannheim, *Ideology and Utopia*, London 1936. It contained a preface by Louis Wirth, an additional introductory chapter by Mannheim and his encyclopaedia article on the sociology of knowledge. On the significance of the changes in the English translation, see D. Kettler, 'Rhetoric and Social Science: Karl Mannheim adjusts to the English-speaking World', unpublished ms., p. 2.
193. K. Mannheim, *Ideologie und Utopie*, pp. 49–50.
194. Ibid., p. 52.
195. Ibid., p. 53.
196. Ibid., p. 54. In the English translation 'co-constitutive' is reduced to 'influence'; see K. Mannheim, *Ideology and Utopia*, p. 50.
197. Ibid., p. 55.
198. K. Mannheim, *Ideology and Utopia*, p. 62. Compare K. Mannheim, *Ideologie und Utopie*, pp. 64–5.
199. K. Mannheim, *Ideologie und Utopie*, p. 67.
200. Ibid., p. 69.
201. Ibid., p. 70.
202. Ibid., p. 72.
203. Ibid.
204. Ibid., p. 76.
205. Ibid., p. 78.
206. Ibid., p. 79.
207. Ibid., p. 82.
208. Ibid., p. 83.
209. Ibid., pp. 83–4.
210. Ibid., p. 86.
211. Ibid., pp. 86–7.
212. Ibid., p. 92.
213. A. Neusüss, *Utopisches Bewusstsein und freischwebende Intelligenz*, p. 40.
214. Ibid., p. 50 f. The two then unpublished essays also suggest that Mannheim was impressed with Heidegger's notion of *Sein*.
215. See D. Kettler, 'Rhetoric and Social Science', loc. cit., p. 5.
216. K. Mannheim, *Ideologie und Utopie*, p. 97.
217. Ibid., p. 100, my emphasis.
218. Ibid., p. 128.
219. Ibid., pp. 131–2.
220. Ibid., p. 134.
221. Ibid., p. 136.
222. Ibid., p. 141.
223. Ibid., p. 149.
224. Ibid., p. 163.
225. See, for example, T. Geiger, *Ideologie und Wahrheit*, Stuttgart/Vienna 1953. For a critique of Geiger's position on the sociology of knowledge see K. Lenk, *Marx in der Wissenssoziologie*, pp. 291 ff.
226. K. Mannheim, *Ideologie und Utopie*, p. 165. My emphasis.
227. K. Lenk, *Marx in der Wissenssoziologie*, p. 76.
228. Ibid., p. 78.

229. G. Lukács, 'Moses Hess und das Problem der idealistischen Dialektik', *Archiv für die Geschichte des Sozialismus und der Arbeiterbewegung*, vol. 12, 1926, p. 123.
230. The affinities are even closer if one accepts Macpherson's argument concerning the latent market model of society in Hobbes' work. See C.B. Macpherson, *The Political Theory of Possessive Individualism*, Oxford 1963.
231. F.K. Ringer, *The Decline of the German Mandarins. The German Academic Community, 1890-1933*, Cambridge: Mass., 1969.
232. A. Neusüss, *Utopisches Bewusstsein und freischwebende Intelligenz*, p. 236.
233. Ibid., pp. 112-82.
234. K. Mannheim, *Ideologie und Utopie*, p. 169.
235. Ibid.
236. Ibid.
237. Ibid., p. 171.
238. Ibid., p. 172.
239. Ibid.
240. Ibid., p. 178.
241. Ibid., p. 179.
242. Ibid., p. 181.
243. Ibid., p. 182.
244. Ibid., p. 218.
245. Ibid., p. 220.
246. Ibid., p. 224.
247. Ibid., p. 225.
248. A. Neusüss, *Utopisches Bewusstsein und freischwebende Intelligenz*, pp. 134-6.
249. Ibid., p. 136.
250. On Mannheim's project in this period see the reference to his correspondence with Mohr Verlag in n. 20, earlier. The only other article in any way connected with the sociology of knowledge that was published in this period, aside from the two referred to below, was K. Mannheim, 'Über das Wesen und die Bedeutung des wirtschaftlichen Erfolgsstrebens. Ein Beitrag zur Wirtschaftssoziologie', *Archiv für Sozialwissenschaft*, vol. 63, 1930. English translation by P. Kecskemeti in K. Mannheim, *Essays on the Sociology of Knowledge*, London 1952, pp. 230-75.
251. K. Mannheim, 'Wissenssoziologie' in A. Vierkandt (ed.), *Handwörterbuch der Soziologie*, Stuttgart 1931; reprinted in K. Mannheim *Ideologie und Utopie*, 5th ed., Frankfurt 1969, pp. 227-67. References are to this reprint. The English translation (L. Wirth and E. Shils) is in K. Mannheim, *Ideology and Utopia*, op. cit., pp. 237-80.
252. K. Mannheim, *Die Gegenwartsaufgaben der Soziologie, Ihre Lehrgestalt*, Tübingen 1932.
253. K. Mannheim, 'Wissenssoziologie' in *Ideologie und Utopie*, p. 228.
254. Ibid., p. 229.
255. Ibid., p. 246.
256. Ibid., p. 248.
257. Ibid., p. 258.
258. K. Mannheim, *Die Gegenwartsaufgaben der Soziologie*, p. 4.
259. Ibid., pp. 18-19.
260. Ibid., p. 19.
261. Ibid., p. 20.
262. Ibid., pp. 39-40.

263. Ibid., p. 41.

5 The Contemporary Controversy

1. See S. Kracauer, 'Die Wissenschaftskrise', *Das Ornament der Masse*, Frankfurt 1963; also, E. Wittenberg, 'Die Wissenschaftskrise in Deutschland in Jahr 1919. Ein Beitrag zur Wissenschaftsgeschichte', *Theoria*, vol. 4, 1938, pp. 235-64.
2. *Verhandlungen des 4. Deutschen Soziologentages 1924*, Tübingen 1925.
3. *Verhandlungen des 6. Deutschen Soziologentages 1928*, Tübingen 1929.
4. A.V. Schelting, 'Zum Streit um die Wissenssoziologie', *Archiv für Sozialwissenschaft*, vol. 62, 1929.
5. See E. Wittenberg, 'Die Wissenschaftskrise in Deutschland in Jahr 1919', loc. cit.
6. Ibid., p. 238.
7. S. Kracauer, 'Die Wissenschaftskrise', loc. cit., p. 197.
8. E. Wittenberg, loc. cit., p. 254.
9. Ibid.
10. Ibid., p. 256.
11. T. Veblen, *The Higher Learning in America*, New York 1918.
12. J. Habermas, *Theory and Practice*, (trans. J. Viertel), London 1974, p. 254.
13. M. Weber, 'Science as a Vocation' in H. Gerth and C.W. Mills (eds.), *From Max Weber*, New York/London 1948.
14. M. Bracht, *Voraussetzungen einer Soziologie des Wissens*, p. 22 f.
15. Ibid., p. 24.
16. Ibid., p. 60.
17. Ibid., p. 56.
18. S. Kracauer, 'Katholizismus und Relativismus', in his *Das Ornament der Masse*, Frankfurt 1963, pp. 187-196.
19. For Adler's contribution to the sociology of knowledge see M. Adler, *Das Soziologische in Kants Erkenntniskritik*, Vienna 1924; M. Adler, 'Soziologie und Erkenntniskritik', *Jahrbuch für Soziologie*, vol. 1, 1925. See also the recent collection, T. Bottomore and J. Goode (eds.), *Austro Marxism*, Oxford 1978, as well as the discussion of his work in P. Heintel, *System und Ideologie*, Munich 1967.
20. M. Adler, 'Wissenschaft und soziale Struktur' (Referent), *Verhandlungen des 4. Deutschen Soziologentages* 1924, p. 184.
21. Ibid., p. 190.
22. Ibid., p. 187.
23. Ibid., p. 199.
24. Ibid., p. 210.
25. M. Adler, *Kausalität und Teleologie im Streite um die Wissenschaft*, Vienna 1904.
and M. Adler, *Kant und der Marxismus*, Berlin 1925; M. Adler, 'Soziologie und Erkenntniskritik', *op. cit.*
26. S. Marck, 'Marxistische Grundprobleme und der Soziologie der Gegenwart', *Die Gesellschaft*, vol. 1, 1927.
27. H. Marcuse, 'Transcendentaler Marxismus?', *Die Gesellschaft*, vol. 7, 1930, pp. 304-26.
28. M. Adler, 'Wissenschaft und soziale Struktur', loc. cit., p. 212. See also

Bottomore's introduction to the selections from this tradition.
29. Ibid., p. 207.
30. Ibid., p. 201.
31. Ibid., pp. 201-2.
32. Ibid., p. 202.
33. 'Diskussion über "Wissenschaft und soziale Struktur', *Verhandlungen des 4. Deutschen Soziologentages*, op. cit., p. 217.
34. Ibid., p. 218.
35. Ibid., p. 221.
36. Ibid., p. 223.
37. 'Diskussion', loc. cit., p. 225.
38. Ibid., p. 227.
39. Ibid., p. 232.
40. Ibid., p. 234.
41. K. Mannheim, 'Die Bedeutung der Konkurrenz im Gebiete des Geistigen', *Verhandlungen des 6. Deutschen Soziologentages 1928*, Tübingen 1929, pp. 35-83.
42. A.V. Schelting, 'Zum Streit un die Wissenssoziologie', loc. cit.
43. A. Meusel, 'Die Konkurrenz in soziologischer Betrachtung', loc. cit.
44. 'Diskussion über "Das Verstehen" ', *Verhandlungen des 6. Deutschen Soziologentages*, pp. 238-43.
45. Ibid., pp. 35-8.
46. Ibid., p. 38.
47. Ibid., p. 89.
48. Ibid.
49. Ibid., p. 90.
50. Ibid.
51. Ibid., p. 91.
52. Ibid.
53. Ibid., pp. 91-2.
54. Ibid., p. 93.
55. Ibid., p. 94.
56. Ibid., p. 95.
57. Ibid., p. 97.
58. Ibid., p. 108.
59. Ibid., p. 110.
60. Ibid., p. 112.
61. Ibid., p. 112.
62. Ibid., p. 113.
63. Ibid., p. 114.
64. See T. Geiger, *Ideologie und Wahrheit*, Stuttgart/Vienna 1953; T. Geiger, 'Bemerkungen zur Soziologie des Denkens', *Archiv für Rechts-und Sozialphilosphie* vol. 45, 1959. For a critique of Geiger's position see K. Lenk, *Marx in der Wissenssoziologie*, op. cit., pp. 291 ff.
65. 'Diskussion über "Die Konkurrenz" ', loc. cit., p. 114.
66. Ibid., pp. 119-20.
67. Ibid., pp. 120-1.
68. Ibid., p. 122.
69. Ibid., pp. 123-4.
70. 'Diskussion über "Das Verstehen" ', loc. cit., p. 239.
71. Ibid., p. 242.

72. A.V. Schelting, 'Zum Streit um die Wissenssoziologie'.
73. Ibid., p. 12, n. 18.
74. Ibid., p. 9.
75. A. Meusel, 'Die Konkurrenz in soziologischer Betrachtung', loc. cit.
76. Ibid., p. 338.
77. Ibid., p. 341.
78. P. Tillich, 'Ideologie und Utopie', *Die Gesellschaft*, vol. 6, 1929, pp. 348-55. This review and the others listed here are discussed in this chapter. For another overview of the reception of *Ideologie und Utopie*, see K.H. Wolff, 'Karl Mannheim', in D. Käsler (ed.), *Klassiker des soziologischen Denkens*, vol. 2, Munich 1978, esp. pp. 365-71.
79. H. Arendt, 'Philosophie und Soziologie', *Die Gesellschaft*, vol. 7, 1930, pp. 163-76.
80. H. Marcuse, 'Zur Wahrheitsproblematik der soziologischen Methode', *Die Gesellschaft*, vol. 6. 1929, pp. 356-69.
81. A. Kleinberg, 'Bürgerliche und marxistische Kultursoziologie', *Die Gesellschaft*, vol. 9, 1932, pp. 252-63.
82. H. Speier, 'Soziologie oder Ideologie? Bemerkungen zur Soziologie der Intelligenz', *Die Gesellschaft*, vol. 7, 1930, pp. 357-72.
83. A. Wittfogel, 'Wissen und Gesellschaft', *Unter dem Banner des Marxismus*, vol. 5, 1931, pp. 83-102.
84. A. Fogarasi, 'Die Soziologie der Intelligenz und die Intelligenz der Soziologie', *Unter dem Banner des Marxismus*, vol. 4, 1930, pp. 359-75.
85. E. Lewalter, 'Wissenssoziologie und Marxismus', *Archiv für Sozialwisschnaft*, vol. 64, 1930, pp. 63-121.
86. H. Plessner, 'Abwandlung des Ideologiegedankens', *Kölner Vierteljahreshefte für Soziologie*, vol. 10, 1931/32, pp. 147-70.
87. F. Stern, 'Über die sog. "Seinsverbundenheit" des Bewusstseins', *Archiv für Sozialwissenschaft*, vol. 64, 1930, pp. 492-509.
88. J. Kraft, 'Soziologie oder Soziologismus?', *Zeitschrift für Völkerpsychologie und Soziologie*, vol. 5, 1929, pp. 406-17.
89. K. Dunckmann, 'Ideologie und Utopie', *Archiv für Angewandte Soziologie*, 1929, pp. 71-84.
90. S. Marck, 'Zum Problem des "seinsverbundenen Denkens" ', *Archiv für systematische Philosophie und Soziologie*, vol. 33, 1929, pp. 238-52.
91. S. Landshut, *Kritik der Soziologie*, Munich/Leipzig 1929, pp. 84-96.
92. M. Horkheimer, 'Ein neuer Ideologiebegriff?', *Archiv für die Geschichte des Sozialismus und der Arbeiterbewegung*, vol. 15, 1930, pp. 33-56. Reprinted in K. Lenk (ed.) *Ideologie*, Neuwied/Berlin, 1967 (3rd ed.), pp. 283-303. References are to this reprint.
93. T.W. Adorno, 'Die Aktualität der Philosophie' (Antrittsvorlesung, 7.5.1931), in T.W. Adorno, *Gesammette Schriften*, vol. 1 Frankfurt 1973, pp. 325-44, especially 340 f.
94. E.R. Curtius, 'Soziologie Die und ihre Grenzen', *Neue Schweizer Rundschau*, vol. 23, 1929, pp. 727-36.
95. E.R. Curtius, loc. cit., p. 728.
96. Ibid., p. 729.
97. Ibid., p. 736.
98. K. Mannheim, 'Zur Problematik der Soziologie in Deutschland', *Neue Schweizer Rundschau*, vol. 23, 1929, pp. 820-29; English trans. in K.H.

Wolff (ed.), *From Karl Mannheim*, New York 1971, pp. 262-70. References are to this translation.
99. K. Mannheim, loc. cit., p. 266. Translation amended.
100. Ibid., p. 267.
101. Ibid., pp. 269-70.
102. H. Arendt, 'Philosophie und Soziologie', loc. cit., pp. 163-76.
103. Ibid., p. 163.
104. Ibid., p. 165.
105. Ibid., p. 167.
106. Ibid., p. 168.
107. Ibid., p. 170.
108. Ibid., p. 171.
109. Ibid., p. 175.
110. See A. Gurwitsch, 'Grundsätzliches zur Soziologie des Wissens' *Die Volkswirte*, vol. **19**, 1930, p. 141.
111. S. Marck, 'Zum Problem des "seinsverbundenen Denkens" ', *Archiv für systematische Philosophie und Soziologie*, vol. 33, 1929, pp. 238-52.
112. S. Marck, 'Zum Problem des "seinsverbundenen Denkens" ', loc. cit., p. 240.
113. Ibid., p. 244.
114. Ibid., p. 248.
115. Ibid., p. 251.
116. P. Tillich, 'Ideologie und Utopie', *Die Gesellschaft*, vol. 6, 1929, pp. 348-55.
117. J. Kraft, 'Soziologie oder Soziologismus?', *Zeitschrift für Völkerpsychologie und Soziologie*, vol. 5, 1929, pp. 406-17.
118. J. Kraft, 'Soziologie oder Soziologismus?', loc. cit., p. 411.
119. G. Stern, 'Über die sog. "Seinsverbundenheit" des Bewusstseins', *Archiv für Sozialwissenschaft*, vol. 64, 1930, pp. 492-509.
120. G. Stern, 'Über die sog. "Seinsverbundenheit" des Bewusstseins', loc. cit., p. 497.
121. Ibid., pp. 498-9.
122. Ibid., p. 493.
123. Ibid., p. 502.
124. Ibid., p. 503.
125. Ibid., p. 508.
126. H. Plessner, 'Abwandlungen des Ideologiegedankens', *Kölner Vierteljahreshefte für Soziologie*, vol. 10, 1931/32, pp. 147-70.
127. H. Plessner, loc. cit., pp. 151-2.
128. Ibid., p. 152.
129. Ibid., pp. 152-3.
130. Ibid., pp. 159-160.
131. Ibid., p. 169.
132. Ibid., p. 170.
133. K.A. Wittfogel, 'Wissen und Gesellschaft', *Unter dem Banner des Marxismus*, vol. 5, 1931, pp. 83-102. The review also discusses works by Troeltsch, Max Weber, Tönnies, Scheler and Sombart.
134. K.A. Wittfogel, loc. cit., p. 100.
135. Ibid., p. 102.
136. A. Fogarasi, 'Die Soziologie der Intelligenz und die Intelligenz der

Soziologie', *Unter dem Banner des Marxismus*, vol. 4, 1930, pp. 359–75, especially p. 359.
137. Ibid., p. 363.
138. Ibid., p. 366.
139. Ibid., p. 369.
140. E. Lewalter, 'Wissenssoziologie und Marxismus', *Archiv für Sozialwissenschat*, vol. 64, 1930, pp. 63–121.
141. E. Lewalter, 'Wissenssoziologie und Marxismus', loc. cit., p. 99.
142. Ibid., p. 103.
143. Ibid., p. 108.
144. Ibid., pp. 114–5.
145. The reception of Mannheim's work by the Frankfurt School has recently been reviewed by Martin Jay. See M. Jay, 'The Frankfurt Critique of Mannheim, *Telos*, no. 20, 1974, pp. 72–89. But see also the critical rejoinder: J. Schmidt, 'Reply to Martin Jay', *Telos*, no. 21, 1974, pp. 168–81. For another brief overview, see also H. Dubiel, 'Ideologiekritik versus Wissenssoziologie', *Archiv für Rechts-und Sozialphilosophie*, vol. 61, 1975, pp. 221–36.
146. H. Marcuse, 'Zur Wahrheitsproblematik der soziologischen Methode', *Die Gesellschaft* vol. 6, 1929, pp. 356–69.
147. Ibid., p. 363.
148. Ibid., p. 364.
149. M. Horkheimer, 'Ein neuer Ideologiebegriff?', *Archiv für die Geschichte des Sozialismus und der Arbeiterbewegung*, vol. 15, 1930, pp. 33–56. Reprinted in K. Lenk (ed.), *Ideologie*, 3rd ed., Neuwied/Berlin, 1967, pp. 283–303. References are to this reprint.
150. M. Horkheimer, 'Ein neuer Ideologiebegriff?', loc. cit., p. 283.
151. Ibid., pp. 287–8.
152. Ibid., p. 298.
153. Ibid., p. 302.
154. Ibid., pp. 302–3.
155. O. Neurath, 'Bürgerlicher Marxismus', *Der Kampf*, 1930, p. 227 f.
156. A. Neusüss, *Utopische Bewusstsein und freischwebende Intelligenz. Zur Wissenssoziologie Karl Mannheims*, Meisenheim 1968, pp. 17–18.
157. G. Eisermann, 'Die deutsche Soziologie in Zeitraum von 1918 bis 1933', *Kölner Zeitschrift für Soziologie*, **11**, 1959, p. 63.
158. E. Troeltsch, *Der Historismus und seine Probleme*, Tübingen 1922, p. ix.

Conclusion

1. K.H. Wolff, 'The Sociology of Knowledge in the United States of America. A Trend Report and Bibliography', *Current Sociology*, vol. XV, no. 1, 1967, p. 7.
2. Ibid.
3. Ibid., p. 9.
4. P. Berger and T. Luckmann, *The Social Construction of Reality: A Treatise in the Sociology of Knowledge*, Garden City, New York 1966, p. 3.
5. Ibid., p. 4.
6. Quoted in K.H. Wolff, 'The Sociology of Knowledge and Sociological Theory', in L. Gross (ed.), *Symposium on Sociological Theory*, New York 1959, p. 572.

7. For a recent plea, not merely for the phenomenological approach to the sociology of knowledge but also Max Scheler's standpoint, see I. Srubar, 'Max Scheler: Eine Wissenssoziologische Alternative', in *Kölner Zeitschrift für Soziologie und Sozialpsychologie, Sonderheft* 22, 1980, pp. 343-59.
8. See M. Horkheimer, 'Traditional and Critical Theory', in M. Horkheimer, *Critical Theory* (trans. M.J. O'Connell *et al.*), New York/St. Louis/San Francisco/Toronto, 1972, p. 213.
9. M. Horkheimer and T.W. Adorno, *Dialectic of Enlightenment* (translation J. Cumming), New York/London 1972.
10. See W. Benjamin, *Gesammelte Schriften*, V, (Das Passagen-Werk), Frankfurt 1982. There are no direct references to Lukács in Benjamin's notes to his monumental project. Instead, as an important Marxist source, there are frequent references to Karl Korsch's work on Marx.
11. On the relationship between Mannheim and the Frankfurt School see M. Jay, 'The Frankfurt School's Critique of Karl Mannheim', *Telos*, **20**, 1974, pp. 72-89, and J. Schmidt, 'Reply to Martin Jay', *Telos*, **21**, 1974.
12. See K.O. Apel 'Reply to Lessnoff', in S. Brown (ed.), *Philosophical Dispute in the Social Sciences*, Sussex, 1979.
13. See A.P. Simonds, *Karl Mannheim's Sociology of Knowledge*, Oxford 1978. Also Z. Bauman, *Hermeneutics and Social Science*, London 1978.
14. See, for example, K. Mannheim, *Structures of Thinking* (trans. J. Shapiro and S. Weber-Nicholsen), London/Boston 1981, for the frequency of references to Heidegger's work. Mannheim had also attended Heidegger's lectures.
15. See J. Mepham and D.H. Ruben (eds.), *Issues in Marxist Philosophy*, **3**, Sussex 1979, pp. 141 f; also, D. Sayer, *Marx's Method*, Sussex 1979.
16. A. Gurwitsch, 'Grundsätzliches zur Soziologie des Wissens', *Die Volkswirte*, **29**, 1930, p. 141.
17. The tragic consciousness thesis, derived from Lukács version, played a crucial role in a different context in the work of Lucien Goldmann. See especially L. Goldmann, *The Hidden God* (trans. P. Thody), London 1964. For a discussion of Goldmann's work as a whole see M. Evans, *Lucien Goldmann: An Introduction*, Sussex/New Jersey 1981.

Bibliography

This is not intended as a comprehensive bibliography on the sociology of knowledge since the present study has only been concerned with the German tradition. It does provide, however, a guide to the central original sources in this area. A selected guide to secondary sources is also included but useful more general bibliographies may be found in the following:

N. BIRNBAUM, 'The Sociological Study of Ideology (1940-60): A Trend Report and Bibliography', *Current Sociology*, vol. 9, no. 2, 1960.

Groupe de sociologie de la connaissance et de la vie morale 'Bibliographie de la sociologie de la connaissance'. *Cahiers internationaux de sociologie*, vol. 32, 1962.

K. LENK (ed.), *Ideologie*, Neuwied/Berlin 1961, pp. 429-50.

K. LENK, *Marx in der Wissenssoziologie*, Neuwied/Berlin 1972, pp. 306-39.

K. MANNHEIM *Ideologie und Utopie* (5th ed.) Frankfurt, 1969, pp. 269-99.

G. REMMLING *Karl Mannheim*, London/Boston 1974.

K. WOLFF 'The Sociology of Knowledge in the United States of America. A Trend Report and Bibliography', *Current Sociology*, vol. 15, no. 1, 1967.

Selected Works of Max Scheler

M. SCHELER, *Gesammelte Werke*, Bern 1954 to present.

_____ *Der Formalismus in der Ethik und die materiale Wertethik*, 4th ed., Bern 1954.

_____ *Vom Umsturz der Werte*, 4th ed., Bern 1955.

_____ *Vom Ewigen im Menschen*, 4th ed., Bern 1954.

_____ *Schriften zur Soziologie und Weltanschauungslehre*, 2nd ed., Bern 1963.

_____ *Die Wissensformen und die Gesellschaft*, 2nd ed., Bern 1960.

_____ *Die philosophische Weltanschauung*, 3rd ed., Bern 1968.

M. SCHELER (ed.), *Versuche zu einer Soziologie des Wissens*, Munich/Leipzig 1924.

M. SCHELER, 'Wissenschaft und soziale Struktur', in *Verhandlungen des 4 Deutschen Soziologentages 1924*, Tübingen 1925.

_____ 'Die positivistische Geschichtsphilosophie und die Aufgaben einer Soziologie des Erkenntnis', *Kölner Vierteljahreshefte fur Soziologie*, vol. 1, no. 1, 1921.

_____ *Die Stellung des Menschen im Kosmos*, 7th ed., Bern/Munich 1966.

Selected Works of George Lukács

A full bibliography of Lukács' early writings down to 1918 may be found in Georg Lukács', *Text und Kritik*, **39/40**, 1973, pp. 81-4. For Lukács' writings from 1919 to 1929 see J. Kammler, *Politische Theorie von Georg Lukács*, Darmstadt/Neuwied 1974, pp. 350-9.

G. LUKÁCS, *Die Seele und die Formen*, Berlin 1911.

_____ 'Zur Soziologie des modernen Dramas' in *Archiv für Sozialwissenschaft*, **38**, 1914, pp. 303-45; 662-706.
_____ 'Zum Wesen und zur Methode der Kultursoziologie', *Archiv für Sozialwissenschaft*, **39**, 1915, p. 216 ff.
_____ 'Rezension von B. Croce', *Archiv für Sozialwissenschaft*, **39**, 1915, p. 878 ff.
_____ 'Die Subjekt-Objekt Beziehung in der Ästhetik', *Logos*, vol. 7, 1917/18 pp. 1-39.
_____ 'Georg Simmel', *Pester Lloyd*, 2 Oct. 1918; reprinted in K. Gassen and M. Landmann (eds.) *Buch des Dankes an Georg Simmel*, Berlin 1958, p. 174 ff.
_____ 'Emil Lask. Ein Nachruf', *Kant-Studien*, **22**, 1918, pp. 349-70.
_____ *Die Theorie des Romans*, Berlin 1920.
_____ *Geschichte und Klassenbewusstsein*, Berlin 1923; Reprinted in G. Lukács, *Werke*, vol. 11, Neuwied/Berlin 1968.
_____ 'Moses Hess und die probleme der idealistischen Dialektik', *Archiv für die Geschichte des Sozialismus und der Arbeiterbewegung*, vol. 12, 1926, p. 105 ff.
_____ *Heidelberger Philosophie der Kunst (1912-1914)*, Neuwied/Darmstadt 1974.
_____ *Heidelberger Ästhetik (1916-1918)*, Neuwied/Darmstadt 1974.
_____ *Taktik und Ethik. Politische Aufsätze I 1918-1920*, Darmstadt/Neuwied 1975.
_____ *Revolution und Gegenrevolution. Politische Aufsätze II 1920-1921*, Darmstadt/Neuwied 1976.
_____ *Organisation und Illusion. Politische Aufsätze III 1921-1924*, Darmstadt/Neuwied 1977.

Works of Karl Mannheim

K. MANNHEIM, *Lélek és Kultura*, Budapest 1918; German translation, E. Mannheim in K. Mannheim, *Wissenssoziologie*, Neuwied/Berlin 1964, pp. 66-84.
_____ 'Rezension von Georg Lukács, Die Theorie des Romans', *Logos*, **9**, 1920-1, pp. 298-302; English trans. K.H. Wolff in his *From Karl Mannheim*, New York 1971, pp. 50-3.
_____ 'Beiträge zur Theorie der Weltanschauungs-Interpretation', *Jahrbuch für Kunstgeschichte*, vol. 15 1921-2, pp. 236-74; English translation P. Kecskemeti in K. Mannheim, *Essays on the Sociology of Knowledge*, London 1952.
_____ 'Zum Problem einer Klassifikation der Wissenschaften', *Archiv für Sozialwissenschaft*, **50**, 1922, pp. 230-37.
_____ 'Die Strukturanalyse der Erkenntnistheorie', *Kant-Studien*, Ergänzungsheft **57**, 1922; English translation, E. Schwarzschild and P. Kecskemeti in K. Mannheim, *Essays on Sociology and Social Psychology*, London 1953.
_____ *Über das Eigenart kultursoziologischer Erkenntnis*, ms. 1922. Now in K. Mannheim, *Structures of Thinking*, (translation J. Shapiro and S. Weber Nicholsen) London/Boston 1981.
_____ 'Historismus', *Archiv für Sozialwissenschaft*, **52**, 1924,

pp. 1-60; English translation P. Kecskemeti in K. Mannheim, *Essays on the Sociology of Knowledge*, London 1952.

──────────── *Eine soziologische Theorie der Kultur und ihrer Erkennbarkeit (Konjunktives und kommunikatives Denken)*, ms. c. 1924-5. Now in K. Mannheim, *Structures of Thinking*, op. cit.

──────────── 'Das Problem einer Soziologie des Wissens', *Archiv für Sozialwissenschaft*, **53**, 1925, pp. 577-652; English translation P. Kecskemeti in K. Mannheim, *Essays on the Sociology of Knowledge*, op. cit.

──────────── 'Ideologische und soziologische Interpretation der geistigen Gebilde', *Jahrbuch für Soziologie*, **2**, 1926, pp. 424-40; English translation K.H. Wolff in his *From Karl Mannheim*, op cit.

──────────── 'Das Konservative Denken', *Archiv für Sozialwissenschaft*, **57**, 1927, pp. 68-142; 470-95.

──────────── 'Das Problem der Generationen', *Kölner Vierteljahrshefte für Soziologie*, **7**, 1928, pp. 157-85; 309-30; English translation P. Kecskemeti in K. Mannheim, *Essays on the Sociology of Knowledge*, op. cit.

──────────── 'Die Bedeutung der Konkurrenz in Gebiete des Geistigen', *Verhandlungen des 6 en deutschen Soziologentages 1928*, Tübingen 1929, pp. 35-83.

──────────── 'Zur Problematik der Soziologie in Deutschland' *Neue Schweizer Rundschau*, **22**, pp. 820-9; English trans. K.H. Wolff in his *From Karl Mannheim*, op. cit.

──────────── 'Über das Wesen und die Bedeutung des wirtschaftlichen Erfolgsstrebens', *Archiv für Sozialwissenschaft*, **63**, 1930, pp. 449-512.

──────────── *Ideologie und Utopie*, Bonn 1929; reprinted, 5th ed., Frankfurt 1969 (with additions).

──────────── 'Wissenssoziologie' in A. Vierkandt (ed.), *Handwörterbuch der Soziologie*, Stuttgart 1931, pp. 659-680; reprinted in K. Mannheim, *Ideologie und Utopie*, 5th ed. Frankfurt 1969.

──────────── *Die Gegenwartsaufgabe der Soziologie. Ihre Lehrgestalt*, Tübingen 1932.

──────────── 'American Sociology', *American Journal of Sociology*, **37**, 1932, pp. 273-82; reprinted in K. Mannheim, *Essays on Sociology and Social Psychology*, op. cit.

──────────── 'German Sociology (1918-1933)', *Politica*, vol. 1, 1934 pp. 12-33; reprinted in K. Mannheim, *Essays on Sociology and Social Psychology*, op. cit.

Contemporary contributions to the sociology of knowledge debates in Germany (1918-33)

M. ADLER, 'Wissenschaft und soziale Struktur' *Verhandlungen des 4. Deutschen Soziologentages, 1924*, Tübingen 1925.

──────────── 'Soziologie und Erkenntniskritik', *Jahrbuch für Soziologie*, vol. 1, 1925.

H. ARENDT, 'Philosophie und Soziologie', *Die Gesellschaft*, **7**, 1930.

E. BLOCH, *Geist der Utopie*, Munich/Leipzig 1918.

E. R. CURTIUS, 'Die Soziologie und ihre Grenzen', *Neue Schweizer Rundschau*, **10**, 1929.

K. DUNKMANN, 'Ideologie und Utopie', *Archiv für angewandte Soziologie*, **2**, 1930.

K. DUNKMANN, 'Die soziologische Begründung der Wissenschaft' *Archiv für systematische Philosophie und Soziologie*, vol. 30, 1927.

H. EHRENBERG, 'Ideologische und soziologische Methode', *Archiv für systematische Philosophie*, **30**, 1927.
A. ELEUTHEROPOULOS, 'Sozialpsychologie und Wissenssoziologie', *Zeitschrift für Volkerpsychologie und Soziologie*, **3**, 1927.
A. FOGARASI, 'Die Soziologie der Intelligenz und die Intelligenz der Soziologie', *Unter dem Banner des Marxismus*, **4**, 1930.
H. FREYER, *Soziologie als Wirklichkeitswissenschaft*, Leipzig/Berlin 1930.
E. GRÜNWALD, *Das Problem der Soziologie des Wissens*, Vienna/Leipzig 1934.
A. GURVITCH, 'Grundsätzliches zur Soziologie des Wissens', *Die Volkswirte*, **29**, 1930.
M. HORKHEIMER, 'Ein neuer Ideologiebegriff?' *Archiv für die Geschichte des Sozialismus*, **15**, 1930.
W. JERUSALEM, 'Soziologie des Erkennens', *Kölner Vierteljahrshefte für Soziologie*, **1**, 1921.
J. KRAFT, 'Soziologie oder Soziologismus', *Zeitschrift für Völker psychologie und Soziologie*, **4**, 1929.
P. LANDSBERG, 'Zur Soziologie der Erkenntnistheorie', *Schmollers Jahrbuch*, **55**, 1931.
S. LANDSHUT, *Kritik der Soziologie*, Munich/Leipzig 1929.
G. LEHMANN, 'Soziologie der Kultur und Wissenssoziologie' in K. Dunkmann (ed.), *Lehrbuch der Soziologie und Sozialphilosophie*, Berlin 1931.
E. LEWALTER, 'Wissenssoziologie und Marxismus', *Archiv für Sozialwissenschaft*, **64**, 1930.
S. MARCK, 'Zum Problem der Seinsverbundenheit des Wissens', *Archiv für Philosophie und Soziologie*, 1929.
H. MARCUSE, 'Zur Wahrheitsproblematik der soziologische Methode', *Die Gesellschaft*, **6**, 1929.
A. MEUSEL, 'Die Konkurrenz in soziologischer Betrachtung', *Die Gesellschaft*, **6**, 1929.
H. PLESSNER, 'Abwandlungen des Ideologiegedankens', *Kölner Vierteljahrshefte für Soziologie*, **10**, 1931.
G. SALOMON, 'Historischer Materialismus und Ideologienlehre', *Jahrbuch für Soziologie*, vol. 2, 1926.
A. V. SCHELTING, 'Zum Streit um die Wissenssoziologie', *Archiv für Sozialwissenschaft*, **62**, 1929.
H. SPEIER, 'Soziologie oder Ideologie?', *Die Gesellschaft*, **7**, 1930.
P. SZENDE, *Verhüllung und Enthüllung*, Leipzig 1922.
P. TILLICH, 'Ideologie und Utopie', *Die Gesellschaft*, **6**, 1929.
A. WEBER, 'Prinzipielles zur Kultursoziologie', *Archiv für Sozialwissenschaft*, **54**, 1920.
K. WITTFOGEL, 'Wissen und Gesellschaft', *Unter dem Banner des Marxismus*, **5**, 1931.
H. ZIEGLER, 'Ideologienlehre', *Archiv für Sozialwissenschaft* **57**, 1927.
V. MEJA and N. STEHR (eds.) *Der Streit und die Wissenssoziologie*, Frankfurt 1982 (Contains many of these essays and other contributions).

Selected Bibliography of Secondary Sources
T. W. ADORNO et. al., *The Positivist Dispute in German Sociology*, (translation G. Adey and D. Frisby), London 1976.

T. W. ADORNO, 'Das Bewusstsein der Wissenssoziologie', *Prismen*, Frankfurt 1955.
C. ANTONI, *From History to Sociology*, (trans. H.V. White), London 1962.
K.-O. APEL et. al., *Hermeneutik und Ideologiekritik*, Frankfurt 1971.
K.-O. APEL, *Transformation der Philosophie*, Frankfurt 1973.
─────── *Towards a Transformation of Philosophy*, (translation G. Adey and D. Frisby) London/Boston 1980.
U. APITZSCH, *Gesellschaftstheorie und Ästhetik bei Georg Lukács bis 1933*, Stuttgart 1977.
H. BARTH, *Wahrheit und Ideologie*, Zürich 1945.
Z. BAUMAN, *Hermeneutics and Social Science*, London 1978.
D. BÖHLER, *Metakritik der Marxschen Ideologiekritik*, Frankfurt 1971.
H. BOSSE, *Marx–Weber–Troeltsch*, Munich/Mainz 1970.
M. BRACHT, *Voraussetzungen einer Soziologie des Wissens*, Tübingen 1974.
W. DILTHEY, *Gesammelte Schriften*, 12 vols, 2nd ed. Stuttgart/Göthingen 1958 ff.
─────── *Der Aufbau der Geschichtichen Welt in den Geistewissenschaften*, (M. Riedel, ed.) Frankfurt, 1970.
─────── *Weltanschauungslehre*, Stuttgart/Göttingen 1960.
─────── *Selected Writings* (trans. and ed. H.P. Rickman), Cambridge 1976.
H. DIWALD, *Wilhelm Dilthey*, Göttingen/Berlin/Frankfurt 1963.
C. V. FERBER, 'Der Werturteilsstreit 1909/1959', *Kölner Zeitschrift für Soziologie*, **11**, 1959.
I. FETSCHER, 'Das Verhältnis des Marxismus zu Hegel', *Marxismusstudien*, 3rd series, Tübingen 1960.
─────── 'Zum Begriffe der "objektiven Möglichkeit bei Max Weber und Georg Lukács', *Revue Internationale de Philosophie*, **27**, 1973.
M. FUNKE, *Ideologiekritik und ihre Ideologie bei Nietzsche*, Stuttgart 1974.
J. GABEL, *False Consciousness* (translated K. Thompson), Oxford 1975.
H. G. GADAMER, *Truth and Method*, (Trans. G. Barden and J. Cumming), London 1975.
A. GRUNENBERG, *Bürger und Revolutionär*, Cologne/Frankfurt 1976.
J. HABERMAS, *Knowledge and Human Interests*, (translated J. Shapiro), Boston/London 1971.
─────── *Theory and Practice*, (translated J. Viertel), Boston/London 1974.
P. HAMILTON, *Knowledge and Social Structure*, London/Boston 1974.
A. HELLER et al., *Die Seele und das Leben*, Frankfurt 1977.
K. HEUSSI, *Die Krisis des Historismus*, Tübingen 1932.
W. HOFMANN, *Gesellschaftslehre als Ordnungemacht. Die Werturteilsfrage — heute*, Berlin 1961.
M. HORKHEIMER and T. W. ADORNO, *Soziologische Exkurse*, Frankfurt 1956.
J. KAMMLER, *Politische Theorie von Georg Lukács*, Darmstadt Neuwied 1974.
D. KETTLER, *Marxismus und Kultur*, Neuwied/Berlin 1974.
─────── 'Sociology of Knowledge and Moral Philosophy', *Political Science Quarterly*, **82**, 1967.
─────── 'Rhetoric and Social Science: Karl Mannheim Adjusts to the English-Speaking World', *unpublished ms*.
K. LENK, *Von der Ohnmacht des Geistes*, Tübingen 1959.

K. LENK (ed.) *Ideologie*, 5th ed., Neuwied/Berlin 1971.
_____ *Marx in der Wissenssoziologie*, Neuwied/Berlin 1972.
H.-J. LIEBER, 'Zur Problematik der Wissenssoziologie bei Max Scheler', *Philosophische Studien*, **1**, 1949.
_____ *Wissen und Gesellschaft*, Tübingen 1952.
H.-J. LIEBER (ed.) *Ideologienlehre und Wissenssoziologie*, Darmstadt 1974.
_____ *Kulturkritik und Lebensphilosophie*, Darmstadt 1974.
M. LÖWY, *Georg Lukács: From Romanticism to Bolshevism*, London 1979.
G. LUKÁCS, *Die Zerstörung der Vern unft*, Berlin 1954.
W. MOMMSEN, *The Age of Bureaucracy*, Oxford 1974.
A. NEUSÜSS, *Utopische Bewusstsein und freischwebende Intelligenz. Zur Wissenssoziologie Karl Mannheims*, Meisenheim 1968.
F. NIETZSCHE, *Werke* (edited by K. Schlechta), Darmstadt 1966.
G. REMMLING, *Karl Mannheim*, London/Boston 1974.
D. RÜSCHEMEYER, *Probleme der Wissenssoziologie*, Dissertation, Cologne 1958.
J. SCHAAF, *Grundprinzipien der Wissenssoziologie*, Hamburg 1958.
A. V. SCHELTING, *Max Webers Wissenschaftslehre*, Tübingen 1934.
H. SCHNÄDELBACH, *Geschichtsphilosophie nach Hegel*, Freiburg/Munich, 1974.
H. SCHOECK, 'Die sozialökonomische Aspekte in der Wissenssoziologie Karl Mannheims', *Zeitschrift für die gesammte Staatswissenschaften*, **106**, 1950.
A. P. SIMONDS, *Karl Mannheim's Sociology of Knowledge*, Oxford 1978.
G. SIMMEL, *The Philosophy of Money* (translated T. Bottomore and D. Frisby), London/Boston 1978.
W. STARK, *The Sociology of Knowledge*, London 1958.
J. STAUDE, *Max Scheler*, New York 1968.
E. TROELTSCH, 'Die Krisis des Historismus', *Die Neue Rundschau*, **33**, 1922.
E. TROELTSCH, *Der Historismus und seine Probleme*, Tübingen 1922.
_____ *Der Historismus und seine Überwindung*, Berlin 1924.
A. WEBER, *Ideen zur Staats- unk Kultursoziologie*, Karlsruhe 1927.
M. WEBER, *Gesammelte Aufsätze zur Wissenschaftslehre*, 3rd ed., Tübingen 1968.
E. WITTENBERG, 'Die Wissenschaftskrise in Deutschland in Jahr 1919', *Theoria*, 4, 1938.
K. H. WOLFF, *From Karl Mannheim*, New York 1971.
K. H. WOLFF (ed.), *Karl Mannheim: Wissenssoziologie*, Neuwied/Berlin 1964.

Index of Names

Adorno, T.W., 198, 226
Adler, M., 26, 65, 69, 136, 178-84, 195, 218
Ady, E., 72, 112
Antal, F., 81
Apel, K.-O., *viii*, 119, 124, 136, 227
Apitzsch, U., 93-4, 115
Arato, A., 73, 75, 93
Arendt, H., *ix*, 201-4
Augustine, Saint, 4
Avenarius, R., 59

Bacon, F., 56
Balazs, B., 72, 109
Barth, H., 4, 5, 8, 9, 54
Bartok, B., 110, 112
Becker, O., 65
Benjamin, W., 226-7
Berger, P., 51, 65, 225
Bergson, H., 4, 213
Bloch, E., 69, 70
Böhler, D., 5
Boltzmann, K., 60
Bosse, H., 6-7
Bracht, M., 31, 177
Breines, P., 71, 75, 77
Bühl, W., 27, 64

Cassirer, E., 30
Coletti, L., 75
Comte, A., 21, 27, 36, 38, 40, 53, 59
Coser, L., 3
Croce, B., 213
Curtius, E.R., 199-201, 207

Dahlke, O., 65
Dilthey, W., *viii*, 1, 3, 4, 10-14, 68, 80, 106, 113, 118, 119, 120, 121, 122, 127, 128, 147, 175, 189, 220, 223
Dostoyevsky, F., 109, 112
Dunkmann, K., 178, 181, 182, 184, 198
Durkheim, E., 48, 137

Einstein, A., 39, 40, 49
Eisermann, G., 223
Eleutheropulos, A., 64
Elias, N., 189, 190
Engels, F., 5, 6
Epstein, P., 192
Ernst, P., 97, 112

Fehér, F., 97
Fetscher, I., 89, 91-3
Feuerbach, L., 89, 217
Fichte, J.G., 21
Fiedler, K., 195
Fogarasi, B., 109, 110, 198, 201, 212, 213-14, 222
Francis, Saint, 4
Freud, S., 165
Fülep, L., 109

Gadamer, H.G., 13, 131
Geiger, T., 160, 192
George, S., 34
Goldmann, L., 75, 114
Gramsci, A., 68, 93
Grunenberg, A., 87, 89, 96-7, 99, 100
Grünwald, E., 3, 10, 27, 29

Gurvitch, G., 42
Gurwitsch, A., 204, 229

Habermas, J., *viii*, 6, 119, 176, 224
Hauser, A., 81, 109, 110
Hegel, G.W.F., 10, 21, 36, 68, 70, 79, 80-1, 85, 86, 88-9, 119, 183
Heidegger, M., 107, 140, 149, 201, 202, 218, 228
Hilferding, R., 198
Hintze, O., 38, 64
Hobbes, T., 50, 162
Honigsheim, P., 31, 66
Horkheimer, M., 198, 199, 201, 217, 219-22, 226, 227
Huaco, G., 72-3
Husserl, E., 4, 31, 65, 80, 106, 118

James, W., 60
Jaspers, K., 109, 202
Jerusalem, W., 26, 48, 66, 123, 189
Jonas, H., 190-2

Kammler, J., 75, 76, 78, 79, 81, 83, 85, 86, 87, 89, 96, 100
Kant, E., 10, 21, 49, 71, 180, 184, 188
Kautsky, K., 70
Kettler, D., 71-2, 73, 107, 109, 131
Kierkegaard, S., 112, 199
Kleinberg, A., 198
Kodály, Z., 110
Korsch, K., 68
Kracauer, S., 16, 178
Kraft, J., 198, 201, 206-7
Kries, J. von, 91
Kuhn, T., 113, 136, 170
Kun, B., 2

Landsberg, P., 66
Landshut, S., 198
Lask, E., 68, 71, 86, 107, 109, 112, 113, 213, 214
Lederer, E., 20, 189
Lenin, V.I., 93, 217
Lenk, K., *ix*, 5, 6, 13-14, 14-15, 16, 17, 25, 28, 30, 34, 67, 68, 72, 100, 161, 229
Lesznai, A., 109
Lewalter, E., 198, 201, 212, 215-17, 222
Lieber, H.-J., 11, 12, 13, 29, 72, 129
Löwe, A., 189-90
Löwith, K., 7
Löwy, M., 71, 75
Lukács, Georg, *vii*, *viii*, *ix*, 1, 2, 3, 6, 7, 17, 22-3, 25, 56, 58, 67, 68-106, 107, 109, 110-11, 112, 113, 114, 115, 116, 119, 124, 131, 132, 134, 142, 146, 147, 152, 157, 161, 165, 182, 183, 187, 198, 201, 206, 214, 216, 217, 219, 222, 223, 224, 225, 226, 227, 228, 229
Luckmann, T., 51, 65, 225
Ludz, P., 81
Luxemburg, R., 93

Mach, E., 59, 60
Maier, H., 71
Mannheim, Karl, *vii*, *viii*, *ix*, 1, 2, 3, 6, 7, 9, 12, 13, 14, 17, 18, 19-21, 22, 24, 28, 29, 54, 57, 65, 66, 68, 69, 72, 73, 75, 81, 100, 101, 104, 105, 107-73, 174, 175, 178, 185-98, 198-224, 225, 226, 227, 228, 229
Marck, S., 66, 69, 180, 198, 201, 204-6
Marcuse, H., 99, 180, 198, 201, 217, 218-19, 222

Index of Names

Marcuse, L., 16
Maretsky, K., 99–100
Markus, G., 71, 110, 111
Marx, Karl, vii, 3, 4, 5, 6, 7, 16, 23, 36, 43, 50, 56, 68, 70, 71, 72, 73, 74, 77, 82, 85, 88, 94–6, 99, 100, 102, 112, 123, 127, 152–3, 157, 178, 180, 183, 184, 189, 190, 197–8, 206, 209–11, 212–13, 214, 215–16, 217, 220, 222, 226
Mead, G.H., 225
Meusel, A., 182–3, 185, 189, 190, 196–8
Michels, R., 182
Mill, J.S., 59
Mommsen, W., 18
Müller-Freienfels, R., 64–5
Musil, R., 140

Neusüss, A., 127, 149, 162, 167–8, 222–3
Newman, Cardinal, 4
Nietszche, F., viii, 1, 3, 4, 7–9, 31, 32, 34, 199

Oppenheimer, F., 169

Pareto, V., 165, 166
Pascal, B., 4
Pascal, R., 80–1
Plessner, H., 66, 198, 199, 201, 206, 209–12, 219
Popper, K.R., 136, 149

Radbruch, G., 91
Rathenau, W., 34
Reich, W., 88
Remmling, G., 107–8
Rickert, H., 68, 71, 103, 107, 113, 120
Riegl, E., 112
Ringer, F., 162, 200
Rousseau, J.-J., 50

Salin, G., 182
Salz, A., 183
Scheler, Max, vii, viii, ix, 2, 3, 4, 6, 7, 9, 15, 17, 18, 20, 21–2, 25, 27–67, 68, 69, 75, 76, 100, 104, 107, 109, 118, 123, 128, 135, 174, 175–8, 178–84, 191, 195, 199, 202, 207, 212, 213, 223, 224, 225, 226, 228, 229
Schelting, A. von, 185, 196, 198
Schiller, F., 60
Schilpp, P., 45, 52
Schmoller, G., 78, 189
Schnädelbach, H., 10
Schutz, A., 51, 64, 65, 136
Simmel, G., viii, 1, 5, 7, 15–17, 68, 70, 71, 75, 76, 77, 78, 79, 80, 81, 83, 84, 89, 95, 97, 99, 107, 110–11, 132, 137, 150, 171, 184, 215, 226
Simonds, A.P., 227
Sombart, W., 34, 132, 187–8, 190, 194, 197
Spann, O., 165
Speier, H., 198
Spencer, H., 32, 40, 53, 59
Stark, W., 51, 65
Staude, J., 58
Steadman-Jones, G., 75
Stern, G., 198, 201, 206, 207–9
Stikkers, K., 27
Sulzbach, E., 181–2
Szabo, E., 72, 110

Tillich, P., 19, 201, 206
Töinnes, F., 33, 83, 135
Tolnay, K., 81
Troeltsch, E., 1, 5, 7, 14, 34, 39, 109, 128, 130, 165, 212, 223–4

Vierkandt, A., 169

Weber, A., 63, 76, 83, 115–16, 135, 165, 182, 185–7, 190, 195, 196, 197
Weber, Max, *viii*, 1, 5, 7, 15, 17–19, 44, 61, 68, 70, 71, 79, 80, 91–3, 99, 109, 121, 124, 128, 132, 136, 137, 140, 144, 161, 165, 166, 174, 175–6, 190, 194, 197, 212, 226

Wellmer, A., 5, 6
Wiese, L. von, 66, 171
Wilbrandt, E., 188–9
Windelband, W., 175
Wittenberg, E., 176
Wittfogel, K., 198, 201, 212–13
Wolff, K.J., 224–5

Zalai, B., 112, 214